AF335339

THE NATURAL BASIS

OF

SPIRITUAL REALITY

THE NATURAL BASIS
OF
SPIRITUAL REALITY

by
Norman J. Berridge

Swedenborg Scientific Association
Bryn Athyn, Pennsylvania
1992

Library of Congress Cataloging-in-Publication Data

Berridge, Norman J., 1916-
    The natural basis of spiritual reality / by Norman Berridge
        p.   cm.
    Includes bibliographical references and index.
    ISBN 0-915221-69-1
    1. New Jerusalem Church—Doctrines. 2. Body, Human—Religious
  aspects—New Jerusalem Church. 3. Spirits. I. Title.
  BX8729. B63B47 1993
  230' .94—dc20   91-39175
                                                            CIP

ISBN: 0-915221-69-1

TABLE OF CONTENTS

Figures vii

Preface ix

Abbreviations used in this work xiv

Chapter

I   New Ideas in Accordance with Cherished Beliefs
(nos. 1-15) 1

II   Seeing and Understanding Require the Light of Truth from
God (nos. 16-38) 11

III   Thinking from Correspondences (nos. 39-53) 23

IV   Correspondence of the Heart and Lungs—Part 1. The
Church and the Human Race (nos. 54-84) 31

V   Correspondence of the Heart and Lungs—Part 2. The Will
and the Understanding (nos. 85-112) 47

VI   Correspondence of the Heart and Lungs—Part 3. Conjunctions Between the Will and the Understanding (nos. 113-154) 63

VII   Correspondence of the Heart and Lungs—Part 4. The Giving
of a New Will (nos. 155-195) 97

VIII   The Lymphatic System (nos. 196-224) 127

IX   The Spleen (nos. 225-250) 145

X   The Thymus Gland (nos. 251-269) 159

XI   The Brain—Part 1 (nos. 270-307) 173

XII   The Brain—Part 2. The Infundibulum and the Hypophysis
         Cerebri (nos. 308-334) 199

XIII   The Brain—Part 3. Decussations (nos. 335-355) 221

XIV   Correspondences of the Eye (nos. 356-374) 233

XV   Correspondences of the Ears and the Organs of Balance or
         Orientation (nos. 375-392) 245

XVI   Perceptions, Delights, Odors, and the Sense of Smell
         (nos. 393-430) 259

XVII   Eating and Digestion—Part 1. A Brief Account of Bodily
         Digestion (nos. 431-444) 285

XVIII   Eating and Digestion—Part 2. Correspondences of Digestion
         (nos. 445-487) 293

XIX   The Interface Between the Spiritual and the Physical
         (nos. 488-500) 313

         Appendix: Sight, The Visual Process, and Doctrine 319

         Bibliography 349

         Index 351

FIGURES

1. Capillaries 42

2. Circulation of the Blood 59

3. The Heart 60

4. Pulmonary and Bronchial Arteries 65

5. The Three Conjunctions of DLW 404 67

6. Factors in Respiration Control 80

7. Fetal Circulation. Block Diagram 112

8. Heart of the Fetus 113

9. Lymphatic System 130

10. Lymph Node 133

11. The Spleen 147

12. The Thymus 161

13. Tissues of the Thymus 162

14. Neurons 175

15. Meninges 180

16. Base of Brain 200

17. Hypophysis 202

18. Cerebral Ventricles 206

19. Decussations 222

20. Optic Pathways 238

21. Development of Eye 240

22. The Inner Ear 251

23. Olfactory Mucosa (1) 268

24. Olfactory Mucosa (2) 271

25. Olfactory Lobes & Nerves, etc. 273

Preface

In the first place, it is my pleasure to thank my wife Olga for her typing and constructive criticism during the writing of the early versions of several chapters which were published in *The New Philosophy*.

Mr. Charles Cole Jr., President of the Swedenborg Scientific Association, played the leading role in the production of this book. It was he who actually invited me to write it although Mr. Lennart Alfelt, the late editor of *The New Philosophy*, had previously mentioned the possibility. He also warned me that some rewriting might be necessary and I would have to submit to a certain amount of editing. I greatly enjoyed the rewriting and I took the opportunity to include more material as well as to attempt an improved presentation of what had already been published. It turned out that the editorial discipline was encouragement of an almost intoxicating quality, administered by Professor Cole himself with great generosity of time and travel during his brief visits to this country. He also organized the production of the figures which, we hope, will do much to widen the use of the work. I ask him to accept my warmest thanks.

I am grateful also to the Rev. Willard L. D. Heinrichs, for a careful and detailed criticism of chapter VII which enabled me to improve it considerably. I also record my gratitude to the Editorial Board of *The New Philosophy* for their work on my contributions, and to Mrs. Kirsten Gyllenhaal and Mr Alan Laidlaw for their development of the Swedenborg Scientific Association's desktop publishing capability, of which this book is the first test-case result.

Mrs. Linda Odhner deserves special thanks for her painstaking drawings of most of the illustrations as does Rev. T. S. Rose for figures 4 and 13, the latter modified by the editor using Alan Laidlaw's skills at computer graphics. I also thank Richard Morris of Oxford University Press for preparing figures 2 and 7 from my drawings. In addition to the above there are many New Church people who have helped by their kind interest and approval. My work would have been much less joyful without them.

Throughout this work I have used a mental microscope. I have selected a few promising fields and studied them in detail. The number of such fields is very great and much greater than at first appears. As an example, take the eye (chapter XIV). While that chapter was being written, several papers on "Sight, the Visual Process, and Doctrine" were published by Dr. Aubrey Allen in *The New Philosophy* (Vol. 84 and 85; see also Vol. 83). Dr. Allen and I had a similar aim, namely to show the spiritual reality within the natural phenomena, yet we scarcely overlap. Such is the spaciousness of the subject. His treatment complements my own, and I am delighted that he has given permission to include his papers as an appendix in this book. Some other New Church writers have adopted a similar approach. The attitudes we have in common include the trust that when all the available trustworthy knowledge on any particular subject is illuminated by the truths of the Writings, then those knowledges enable the mind to see even the Writings themselves more clearly. How much more clearly obviously depends on many factors, including the availability of knowledge. Often the knowledge is scarce and particular beliefs must look to the future.

That trust began with me as an attitude of mind—a sort of faith in the Writings. I felt that such a learned, detailed, marvelous opening of the sacred scripture (which had been closed to me) must be fundamentally right. I felt that it must all be true in some way. I do not know how that faith began but it was strongly confirmed when I read AC 9300:3. It was not my first reading of that passage. I am quite sure that the first reading was as most first readings of the *Arcana* are: scarcely understood! As the years went by correspondences became more and more a habitual way of thought. When the writing was needed this passage became incandescent.

AC 9300:3 teaches us how to view nature. It also teaches us how to look at the Word in all its forms. It can especially be applied to the Writings themselves. Sometimes it even seems as though correspondences are being used in the Writings in their spiritual meanings, for example lungs to mean the understanding. This same passage gives us courage to attempt the kind of work shown in this book. The task is not easy. I have had periods when I could not see how to proceed, but then something has fallen into place, and stumbling blocks have become stepping stones. One pretends to oneself that one's faith is firm, but temptations (and even some fermentations as in DP 25) are accompanied by doubts about the outcome, and, as we know, the doubt and sorrow are changed into joy when they are dissipated. For the most part I have written the following chapters in an impersonal, academic, detached style. But the experience was quite different. Often it was even a matter of surprise, as well as delight, that modern science could agree so well with the Writings, but now I expect that everything will fall into place in the Lord's good time. At present, of course, it is sometimes difficult. How, you may ask, can an account of spirits from the moon fall into place in view of what we know now? It has been suggested that perhaps the people live underground for they are said to be "in" the moon. But there is another way of looking at the problem. AC 9300:3 is one of the most strongly worded passages of the Writings. It warns us (suggests) that unless we think from correspondences we shall inevitably go wrong. Applying that to the case in point: we know what the moon signifies and what people are like who dwell in it. We have met some! There is also the cold, the light without heat and the absence of wind. It also seems not really to matter where such spirits lived when in the body. It is their minds which are in the moon.

Something similar may actually apply to spirits from planets other than ours. A great deal of careful study of this aspect of the Writings is needed. A cursory reading suggests that the location of the planet has no relevance to the spiritual wisdom that is to be imparted or exemplified. Since the names of the planets go back to mythology they might be important.

Any improvement in our delight in, or understanding of, the Word (whether we include the Writings themselves in the Word or not) is of greatest importance. Studies like these in the following chapters do contribute to such a delight or understanding for some people. If they do not do it for you, dear reader, you will hardly have got this far. Most of this book is not for you and there are other ways of thinking from correspondences, as I have shown (no. 44, chapter III). The Word has internal senses that open upwards, even to the Lord. Practically speaking it often doesn't matter whether you think this applies to the Writings themselves or to the older Word opened by their means. The important thing is to be led nearer to the Lord. Our need for a growing detail and an increasing understanding is always with us because the Word always transcends our appreciation. The Lord allows us—leads us—to understand enough to rouse our interest and love, but much remains hidden by falsities that take a lifetime to dissipate. They are hidden even more by false attitudes: the residues of old doctrines, hereditary opinions and evils; things that might be called "anti-remains." Perhaps it is because of our merely spiritual quality, as contrasted with celestial perception, that we need the reflection from natural knowledges to help us in our appreciation of spiritual verities. If we had the celestial mentality we would see unlimited glory in the Word at once. But even then we might enjoy the detail of natural correspondences better if we also had the detail of natural knowledges. What a vista this reveals! Instead of merely seeing men as trees walking (Mark 8: 23-25), we can see how their spiritual activities are related to the physiology of plants as well as to their general appearance and use. Even celestial angels are instructed by spiritual ones and it is therefore clear that the celestial transcends, without including, the spiritual and natural but still it can be enriched by them.

The body of man is the natural object corresponding most closely to heaven and having the greatest relevance to the truly human form. Hence it is that human anatomy and physiology facilitate our understanding of the doctrine of the Grand Man. How delightful it is to think about the beauty and wonder of the bodily structure and function and at the same time to realize that it is the product of the Lord's Love and Wisdom descended by degrees through heaven, even to the minerals; to the stones, water and air of the lowest level of creation. One may easily be lost in wonder and praise. Yet this joyful experience is only a small trace of what it could be if more study, more time and more people were devoted to building temples of wisdom on the foundations of nature. In Swedenborg's time even the angels were interested in what was going on in this planet, and since the whole of nature is a theatre representative of the Lord's kingdom, there is nothing in nature which cannot be instructive once its representation is adequately understood.

The study required for this work has shown me that every time one reads the Writings, especially *Arcana Coelestia* and *The Apocalypse Explained*, some additional meaning appears. Other people, including my editor himself, have confirmed this. These experiences suggest that the voluminous and sometimes apparently contradictory nature of the Writings may enable us to absorb spiritual matters which are too subtle and complex to take in in a complete and concise form. What looks like a repetition may be an increase in detail or a different aspect of the same truth but still seen from a similar point of view. If seen from a different point of view it can look like a contradiction. It looks different but it is still the truth. The image in a plane mirror is correct, and also true in some respects. It can even bring out facts which might not otherwise be clear.

When I remember these things and realize that the Writings were given by the Lord through a man—whom He had specially prepared - I wonder how I dare to take the Writings to bits, quoting a sentence here, a few words there. How can any pastiche formed in such a way retain any part of the glory now to be seen in the clouds of the Word? I am glad to say that sometimes I have been allowed to quote long passages; such as were irresistible. I hope that you will be dissatisfied with the shorter quotations and will take delight and instruction by reading (again?) the whole numbers. Almost always it gives a different "feel" and an enhanced perception of the truth.

It is also the only way to avoid being led astray by a merely human writer!

Abbreviations used in this work

The Works of Emanuel Swedenborg:

AE	Apocalypse Explained
Arcana, AC	Arcana Coelestia
CL	Conjugial Love
Diary, SD	Spiritual Diary
DLW	Angelic Wisdom Concerning the Divine Love and Wisdom
DP	Angelic Wisdom Concerning the Divine Providence
DW	The Divine Wisdom (Bound with AE Vol VI)
HH	Heaven and Hell
TCR	The True Christian Religion

Other Abbreviations:

c	corresponds
ed.	editor
Fn	footnote
KEM	Knowledges of the External Memory
trans.	translator
MAC	Most Ancient Church

Note: All numbers refer to paragraphs, not to the Writings, unless preceded by the above abbreviations.

CHAPTER I

NEW IDEAS IN ACCORDANCE WITH CHERISHED BELIEFS

1. All Christians, and many others, believe the world was created by God. The idea that creation is a continuing process is less widely held, but many people are familiar with the view that the world we see and touch is but the outer garment of a more real world of the spirit. Some who believe and feel that it is so do not have any definite and detailed theory as to how this garment is worn or as to how the inner reality expresses itself in the external things which impinge upon our senses. Others have adopted clear ideas; it has been said that the world of the spirit represents itself in nature (Stanley, 1977) and it does so in a consistent and orderly way. This means that the properties of one may be realistically illustrated by those of the other.

2. Thus it was that the Lord chose illustrations from nature to teach us about the kingdom of heaven. The obvious content of His teaching was limited to the capacity of His hearers. The less obvious content can be revealed in ever-increasing richness and detail as the human race (or at least part of it) increases in intelligence and wisdom. The work that follows will demonstrate that we are now in a position to learn much more detail about the world of the spirit; for if all the world of nature is a representation of the spiritual world, our scientific knowledge should enable us to appreciate more keenly the relation between the spiritual and the material. We will then be able to understand more clearly what has been revealed concerning spiritual things.

A knowledge of the relation between natural and spiritual things can be used to present spiritual truths clearly to the affirmative rational mind

3. The relation between natural and spiritual things is sometimes fairly obvious, as in most of the Lord's parables. However, once it is accepted that it is a consistent and orderly functional relationship rather than merely a matter of poetical imagery, it becomes possible to see more clearly what is involved in many doctrines of faith by means of our knowledge of the facts of nature in which spiritual truths are represented.

4. A simple example will make this clear. An important teaching is presented in the parable of the sower and the explanation of it (Matt. 13: 3-9, 18-23). It is possible, however, to go further by considering the role of water in the germination of seed and its subsequent growth. The Lord spoke of the water of life (John 4: 10, 14). Our knowledge of the growth of plants makes it clear that the seed He sows will not be fruitful unless the recipient approaches Him for that spiritual thing which corresponds to water. The natural knowledge behind this is not new; what is new is our understanding of what water does for the plant by dissolving nourishing materials out of the earth, carrying them throughout the plant and, in part, combining with carbon dioxide in photosynthesis to produce the actual tissues of the growing plant. An account of the spiritual counterparts of these things will, it is hoped, be presented later. It will show how the processes that go on in plants can be related to those in the mind of man during his spiritual growth. The correspondence between these two different living systems emphasizes the importance of love and wisdom, shows how the Lord is all-in-all, and at the same time indicates the importance of man's own free response. At present, however, we confine our attention to a general consideration of correspondences as a whole.

The relation between the spiritual and the natural is an orderly and consistent one of cause and effect

5. Science has advanced to its present state on the assumption that the laws of nature operate all the time and without any exceptions. Apparent exceptions have always pointed the way to further discoveries. Once it is accepted that spiritual things are within, it is easy to adopt the view, at least as a hypothesis, that they act in an orderly and consistent way to produce effects in the visible things of nature. It is important to emphasize that the orderly and consistent operation of spiritual things directs our attention for the time being away from unusual phenomena such as ghosts, poltergeists and other similar occurrences. Our hypothesis is that spiritual things do not occasionally make use of natural things independently present, but that all the natural things are produced and activated by the inflowing of spiritual things; thus, no flower blooms, no star glows, except as a result of spiritual entities acting according to established laws. This can be a matter of faith to those who prefer to make it so rather than to think more deeply, but for those who wish for confirmation, there is at least one place where happenings of this kind can actually be observed, and that is in man himself.

The actions of human beings illustrate the production of material effects by spiritual causes

6. In a man we have many spiritual forces which are things of the mind or spirit. Love is one example. Love makes a man's material body act in many ways in the material world. A spiritual thing causes natural things to happen. The relation between the spiritual cause or love and the natural effect or bodily action is a relation of consistent laws. The fact that the laws are very numerous and that their interplay is complex does not take away their consistency. Even the simple act of a loving father smiling at his child is governed by consistent laws, although it requires an interplay of many nerve impulses within the brain and between the brain and the face.

There is a discrete distinction between the spiritual and material. How they can still be related as cause and effect is illustrated by the action of nerves on muscles

7. It is important to emphasize at this point that we have just been thinking of two very different levels within a series of events follow-

ing a single cause, the cause being love, the final event being a smile. The smile can be seen; the nerve impulses can be detected by scientific apparatus. The love can be inferred or deduced but not detected directly by any physical means. It is discretely different. Although it acts as a cause, it is distinct and separate. A physical image of the discrete difference can be seen in the relation between nerves and the muscles they activate. Although both are physical and both use proteins, enzymes, and other biochemical substances, they differ so markedly that one cannot pass gradually into another. Special "end plates" with special enzymes must be present to act as an interface. Of the more subtle interface between love and the brain we are as yet profoundly ignorant.

8. As with the brain, so with nature. We have a philosophy by which we can relate many things in nature to the spiritual things which we believe cause them, but as yet we do not know the mechanics of the interface. At present this is a small handicap, for we have only just begun to tackle the immense but fascinating task of relating the vast range of scientific knowledge to the newly available knowledge of spiritual things. (Of this last knowledge, more below.) The much smaller range of natural knowledge that has been with men for several thousand years has often (or even always) been more or less vaguely related to spiritual matters, as mentioned above in connection with parables. However, it can now be shown that the relationship that exists between the spiritual world and the natural can be observed in many other spheres: for example, in all the Divinely inspired books of the Bible, in Greek mythology, and even in common speech.

An example from common speech of the representation of an imponderable by a physical organ of the body. The extension of this representation to spiritual matters

9. It is quite usual to say we "see" when we mean we "understand." The eye, then, corresponds to the mind's ability to understand. The old saying of "an eye for an eye" (Exodus 21: 24) shows that anyone who tries to destroy the ability of another to understand by misleading him will himself be misled. The same words, however, can have a positive meaning which is also quite well-known, namely, that he who labors to encourage the understanding of others has his own understanding improved. A little thought shows that there is not, and cannot be, any end to this kind of interpretation. The eye sees by means of light. The Lord said, "I am the light of the world." Light comes from the sun. So! Moreover, as the eye corresponds to the understanding, so the anatomy and physiology of the eye can teach us much about the true function of our faculty of understanding. So we have much to think about, even if we cannot say how the Lord created the material universe or how the "light of the world" produces that huge atom bomb which is our source of physical light and energy.

It is possible to understand partially the causative relationship between spiritual and natural things although it is not possible to explain it in natural language

10. Although we cannot explain how love activates the brain to cause the face to smile, we still accept the causative relationship. It is the same with the relation between the natural and the spiritual. We may understand and accept even if we cannot explain. For a long time men have been able to see that there is a causative relationship only in general and have not realized that the general must fail if the particulars do not conform. Ignorance of both spiritual things and natural things has contributed to an inability to relate them to one another in detail. The belief in a detailed relationship becomes a conviction when certain lines of study are followed. The need for special study is made clear when one considers how impossible it would be to believe (did we not know it already) that a complex pattern of changing electric potentials on the interfaces of microscopic fibres (the nerves) in one being could produce a sign (the smile) that would give joy to another yards away (or even miles with the help of television). Even more so, were it not a matter of experience, we would find it quite beyond credence that a mere imponderable thing like the emotion of love could have the tremendous material consequences that often follow. It is, then, not surprising that we should need some preparation in order to appreciate a connection between the wonderful material universe and the even more wonderful universe of the spirit.

The spiritual and natural worlds are both vast and complex. A knowledge of both is required if their relationship is to be expounded, and this can only be achieved by a man whose mind is properly prepared so that it can receive Divine instruction concerning the meanings of spiritual experiences and of many other things

11. The ordinary material world is so vast that a detailed knowledge of it is beyond the capacity of any one man. There is even more in the spiritual world of causes. So complex are both worlds that we might be forgiven for thinking that the connection between them is beyond the grasp of the merely natural man. However, if the Divine who made them both would vouchsafe a few hints, it might then be possible for man to see, or perhaps become vaguely aware of, the connection. But the Divine can do more. In His wisdom He always adapts His revelation to the man or society of men to whom it is made. Thus men can be made aware of many things they did not formerly know, if they are willing to be made aware, and if they are of such a character that the knowledge will not be misused. It is within the bounds of possibility for God to reveal a great deal more about the expression of spiritual verities in natural and material objects and activities than the world is yet aware of.

12. But consider the requirements! We are not talking about a mere revelation of simple previously unknown facts, but about being able to understand subtle and complicated relationships that had not as yet entered the mind of any man. Take again the example of a smile. Even leaving out the more complex operation of the love itself we have a

process in the brain and between the brain and the face that is quite difficult to comprehend.

13. To know how the brain activates the face to smile one must know a great deal about the brain itself, not only which parts are connected to the face, but how they are connected with one another and with other parts of the brain, including those where memory resides, and many other details. This is one side of the necessary knowledge. On the other side one must also know a great deal about the muscles and the face; what a nerve impulse is and how it can make a muscle contract or relax, which muscles are to act, and by how much. The eyes, too, will be involved, and more besides. To trace the smile back to the love would involve even greater understanding. This example shows that anyone who is to reveal the relation between spiritual and natural phenomena must understand the natural world of effects as well as the spiritual world through which the effects are produced. Thus a knowledge of both is required. This criterion was met by Emanuel Swedenborg (1688-1772). He was a Swedish scientist and engineer whose achievements caused him to be regarded very highly. He received many honors and was greatly respected by knowledgeable people of his day (Sigstedt,1952). He led a useful, practical life, but his chief interests were in fundamental causes, even when his attention was focussed on physics and "as his thought began to plumb ever deeper depths he left his contemporaries behind and was in turn neglected by them" (Stanley,1977). His deeper thought and his spiritual experiences took place, so he said, under Divine auspices, about which he was completely modest. His experiences and his knowledge enabled him not only to look into the spiritual world but to understand what he saw.

14. Many people have seen the spiritual world and some of their experiences are on record, for example, those of John (in Revelation), Paul (a very brief experience), the disciples, Ezekiel, and other prophets. These seers, however, knew little about the world of nature and almost nothing about the relation between it and the world of the spirit, so that they could not at all explain what they had seen. On the other hand, Swedenborg became expert in most branches of the science of his day (it was possible two hundred years ago!), but especially in anatomy and physics. "His prophetic insight into the fundamental nature of matter" can only be appreciated now, after two hundred years of experimental science. However, although these insights were nearer modern physics than Newton's, Swedenborg had no miraculous knowledge of future science, and his encyclopaedic knowledge of the spiritual world was related to selected natural knowledge of his time. His own "prophetic insights" were largely laid aside and knowledge that was already widely accepted among the educated was used. Some of that knowledge has been discredited; much of the rest has been superseded by more accurate and more detailed knowledge. How can a revelation linked with inadequate, outdated knowledge remain viable? It remains not only viable but increases in vigour, for the newer knowledge is more correct and therefore it forms an even better basis for spiritual truths, and shows more clearly than before the orderly links between the spiritual and the natural. (Of course, this claim can be substantiated only by detailed study such as that which follows in later chapters.)

A true revelation is more and more confirmed as scientific discovery progresses, providing the relationship between scientific fact and spiritual knowledge is known

15. The phoenix-like renewal mentioned above is only to be expected because the spiritual revelations were made more closely under the Divine auspices than the acquirement of natural knowledge by the world at large, which had necessarily to proceed at the pedestrian pace of experimental investigation. On the other hand, spiritual advancement, in general, had seemed to be going backwards; but when a knowledge of spiritual things was revealed the result was a tremendous leap forwards. A new revelation from God is sure to be in

greater perfection than any merely natural knowledge. In such a case, an improvement in natural knowledge by two centuries of patient, painstaking experimental investigation should lead to a body of science more capable of supporting the spiritual revelation than was the knowledge it displaced. Because Swedenborg learned many things under Divine auspices, he was able to reveal the relationships between spiritual and natural things, i.e., to expound the theory of correspondences. Correspondences indicate the means of creation and provide the interpretation of the Divine Allegory, i.e., of the whole Word of God, as we have it in the Bible. In the view of many people, the work of Swedenborg in laying before us the inner meaning of the Scriptures was his most important task. It is particularly remarkable that the correspondences by which this was done are exactly those by which the material universe was created and continues. Thus it was that most of Swedenborg's effort was in interpreting the Word; yet so closely do the two facets of reality march together that neither can be studied without, inadvertently as it were, learning much about the other. Spiritual thought could not exist without the Word of God, and the natural basis would be pointless without a Spiritual superstructure. The concepts of spiritual matters which are necessary for understanding what follows are fully explained in those of Swedenborg's works written after he was called to his spiritual task. These works as a whole are called "The Writings." The full titles and the abbreviations of Swedenborg's works referred to herein are given in the List of Abbreviations, xiv; and in the Bibliography, p. 350.

CHAPTER II

SEEING AND UNDERSTANDING REQUIRE THE LIGHT OF TRUTH FROM GOD

Sight corresponds to many mental concepts connected with under–standing

16. It has already been noted (No. 9) that even in ordinary conversation "to see" often means "to understand." The Writings make it clear in *Arcana Coelestia* (AC) that sight is universally accepted as a symbol of understanding because there is, in the human race, an awareness, though often vague and weak and sometimes denied, of the most pervading effects of the spiritual world (AC 4406). So sight is more than a mere symbol of understanding because it is an actual correspondence. In fact, the closeness of the correspondence and its acceptance into the language make it difficult to write about understanding without using correspondences based on sight and light. This can be seen (!) from a short list of words frequently used in relation to mental things, e.g.: clear, dull, bright, short-sighted, point-of-view, imagine (from image), project, show, outline, adumbrate, black-and-white.

17. The complete process of seeing also involves understanding even on the natural level, for, unless the patterns of light, shade, colour, and the stereoscopic results of using two eyes are properly interpreted, there will be no apprehension of the surroundings; no real seeing. It is therefore true to say that sight not only corresponds to the understanding, but that it *is* understanding, though of a limited kind. This is confirmed by the experience of those born blind and later cured by modern surgery. They need to learn what the patterns on their retina mean and to connect them with their previous experience through the other senses.

As an isolated eye cannot see, so neither can a man if isolated from influx

18. At the level of being able to interpret the patterns on the retina, we have much in common with the animals, whose bodily processes are like our own; but in addition we have more interior (i.e., spiritual) things that correspond precisely with bodily processes. Thus we read that unless man's interior sight,

> continually inflowed into his outer sight, which is that of the eye, this latter could not possibly apprehend and discern any object...It is his [man's] spirit that sees, not his eye; the spirit sees through the eye...The case is the very same in regard to this interior sight, or that of the spirit; this again does not see from itself, but from a still more interior sight, or that of man's Rational. Nay, neither does this see of itself, but does so from a still more internal sight, which is that of the internal...man. And even this does not see of itself, for it is the Lord who sees through the internal man, and He is the Only One who sees because He is the Only One who lives, and He it is who gives man the ability to see, and this in such a manner that it appears to him as if he saw of himself. (AC 1954)

Seeing leads the attention away from self into the surroundings and can even make a man feel as though the spirit is being led out of the body

19. Sight can only take place when the eye and the brain function together, and when they do so they constitute a complicated device by which the outside surroundings are as it were brought right into the brain. There is no communication between the separate strands of the optic nerve; they do not divide and rejoin, though it has recently become clear that their inputs are to some extent integrated in the lateral geniculate bodies (See No. 369) and possibly modified from an inflow from the cerebral cortex. Even so, the pictures on the retinae are transferred as a pattern of some kind to the visual cortex, and in the brain there is therefore a stereoscopic representation of the surroundings: a little world in the head corresponding to the big world outside. It is as though we take the environment into ourselves and this, from the point of view of our own experience, is like flowing out of ourselves and pouring and spreading our being into the surroundings. We feel as though we are in the scene we are looking at.

20. This is an emotional, not a factual, experience, but it may have its roots also in correspondence; when we study the internal, i.e. spiritual, sense of "He led him forth abroad and said, `Look now toward heaven'…" we learn that the eye "is properly nothing but the sight of his spirit led forth abroad" (Gen. 15:5; AC 1806). This inward sight occurs whenever things seen by the eye of the body lead the man to think of things concerning the Church or heaven. Perhaps it is not straining the meaning of correspondences to think that by means of the understanding one is liberated and led out of oneself to explore the natural or spiritual world.

The personality absorbs truths through the understanding in the same limited way as the brain absorbs images through the eye

21. It was suggested above that the process of seeing is, as it were, a taking of our environment into our own brain (No. 19). This in turn suggests by correspondences that even in this world the spiritual function of the understanding is to take into the personality a true, useful, necessary representation of spiritual objects in the form of truths. The analogy of sight shows that by understanding these things we are not so much explaining to ourselves how they work as taking them into ourselves in the form of adequate images. An image is adequate when it enables the man to appreciate the real thing and to act appropriately towards it. Thus the humiliating fact is that we can have no real genuine truth in ourselves. We can comprehend only a mere image. Genuine truth is always limited by our own understanding or spiritual sight. Nevertheless, the image is formed according to the orderly way provided by the Lord who designed the eye and also gives the light.

As the eye cannot function without light, so the understanding cannot function without truth

22. No one can know the excellence, paucity, or limitations of his own or his companion's sight unless he knows what there is to be seen. It is the same with the corresponding faculty of the understanding. It is, as already mentioned, the function of the understanding to take in truths and to think about them. We have already considered how the eye takes into the brain an image of its surroundings, by means of light. Similarly, there is a spiritual light which enables the understanding to function. This also is called truth (because of the inadequacy of language). In order to explore the correspondences of sight and understanding we need to turn our attention, for a while, to truth.

23. It is a remarkable fact, and, to those who are unfamiliar with the Writings, somewhat of a puzzle, that the internal or spiritual sense of the Word is so often shown to be merely truth, or concerning truth. It is even said in the Writings that everything has relation to good and truth (AC 4409) and, further, that truth is the form of good (AC 3049). This means that, as to essentials, everything is good. Such a general statement needs particulars to make the meaning richer.

The purpose of truth is to introduce good

24. Truth itself is an empty abstraction. Without some connection with good or use it means nothing. Therefore let us consider good for a moment. The purpose of truth (or its use) is that we may receive good. The Lord is good. It is His aim to bring us nearer to Himself so that we may delight in His good. As truth is the form of good, we may make use of the truth; by studying it with love and reverence we may approach a little nearer to the good which is its essence, and so to a life in which the truth is obeyed because the good within it is loved.

There are many varieties of truth

25. Truth is often thought to be a simple thing. It is so considered in the Courts of Law: "the evidence I shall give shall be the truth, the whole truth…etc." People tend to think like this because they tend to confuse truthfulness with truth in spite of knowing that there are many truths. Correspondences show that there are many different kinds of truth. For example, stone, iron, silver, water, light, a son, a king, all correspond to truth, and as correspondences are not merely fanciful poetic metaphors but are the relation between natural things and the spiritual things that cause them, it must follow that there is a wide variety of truths. That which produces light cannot be the same as that which produces a stone, even though physics shows us the interconversion of matter and energy.

The lowest form of truth is about physical things

26. It is perhaps useful to begin a consideration of truth by taking it first at its lowest level. This level probably corresponds to stone. (Yet there are also many kinds of stone. Even gems are only stones; but at the moment we think of common pebbles or pieces of rock.) The lowest level of truth is the property of an ordinary factual statement, that it is true. It is interesting to note that even at this level the truth is abstract, but the test of it is concrete! At this level the statement to be tested will be about concrete things, and if the statement is true it can be used to plan successful manipulations of concrete things. For example, it is true that ice will melt if warmed above zero degrees Centigrade. So the Eskimo knows how to get a drink. It is also true that ice will melt a little below zero degrees Centigrade if salt is added to it. So after a frost, the skidding of a motor vehicle can be controlled because of the abstract quality of the truth in this statement.

The highest form of truth is an Emanation from God in which He is also present

27. We now contrast the lowest factual truths with the highest idea of truth that is available to us. The Lord Himself says that He is the truth and that He is the light. We learn also from the Writings that the Divine Wisdom goes forth from the spiritual sun (in which the Lord is) as light; yet it is not Wisdom alone, for as it proceeds, it is perfectly united with Love. This kind of Wisdom, Truth and Love is far more than a mere abstraction. We are accustomed through the Writings to think that the Lord Himself is in, or actually is His Love and Wisdom. For example, "as all Love is from the Lord it is the Lord Himself" (AC 1873); and "the things that are from Him, or which are of Him, are also Himself" (AC 10,336). Now this may be a difficult concept. How can that which proceeds from the Lord be the Lord Himself? Obviously, such Divine things will always be beyond our grasp and the Writings warn us not to try too hard to grasp them. For example we read: "But how the Divine Good of the Lord's Divine Love is accommodated to reception cannot be known by anyone, not even by the angels in heaven, because it is an accommodation of the Infinite to the finite; and the Infinite is such as to transcend all finite intelligence, so much so that when the understanding of the finite desires to direct its intuition thither it falls like one who falls into the depths of the sea and perishes" (AC 8644). Such a warning does not mean, however, that we are not to attempt to form some ideas about the subject, and we are instructed that correspondences are the means whereby we can form such ideas (AC 9300).

28. The Writings frequently use the correspondence of the natural sun to explain the nature of the spiritual Sun, of the Divine Good of the Divine Love which is in it, and of the Divine Truth and Divine Good

which are from it. Thus we may use our knowledge of the sun and its light to help us visualize something of the Divine Love and Wisdom even if we can never fully understand them. We may, for example, form an idea of how that which proceeds from the Lord can also be the Lord Himself. We first call to mind the present general ideas in physics about the conversion of matter into energy and Einstein's famous equation (Energy = Mass multiplied by square of velocity of light). From this, we think about the sun where matter is converted into energy and is radiated. Thus every bit of sunshine we receive is really a little bit of the sun itself, which means that the sun is busily making itself into innumerable little packets (quanta) which travel out across space (but the packets are so small and so numerous that the light appears continuous). Similarly, but more perfectly, The Lord is able to send us something of Himself in His truth and good. As we can not be near the sun but must have the sunshine accommodated for our reception, so also the Lord's Love and Wisdom must be accommodated to our reception. There is much difference, however, between every natural thing and every corresponding spiritual thing. Thus the sun will expend itself and be used up in x million years, but the Lord is infinite. Nevertheless, the fantastically huge amount of energy in the sun compared with the tiny quantity we need for sight can give us an idea of the Lord's infinity; for although the sun is finite, the number of quanta it can produce is so large that for practical purposes we regard it as inexhaustible and thus, as it were, infinite.

29. In providing us with "inexhaustible" warmth and light (including that stored in fossil fuels), the sun is like an image of the Lord's Love. He has made a device which shall show His Love on the natural plane. Its distance from us, the intervening atmosphere, and especially clouds, show how the Lord accommodates His Love and Wisdom to our reception for the sake of our freedom. In His creation, especially in the sun, we see the Lord striving with all His power to show us His Love, to woo us to Himself. Yet, at the same time, He withdraws and hides lest His ardour should wipe us out or destroy our freedom, converting us into automata in which there could be no joy of life.

Every man needs at least a trace of the Divine Emanation to enable him to think

30. Returning now to the correspondence between the sun's radiation and the Divine Truth, we see that the highest kind of truth is something of the Lord that is continually flowing towards all of us, as AC 9399 states: "for the Divine Truth which is from the Lord flows in continually with man." We learn about its properties in many places in the Writings, e.g., AC 6032. We find that this Divine Truth not only illuminates the mind of man but also constitutes his intellectual or his internal sight which is understanding (AC 9399). It adapts or fits every one for reception. Without it man would be unable to perceive or understand anything whatever.

31. Even with the fallen natural man, the faculty of thinking and speaking depended upon the influx of such spiritual light "as could enter as it were through chinks" (AC 3167). Moreover, the evil spirits in the other life see by the light of heaven, except that with them it is changed into a light like that from a charcoal fire (AC 3195).

32. Even in hell the light still comes originally from the Lord, but by so many derivations that its character is changed. (We know that coal contains solar energy trapped by plants that have then become fossilized) (AC 4531).

The man of the Church enjoys the sight of truths according to his own quality

33. It is obvious that in ordinary daylight we see by the sun's light, even if it is diffused by clouds or reflected from the walls of a room. In the same way, the image on our spiritual retina is formed by the radiating Divine Truth after it has been reflected by spiritual objects

which are truths. Our spiritual eyes cannot otherwise receive this form of Divine Truth, just as we cannot gaze at the sun without being blinded. Many truths are necessary to provide a healthy spiritual environment, as well as beneficent scenery. Doctrine provides such truths; the Divine Truth shines on them and our understanding accepts an image of them. This concept is explained in beautiful and vivid language in AC 8707, part of which is as follows:

> The understanding which the man of the spiritual church has is from the immediate influx of Truth from the Lord, from which there is no apperception of truth, but a light which gives the capacity of understanding. It is with this light as with the light of the sight of the eye; in order that the eye may see objects, there must be a light from which there is general illumination. In this light the eye sees and discerns objects, and is affected with beauty and delight according to their conformity with order. The case is similar with the sight of the internal eye, which is the understanding; in order that this may see, there must also be a light from which there is general illumination, in which appear the objects which are the things of intelligence and wisdom. This light is from the Divine Truth which proceeds immediately from the Lord (see AC 8644e). The objects presented in this light appear beautiful and delightful according to their conformity with the good anyone has.

The last remark shows that the image we form for ourselves is always more or less inadequate since no one is perfect, but as our spiritual sight grows stronger the image becomes less inadequate. As our lives improve we move into regions where the Divine Sun is less obscured by clouds or the day advances and the light grows stronger.

The act of seeing spiritual truths is an advent of the Lord

34. In all our seeing it is really the Lord who is coming, in the form of His Light, into our understandings. The reflection of daylight by objects in the world does not destroy the daylight. Neither is the Lord's light destroyed by reflection from the truths of His Word, by which He chooses to reveal Himself. It is solely by His light that these truths can be seen, and they are there so that they may reflect His Light. Our attention focusses the light on the retina which then gives an image of the truths. The image even gives the relationships among the truths, which are near each other, above, below, behind, joined, or separated. This image is not the same as the truths themselves. In some ways it is less. In another way, it is more, for it is formed by the Divine Light. We have, then, in our "eye" not the truths but something of the Lord sent to us *via* the truths. In such a way even incorrect beliefs can mediate to us something of the Light which is the Lord, providing we are living where the Daylight is.

35. There seem to be no words for this substance that flows out from the Lord other than spiritual light or Divine Truth. We usually think of Divine Truth in connection with salvation and spiritual and celestial things. It seems very different from that quality in man which distinguishes a fact from a non-fact but, all the same, it is that exact quality.

36. The interior sight referred to here (Nos. 31-35) is the sight of the spirit, i.e., intellectual sight, which, as we have seen, is understanding. Thus we arrive once more at the point of AC 9399, namely, that without Divine Truth man would be unable to perceive and understand anything whatever.

Even simple facts can be discerned only by means of the Divine Truth "which lighteth every man that cometh into the world"

37. We are now in a position to notice clearly the difference between facts and Divine Truth. The facts are the objects of the internal sight. Divine Truth is the light by which they are seen. The same applies to spiritual things. They also appear only in the Divine Light but in a brighter light by which only those who are in love to the Lord can see.

38. So we have the Truth which is the light and the truths which are the objects seen by that light. (These objects are really goods, but truths are their forms and appearances.) Since truths are innumerable there is no limit to the variety of intellectual objects that may be seen. There is only one Truth *by which* they are seen. This is the light "which lighteth every man that cometh into the world" (John 1:9).

CHAPTER III

THINKING FROM CORRESPONDENCES

Correspondences reveal the spiritual sense of the Word only to those who are led by the Lord

39. Having now seen from a few examples how correspondences can help in the understanding of spiritual things, we turn our attention to the more general question of whether it is wise to assist thought in this way. We have the Word of the Lord, the commandments and our faith. Do we go astray if we look for more?

40. It is certainly possible to go astray, for we are warned in *The True Christian Religion* that no one can see the spiritual sense of the Word except from the Lord alone and that anyone who wishes to investigate it from his own intelligence by means of a few correspondences will probably violate it (TCR 208).

41. From the above, we might think it better to diminish our study of spiritual things. There are many people who live good lives without needing a great deal of intellectual justification. On the other hand, many good folk are misled because they lack true knowledge and their efforts (which are in themselves good) actually produce evil. This is true in practical affairs and even more true in the inner life of the soul where temptations and battles between right and wrong go on. Probably every person who receives good would be better if he could improve the quality and quantity of the truth according to which he lives. Correspondences, more or less remote, inevitably take part in such improvement.

Thinking from correspondences is necessary because man's mental faculties begin with sense experiences and always rest upon them

42. The truth in a man's mind may seem far from the objects of the world around him. His life may be ruled by ideas of sincerity and unselfishness which seem so abstract as to have no connection with natural objects. However, the connection is really there and can easily be traced; from earliest infancy he has learned to deal with material objects, and much of his way of thinking has arisen as a result of such experience. Probably everyone who has learned not to steal has his first prohibition related to some particular object. Thus we read:

> It is known that man is not born into any knowledge, nor into anything rational, but only into the faculty of receiving them; also that he afterwards learns and imbibes all things by degrees, and this especially by means of the sensuous things of hearing and sight, and as he learns and imbibes he becomes rational. That these things are effected by the way of the body, that is, by an external way, since they are effected by hearing and sight, is evident. (AC 2557:2)

Thus we also read:

> Apart from an idea drawn from things knowable and capable of being seized by the senses, a man cannot think with himself; and he then thinks correctly, even concerning the things which belong to faith and love, when he thinks of them from correspondences; for correspondences are natural verities in which, as in mirrors, spiritual verities are represented. Wherefore so far as the ideas of thought concerning spiritual things are formed independently of correspondences, so far they are formed either from the fallacies of the senses or from things incongruous. (AC 9300:3)

This strong statement must, however, be viewed in the light of many other passages in the Writings which point to the need for an acceptance of truth primarily because it is from the Lord. In the story of the sterility of Abimelech's wife and household on account of Sarah, Abraham's wife, we learn from the following passage that when the doctrine of faith is viewed from Divine truths, that is, from the Word, then all things confirm it. But when viewed from human things, that is, from reason and knowledge, nothing of good and truth is conceived:

> for to view it from the Word is to view it from the Lord, but to view it from reason and science [i.e., external knowledges] is to view it from man; all intelligence and wisdom are from the Word, and all insanity and foolishness are from reason and science… (AC 2584:3)

Nevertheless it is quite clear that reason and external knowledge have a very important role to perform, and as long as they are in their proper place of subservience to higher faculties, insanity and foolishness are not allowed to develop from them.

43. There was a time in the Christian Church when great emphasis was placed on the abstruse nature of Divine mysteries; men were taught that they could not understand them and must accept them without trying to understand. This attitude of mind leads to blind, mechanical, superstitious, merely animal obedience, far from the Lord's "and the truth shall make you free." No idea at all can be of use to a man if he does not think about the Lord's truth. Moreover, there are many passages in the Writings making it clear that any one who has an affirmative attitude towards the Lord's teaching is allowed to confirm his faith by whatever ideas and knowledges appeal to him for that purpose, even quite external ones. So we return to our last quotation: "so far as the ideas of thought concerning spiritual things are formed independently of correspondences, so far they are formed either from the fallacies of the senses or from things incongruous." This means that it is not only allowable but necessary to think from correspondences.

It is not difficult to think from correspondences

44. Thinking from correspondences is easy because, owing to influences from the spiritual world, we all think from correspondences, to some degree, without knowing it, as when we say "see" for understand, or when we talk about the warmth of love. Clearly an expert knowledge is not necessary to enable anyone to think from correspondences.

45. Many people have an emotional response to a glorious sunset; they enjoy the colours and perhaps the peaceful evening and leave it at that. But there is something heavenly about a colourful sunset and even more so about a colourful dawn. You only have to remember that the Lord is the Sun of heaven, that the light corresponds to His Divine Wisdom and the warmth to His Divine Love. You might even remember that the flaming red colour corresponds to celestial love and that the changing colours of the setting sun fill you with joy because they show the delight when celestial love flows into spiritual love. There is no intellectual exercise here, and yet merely by allowing a few such ideas to flow into your mind you are thinking with the angels!

46. Perhaps, however, the sunset does not thrill you. Maybe you like flowers (even if you like sunsets as well). Then you will find greater joy in them when you think that their beauty represents the delights and blessedness of conjugial love.

47. Everyone who is healthy enjoys good food. People of some religions tend to feel a little guilty about it, as it can easily become a matter of self-indulgence. If you think from correspondences, however, you know that it is orderly to enjoy your food, that the Lord also provides food and drink for the soul in the form of good loves and truths, and that the two kinds of food correspond. We can eat wisely (and nothing destroys the enjoyment of good food more certainly than eating unwisely!) in order to have a sound body as a fitting and useful home for a sound spirit which can serve the Lord in this life and in the next as well.

48. It requires no effort at all when you see mountains to think of their tops being in the sky and so corresponding to the loves or delights which raise us towards heaven and nearer to the Lord. Perhaps this is the real reason why people climb mountains, and it suggests that correspondences are effective even in those people who are not conscious of them. When you see a beautiful tree and take delight in it, what you are really doing is enjoying the delight from the spiritual world which flows into the corresponding thought. In the words of the once-popular song, "Only God can make a tree"; and the much older song (Psalm 1) which says of the man, whose delight is in the law of the Lord, "he shall be like a tree planted by the rivers of water." This unconscious appreciation of correspondences probably explains the popularity of Psalm 23. There the correspondences are easily understood and accepted.

Correspondences are the only means used in the Word to express inner meanings in outer forms

49. Like Psalm 23, many other parts of the Bible are very poetic (despite what some people may think of the language itself) but it is necessary to realize that it is not merely poetic. The imagery in poetry can be according to the genius of the poet, but the imagery in the Word of the Lord is according to correspondences and precise representations which consistently express the inner sense in outer ideas (See Nos. 1-5, 15, 52).

50. We conclude, then, that thinking from correspondences is for everyone, and is the only sound way to elevate our thought to spiritual things. We may think from correspondences either by means of familiar things of daily life or by special knowledges. Each approach has its use.

Accurate knowledge is advantageous when thinking from correspondences

51. We have seen already that modern science forms a better basis for revelation than did the lesser knowledge of earlier times (Nos. 3, 4, 15). This is because the correspondence is between spiritual things and natural things as they actually are. Thus the correspondences from which we think must be based as far as possible on true and accurate natural knowledges. Providing our method of seeing spiritual things reflected in natural things is sound, the wider and truer our natural knowledge, the better will be our vision of spiritual things. If we can make proper use of the current tremendous growth in scientific knowledge, the Church will have a better understanding of spiritual matters than ever before; whereby also its love will be strengthened.

Significatives and representatives are not always the same as correspondences

52. Since our theme is thinking from correspondences, it is important to consider the meaning of the word "correspondence" and to understand it as accurately as possible. In the Writings correspondences, representatives, and significatives are most frequently mentioned and usually the meanings appear almost the same. However, we occasionally need to distinguish between them because, although they are usually the same as to essential meaning, this is not always the case. If we imagine they are always the same we may go astray. For example, an evil priest in the representative church was able to represent the Lord although there was no correspondence. We read, for example that "evil men equally with good men can represent and have represented the Lord's Divine" (AC 3670), and "they who are in things contrary to love and charity are not in correspondence" (AC 3484). The general law is nicely summarized as follows: "The things which flow in out of the spiritual world and are presented in the natural are in general representations; and so far as they agree together they are correspondences" (AC 2990). The words which are used in the Scriptures are symbols of natural representatives and they (i.e., the words) are then said to signify the spiritual things. There is obviously a world of difference between *signify* and *correspond* inasmuch as the former relates to the relationship between a word and a spiritual thing, whereas the latter relates to the relationship between two actual things, one of which is a cause and the other an effect.

The inevitable limitations of knowledge and intelligence ought not to deter anyone from undertaking spiritual studies

53. Obviously our progress in thinking from correspondences will be limited by our own knowledge and intelligence. Our knowledge can never approach the Divine Wisdom, and our intelligence is feeble and blind compared with the Divine Providence which has been used in the design of all things. It may well be that there is no particular so small or simple that it fails to embody all the Divine Wisdom. Thus, whatever subject we select for thought, we inevitably reach the limit of both our knowledge and our understanding. Until we realize its inevitability, this limit is depressing and tends to undermine our faith. It should do just the opposite! We should delight in the heavenly vistas extending beyond our sight and beyond our imagination. They confirm all we have been taught about the infinity of the Lord, and we should feel secure in the knowledge that such an infinite Creator is our Heavenly Father and our constant and closest companion. We undertake our exploration then with these limits constantly in mind; we rejoice at whatever is revealed and are in no way downcast at the things which remain hidden.

CHAPTER IV

CORRESPONDENCE OF THE HEART AND LUNGS—PART 1
THE CHURCH AND THE HUMAN RACE

Correspondences are seen in their most excellent forms in man

54. Although the whole realm of nature exists from the spiritual world by means of correspondences, some natural things are more remote than others. Mineral matters are most remote, plants less so, and human beings the least remote because nearest to the Lord. Thus the human and animal body derives its existence from the spiritual forces that flow into it, but these forces are not merely general influences, like gravity for example, but most particular and minute. Every smallest part of the human body represents some specific spiritual thing and much may be learned about the spiritual world from the uses of the various organs of the body, as has already been suggested with regard to the eye. These uses are reflected in the anatomy and physiology of each organ; therefore, these sciences also contribute to an understanding of the correspondences. Before entering in detail into the correspondences, it is useful to consider an aspect of the subject in which a result of correspondence or a derivation of it is seen rather than the correspondence itself as precisely understood. This aspect involves the idea that the human race can be seen spiritually as one body, different groups constituting different members. A perception of this truth was probably the origin of the famous chapter XII in Paul's first letter to the Corinthians; and now, by correspondences and the sciences, we can follow the theme in greater detail.

The whole human race is like one man, and the Church is like the heart and lungs of that man

55. In considering the human race as a whole, we nevertheless distinguish between the good and the evil, calling the former the Church Universal, irrespective of their religious loyalties. The Church Universal and Specific is described as follows:

> Those who are outside the Church, and yet acknowledge one God, and live according to their religion in a kind of charity towards the neighbor, are in communion with those who are in the Church; because no one who believes in God and lives well is condemned. From this it is evident that the Lord's Church is everywhere throughout the whole world, although it is specifically where the Lord is acknowledged, and where the Word is. (AC 10765)

Further details are to be found in AC 3263 which includes the following specially beautiful and poetic passage:

> The Lord's spiritual Church...extends throughout the whole globe; for it is not limited to those who have the Word, and who thereby know the Lord, and some truths of faith; but it is also amongst those who have not the Word, and who therefore are altogether ignorant of the Lord, and consequently do not know any truths of faith (for all the truths of faith have respect to the Lord), that is, it is amongst the Gentiles remote from the Church. For there are many amongst them who know by rational enlightenment that there is one God, that He created all things, and that He preserves all things, likewise that from Him comes all good, consequently all truth, and that likeness with Him makes man blessed; and who moreover live according to their religion, in love to that God, and in love towards the neighbor; from the affection of truth they worship the Highest. They who

are such amongst the Gentiles are those who are in the Lord's spiritual Church; and although they are ignorant of the Lord during their abode in the world, still they have in themselves the worship and tacit acknowledgement of Him, when they are in good, for the Lord is present in all good.

56. So we call the Lord's spiritual Church, which extends throughout the whole globe, the *Church Universal* and we call that Church, which is specifically where the Word is, the *Church Specific*. For example, we find in *Heaven and Hell*:

The universal Church on earth in the sight of the Lord resembles one man just as heaven does…but the Church where the Word is and where the Lord is known by means of it is like the heart and lungs in that man. It is known that all the viscera and members of the entire body draw their life from the heart and lungs through various derivations; and it is thus that those of the human race live who are outside the Church where the Word is, and who constitute the members of that man. (HH 308)

and in TCR there is this passage:

[The Church] is like the heart and lungs; the Lord's celestial kingdom like the heart and His spiritual kingdom like the lungs. As from these two fountains of life in the human body all other members…live, so also do all those people in every part of the earth who…worship one God and live good lives…live from the conjunction of the Lord and heaven with the Church by means of the Word. (TCR 268)

A starker aspect of the same truth is seen in AC 637:

The Lord's church on earth is as the heart whence the human race, even that part of it which is outside the church, has life…the whole human race on earth is as a body with its parts, wherein the Church is as the heart; and…unless there were a Church with which as with a heart the Lord might be united through heaven and the world of spirits there would be disjunction; and…the human race…would instantly perish…because regarded in himself man is much viler than the brutes…every one loves himself more than others, and thus hates all others…Therefore unless the Lord should have compassion on him and conjoin him with Himself through angels, he could not live a single moment…

The Church functions spiritually as a heart and lungs because the heart corresponds to love and the lungs to wisdom

57. We note that the Church is "like" the heart and lungs, but correspondences are behind this similitude, and we remember what is said perhaps even more often, namely, that "the heart corresponds to love and the lungs to wisdom" (TCR 37). Thus it is only according to the measure of their love and wisdom that members of the Church can function as heart and lungs to the rest of the human race.

58. Some of the quotations given above indicate that the Church where the Word is constitutes the heart and lungs of a man formed by all who are in good, but AC 637 indicates that the Church is a heart to the whole human race. In another place we are told that unless there were communication of heaven with man by means of the Church the human race would annihilate itself (AC 4545:7).

59. From these passages it is difficult at first to decide whether the Church specific is as a heart in the Church universal or in mankind as a whole. However, there is no real contradiction. Life from the Lord descends even to hell. So it descends even to the most evil on the earth. Evil men, however, are not in the Grand Man. They "do not correspond to any organs and members in the body but to various corrup-

tions and diseases induced in them" (AC 4225). The body all too often includes diseases and disorders of various kinds. Many of the bacteria and other organisms that cause these diseases derive their nourishment from the blood or from tissues built up by the blood. Moreover, the organisms are usually controlled by antibodies and other defence mechanisms provided by the blood. Thus we have a clear illustration of the function of the Church specific in preventing the human race from annihilating itself. This concept in no way weakens the correspondences between the Church as a whole and the body itself which lives according to order by means of the blood and the heart.

60. But let us consider in more detail how the Church functions as heart and lungs. The most obvious action of the heart is in pumping the blood (although it was not obvious before Harvey, and he was not so very long before Swedenborg!). So we need to know something about the correspondence of the blood.

Something in the Church or in Love and Wisdom corresponds to the blood in the heart and vessels

61. In the first and most general sense the correspondence of blood can be the same as that of the heart, for "containing vessels in the Word signify the same as their contents: thus a cup signifies the same as the wine, and a platter as the meat" (AR 672). In *Angelic Wisdom Concerning Divine Love and Wisdom*, we sometimes find "blood" being used in the same sense that "heart" has been used previously (DLW 419, 420). It is clear, however, that the correspondence, or cause of the existence, of a vessel cannot be exactly the same as that of its contents (although the end or purpose may be the same). The signification may be the same but, as already mentioned, there is sometimes a difference between signification and correspondence. So if we look more closely we find differences between the correspondences of the vessels and of their contents. Generally vessels mean scientifics (i.e., knowledges) because "every scientific is a vessel of truth and every truth is a vessel of good" (AC 3068; see also 3079). This suggests, as does common sense, that the contents correspond to something higher or more important than the vessel, though very probably something of the same type. If this is true of inanimate vessels it can be equally true of living ones, but it is likely that the relation between the vessels and contents will be more specific. A heart cannot live long if it contains anything other than blood.

62. We may think, then, that in terms of general ideas blood corresponds, as does the heart, to the celestial or to love and to those in the Church who have it. For more particular detail we may look in *Arcana Coelestia*, where we find that blood *signifies* celestial things which are of the Lord alone, and thus, relative to man, the celestial things he receives from the Lord (AC 1001); that blood (or wine) *represents and signifies* spiritual Divine Love (flesh or bread representing celestial Divine Love) (AC 4735:2); that blood *signifies* the holy of love, consequently charity and faith, for these are the holy things of love, consequently blood *signifies* holy truth proceeding from the Lord (AC 7326); that blood *means and signifies* Divine Truth proceeding from the Divine Good of the Lord (AC 7850, 10026). Here we have *signifies and represents*, which are not always the same as *corresponds to*, but here, where there is agreement, the terms are probably equivalent. This is confirmed when we read from *Apocalypse Explained*, "Flesh corresponds to good, and therefore in the Word signifies it, and blood to truth and hence signifies it" (AE 962:9), but we also have "the affections of love…correspond to the blood" (DLW 423).

63. As we might expect when we move from generals to particulars, some different details emerge which at first look like contradictions: the blood corresponds to love, to affections of love, and also to truth; and truth seems to be so different from good! Nevertheless, truth is only separable from good in the thought of man. In reality, genuine truth always has good or love actually inside it. ("Truth is a vessel of good") It is much the same with blood. Although it is mostly water (corresponding to truth), it includes sugar and fat (corresponding to good) and many other good things which it takes to the parts of the body which need them.

The many functions of blood show the variety and importance of its correspondences

64. It is impossible to realize the scope of the correspondences of the blood without looking at its functions. As it would require a whole treatise to describe them in detail, a brief list of the more obvious ones must suffice. They are as follows:

1. The control of the amount of water in tissues by providing it where needed and removing it if it is present in excess (with the aid of the kidneys).
2. The transport of numerous items of nourishment (sugars, fats, amino acids, vitamins, minerals) from sites of absorption or storage to sites where they are required.
3. Transport of oxygen to all living tissues.
4. Removal of carbon dioxide from all living tissues.
5. Removal of numerous more or less toxic breakdown products produced by wear and tear.
6. Combat of infection (by antibodies and leucocytes).
7. Plugging of leaks (by clotting which includes a mechanism for directing the laying down of new tissues in scars to give extra strength in the directions of greatest stress).
8. Transport of hormones from the glands where they are made to the tissues to be subjected to their control.
9. Temperature regulation.

65. It does not require much imagination to translate these functions in a general way into their corresponding functions in the spiritual world, and by doing so one can get a clearer picture of the conditions there. For example we are told that each individual in heaven is the centre of all influxes (AC 4225:3). Any attempt to picture this paradox in the terms of geometry whether two-dimensionally, three-dimensionally or n-dimensionally, is likely to produce nothing but confusion. But in terms of the body and its blood we can see that every cell is in "contact" with every other cell via the blood and so can receive from all and give to all. Moreover, the numerous functions we have just listed indicate the richness and abundance of the types of communication.

The Lord blesses the Church Universal with good and truth as far as it can receive. This good and truth corresponds to blood which is made in various organs and not in the heart and lungs

66. It was noted above (No. 62) that blood signifies the celestial things a man receives from the Lord, but this is not saying that things corresponding to blood flow into man directly from the Lord. There is much to be deduced from the correspondences of the bodily origins of the blood; it is a vast and wonderful subject. We can only hint at a few possibilities here. Others will be mentioned when we consider the lymphatic system which contributes much to the blood (See Chapter VIII).

67. It is a brute fact of physiology that the blood is made in various parts of the body other than the heart (e.g., the red cells and some of the white cells in the bone marrow, other cells in lymphoid tissue, proteins responsible for clotting in the liver). How are we to understand the correspondences of these facts? If we think merely of the "blood" being the Lord's or of its being made in heaven, we run into difficulties regarding the function of the Church (but see also Nos. 77-83).

68. Although we have the simple statement that blood corresponds to truth (AE 962:9), most of the references indicate a correspondence to truth from good from the Lord, suggesting perhaps that it comes directly from the Lord, though often indicating through heaven. Neither of these ideas agree very well with the fact that blood in the body is manufactured in organs other than the heart and lungs. Thus if the Church Specific is as a heart and lungs in a man to which the Church Universal corresponds, we must accept that the "blood" is made in the Church Universal and not in the Church Specific. However, correspondences exist at various levels (and the Writings seldom give the whole series in one place). Thus the spiritual heaven is in correspondence with the celestial. Representatives corresponding to the ideas of angels appear in the lower spiritual world. There are also numerous degrees between which correspondences may occur. The three degrees of celestial, spiritual and natural are only general ones. Each contains subdivisions.

69. We have, for example, "good seeks to live in truths, and truths seek to live in scientifics, and these in things of sense, and things of sense in the world" (AC 6077). We are also instructed that good produces truths and disposes them into a heavenly order by means of which further good is produced, and from this further truths (AC 3579). These series show life flowing down, or causes producing effects, and are thus examples of correspondences, although this word itself is not used in these passages.

70. In natural good there are also civil good and moral good. We may, therefore, accept that there is a kind of good-and-truth corresponding to blood which may come to us from the non-specific (universal) Church. It is really from the Lord, of course, since all good and truth are from Him. And indeed the most external kind of "blood" from the Church Universal must exist with them from a celestial inmost, even with those who have no knowledge of such things. This is the higher "blood" which can be directly from the Lord and of which the Church Specific can have some little knowledge. It may well be that there is a whole series of degrees of good-and-truth to be thought of as correspondences of blood of different apparent origins.

As "blood" which can originate in the non-specific Church, we have all those civil laws made for the purposes of true justice and equity; the honor and morality to be found in many communities and the good-neighbourliness we so often meet in everyday life.

71. These ideas suggest that civil and moral good-and-truth cannot originate within the Church. This is a shocking conclusion until we realize that it applies only to *merely* civil and moral matters and that within the Church nothing of the kind can exist because all moral and civil good-and-truth must be an expression of spiritual good-and-truth. The importance of the teaching to be derived from the correspondence is that we should in no way despise the merely civil and moral goods, but play our spiritual part as a heart and do our best to pump them around the community, and as lungs to freshen them with God's good air.

The kingdom of the heart includes all the blood vessels and the blood itself which permeates every organ

72. A further step in the development of the subject is to understand what is involved in the teaching that the heart rules throughout the body. It is said in DLW that the heart rules throughout the body by means of the blood vessels; also, that "the whole angelic heaven resembles one man and so appears in the Lord's sight. Consequently its heart makes one kingdom and its lungs the other" (DLW 381).

73. We also have: "for by means of the blood vessels the heart rules in the whole of the body and in all its parts; and the lungs in all its parts by the respirations" (AC 3887). So what are we to think about the rest of the organs? Further reading makes it clear that to whatever province (organ) an angel or spirit belongs, he is also either in the heart or lungs or both. Thus those of the province of the head are divided into celestial and spiritual, the celestial belonging to the province of the heart and the spiritual to the province of the lungs (AC

3886). And there are "spirits of the middle sort belonging both to the province of the heart and that of the lungs" (AC 4046).

74. The picture now emerging is that the heart "rules in" all the other organs. As confirmation of this idea we read: "all things of the body (have relation) to the heart and lungs" (DLW 374). A clearer statement reads: "the heart and lungs are the two things which reign...in the body" (DLW 382). The heart is then thought of as extending throughout the body, as in the following: "the heart and its extension into the body through arteries and veins..." (DLW 399).

75. We have already noted the similarity in correspondences of the heart and blood. It is now clear that arteries and veins are to be included with the heart, and it seems reasonable to add the smaller arteries, veins (arterioles and venules), capillaries, and other spaces occupied by the blood. We now begin to see what is involved in the idea of the heart "ruling" throughout the whole body. It becomes even more clear if we consider a few details.

76. In most organs the arterioles divide into capillaries which are not only microscopic but also extremely thin walled. Many, though not all, constituents of the blood can pass through the walls and actually do so to feed, cleanse, and help to control the tissues. The simple picture we are sometimes given of the blood passing through the capillaries to be collected again in the venules and then veins and so back to the heart tends to obscure the essential details. With respect to the numerous constituents of the blood that have small molecules (e.g., water, salts, glucose, oxygen, carbon dioxide, hormones), it is more true to think of the blood as permeating the whole organ, and continually soaking through it. Thus it provides all the cells with a continually-changing liquid environment from which they take nourishment and into which they discharge waste products. So we can see how intimate is the connection between the cardiovascular system and the rest of the body. See Figure 1 for an illustration of the capillar-

FIGURE 1

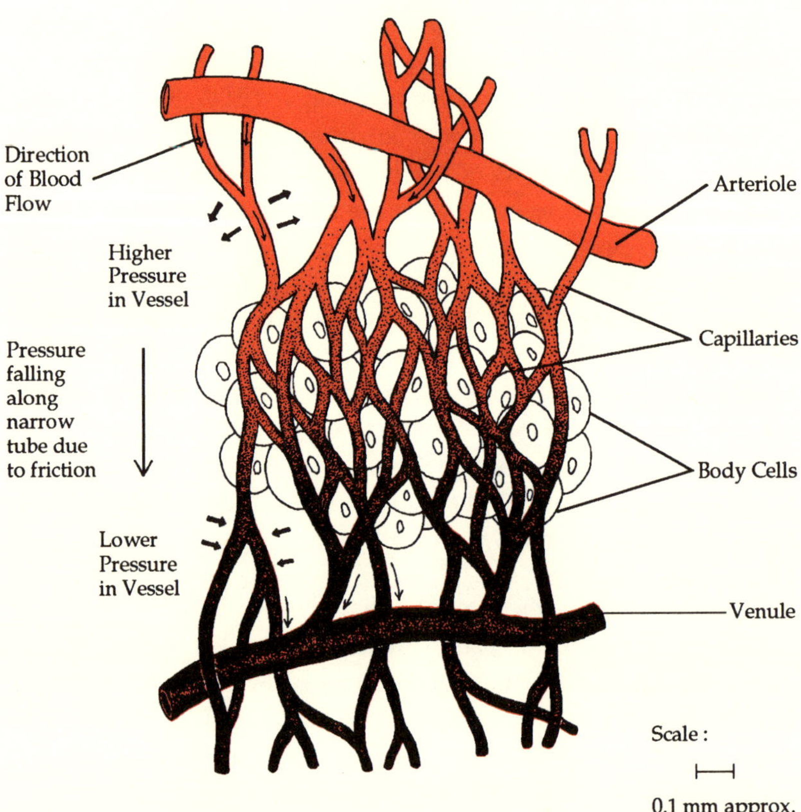

Figure 1: **Capillaries**

A simplified diagram showing how capillaries branch from an arteriole and pass between body cells, dispensing nutrients and other substances (eg. hormones) in the water that exudes where the blood pressure is highest. The capillaries are so narrow, (see scale), that there is a great drop in pressure along their length so that water in the tissue spaces can flow back into the bloodstream in capillaries at some distance from the origins, (which are different for different capillaries, as the diagram shows). The capillaries pass between the body cells, but here the cells in front have been omitted for clarity. They also vary in shape and size. Very few are spheres. Some of the watery liquid which exudes from capillaries will pass into the lymphatic system. (See Chapter VIII).

ies. Regarding that system and its blood as one, we can see more clearly now than anyone could in Swedenborg's time how the heart permeates every other organ, and rules in the whole body.

The heart rules the whole body by being the servant of all

77. Although it was stated above (No. 57) that the heart corresponds to love, it has perhaps not been made sufficiently clear that because of that correspondence the heart also corresponds to the will, which is the residence of love, and to the celestial heaven which is also a residence of love since all the angels there are primarily in love to the Lord. Since the celestial heaven is the highest heaven, it can be thought of as ruling the rest of the spiritual world. In the individual man it is his will or love that effectively rules in him (although he often tries to make it appear otherwise). Now, as love rules spiritually, we would expect the heart, by correspondence, to rule naturally or, if you prefer it, physiologically. This is what the Writings teach. It is not what medical science teaches. Yet both are true, and by bringing them together we can see several points of doctrine which might otherwise be less clear.

78. We hesitate first at the use of the word "rule." We do not observe any rule of the body by the heart except when it is inadequate. Yet according to the heavenly order from which the correspondence comes, it is quite clear. The heart rules, or is greatest, because it serves all the other organs. As the Lord teaches: "He that is greatest among you shall be your servant" (Matt. 23:11 and similarly in 20: 27).

The rule of the heart in the body shows the ruling influence of love or the will in the mind, and of the Church in the world

79. The correspondence of the rule of the heart which has just been described confirms a very important teaching that recent writers are

putting forward to counteract a tendency some of us have to think we can be just intellectual. They point out that experience and the Writings both indicate the importance of love, affection, or feeling in every aspect of our lives. The Rev. P. V. Vickers shows in *God-Talk and Man-Talk* (Vickers, 1970) that no matter how intellectual we may be nor how carefully we marshall truths and deduce conclusions, what really rules with us is our affections. And in an essay devoted mainly to demonstrating the unity of love and wisdom and all their derivative functions, Dr. Wilson Van Dusen emphasizes the importance of love, affection, and feelings (Van Dusen, 1975, p. 401). These teachings are not new, of course, but the awareness of them seems to have become somewhat keener recently, and it is gratifying to find them so vividly portrayed in anatomy and physiology.

80. The correspondences also help us to gain a clearer idea of heaven. Although we are taught to remove ideas of space and time, we are also told that the celestial live on the mountains; and we (or at least I) had an idea of the celestial as "way up there" beyond our reach, of the spiritual as lower, and of the natural as lower still. We see, however, from the correspondence with the body, that the celestial, in the kingdom of the heart, are in the closest possible relation with all the other provinces, so close in fact that the use of the word "other" is difficult to justify.

81. We must similarly consider the place of the Church Specific in the Church Universal. The correspondence indicates an extremely close relationship, since the Church Specific is as the heart and lungs and the Church Universal as the rest of the body, or even the whole of mankind on the earth as the rest of the body. We can discover something more about this relationship from certain passages of the Writings.

82. From the *Apocalypse Explained* we receive a picture of a continuous flow of life (i.e., of love) from the Lord through heaven and then

through the Church Specific into all mankind, for we read:

> all in the whole earth, those who constitute the universal church,
> [live] from the church where the Word is; for thence the Lord
> flows in with love and with light, and vivifies and enlightens all
> who are in any spiritual affection of truth… (AE 351:2).

We have already seen that without this relationship (or association) mankind could not live for a single moment, or that the race would "instantly perish" (AC 637). The instantaneous result of the severing of the association shows that it cannot be a natural one based on teaching and example but something taking place in the spiritual world (in which, of course, we are all living). Thus there is an occult influx of life through the Church into the rest of the human race, and by its means the evil are restrained. How this may function can be deduced from what we are told about the representatives of a Church amongst the Jews. The representatives affected the spirits who were with men and thereby the angels in heaven (AC 4545:6). Thus we may expect that anything of a Church in man will affect the spirits with him, and these spirits will communicate with others who are associated with people outside the Church and will have some influence upon them.

83. Let us now return to the fact that blood is not made in the heart-and-lungs. We have seen how the "kingdom of the heart" extends throughout the whole body, and it would seem that when "heart" is mentioned in the Writings it is usually the "kingdom of the heart" which is meant, or, as we would now call it, the cardiovascular system. Thus it may be correct to place the various organs which manufacture the various constituents of the blood in the kingdom of the heart, and we could then account for the many civil, moral, and natural goods that "originate" in the Church Specific. Indeed in one way the matter is quite simple for, although at one level the Church Specific may be as the heart and lungs, at another level it is as a whole man.

84. The effect of the Church through associated spirits does not, of course, preclude the more obvious effects of the church in disseminating truth and encouraging good. We have already referred to the several degrees of correspondence and these more obvious effects are clearly like the pumping out of blood, which concept brings us again to that most essential teaching that the Church Specific should rule in the Church Universal by being the servant of all. How the Church Specific serves the Church Universal at a practical level varies according to the loves and abilities of different groups and individuals. Perhaps it is a matter that ought to receive greater attention.

CHAPTER V

CORRESPONDENCES OF THE HEART AND LUNGS—PART 2
THE WILL AND THE UNDERSTANDING

85. We have already noted that the rule of the heart in the body corresponds to the rule of love in the mind of an individual, but most of our attention in the previous chapter was focused on applications to the Church as a whole. We have seen that the Church functions spiritually as a heart and lungs because its love corresponds to a heart and its wisdom to lungs for the service of the human race as a whole (Nos. 57 and 84). The quality of the Church is an integration of the quality of its individuals, and it is for this reason that the correspondences in each man apply also to the Church. But there is a further spiritual reason, namely, that the Lord organizes each heavenly society (of which the Church is one) into a human form. Thus there is no fundamental difference between the application of correspondences to an individual man and their application to the Church. It seems easier to envisage their application to the individual, especially when, as now, we attempt to relate particular functions in the body to those in the mind, or spirit.

86. There is a spiritual universe between the innermost soul of man and the living organs of the body (man is a microcosm, AC 6057). But every level of this universe is related to every other by correspondences. By making use of this relationship our merely natural minds can grasp spiritual verities which intuition or the rational mind urges us to accept.[1]

---

[1] Rational is here used to mean a higher or spiritual level of the mind, not as used in the everyday sense—of a mind that thinks only from physical or sense experience and knowledge derived therefrom.

87. From common speech we are ready to accept that the heart is love, for as we have seen, common metaphors are often derived from correspondences (AC 4406). It is not so generally accepted that the lungs correspond to the mental faculty of understanding, perhaps because most people are confused regarding will and understanding (AC 634; DLW 361). However, it will become clear from what follows that the correspondence of the lungs is with the understanding. In the Writings, will is often used to mean love, for it is the receptacle of love, so we begin with the concept that the heart corresponds to the will or love, and the lungs to understanding or wisdom. It is therefore important to form serviceable ideas of what the will and understanding are.

The meaning of will and understanding

88. Thoughtful people of all persuasions are accustomed to distinguish between the emotions and the intellect. They know that the two interact to some extent and that it is often wise to control the former by means of the latter. From this beginning one may step into the New Church world of will and understanding by regarding the will as the seat of the emotions and the understanding as the intellect. However, this is only a most external view and if not opened it can be quite misleading; emotions, for example, can sometimes be largely a condition of the body-brain unit. A truer view is to see that the will is that inmost part of man into which the Lord flows with life which expresses itself in love, and that the understanding similarly receives wisdom from Him.

89. It is difficult for man to grasp the real meaning of the understanding of truth and the will of good. The reasons for the difficulty and some aid in overcoming it are to be found in AC 634, but the angelic way of thinking about these things is described as far as natural language allows in DLW, part V. This opens with the following heading:

Two receptacles and dwellings of His own, called will and understanding, have been created and formed by the Lord in man; the will for His Divine Love, and the understanding for His Divine Wisdom.

As explained in AC 634 and elsewhere, these Divine qualities received in the highest part of a man's mind are above his consciousness, and they descend by degrees to the conscious mind where they are received according to the quality of that mind. Thus it is that will and understanding sometimes mean such qualities of love and wisdom as are within our conscious grasp. But again, as they are received according to the form of each man's mind, they can even mean the opposite, when will is self-will and understanding is folly. In the Writings such variant meanings are always quite clear from the context.

The will is the receptacle of love but it is not identical with love neither is the understanding identical with wisdom

90. As the will is the receptacle of love it is often used to mean love. The Writings state that we may equate will and love, but this is probably only as a first approximation, for it is introduced by "Whether you say." The whole sentence is "Whether you say love or will it is the same since the will is the receptacle of love" (DLW 378 at the end).

91. There are a number of reasons for regarding this statement as a first approximation (or a general truth), but as an example of the difficulties that arise if it is applied too rigidly, consider the following.

Just as the heart produces such things [other organs] on account of the varied activities it is about to perform in the body, so love produces corresponding things in its receptacle, the will, for the sake of the various affections that make up its form. (DLW 410)

From this we get an idea that love acts in the will as the heart acts in the body, thus that the will corresponds to the whole body, and this is confirmed in DLW 403 where we read, "the will is the whole man." But we read elsewhere "The will corresponds to the heart" (DLW 371:iii).

92. In trying to understand these things more clearly, we wish to distinguish between the vessel (the will) and what it contains (the love). This is not now difficult for we have already seen how, in the language of the Writings, the kingdom of the heart includes the blood vessels and the blood, and thus how the heart is united with the whole body, and rules all the other organs by serving them (Nos. 74-78). This means that in our reading we must not always confine our ideas of the heart to that particular organ itself. Instead, we may think of the correspondence of the will with the kingdom of the heart as it extends throughout the whole body, and of the correspondence of love with the heart itself within the chest. In other words, as the whole body is full of blood vessels and blood within different organs, so the will is full of loves of many kinds, yet all with a common purpose depending on the ruling love. There has been occasion earlier (No. 61) to distinguish between a vessel and its contents (although vessels are so often used in the Word to signify the contents). But the vessel is external and so, in our thoughts as we pass from the vessel, e.g., "a cup," to the contents, e.g., "cold water," we are led from externals towards internals, and thus in the direction of heaven and the Lord.

93. Similarly, when we read of the heart we may think of the will, and when we think of the will we may think of the love it can receive from the Lord and how He dwells with man. From contemplating these things we may, at times, be led to think of the Lord's love as being for the whole human race, and as expressing itself through individuals and their uses towards the neighbor. So we become concerned with how love can express itself in use. Then our concept of the will as being the whole man and as corresponding to the heart, and blood vessels, and blood itself throughout the whole body helps us to realize the richness and variety of the uses that love can perform, although enthroned, as it were, and protected in the chest. In this way a distinction between love and the will can be useful. However, whenever we observe such a distinction it is important to remember that love is not in its receptacle, the will, as water in a cup, but that it penetrates and activates because it is life from the Lord. The will without love would be a corpse.

94. A similar distinction must apply to the understanding and wisdom, but it is not so obvious, for as the lungs cannot work without blood from the heart, so neither can the understanding work unless impelled by some form of love from the will. Since, however, the understanding may be filled with foolishness which it may later replace with wisdom, it is clear that the understanding is also a kind of receptacle or organ.

95. Although it seems important to make these distinctions if we wish to think deeply, the Writings often do not do so, perhaps because a true understanding must necessarily house wisdom and a genuine will must necessarily be the dwelling of a good love. We may therefore continue to say the heart corresponds to love and the lungs to wisdom, invoking the distinctions only where necessary.

The correspondences of the heart and lungs include all psychology

96. This is because psychology means knowledge of the psyche (or soul), and we read:

> All the things which can be known…of the soul of man may be
> known from the correspondences of the heart with the will and
> of the understanding with the lungs. (DLW 394)

In view of the complexities of the human mind, how can such a statement be justified? The things that follow in DLW concerning the heart and lungs are relatively simple, and what we are taught about will and understanding in the Writings, are vast, complex, and difficult to understand. It is clear that in the Writings the Lord was providing for the future, when much more would be known about the heart and lungs. But even now all the known detail of the anatomy of these organs could scarcely suffice to illustrate what the Writings teach. Other sciences have their role, and it is one of the delights and uses of the New Church scientist to show how knowledge of the ultimates amongst which we live can provide, through correspondences, a more vivid picture of spiritual reality.

97. The assertion which provides the heading just above can only be proved by one who knows all "which can be known," etc., but it is hoped that the chapters which follow will demonstrate some of the things which can be known from the correspondences and that many more remain to be discovered.

98. Until now we have been concerned mostly with correspondences of the heart, but we need to think a little more about the lungs if we are to achieve a portion of the knowledge promised in the quotation above.

99. The correspondence of the lungs has already been mentioned because in so many places in the Writings the heart and lungs come together. Anatomically and physiologically this is an obvious convenience, because they are so closely associated, and as we would expect, the association extends into the correspondences also, since the lungs correspond to wisdom, and love without wisdom is as useless as a heart without lungs.

Only active lungs correspond to wisdom

100. To be precise, we say that the understanding (or wisdom) corresponds to the respiration of the lungs. This is as stated in AC

3888. However, lungs are often spoken of without mention of respiration, for (as before noted) correspondences are really with the use or function; what are lungs apart from the respiration? It is obvious that it is only normal, healthy, active lungs that correspond to wisdom. Active lungs require a good supply of blood from the heart (which is love). The correspondence of this is that, although wisdom can only exist when truth is in the understanding (the lungs), love also is necessary, for we read that "he is wise who lives the truth from love" (AC 10331:2). We see, then, that when the truth is activated by love so as to be useful, then it is not merely truth but wisdom. Truth activated by an evil love becomes folly. Truth not activated by any love is not anything at all. It is, however, an abstraction which, if not destroyed, may become something. We see this in the state of the lungs in the embryo. Their union with the heart is sufficient only for their preservation and growth. They do not function. Most of the blood by-passes them. So we have a picture of man at the beginning of regeneration. His love is sufficient to cause the truth with him to grow and to maintain it in a potentially useful form, but it does not as yet function in his life. It is not wisdom. His "heart's blood," the driving force of his life, by-passes the truths stored in his memory, and his life is not really good.

101. In some such way as this we must distinguish between truth and wisdom. Nevertheless, in order to study the ways in which truth is united with good, and so becomes wisdom, we often speak of it as though it were already wisdom; prolepsis rather than inaccuracy.

The importance of the understanding to the life of the mind is shown by the importance of the lungs to the life of the body

102. This statement is the obverse of DLW 399 which says, "the love or will is the very life of man." This is so true that we cannot but assent to it wholeheartedly, but the facts brought forward in support of it introduce a soupcon of doubt. They are like salt in food; clearly they are deliberately introduced, as salt is deliberately added to food. We therefore examine them more closely.

103. At first we receive an impression that the importance of the understanding is being depreciated. It seems to be established that the life of the mind depends on the will alone:

> [The heart] may act apart from the cooperation of the lungs [as] is evident from cases of suffocation and swooning. From this it can be seen that, as the subsidiary life of the body depends on the heart alone, so likewise the life of the mind depends on the will alone, and in the same way the will lives when thought has ceased… (DLW 399)

But one may be excused for thinking that the life of the body does not depend on the heart alone. Many other organs are necessary, as is also pointed out in DLW 367 in which we read, "the whole exists from the parts, and the parts continue to exist from the whole."

104. Swooning and suffocation are temporary conditions; a drowned man will not survive unless he receives artificial respiration promptly. Swooning and suffocation are usually the result of sickness or accident, and we may therefore think of them as disorderly as well as temporary. Translating by correspondences, we deduce that the life of the will when thought has ceased is temporary and disorderly. We therefore conclude that, as a man cannot continue a normal life if his lungs are not working, so neither can he do so if his understanding does not function. Those whose will is not assisted by the understanding are of unsound mind.

A life of the body unassisted by its own lungs, yet not disorderly, is that of the embryo. We know that celestial angels have charge over this, and our thoughts are hence led also to the Most Ancient Church, their celestial character, and their internal respiration. It would seem that internal respiration means that their understandings did not need to labour (as a man panting for breath) as ours do, but the Lord flowed into their minds by an internal way; but these things are considered in more detail in Chapter VII.

105. Thus we can see more in DLW 399 than at first appears. As stated there the will can live when thought has ceased, but this is only for certain types and conditions of men and angels, and for us, activity of the understanding is necessary most of the time.

The "joint rule" ascribed by the Writings to the heart and lungs can be understood only in terms of physiology and biochemistry

106. One of the most interesting problems arising during a study of the heart and lungs involves the predominance the Writings give to the heart. At the same time, a ruling influence is ascribed to the lungs throughout the body; that is to say, the lungs join the heart in its rule but the heart is the senior partner. It is difficult to envisage this role of the lungs without the aid of a little biochemistry, even though every-one knows that normally the whole body dies if the lungs cannot function.

107. Several passages in DLW explain the primary importance of the heart compared with the lungs, and show that this is in correspon-dence with the primary importance of the will compared with the understanding. There are passages which emphasize that, as the will does nothing without the understanding, so the heart does nothing without union with the lungs; it is together that they "rule" through-out the body. Some ideas about the movements of the lungs and how such movements affect the rest of the body are brought out to show how it may be that the lungs have their part to play in the joint "rule" with the heart. Here we wonder whether the limitations of natural knowledge in Swedenborg's time made it difficult for him to find the natural facts to which the wisdom of the angels corresponds.[2] We read that:

> All things in the body are connected so that when the lungs breathe, each and all things of the whole body are moved thereby, while at the same time also they are moved by the beating of the heart. (DLW 403)

The union of the heart and lungs by blood vessels is next mentioned. This is followed by a statement about ligaments joining the cavity of the chest and other viscera:

> [They are]...so joined that when the lungs breathe, each and all things in general and in detail receive something from the respiratory motion...all the lower parts of the body...receive some movement through the action of the lungs.

108. The union of the heart and lungs is also mentioned in *Arcana Coelestia*, where we find:

> By means of the blood vessels the heart rules in the whole of the body and in all its parts; and the lungs in all its parts by the respiration. Hence there is everywhere in the body as it were an

---

[2] Clearly Swedenborg was obliged to write according to the knowledge his readers would have. Had he written according to the knowledges we now have, his works could not have been understood in his own time.

In writing, the first necessity is to use a language the readers will understand. The second necessity is to use acceptable idioms; the third is a style of thinking not too foreign; the fourth is a background of beliefs and opinions that will not be offensive; the fifth—but how far can we go? It may even be necessary to include some erroneous beliefs to avoid becoming entirely incomprehensible to those who hold such beliefs. It has been said that a perfect revelation would be a miracle forcing belief and destroying freedom, but probably it would not do so. It merely would be incomprehensible, useless, a failure. The Word in Greek and in Hebrew contains many examples of Divine Truth accommodated in erroneous beliefs.

influx of the heart into the lungs; but according to the forms there and according to the states. (AC 3887; see also 3889)

109. But, one may ask, How can the heart flow into the lungs in remote parts of the body, even "as it were"? How can the lungs rule in remote parts of the body by respiration? Can "some movement" be enough for "rule"? What is meant by "according to the forms and according to the states"? How can "some movement through the action of the lungs" be interpreted as a union of heart and lungs? We hesitate to ask such critical questions but it seems as though it was foreseen that many of us would ask questions, and that we would feel diffident in so doing, for at the end of DLW 403 we are encouraged by these words:

> but examine the connections well and survey them with anatom-
> ical eye, and afterwards, according to the connections, observe
> their cooperation with the breathing lungs and with the heart,
> and then think of understanding in place of lungs, and of will
> instead of heart, and you will see.

If with "anatomical eye," why not also with the physiological, biochemical and, in general, scientific eye?

110. We read, "all things receive something from the respiratory motion" (DLW 403). What is the something they receive? The reduction of pressure in the chest during inspiration of air is believed to help in the return of venous blood to the heart. This could be considered one way in which the lungs cooperate with the heart (although it is really the chest rather than the lungs). But it can hardly be the "something" that *all parts* receive. Later it is said that they receive "some movement." Now, it would seem that "movement" in the sense of a small displacement in space, such as, for example, the pulse in an artery, would be a trivial matter, apart from the actual pumping effect. From his knowledge of spiritual things, it was very clear to Swedenborg that a union of love and wisdom takes place in every one of the most minute sections (if I may use the word) of the mind. Therefore, he was sure that a similar union of heart and lungs must take place in the body. In the absence of modern science, motion was the nearest he could get to actuality. Motion was, under the circumstances, a good word to choose, for it has suitable metaphorical meanings, e.g., "they were moved by the music"; "she put the motion before the meeting." So we are only supplying the necessary facts for the correspondence when we suggest that the motion is that of various components of the cells when, via the heart and blood, they receive oxygen supplied by the lungs. (The kind of motion we are thinking of here is not, of course, the Brownian motion by which diffusion takes place, but the many more special motions. An example is the movement of a phosphate group on to a glucose molecule, which occurs at the beginning of the cycle of events leading to oxidation of the glucose and a supply of energy to, say, a muscle.)

111. Can we imagine a more complete union between the lungs and the heart than this: that the heart pumps the blood through the lungs and then through the body, enabling the lungs to supply the essential oxygen (as well as to remove the carbon dioxide)? See Figure 2. And can we imagine a more complete dependence of every part of the body on the lungs as well as the heart beyond this: that without the oxygen from the lungs, brought by the blood, no part could move (in any sense) or exercise any orderly function or remain alive?[3] See Figure3. The collaboration of heart and lungs to bring refreshment to every smallest part of the body by means of the circulation is, I submit, a sufficient enough approximation to "influx" to be called "as it were an influx." Clearly also, the lungs rule, i.e., serve, all parts by means of the

---

[3] It is not surprising that, in an age when oxygen was not known and oxidation was not understood, the word "lungs" could be used to cover the whole phenomenon of respiration, and their movement could be regarded as of importance to the whole body. Even now, we find "lungs" being used in a vague way to mean apparatus for breathing, as in "iron lungs," for patients with paralysis of the muscles needed for breathing.

FIGURE 2

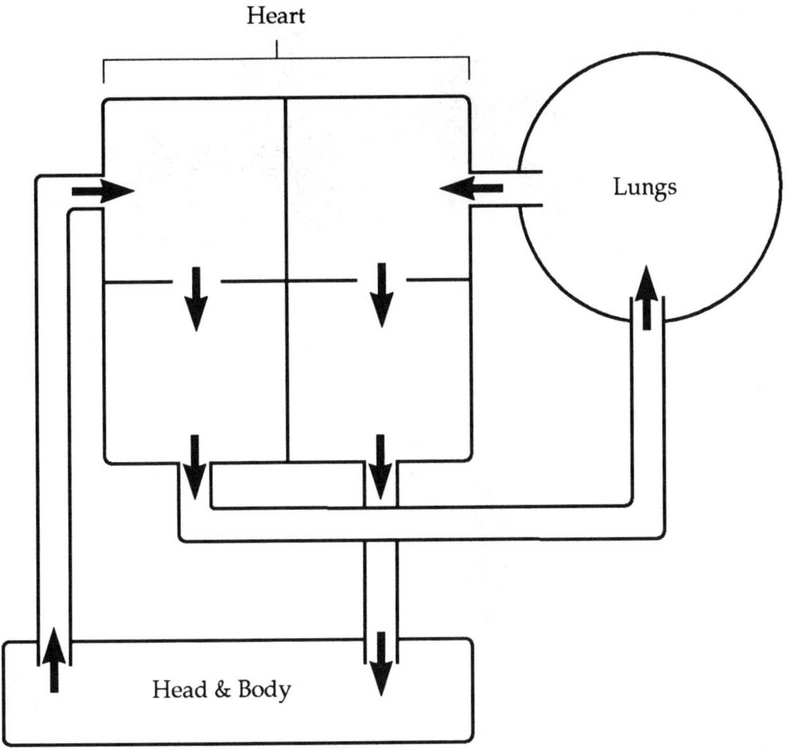

Figure 2: **Circulation of the Blood**

Block diagram of circulation to show the separation of the two routes, lungs and body, and to illustrate that blood from the body cannot return to the body until it has passed through the lungs. See also Figure 3.

The bronchial arteries and veins which also connect the heart with the lungs are not represented here because (a) the volume of blood conveyed is relatively small, (b) they do not connect with the air saccules where oxygen is taken up, and (c) their blood is returned to the right side of the heart with that from the rest of the body (except for a very small leak of about 1% which passes to the pulmonary vein).

Drawn by Richard Morris.

FIGURE 3

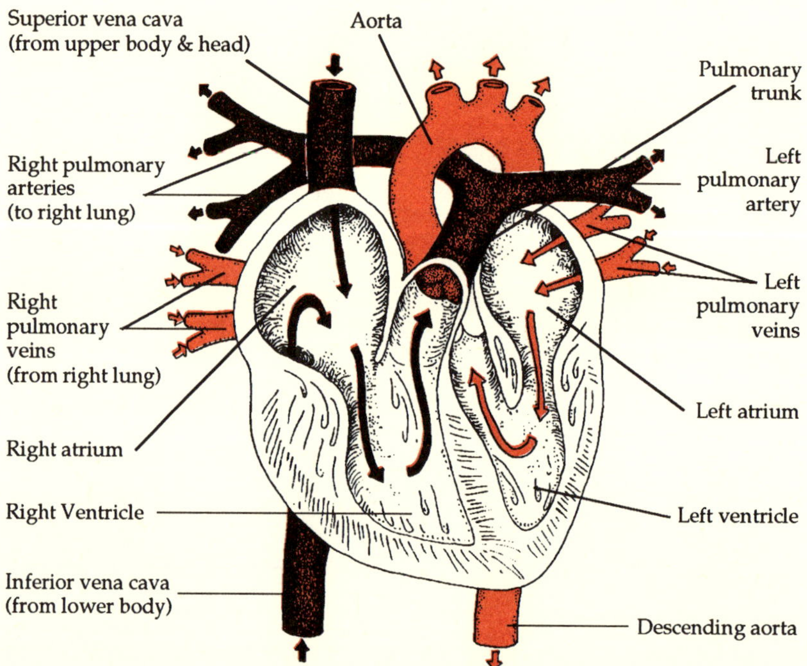

Figure 3: **The Heart**
 A simplified drawing with certain details omitted because it is impossible to represent the heart completely in a single drawing. The valves between the atria and the ventricles are also not shown. Only part of the front of the heart has been removed, and the full volume of the ventricles (when relaxed) is not apparent. The marks inside the ventricles represent muscular strands and tendons. Blood flows through the heart twice in each cycle. Depleted blood (dark red in the diagram) enters the right atrium from the venae cavae, is sent into the right ventricle, and is then pumped to the lungs through the pulmonary arteries when the ventricle contracts. Oxygenated blood (bright red) returns from the lungs through the pulmonary veins into the left atrium. The contraction of this chamber sends the blood into the left ventricle which them pumps it to the rest of the body via the aorta. The aorta emerges from the heart behind the pulmonary trunk, passes in front of the right pulmonary artery, and then curves over to pass behind the heart itself.

Source: Anthony and Kolthoff, *Textbook of Anatomy and Physiology*, figs. 13-15.

respiration, for even the extremities must receive their oxygen and be relieved of the carbon dioxide through the lungs. "According to the forms and according to the states" is simple enough from the physiological point of view. A muscle is a form different from bone. It requires more oxygen, and this requirement will depend on the state of the muscle, i.e., whether it is working or relaxed. These ideas can be pursued down to the molecular level, where a molecule will receive oxygen in one state, but not in another; but there is no need to go into detail. Thus, we find that the lungs ruling by the respiration agrees fully with modern thought, especially since, in a biochemical context, respiration refers to the exchange of oxygen and carbon dioxide at the cellular level.

These examples show how natural knowledges can lead to a more internal appreciation of truth

112. Although in the last section we have done no more than confirm what certain passages from the Writings say about the heart and lungs of the body, the exercise is more than mere confirmation. Confirmation is certainly not to be despised, but having been given it, we are emboldened to step out further. "The simplest statements [of the Writings] explored in depth, yield arrangements of ideas which appear to stretch to infinity. Many of these ideas may be understood only in terms of facts which Swedenborg the man could not have known" (Newton, 1981). Hence, with the aid of doctrine, and under Providence, we may use our natural knowledges to discover spiritual truths reflected in natural facts (DLW 385)[4], and to see truths which we might otherwise accept blindly. In such a way we may gradually progress from external representatives towards more internal, and therefore more excellent truths that we did not understand before. Then we do not merely acquiesce in the truths of the Writings, but with joy "draw water out of the wells of salvation" (Isaiah 12:3).

---

[4] See also (Newton, 1981, p. 75).

CHAPTER VI

CORRESPONDENCES OF THE HEART AND LUNGS—PART 3 CONJUNCTIONS BETWEEN THE WILL AND THE UNDERSTANDING

113. The conjunctions between the will and the understanding, which are almost too wonderful to comprehend, can be illustrated by the way the heart and lungs act together.

114. Perhaps there are people to whom this subject seems simple and straight forward. Others may experience difficulty. But for all, a reading or re-reading of Part V of DLW is highly recommended. The wisdom therein is often transcendent, and there are numerous cherubim (see AC 308). However, the prepared mind can enjoy many fascinating walks in paradise, and even see birds of paradise (DLW 374). In what follows we descend somewhat to natural and scientific things, for we are so constituted that it is necessary for us to keep our feet on the ground (AC 4939; 2557:2). This we do with the aid of correspondences (AC 9300:3), and we hope to progress by walking (AC 519). Our need to think from correspondences is also spelled out in DLW 402, where we read:

Why it is so cannot be fully described except in spiritual language because love and wisdom, and will and understanding therefrom, are spiritual concepts, which can indeed be taught in natural language, but only so as to be vaguely perceived on account of the ignorance of what love, wisdom, affections of goodness, and affections of wisdom which are affections of truth, are. Yet one can see the nature of the betrothal and of the marriage of love with wisdom, or of the will with understanding, through the parallelism that exists in their correspondence with the heart and lungs. For it is the same with these as with love and wisdom, so much so as to make absolutely no difference except that one is spiritual and the other natural.

This statement (like several others) encourages us to attempt to see the spiritual in the natural, and we hope that our modern knowledge of the natural will enable us to picture the spiritual more clearly. But for our knowledge of the spiritual itself we are still dependent on the natural language in the Writings and it is inevitable that we shall be labouring with spiritual concepts "vaguely perceived."

The conjunction of the heart with the lungs by arteries and veins portrays the way the will acts into the understanding causing affection, perception and thought

115. We have contemplated the activities of the heart and lungs in the body as a whole and we have seen how these activities are integrated so closely that they form one service to the body and reflect the far-reaching influence of love united with wisdom in the whole mind (Nos. 77, 78, 106-111). It is obvious, however, that this unity in service could not exist without that other union within the chest through arteries and veins. A general idea of how the heart is joined to the lungs through arteries and veins can be obtained from Figure 2. This is to give a first, most general picture of the whole heart-lung system. A more detailed anatomical drawing of the opened heart has been presented in Figure 3. Figure 4 shows a more accurate but still modified drawing of the arterial connections to the left lung. The conjunction of the heart and lungs through their blood vessels enables them to be together in their effect, which is the maintenance of conditions necessary for the life of all the tissues in the whole body. Similarly, the will and understanding provide conditions for the life of the whole mind, and nothing is more important than their life together which develops through three conjunctions (DLW 404). These conjunctions take place

FIGURE 4

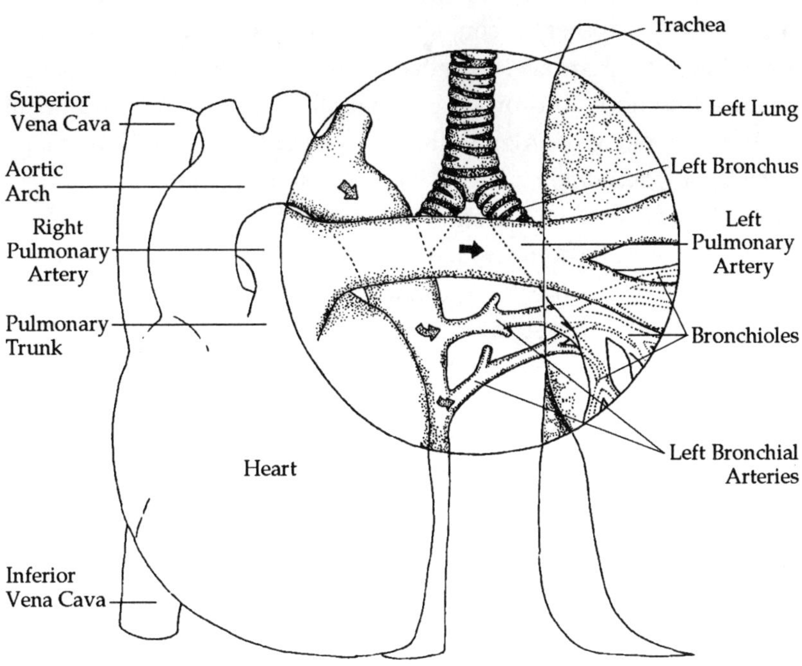

Figure 4: **Pulmonary and Bronchial Arteries**

Schema to illustrate the difference between the pulmonary and bronchial arteries (left side only). The trachea and lung have been displaced far to the right of the diagram, and the arteries have been correspondingly lengthened. There are usually two left bronchial arteries (as shown) but only one to the right lung. It arises from the third intercostal artery which is, itself, a branch from the aorta.

Source: Clemente, *Gray's Anatomy*, 30th American ed., figs. 7-25, 8-53, 15-24, text pp. 729, 1398.   Based on sketch by N. J. Berridge.

"after the nuptials," but as the nuptials mean man's state from ignorance to intelligence and thence to wisdom, they would seem to cover the whole of man's mental progress. The conjunction of the will and the understanding is compared to a marriage, and the definition of nuptials suggests that the conjunctions should always be preceded by something of a marriage. Also that a binding covenant is not merely entered into once and for all, but that all conjunction should begin with a wooing, and progress through consent to a holy agreement. Such a sort of wooing may even be considered relevant on the merely physiological level of the operation of the lungs; for in disorderly states there can be so much tension and constriction of arteries and chest muscles that breathing cannot function properly. In states of good order the "request" by the control centres (see No. 124) for more air is quickly met by increased ventilation in the lungs.

The will and the understanding are joined by three affections corresponding to blood vessels and three offspring are produced corresponding to structures in the lungs

116. The three conjunctions of the will with the understanding arise through three affections: (1) for knowing, (2) for understanding, (3) for seeing truth. Each conjunction produces its particular offspring: (1) affection for truth, (2) perception of truth, (3) thought. We now consider each conjunction in more detail, as diagrammed in figure 5, and find that the first conjunction takes place through an affection for knowing, as already said, but this leads to an affection for reasoning and forming conclusions on matters the person delights in. When this latter affection is exalted to spiritual things it becomes the affection for truth. These various affections are from the will in the understanding and thus correspond to blood vessels in the lungs.

117. The second conjunction takes place through an affection for understanding which gives rise to the perception of truth. The affection and the perception are so related that we may conclude that one

FIGURE 5

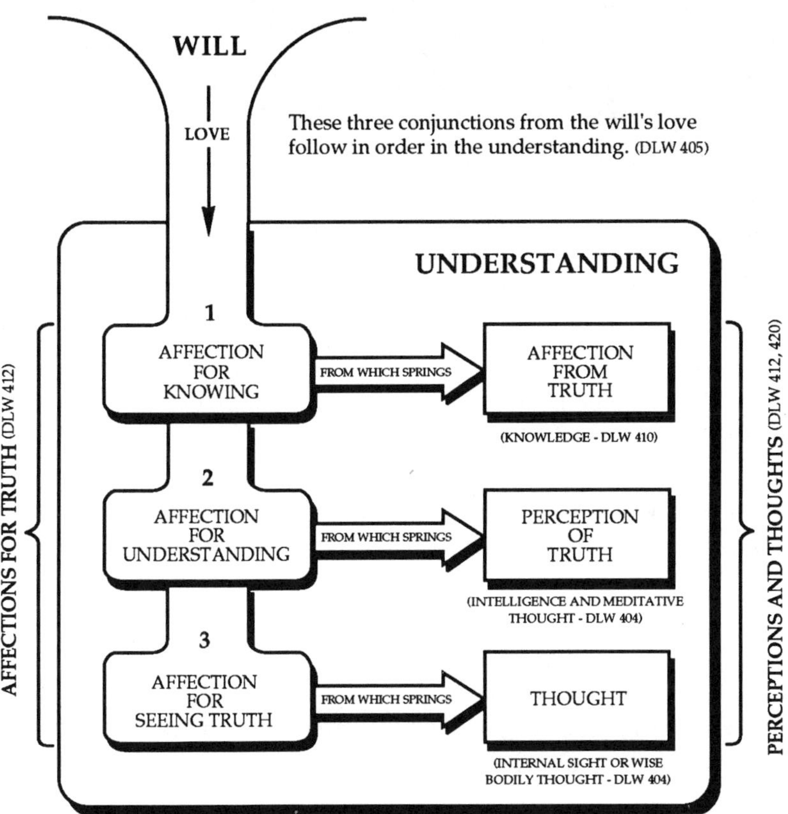

Figure 5: **The three conjunctions of Divine Love & Wisdom 404 - 420**
It can be seen by the flow of the blood out of the heart into the lungs how the will flows into the understanding and produces these results. (DLW 405)

Drawn by Tony Rose with Rev. Thomas Rose.

who loves to understand can perceive truth according to the extent of his love. Again the affection corresponds to blood vessels, but perception and the thoughts from it correspond to the branches of the air ducts or bronchia (DLW 405).[5]

118. The third conjunction takes place through an affection for seeing truth, from which springs thought. Once more, affection corresponds to blood vessels, but thought in this context seems to correspond to the air saccules. We find in DLW 413:

> The minutest air cells, which are receptacles for the air used in breathing; these are the things with which the thoughts act in conjunction by correspondence.

The minutest air cells are a sort of continuation of the branches of the bronchia, for these continue to divide until they reach the microscopic size of the air cells. Thus the perception from the second conjunction is related to the thoughts from the third.

There are three conjunctions between the will and the understanding but only two sets of arteries between the heart and lungs

119. While this section of DLW repeatedly invites us to study the anatomy of the lungs and heart and their conjunction, the exact correspondence between the mental or spiritual things and the bodily things is not always clear, and it is difficult to relate DLW 405 precisely to No. 404. It is said in 405:

> It may be seen from the influx of the blood from the heart into the lungs, how the will inflows into the understanding and

---

[5] It is important to distinguish between the bronchia which are air tubes and the bronchial arteries and veins which are blood vessels. Failure to do so can lead to confusion. The mere omission of the final letter 'l' can easily happen as a misprint. This seems to be the case in the 1969 Swedenborg Society edition of DLW (p. 184).

brings to pass those effects...relating to the affection and perception of truth and relating to thought.

Still, the bodily correspondence of the three conjunctions eludes us. For we have three affections: (1) for knowing, (2) for understanding, (3) for seeing truth; but in DLW we have only two routes of corresponding arteries: (1) the bronchial, (2) the pulmonary (and the veins we need not consider, as they merely provide for the return flow).

120. When we consider the pulmonary arteries we find with surprise that there is no comment in DLW on the fact that the pulmonary arteries take the whole stream of blood (for it comes together into the right side of the heart and is then all discharged through the lungs). Perhaps this is meant when it is said that the pulmonary arteries come from the heart alone (This point is further discussed in No. 172). The way the blood flows can be imagined from Figure 2. The actual anatomic arrangement within and around the heart is shown in Figure 3. No organ other than the lungs takes the whole of the blood supply in this fashion. Although so little is said about this peculiarity of the pulmonary circulation, the correspondence of it is described where it is said that the love does nothing except in conjunction with wisdom (DLW 409). Thus pulmonary and bronchial arteries differ from one another more than one might imagine from a reading of the text; indeed they could not be more different: The pulmonary arteries take all the output from the right ventricle and direct it to the air-saccules of the lungs, while the bronchial arteries take a little of the output from the left ventricle and direct it to the bronchial tubes and associated structures as well as to the surface of the lungs beneath the pleura, but not to the air saccules (alveoli). Figure 4 assists visualization. The bronchial arteries are for the nutrition of the lungs; the pulmonary arteries are for making use of the lungs to refresh the whole of the blood before it is re-distributed to the body. So we have two very different circulations; but we need a third if we are to have a special circulation to correspond with each conjunction. In DLW we are not told that either of the two sets of arteries corresponds to a particular conjunction. This reticence probably arises from the need for accommodation to the limited knowledge of the period (see, e.g., DLW 405, 512). A brief survey of modern knowledge shows the subject to be sufficiently complex and makes clear the need for reticence at that time. However, complexity need not induce us to fear making a search for a third circulation which we would hope to be so different from the other two that it could easily be recognized as a third, and not merely as a subdivision of either of the others. It may nevertheless be possible that one or other of the two systems we already have could be clearly divided to make three in all. This possibility must not be ignored and, therefore, we must look more closely at the anatomy of the pulmonary and bronchial arteries.

121. The branches of the bronchial artery become more numerous and finer as they ramify along the bronchia and bronchioles among other structures. The finest branches are, of course, the capillaries through which nourishment passes to the various tissues other than the air saccules. The bronchial system does not reach to these. However, there is a very abundant blood supply to the air saccules through the pulmonary system which must therefore supply nourishment to them. Although the blood in the pulmonary artery is depleted in oxygen, it is not likely to be so depleted in other nutrients (amino acids, glucose, vitamins, minerals) that the abundant flow will not compensate for the lower level of those nutrients.

122. Soon after leaving the heart, the pulmonary arteries form several branches which differ merely in supplying different segments of the lungs, and it would be difficult to justify a division into two systems rather than several, especially as this would merely be a minor subdivision.

122A. The bronchial arteries can be divided into three groups and the veins into two. The three groups of arteries supply the walls of the bronchia, the areolar tissue between the lobes of the lungs, and the surface of the lungs beneath the pleura. The veins fall into two systems, one of which empties into pulmonary veins or the left (!) atrium, the other into one of the azygous veins or an intercostal vein, but also communicating with the pulmonary veins. Thus, some of the blood flowing into the bronchial arteries finds its way into the pulmonary veins rather than the bronchial veins and thus returns to the same side of the heart that it left. Branches of the bronchial arteries also join those of the pulmonary arteries in parts of the pleura and smaller bronchi.

But these are clearly not the two ways in and the two ways out referred to in DLW 405, and the complexity of the whole system prevents our dividing it into two groups with any degree of confidence. Thus we are still left with only two circulations and our search for a third must take us farther afield.

A proposition concerning the three correspondences requires further study

122B. A proposition is developed below with the intention of including other organs that assist the heart and lungs to act jointly. These organs must have their correspondences or they would not exist. Their importance is easily discerned when they are described, but it shows up still more clearly when we think about the development of the embryo, because they help to explain the difference between "the heart first forms the lungs" and "afterwards conjoins itself with them" (DLW 402). The explanation hinges on the fact that the organs to be described are not active in the embryo but, like the lungs themselves, become active after its birth. For one may ask how the heart can first form the lungs without being in some way united with them. Can it do so at a distance? If it does not, one might suggest that the bypassing of the blood flow through the *foramen ovale* and *ductus arteriosus* shows a withholding of the full stream of blood from the heart into the lungs so that the heart could be imagined as drawing back from full conjunction. But then it would be as already suggested, that conjunction could not be represented by the mere presence of arteries in the lungs and scarcely by the mere flow of blood through them on its way to the capillary beds. Nor could we define adequate representations of three conjunctions by the types of arteries present.

122C. We are encouraged by DLW to include the embryo in our studies, for this section of DLW (no. 398) includes 22 propositions. No sooner do we come to the exposition of the second one (DLW 400) than we are invited to consider the embryo as follows:

> It is a known fact that all things of the body are formed in the womb…through fibres from the brains and…blood vessels out of the heart.

In no. 402 near the end we find:

> The heart first forms the lungs; and afterwards conjoins itself with them; it forms the lungs in the embryo, and conjoins itself with them after birth.

There are now many more "known facts" which enable us to add detail to the statement that the heart first forms the lungs and to see by how much or how little the heart first forms the lungs and to see by how much or how little the heart conjoins itself with them during this formation. So we launch into a small bay of the sea of Embryology.

There is close association between heart and lungs before birth

122D. The very young and very small embryo develops quickly. Rapid changes take place during the first few weeks but the fourth seems particularly dramatic. Early in the fourth week, the embryo being only 2.4 mm long, the umbilical arteries and veins are already defined and are beginning to link up with vessels which will complete the chorionic circulation. By comparison with the chick embryo, it is thought that the heart begins to beat at about this time. As the channels for circulation are not yet complete, the fluid in them can only flow to and fro. At this same time, the lungs begin to grow as buds on each side of the oesophagus. They are nourished at this time through a network or plexus of capillaries connected with the aortic sac (which is a relatively wide, odd-shaped vessel between the ventricle and the beginnings of the aorta). There is a well marked dorsal aorta at this time and to this the capillary network (plexus) is eventually connected, and it then grows into a distinct artery, all the time remaining as the route for the supply to the lung buds. The new artery is known at this stage as the 6th aortic arch, but it shortly becomes recognizable as the pulmonary trunk. Connection between the heart and lungs thus begins at a very early stage, as indicated in DLW, though in those days anatomists probably could not see details in the embryo which is only 2.4 mm long. An advanced technique of fixing, staining and serial sectioning is probably needed in addition to a good microscope and observations of living specimens.

122E. Three phases are recognized in the development of the lungs. During the first one, which is known as the *glandular* phase, the lungs are mostly a concentrated mass of tissue with an appearance normally associated with glands. This period lasts from the beginning of embryo development to the 11th week. Thus it includes the development described just above when the pulmonary trunk is being formed. The second phase is the *canalicular*. It lasts from the 16th to the 24th week, and during this time the channels proliferate and branch and some cells become flattened and applied close to capillaries. The third stage is the *alveolar*. It covers the major development of the alveoli. It lasts from the 24th week until after the birth. Although the *foramen ovale* and the *ductus arteriosus* cause most of the heart's output to go into the aorta, the pulmonary arteries are not blocked. There must be some flow through them which may well be enough to provide for the growth of the alveoli and their surrounding capillaries, for these tissues are so delicate that their total mass is small. There is some belief also that in the newborn, the anastomoses, or junctions between the bronchial and pulmonary systems, are more extensive than they are later.

122F. During their development, the alveoli have no air to open them and allow room for proper growth, but they are expanded by fluid from other tissues. Some embryologists believe also that respiratory movements before birth cause some of the amniotic fluid to be drawn into the lungs. Even before full term, i.e. after premature delivery, the lungs are capable of respiration once the efforts, or assisted efforts, of the fetus have ejected the fluid so that air can be drawn in from the surrounding atmosphere. After birth the alveoli continue to develop. They become more numerous and complex in shape as they keep up with the increase of bodily size.

122G. The bronchial arteries arise from the descending aorta (Figure 4) or from the posterior (aortic) intercostal arteries. As previously noted, they supply the various air passages in addition to other tissues. Once circulation is established, new arteries grow out as branches from earlier ones and it is clear that the bronchial arteries will be functioning in the canalicular phase if not sooner. They will be taking their full quota of blood. A limited quantity will also be flowing through the pulmonary arteries and it may seem that conjunction between the heart and lungs is progressing. As for the closeness of conjunction, it seems that from about the fourth week after fertilization of the ovum, if not earlier, conjunction has been very close indeed. It has extended to the intimate relationship necessary for the transfer of so many nutrients and growth factors from the blood to the growing cells. This adumbration of a few facts from the great array in embryology gives us some appreciation of "the heart first forms the lungs."

After birth conjunction is for the sake of use

122H. In view of the close union between heart and lungs for so long before birth, how can we explain an even closer union which conjunction appears to mean? The blood has already been flowing through all the vessels for a long time, though at a slow rate through the pulmonary artery. We need to note that Swedenborg wrote of conjunction after the birth although he obviously knew that the formation of the lungs involved a close association with the heart. Why then did the situation after birth promote conjunctions? The philosophy of the Writings can come to our aid. It need not be brought forward in detail but it seems to show that the normal progression of end to cause to effect occurs only for the sake of use.

122I. If this philosophy be applied to the heart-lung situation, we see that the end or purpose of all development is use in the body, in order that the body may be useful so the neighbor and the Lord may be served. It might be accepted, therefore, that it is use that unites. The heart and lungs cannot be fully united until they are in use. This happens only after birth. Therefore, we then have conjunction, and indeed it is easy to see three conjunctions once it is accepted that use is essential.

It is difficult to decide which order to suggest for the three conjunctions. The first might mean the most important, or the first in time. DLW 404 seems to refer to first in time since it corresponds to the early development of the intellect. We cannot, however, choose a first in time for the correspondences unless we go back to the embryo when conjunction had not taken place. We can choose a first after birth if we are allowed to distinguish different periods separated only by seconds. The bronchial artery has been in full use all the time and after birth it continues to function before the child's first breath, using the residual oxygen supplied a few seconds earlier from the mother's lungs, *via* the placenta. It therefore seems reasonable to place the bronchial artery as corresponding to the affection which produces the first conjunction. Before the first breath the fluid in the lungs must be expelled to make room for the air. This requires the muscles of the chest and probably other muscles of the trunk. These also belong, as it were, to the heart and lungs for they grow and they work only by means of blood sent to them by the heart through the aorta and their work enables the lungs to breathe. They must therefore correspond to the second conjunction or to part of it. It is not, however, until the third conjunction takes place that the other two are valid. Without it they are useless, not actually conjunctions. They fade away. The child dies. But if the pulmonary artery opens and plays its part, the third conjunction is secure. The lungs are opened as to their minutest blood vessels which allow the blood in them to take up oxygen from this the baby's first breath. All the organs in the activities just mentioned, even the heart itself, continue to function after birth by means of the oxygen drawn in and then transferred through the pulmonary vein in blood supplied a few moments before through the pulmonary artery. The exhalation of carbon dioxide is equally important.

Time has been split into small intervals to show an order of first, second and third for the conjunctions. It has also shown how three stands for what is full and complete, for if anything is missing, all the conjunctions come to naught. This concludes the presentation of this particular proposition, but parts of it need to be explained in more detail.

How the chest and its muscles facilitate the breathing of the lungs

122J. The chest and its muscles have only been mentioned in passing, but they must be integrated with the rest of our picture. An obstacle to the clearer understanding of correspondences is the belief that the two arterial systems supplying the lungs enables them to breathe at a different rate from the heart's beat. Let it be understood that what makes the lungs inflate is the contraction of certain muscles of the chest and diaphragm. The cage of ribs is so structured that when certain muscles between them contract, the volume of the chest is increased. The three dimensional geometry behind the movement is subtle but the facts are plain. Other muscles quite nearby can serve to diminish the volume and so expel air, but expulsion is often an effect of relaxation. The muscular diaphragm is effective because its domed shape is flattened when its muscles contract. This is a simplified account from conclusions from a great deal of experimental work published in the medical literature. Some of the evidence varies in detail, but for the picture as a whole, it is uncontroversial and more than adequate. We can therefore allow ourselves to believe that ribs, muscles and diaphragm enable the lungs to be expanded.

Two ways by which blood enables the lungs to be expanded

122K. The need for activity of the diaphragm and chest muscles (intercostals) corresponds well with the spiritual fact that the understanding does nothing of itself (DLW 412). It is added that all the conditions of the lungs depend upon the blood and "when the inflow of blood stops, breathing stops." This is because the lungs can do nothing of themselves. Now we can see more detail of how the blood flow enables them to breathe. As is said in DLW 413, "this cell-like substance [the alveoli] is such that it can be expanded and contracted in twofold fashion." The evidence now is that the bronchial arteries have little to do with the actual mechanics of the expansion, but the alveoli are indeed expanded in two ways as follows: (1) blood from the pulmonary artery causes the expansion of the network of capillaries around each alveolus; (2) blood from the aorta goes to the intercostal muscles (i.e. those between the ribs) and to the diaphragm, enabling them to expand the chest and hence the alveoli so as to draw air into them. (Some readers may like to be reminded that the aorta is the highway for blood travelling to the body from the heart. The intercostal muscles are not supplied through the bronchial artery but through a different one also, of course, branching from the aorta.) These matters of anatomy and physiology show Swedenborg having to write within the scientific limits of his time but being biased towards a correct view by the angelic wisdom. He was allowed to say expanded in two ways (DLW 413), but not to say what the two ways really are.

122L. Perhaps it can now be seen that a better appreciation of the will and the understanding and of their conjunction can be obtained with the help of modern anatomy and physiology if we also widen our field of view according to the hints we find in many places. First, in DLW 408 we read that love introduces wisdom "into many things of its house" and that the house means the whole man, also that "the lungs are introduced into all...[parts of the body] in the same way as the understanding into all things of the mind." Moreover, we have already noted that there is a union of the heart and lungs everywhere in the body (no. 108) though in the AC this is modified by "as it were."

Respiration is regulated according to the state of blood in the aorta

123. The collaboration between heart and lungs in supplying oxygenated blood to the whole organism (no. 115) shows how they work together for the sake of use. What is to be seen of this use in every organ is the last link of a segment of the end-cause-effect chain. There is, however, a link or two missing in the earlier part of this chain as we now view it, because we have not examined adequately the facts concerning the mechanism by which the lungs are expanded and contracted. The diaphragm and the muscles between the ribs have been mentioned as the means whereby the lungs are expanded,[6] but those muscles cannot, of themselves, respond to the varying requirements of the body for air. Therefore, there are special centres which monitor the condition of the blood and provide information enabling the control centres to maintain the activity of the chest muscles and diaphragm at the optimum level. One does not often realize the importance of these centres. It is scarcely possible to imagine the breathing being fixed at a constant amount, for if it were sufficient for vigorous activities there would be drawbacks during quieter periods.

---

[6] Connections of both blood and nerves to the muscles of the ribs and diaphragm are very important, but they are not essential for survival because either the ribs or the diaphragm can be used for breathing, when partial paralysis occurs (as in poliomyelitis, for example) even muscles of the neck can be used to draw up the ribs and expand the lungs.

It would impose unnecessary work loads on the chest muscles and dry out membranes lining the nose, throat and bronchi. It would also remove too much carbon dioxide (CO_2) from the blood, thereby upsetting the very important acid-base relationship (most people have experienced giddiness after blowing too much). It would seem, then, that this control is a most important function to ensure the satisfactory working of the heart and lungs, and it is interesting to look at it a little more closely.

124. What makes a child take its first breath (i.e., the mechanism through which the inflowing life from the Lord operates) is still a matter of speculation. Dejours (1981, p. 169) suggests several stimuli, but once breathing has started, control is necessary. There are structures, probably in the medulla oblongata, certainly in the carotid bodies (see below) and probably elsewhere, that are sensitive to the amount of oxygen (O_2), carbon dioxide (CO_2) and acidity (pH) in the blood. These sensitive structures send impulses to the respiratory centres also in the medulla oblongata. Signals are also received from muscles of the chest, from the lungs themselves, from moving parts of the body by reflex action, and probably from the brain itself. The respiratory centres then presumably process all this information and "instruct" the muscles which expand the chest to make appropriate movements. Figure 6 provides a pictorial summary of this chain of events. The carotid bodies mentioned just above are found in the neck at the junction of the internal and external carotid arteries. They are sensitive to oxygen and carbon dioxide in the blood which circulates through them and although they only control ten to fifteen percent of the breathing (*via* the respiratory centres), this may be enough to maintain a steady state under certain conditions. Control to the extent of one hundred percent is often in command, e.g., in sleep, and it is to be assumed that other monitoring devices contribute. Some, for example, are to be found near the arch of the aorta. All these sensory bodies are in a position that enables them to respond to the chemical composition of the blood soon after it leaves the heart. So they are part of the

FIGURE 6

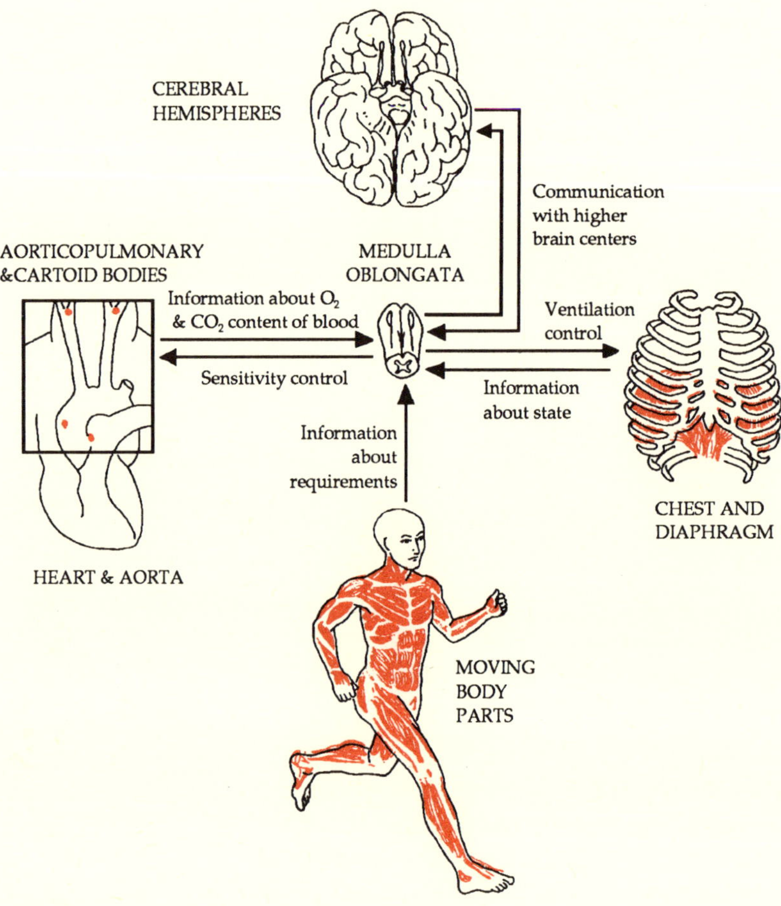

Figure 6: **Diagram of Factors in Respiration Control**

Source: David K. Rubins, *The Human Figure.*

continuous monitoring system that determines how the chest and diaphragm will respond to the needs of the rest of the body by drawing air into the lungs more frequently or less, more deeply or less. From what has already been said it is clear that the muscles which change the volume of the chest are an essential part of this system that is being suggested as a correspondence of the second conjunction (no. 122J). As already stated, the respiratory centres in the medulla oblongata issue instructions, according to the information they receive, thus bringing into being a viable system for the control of breathing.[7]

125. As the medulla oblongata is part of the brain, the respiration depends on fibres from the brain. But we are told (DLW 412) that it is respiration of the *spirit* that depends on fibres from the brains. These fibres are probably of an origin different from that of the former ones. This would enable its main brain (or higher centres, i.e. the cerebrum and cerebellum) to overrule the lower parts of the brain, one of which is the medulla oblongata. Conscious control, which is of the will or spirit, can obviously overrule for a limited period. Unconscious effects such as lead to sighing are well known to result from a state of the spirit.

126. The necessary involvement of the central nervous system corresponds presumably to the impossibility of explaining the activity of man's understanding without involving influences from the spiritual world. It is inevitable that in our thoughts we link the involvement of the nervous system with the more internal activities of will and understanding, for the "messages" from the carotid bodies must

---

[7] The inclusion of this route as important in the relationship between the heart and lungs is precisely a matter of fact, but it is also in harmony with the Writings, for, twice in DLW 412 the aorta only is mentioned as the source of arterial blood other than the heart (the vena cava being merely the return route), and all the arteries of the third system are branches coming from the aorta. Of course, the blood from the aorta comes from the heart, but here, coming from the aorta is contrasted with coming from the heart, because much of the blood coursing through the aorta goes elsewhere, but all the blood from the right side of the heart goes through the pulmonary arteries. This is discussed further in Section 8 of Chapter VII.

go through higher centres before they can affect the lungs. So we immediately think of conscience, and conscience is a species of perception (AC 2144:3). Thus we have arrived at the second conjunction of DLW 404, "from which springs perception of truth." However, we must not forget that what the respiratory centres "perceive" is the state of the blood, not the freshness of inspired air, so their activities including those of the carotid bodies would correspond to a persons perception of his need rather than of Truth from the Lord. We also keep an open mind about the validity of this interpretation, as it is said that, "the branches of the bronchia of the lungs [correspond] to perceptions and thoughts..." (DLW 405). The possibility of different perceptions corresponding to different structures is considered below (No. 139).

Three circulations may correspond to the three affections

127. We now have three clearly defined routes of circulation which are of special importance to the lungs:

1.   the bronchial arteries branching from the aorta (some directly, some indirectly),

2.   the aorta and those of its branches that are necessary for respiration, and

3.   the pulmonary arteries stemming directly from the heart.

It is suggested that these circulations correspond in this order to the three conjunctions of DLW 404. It is the picture as a whole that leads to the choice of this order and it will become clear in what follows, but some of the detailed argument is summarized in footnote 10 in No. 142.

128. In an earlier essay the second conjunction between the will and the understanding was said to correspond to that of the heart with the bronchia through the bronchial arteries (Berridge, 1979B). Perhaps this is true also. Since each part is an image of the whole (HH 58), each conjunction bears a resemblance to all three as they follow one another in due order to make one mind.

129. We may now compare the three arterial systems with the three conjunctions described in DLW 404.

The bronchial arteries correspond to affections by which the understanding is nourished

130. This is clear from what has already been said (120, 121, 122E, and 122G) about the nourishment of the lungs and associated tissues through the bronchial arteries, and about the correspondence of the lungs with the understanding. These arteries are said to be "almost separate from the heart" (DLW 413, 415). Nevertheless, as we have seen, "the heart first forms the lungs" and the arterial connections are very close, though, clearly, not so immediate as those of the pulmonary arteries.[8] This "almost separate" is such an important distinction and yet seems rather artificial, for the blood in the bronchial arteries was in the heart a few seconds earlier. However, it probably refers to the great difference between the bronchial route of circulation and the pulmonary route as already emphasized above (No. 120).

131. The bronchial arteries also nourish structures associated with the lungs, such as the pleura, for example. Thus we see how, in the early stages of the growth of the understanding, the affections producing the growth are slightly different from the main will or perhaps ruling love; various affections also nourish associated things necessary for the proper functioning of the understanding. So the bronchial arteries are complex both in functions purely their own and in their varying connections with the pulmonary arteries and veins. Is not this picture typical of the complexity of the growth of the mind? Obvious-

---

[8] It is said (122D) that the 6th aortic arch of the embryo soon becomes recognizable as the pulmonary trunk, the heart being already clearly linked to the lungs. At this early stage, however, the contribution of the bronchial arteries is difficult to evaluate.

ly, and in agreement with the correspondences, the affections play a predominant part. However, we see in the bronchial system arteries which do not come directly from the heart but from the aorta, and as they branch, so they seem to be further away. This suggests that the understanding grows by many affections, some more nearly, others more distantly related to love. It is obvious that there are many ways by which the growth of understanding is stimulated, and knowledge is sometimes gathered even in spite of the affections. It is not so very long since education by punishment was the vogue, and it was, to some extent, effective. The understanding is sharpened by pain, fear, and many other emotions somewhat distantly related to love. Even boredom will drive some of us to exercise our understanding as a means of escape. Pain and fear have no relation at all to love of the subjects of education, but they are related to the love of self. It may well be that the bronchial arteries, or parts of them, correspond even to affections derived from the love of self, for there is a love of self which is good and useful as long as it is subservient to heavenly loves. So it could be with the bronchial arteries, which are good as long as they serve the lungs for growth and health, but which would be evil if they took too much blood and deprived the other parts of the body.

132. The connections between the blood vessels of the bronchial system and those of the pulmonary system are believed to permit a "leak" of only one or two percent of blood back to the "wrong" side of the heart (Dejours, 1981). The existence of these connections may correspond to a childish state when the understanding is biased by the will and does not work with precision. Such a state is all too common among adults, of course, but it is nevertheless childish. This also agrees with anatomical observations, which show that such connections are fewer in adults than in the very young. (My earlier suggestion (Berridge, 1979B), which was that the connections illustrate how readily the affection for knowing develops into the affection for truth, agrees with the one now put forward, inasmuch as the affection for knowing begins in the childish state and can only gradually become the affection for truth.)

133. The bronchial arteries do not disappear when growth ceases. The living tissues in the lungs still need nourishment, cleansing, refreshment and the replacing of worn out parts by new growth. In the same way, the understanding needs to be continually refreshed; hence the need for recreation and change. These considerations show that the first conjunction of will and understanding is not limited to childhood. It happens all the time. We shall see later (No. 153) how the other conjunctions improve the first and facilitate each other.

134. Since the product of this first conjunction is an affection (which is of love, hence of the heart), we assume that it corresponds to the blood vessels which are being produced in the lungs in accordance with their growth.

135. It is interesting to express some of the phrases of proposition (vi) in DLW 404 in more common if less exact words: "affection for knowing" can be "wanting to know," "affection for reasoning" can be "wanting to know and to argue" and "affection for forming conclusions on matters in which he takes delight" can be "deciding what he wants to do." So we have a series typical of the young child: wanting to know, then to know why and argue, and finally to do something. This series at its own level is very like the series of propositions vi, vii and viii, and we are reminded that in spiritual things the parts are an image of the whole (see for example HH 58).

The aorta and its branches that effect and control breathing correspond, in part, to affections that activate conscience or perception

136. That they correspond to affections is clear from it having been said so many times that arteries "belonging" to the heart correspond in that way. The activation of conscience corresponds to all the parts that cause the chest to expand and draw air into the lungs. The carotid bodies, their nerve connections through the medulla oblongata and the various obedient muscles (see no. 124) must all be part of this system. It is said in part because all the blood courses through the aorta and supplies all parts of the body, which, of course, includes many that have nothing to do with respiration except their dependence on it.

137. With respect to the second conjunction we read in DLW 404 that it "comes through an affection for understanding from which springs perception of truth," and a little later, "everyone has as much perception of truth as he has affection for understanding." From the rest of this paragraph we deduce that anyone of sound reason who loves to understand is able to perceive truth according to the measure of his love. This suggests further that here perception means not that special faculty which is confined to the celestial genius, but something we all have. (On the other hand one may argue that love in the spiritual man is so weak that his perception, which depends on love, is of a different order of magnitude, though of the same kind, as that of the celestial.)

138. In examining the physiological correspondence that I have suggested for this, the second conjunction, we bear in mind that the conjunction depends on an affection, or a will, wish, or desire to understand. How similar is the longing for understanding to the longing for a deep breath of fresh air! The invigorating air enlivens the body as the spirit of the Lord renews the soul of man. But breathing must continue all the time. The blood must be pumped continually to the head through the carotid arteries and past the carotid bodies which in turn will continually "inform" the nerve centres whether more or less air is needed. Perhaps we will not be going far astray if we see here a correspondence of the continual vigilance of conscience. For the love is continually urging many activities and in the regenerating man all the impulses of love cannot avoid being examined to see whether they are acceptable to the conscience. As the "blood" of the spirit is on its way to the "head" we can think that it is being monitored by a higher faculty with celestial affinities. As the carotid bodies are in the neck they might correspond to a faculty that partakes of both the spiritual (chest) and celestial (head) and the longing to understand genuine truth must be an urge from something higher or within.

139. Conscience comes into the picture quite readily, for the product of this second conjunction is "perception of truth," and conscience is a species of perception (AC 2144:3). Now, however, we find that the branches of the bronchia are the things which correspond to perceptions and thoughts from affections for truth (DLW 405). Are these latter perceptions and thoughts different from that perception of truth arising from the second conjunction which is the one we are trying to understand now? They may well be different. We are suggesting that conjunction No. 2, i.e., through affection for understanding, corresponds to the whole operation of the system which controls the breathing. This system ensures the proper working together of the heart and lungs. Thus it is a conjunction. On the other hand, the perceptions and thoughts from affections for truth are mentioned later (DLW 404: viii) and presumably follow the others. So this later perception is different, but the former is equally important, for if the lungs are to breathe there must be ducts for the air to get in. Believing the air corresponds to the Divine Spirit,[9] we can imagine that the ducts leading it in must correspond to a kind of perception other than that which makes man aware of his need. Although there is only one life it is received at many different levels. It is all a highly complex process forming a continual cycle. The life which is within activates the monitoring system which

---

[9] This correspondence may be deduced from the meaning of "wind" as explained in AE 419, for wind is nothing but air in motion. In AE 1012, however, air is said to signify thought. The signification and correspondences are harmonious when man is in order and his thoughts are from truths. In states of disorder a man will seek stale or foul air (falsities) rather than a fresh breeze. The equivalence of breath and spirit is mentioned in AC 9987, and DLW 383 as well as in AE 419.

indicates a demand (or a satisfied demand) for more life. Nevertheless it can be conceived of as one process.

140. In this way the physiology extends our ideas of conscience and perception. The product of the second conjunction between the will and the understanding is "perception of truth." We find this concept difficult to grasp when it refers to the celestial genius, but the perception everyone has is easier to apprehend. If we accept the suggestion that the corresponding product in the body is not merely an organ, nor even the use of an organ, but a whole integrated system of control in addition to the organs mentioned (the bronchia), we can possibly enrich our ideas of perception.

141. Just above, "affection for understanding" was paraphrased by "desire to understand." It is a striking point in the correspondences that the stimulation of the carotid bodies and other sensory organs by vitiated blood produces a desire to draw breath - on occasion an irresistible urge. So we see a perfect parallelism when a man, feeling his lack of truth, draws in the Divine breath or Spirit. For him to have spiritual life he must do this continually, drawing in the breath of God more or less deeply according to his need. But this will do him little good if the air fails to reach the spiritual "air saccules" where it meets the "blood." His perception of truth will be sterile unless he puts it to use. And the difference between a sterile perception of truth and a fruitful one is like the difference between shallow and deep breathing. The breathing gets deeper when the lack of air is felt. The perception of truth gets keener when its absence is troublesome. The lack of air for the body is felt more and more as exercise or work (i.e., application to use) is undertaken. So also as the life of the spirit expresses itself in uses, the soul (will joined to understanding) is stimulated to draw Divine Truth deeply into itself so that it may purify and refresh the blood of the spirit. Here, however, we are already thinking of the third conjunction, for it is from this that thoughts of wisdom and hence of use are born. The affection leading to this third conjunction seems to correspond to the pulmonary arteries, to which we now turn.

The pulmonary arteries correspond to affections that complete the means whereby new life from the Lord can flow into the mind

142. The pulmonary arteries form the third arterial system of special importance to the lungs, so that we consider now how they are related to the third conjunction. Of this we read, "The third conjunction comes through an affection for seeing truth, from which springs thought" (DLW 404, proposition viii). From what follows in that paragraph one is led to infer that the thought referred to is not necessarily merely that kind which shows up in bodily speech and action when anyone is in the company of others. This latter thought is contrasted with the thought a man has when an affection for understanding leads him to perceive truth. This kind of thought is called thought of the spirit or meditation. It also falls into the thought of the body but not obviously so, for it is above thoughts which come from memory and it makes use of them for conclusions or confirmations. It is said to look down on them, but naturally it also influences them greatly in selecting from them according to the use required.[10]

143. It was mentioned above (No. 135) that in spiritual matters each part is an image of the whole (HH 58). It is the same with the affections corresponding to the pulmonary arteries. The fact that the branches of

---

[10] The inferences here drawn are derived in part from the following details. The word "perception" is omitted from the series towards the end of proposition viii (DLW 404, 3rd conjunction) where we find "when love enters into the understanding,…it first begets affection for truth, then affection for understanding what it knows, and finally affection for seeing in bodily thought that which it understands." But we have seen that affection for understanding produces perception of truth (vii), also that this perception is the thought of his spirit, i.e., meditation (vii middle) which falls into bodily thought, but hidden or silent thought. When we compare this with the former quotation we see that the thought mentioned there is not hidden, thus the 3rd conjunction is tending towards producing effects in the natural, and as we have said, the thoughts or meditations it produces make use of ideas from the memory for conclusions or confirmations, which are thoughts of wisdom.

these arteries follow one another so closely suggests that the corresponding affections may also follow very closely, and form a triad like the three conjunctions. The affections for truth, for understanding, and for seeing what is understood are the result of love entering the understanding. It would appear that they follow one another as closely as do the branches of the pulmonary arteries in the lungs. For consider the affection for truth; does anyone love truth and not wish to understand it? When he understands it, does he not love to turn it over in his mind and see it from different points of view? Hence it can be seen that the third conjunction includes elements of the former two.

144. Remembering that thought is the product of this third conjunction, we now come to consider the correspondences and note that thought corresponds to the "minutest air cells, which are receptacles for the air used in breathing" (DLW 413). We read further that thought flows from conscience and it is "little else but an unfolding of the things that are of conscience and thereby the partition of them into ideas and then words" (AC 1919). This unfolding and partitioning reminds one of the repeated branching and dividing of the bronchia until they end in the innumerable "minutest air cells."

145. I have suggested that the affection leading to the third conjunction corresponds to the pulmonary arteries. These undergo repeated branching and dividing more or less as do the bronchia until they end in the minutest capillaries in the surfaces of the minutest air cells. The agreement between the correspondences of the affection (pulmonary arteries and derived capillaries) and those of the thoughts, arising from the conjunction the affection produces (the minutest air cells), is seen in the close association of the two structures. Here we have the closest possible intimacy belonging to the marriage of the heart and lungs. In these minute air cells the blood is separated from the air by the thinnest of membranes; here the capillaries are very densely packed, yet in a single layer, and their walls are exceedingly thin (0.2 micron, i.e. 0.0002 millimeters). Everything is arranged to facilitate the exchange of gases between the blood and the air in the lungs. We see from this how every thought is a marriage of will and understanding: as the oxygen refreshes the blood so the truth enlivens the love, and this takes place in every minutest thought. The blood can receive oxygen only in these minutest air cells. Similarly, love can be enlivened only when truth is present in every least thought. Not that we must think of nothing but doctrine, but that the truth, which is the inflowing of the Holy Spirit of the Lord, gives life to the mind through every minutest thought. Yet there are many thoughts that seem to have little or nothing to do with love, wisdom, or even facts and common sense. Can they correspond? It seems that they can, for during quiet respiration, that is, in the absence of muscular exertion, some parts of the lungs move only slightly, and less than a tenth of the total capacity is emptied and refilled with fresh air. The new air mixes with the stale air remaining, but obviously some air saccules get fresher air than others, and probably some remain closed until the demand increases (Cotes, 1963, p. 415). So we have many thoughts which are not matters of conscience or perception but which can become so during occasions of joy or stress that correspond to muscular exertion.

The understanding of the simultaneous workings of the mind is facilitated by the imaginary separation in time of circulatory functions that are simultaneous

146. We may now reiterate the products of the three conjunctions, namely, affection of truth, perception of truth, and thought. In DLW 404 (proposition viii) these three are repeated in different words which help the reader to grasp the meaning:

It first begets affection for truth, then affection for understanding what it knows, and finally affection for seeing in bodily thought that which it understands.

Since this last is used for conclusions and confirmations, it is the driving force within wisdom of speech and charity of action.

147. The psychology of the three conjunctions is said to be "but dimly seen by those who are unable to perceive the mind's workings separately..." because "the mind's workings are simultaneous in the thought with those who have both affection for truth and the perception of it..." (DLW 404: viii).

This difficulty can be diminished by studying the corresponding heart and lungs, where several processes occur almost simultaneously. We separate them in order to understand them, and as they are relatively easy to consider separately, it may be worthwhile to re-examine the subject from this point of view, although some repetition will be involved.

148. We have first the bronchial arteries in the embryo. By their means the lungs and all accessory tissues are nourished and are able to grow. Also the bronchia, their branches, and the minutest air cells are formed. These last two would correspond, respectively, to means aiding perception, and to thoughts; but as they are not yet in use, they cannot correspond. Just before birth the whole system is ready, but not working. From this we may deduce that the betrothal between the will and the understanding produces in due order all the faculties of the future mind, and facilitates their growth, but not their activity. Obviously, mental growth continues for a long time after activities begin, just as the heart and lungs keep pace with the growth of the body. As the embryo itself has no will and no understanding, it may seem difficult to accept this summary explanation. Nevertheless, there must be some form of correspondence for these things to come into existence. We cannot doubt that the correspondence is with the will and understanding of the angels who are close to the embryo, and perhaps with those of the mother if she is angelic. We remember also that spiritual matters are not bound in with our bodily, four dimensional space-time continuum. What seems future to us is present with the

Lord, and, by derivation, to some extent with angels also. What appears as future can act as a cause in our natural sphere, besides the immediate influx from the Lord.

149. We have, secondly, the carotid bodies together with similar sensitive structures and the nerve centres and muscles through which they operate. Through their means the machinery which has been formed will be animated and controlled. Knowledge will be brought to life, truth will be perceived as something beyond mere fact, but thought in accordance with the truth perceived waits on the third conjunction.

150. We have, thirdly, the pulmonary arteries (The third signifies completion) in full flow after birth. The difference is fantastic! It is the dawn of life, the baby's first cry; it is Man, the work of the Creator. Only now can the other two conjunctions operate fruitfully. Growth and control are meaningless until use follows. The physiology shows it so clearly. Now at last the pulmonary arteries can convey the full flux of blood to the millions of air cells whereby the blood and thence the whole body will receive all the oxygen it needs, and eliminate the carbon dioxide that would poison it. Similarly when the will, as a receptacle of love from the Lord, completes the three stages of its conjunction with the understanding, as the receptacle of wisdom from the Lord, the man can truly begin to live.

151. What is worth contemplating more closely is that, as the whole of the blood must circulate in its turn through the lungs, so all the activities of the will must be subjected to the understanding for purification (corresponding to the elimination of carbon dioxide) and for potentiation (corresponding to the absorption of oxygen). All the blood from the lungs comes back to the heart to be pumped at higher pressure to the heart muscles themselves as well as to the whole body. This must mean that when the understanding has invigorated the thought, the will itself receives invigoration, enabling it, in turn, to fill the whole mind with vigour.

152. What is also very remarkable is that when this refreshed blood is returned to the heart and re-distributed, it is continually assessed to determine whether its refreshment is commensurate with requirements, and if not, higher centres make the necessary adjustments. Similarly, in the mind or spirit, the activities performed by the will with the aid of the understanding are continuously observed by the conscience or perception to determine whether they conform to the standards required. If they do not, the understanding is further stimulated, or, alternatively, commanded to rest. From the correspondence it is clear that conscience and perception are far more than can be put into two simple words. They must be complex sensing and controlling systems through which the Lord works (see for example AC 875).

After sequential development in due order, the three affections, conjunctions, and offspring can occur repeatedly as rapid cycles or spirals whereby the mind develops further and becomes more useful

153. We notice now that although the three conjunctions of heart and lungs follow over a period of time in the embryo and young child, they become simultaneous after birth. So with the spirit; each conjunction must be properly effected in order and its offspring may be produced. After that, affection of truth, perception of truth, and thought follow so closely as to seem simultaneous, but it seems easier to imagine that they form a cycle which can be repeated with great rapidity. The short time required for the circulation of the blood emphasizes this point. A thought will stimulate the affection for truth so that a further perception arises, whence new thoughts originate, and in a few seconds an entirely new mental condition prevails. Changes continue! Thought as an end in itself is useless. The correspondence of heart and lungs by themselves is obvious. The rest of the body is needed for use. The will must be determined into action, but in such a way that "whatever is done from this appears as if by the man's will, but is really done by the Lord" (AC 875).

*The correspondence of a new will (or heart) given through regenera-
tion requires further study*

154. Throughout this chapter we have assumed that we are dealing
with a regenerating man, but in many places we are told that regeneration involves the giving of a new will in place of the old one which is
irredeemably evil. The lack of obvious reference to this part of the
subject in DLW poses a serious problem. This problem is considered
in the next chapter.

CHAPTER VII

CORRESPONDENCE OF THE HEART AND LUNGS—PART 4
THE GIVING OF A NEW WILL

155. The writings show in many places (as we have already seen) that the will corresponds to the heart. In many other places they show that the regeneration of the spiritual man requires the formation of a new will. The student of the Writings may easily become distressed when he finds that these two doctrines are separated and that hardly ever does he learn about the formation of a new heart, although it is mentioned in the literal sense of the Old Testament. It seems as though there ought to be some kind of formation of a new heart to correspond to the new will necessary for regeneration, but a new heart does not grow in the body. As far as I am aware, the only reference in Arcana Coelestia to a new bodily heart is in no. 3470, part of which is as follows.

> Thus also it is with man's Natural while it is being regenerated; for natural good is such, that of itself it is not willing to obey and serve rational good as a servant serves a master, but it wants to have the command. In order therefore that it may be reduced to a state of compliance and service, it is harassed by states of vastation and temptation, until its concupiscences become weakened, and then by an influx of the good of faith and charity through the internal man from the Lord, it is tempted, until the good received hereditarily is by degrees extirpated, and a new will is implanted in its place, into which good the truths of faith are then insinuated, which are like new fibres which are inserted into the heart of man, through which fibres new juice is introduced, until a new heart has grown by degrees.

156. It is well known that new blood capillaries can appear in muscular tissue when there is a need for an improvement in blood supply and that a heart weakened (for example by lack of exercise) can, in this way grow stronger under a healthy regime. Many living tissues are constantly being broken down and renewed and we do not normally regard this repair and growth as producing a new organ.

157. If the whole of AC 3469 and 3470 is studied it appears possible that the correspondence is at a more external level than that concerned with the giving of a new will. We are here dealing with a man whose will has already led him to a religion of a kind (under Providence of course). Such a religion could be like that of people who live in accordance with doctrine from the literal sense of the Word. Such people are already regenerate as regards interior things; they already have a new will or conscience. The regeneration referred to in these two numbers is the reformation of natural good. As it is a process of gradual improvement and re-arrangement, it corresponds to the gradual renewal of an existing organ, not to the creation of a new one. To appreciate the meaning of the new will required for regeneration, we need to examine the fall of mankind and to understand how the Lord saved a remnant and continues to save us.

The fall of man and the end of the Most Ancient Church

158. The fall of the human race reached its tragic end when the Most Ancient Church (MAC) was extinguished among the posterity of the early celestial people. Those people were the wisest of men, for goods and truths flowed into their minds from the Lord as though they had been born with them. For example, in AE 739:6 we read: "For the men of the celestial church are such that they perceive all the goods and truths of heaven from the Lord through influx into their interiors, whence they see goods and truths interiorly, in themselves as though innate,..." The function of truths with them is explained in AC 4489 where it is said that "The varieties and differences of good were to them truths, and hence they knew what all things in general and in particular in the world represented in the Lord's kingdom,..." They acquired cognitions of good and evil from heaven, but they were also allowed to procure knowledges of good and evil from the world. This we learn from AE 739:7 which continues:

> for from [the world] their natural man had its knowledge. But they were forbidden to view their knowledges by a posterior way, because it was granted them to see all things which appeared before their eyes in the world in a prior way. To view the world and everything in it in a prior way, and thence to receive knowledges is to regard them from the light of heaven, and in that way to know what they are. Therefore by means of knowledges from the world they were able to confirm heavenly things and thus to strengthen their wisdom.

We notice in particular the difference between the progress of a person of the Most Ancient Church and that of spiritual people. The former were regenerated by "assimilating from infancy the good of charity" whereas in respect to Noah (the first spiritual church) the necessity of truth is emphasized. An emphasis is also placed on truth as a necessity for the formation of celestial good in AC 10252, 10266 and 10269, but this is obviously a different celestial, as it is formed or grows from below or from exteriors. It seems like the good from a celestial origin which is the Woman clothed with the Sun (Rev 12).

The prior way by which they were to look at the world is also indicated by what we are given of their internal respiration. This respiration is described in AC 1118 in terms which incline a reader to think in terms of parts of the body, (as lips, ear, mouth) but the passage is speaking of *internal respiration*. The bodily parts might easily be ascribed to their spiritual body making it easy to understand why the internal respiration was "more applicable and conformable to the very idea of thought." Furthermore, in AC 1119 it is said, "they respired with the angels," also, AC 1121 says their spirit "by means of internal respiration, was joined to heaven," and AC 805, "breathing similar to the angels."

In this matter, as in many spiritual matters we cannot *prove* anything. This, as we well know in the New Church, is a dispensation of providence to give us the maximum freedom. The ideas we are playing with are "all," as far as we can keep them pure, derived from the internal sense of the Word, "which is more manifold than anyone could believe; and therefore it does not suffer itself to be limited by times and distinctions" (AC 618).

159. In order to understand how the MAC came to an end we need to know more about the structure of the minds of the members of the MAC. This church was celestial so the following from AC 5113:3 applies to it.

> The member of the celestial church was regenerated as to the will part, assimilating from infancy the good of charity; and when he had attained a perception of this, he was led into a perception of love to the Lord, whereby all the truths of faith appeared to him in the intellectual as in a mirror. The understanding and the will made in him a mind completely one; for by the things in the understanding it was perceived what was in the will.

This quality of having "a mind completely one" was inherited by his descendants and, (as we are taught by the internal sense of the early chapters of Genesis) when they fell away from the Lord they could not be rescued because they were so simple minded. When their affections led them astray they could not accept any truths contrary to their affections. Thus they denied themselves the means for correction.

160. At this point the whole human race on earth would have died out owing to the lack of a church through which the Lord could flow to give them life. To avoid that end the Lord made special provision for a change in the state of the human mind or spirit. The change is dramatized in the story of Noah, the Flood, and the Ark, the internal sense of which teaches how the changes were made. Of the many passages in the Writings we note merely two which show that the whole human race would have perished without special intervention. In AC 631 we read, "the end of all flesh has come before me." This means that the whole human race would inevitably perish. AC 637 is, in part, as follows:

That "I will destroy them with the earth" signifies that together with the church the human race would perish, is on this account: If the Lord's church should be entirely extinguished on the earth, the human race could by no means exist, but one and all would perish. The church, as before said, is as the heart: so long as the heart lives, the neighboring viscera and members can live; but as soon as the heart dies, they one and all die also. The Lord's church on earth is as the heart, whence the human race, even that part of it which is outside the church, has life. The reason is quite unknown to anyone, but in order that something of it might be known, it may be stated that the whole human race on earth is as a body with its parts wherein the church is as the heart; and that unless there were a church with which as with a heart the Lord might be united through heaven and the world of spirits, there would be disjunction; and if there were disjunction of the human race with the Lord, it would instantly perish.

It is clear therefore, that provision had to be made for the setting up of a new church.

The formation of a New Church (now called the Ancient Church)

161. The Most Ancient Church was celestial (see also Nos. 188 to 190 below and 158 to 159 above), that is, everything with them depended on love to the Lord (which also flowed into them from the Lord). But when that church declined, the whole of mankind was in peril, as explained just above (No. 160). The Lord foresaw the development, of course, and began the necessary changes well in advance, i.e. before the flood. (See AC 401, 519, 521 and 2896.)

162. Most New Church people are aware of the spiritual history of the Most Ancient and Ancient Churches and of the general signification of The Flood. It is not very easy, however, to understand in detail what happened then nor to envisage its continual influence on our own individual and corporate development. Rational conviction comes from within, but in order to see the doctrines clearly in our own minds we can use correspondences. They are, of course, found in the story of The Flood and the Ark since that is part of the Word. However, the Writings can take us further and they have much to say about the correspondences between the mind or spirit which we cannot see, and the body which we can see.

163. The Writings also teach us about the inheritance of evil tendencies, which would lead us to expect a large residue of such tendencies to be present with Noah, as indeed the internal sense of the story confirms. Scientific knowledge of inheritance leads us to expect that most of the bodily structures of the men of the Ancient Churches would be derived from, and therefore be the same as or similar to, those in men of the Most Ancient Church. Thus when we compare the Ancient and Most Ancient people, we are not dealing with entirely different creatures. It is against a background of inheritance assumed to be reasonably constant that we view the spiritual meaning of the story of Noah. A constant background should render any change easier to observe than if the whole had changed and the earlier forms had disappeared. Now the spiritual meaning of The Flood and the survival of Noah and his family indicates a drastic change in the inherited constitution of the human mind. The change was so fundamental that we would expect some very remarkable change in bodily structure to correspond with it and the relatively constant background should enable us to notice the change. The mental change was an alteration in the relationship between the will and the understanding to which we now direct our attention. The change was instituted by the Lord in a small number of the posterity of the MAC. These few are meant by Noah and are called *spiritual*. Collectively they were the Ancient Church. Spiritual people have a mind which is in two parts: (a) a will part where love resides and (b) an understanding part where knowledge and truth are stored and studied. The dual structure of the mind enables spiritual people to accept truth and instruction even if they don't like it. They can be persuaded by various influences to accept doctrine and learn it and later to love it. The descendants of the MAC could not do this because, as already said, the will and the understanding with them formed a united mind. The importance of the division which produced spiritual people is emphasized in many passages. One would like to quote all of them, but perhaps the following will suffice for the present. First, from AC 875 we have the following:

> The real "ground" with this man is in his intellectual mind, and when it has been prepared the good of charity is insinuated by the Lord, and from this, conscience, from which he afterwards acts, that is, through which the Lord works the good and truth of faith. Thus the Lord makes the intellectual things of this man distinct from those of his will, so they are never united; for if they should be united, he could not but perish eternally. With the man of the Most Ancient Church the things of the will were united to those of the understanding, as they also were with the celestial angels. But with the man of the Ancient Church they were not united, *nor are they with any spiritual man*. It appears indeed as if the good of charity which he does were of the will, but this is only an appearance and fallacy. All the good of charity which he does is of the Lord alone, not through the will but through conscience. If the Lord should relax ever so little

and suffer the man to act from his own will, instead of good he would do evil from hatred, revenge, and cruelty. The case is the same with the truth that the spiritual man thinks and speaks: unless he were to think and speak from conscience, and thus from the good that is of the Lord, he would never think and speak truth otherwise than do the devils of hell when they feign themselves angels of light. All this is clearly manifest in the other life. From these things it is evident in what manner regeneration is effected, and what the regeneration of the spiritual man is: that in fact it is the separation of his intellectual part from the will part, by means of conscience, which is formed by the Lord in his intellectual part; and whatever is done by this appears as if done by the man's will, but is really done by the Lord. (emphasis added)

The change in mental constitution as well as the condition that made it necessary are very clearly described in AC 927. This passage is included in full, for it is a beautiful piece of writing.

"I will not again curse the ground any more on man's account." That this signifies that man would not any more so turn away, as did the man of the posterity of the Most Ancient Church is evident from what has been said before about this posterity. That "to curse" signifies in the internal sense to turn oneself away, may be seen above (n. 223, 245). How the case is with this and with what follows: that man would not anymore so turn away, as did the man of the Most Ancient Church, and that he would not again be able so to destroy himself, is evident from what has already been said about the posterity of the Most Ancient Church who perished and about the new church which is called "Noah." It has been shown that the man of the Most Ancient Church was so constituted that the will and understanding with him formed one mind, or that with him love was implanted in his voluntary part, and thus at the same time faith, which filled the other or intellectual part of his mind. From this their posterity inherited the condition that the will and the understanding made a one; and therefore when the love of self and the consequent insane lusts began to take possession of their will part (where previously there had been love to the Lord and charity towards the neighbour), not only did their voluntary part or will become utterly perverted, but so also together with it did their intellectual part or understanding, and this was still more the case when the last posterity immersed their falsities in their lusts, and so became "Nephilim," for thereby they became of such nature that they could not be restored, because both parts of the mind (that is, the whole mind) had been ruined. But as this had been foreseen by the Lord, He had also provided for man's upbuilding, in this way, that he might be reformed and regenerated in respect to the second or intellectual part of the mind, in which there might be implanted a new will which is conscience, and through which the Lord might work the good of love (that is, of charity), and the truth of faith. Thus of the Lord's Divine mercy has man been restored. These are the things that are signified in this verse by, "I will not again curse the ground any more on man's account; because the imagination of man's heart is evil from his youth; neither will I smite any more everything living, as I have done."

164. From these two numbers (AC 875 and 927) we observe that not only were the will part and the understanding part separated from one another, but also that a new will was implanted in the understanding part. This new will is conscience. It is necessary for the regeneration of all spiritual men. It is described briefly at the end of AC 918 in these words:

The conscience which the Lord grants to the spiritual man is, so to speak, a new will, and thus...a person who has been created anew is provided with a new will and from this with a new understanding.

The continuation of the old will

165. Since it was the inability to receive a new will that led to the extinction of much of the posterity of the MAC it might be thought that the inherited evil will of mankind was then completely destroyed. Only those like Noah (the Ancient Church) survived in whom a new will could be formed; thus that in Noah and every individual after him the old evil will was destroyed and replaced by a new one (AC 4328). But "altogether destroyed" does not here mean "annihilated," but evil, for it is added that the voluntary, that is the will part, "was nothing but evil." It is clear that the evil will was not destroyed, for it was "preserved from inundation" (AC 641, 642). We also find that "though the will part of (regenerated) man is opposed, yet it cannot but be present" (AC 1044:2), and that although actual and hereditary evil can be modified and rendered harmless, it cannot be abolished (AC 719). It is true that we learn from AC 4328 that the black column shown to Swedenborg signified a Voluntary (approximately equivalent to the will) "altogether destroyed." At this point, however, we have already learned that "destroyed" in Genesis VII:4 signifies a proprium that does not appear and is no longer hurtful, and the proprium is not destroyed but remains (AC 731). Here we take proprium to include the old will because: (1) it "is entirely evil and falsity" and (2) the same phrase (Gen. VII:4) also signifies the final vastation of those who were of the MAC. The virtual equivalence of proprium and the old will in this instance is confirmed in AC 1023 where we find that it is the "corrupt proprium of his will part" from which the "proprium of his intellectual part" is separated. Moreover, in the index to AC under "Proprium" we find, "The voluntary, thus the proprium...4328," where "voluntary" is probably the same as the will.

166. The need for persistence of something of the old will in mankind after the Flood, i.e. for the presence of will in each person before regeneration is brought out in AC 657 where we find the following; "Without influx of the Lord's life into the things of the understanding in man—or rather into things of the will and through these into those of the understanding...life would be impossible to man." The old evil will is even necessary in order that man may be led by means of it to learn and do what is good as an essential preliminary to his reformation. For "he must first learn the truths of faith, and assimilate what is intellectual, and thus from truth learn what is good; and after he has thus learnt it, he is able to think it, and then to will it, and at last to do it; and then a new will is formed in him by the Lord in the intellectual part. By this new will the spiritual man is raised by the Lord into heaven, evil still remaining in the will that is proper to him; which will is then miraculously set aside..." (AC 5113:2). We note that the new will is not given before good is done, which must therefore be from an evil will; and that evil remains in the old will which is "set aside," not destroyed.

167. We conclude then that this proprium or will of evil which is "as if destroyed" actually remains and "is no longer hurtful" and is even "vivified" (AC 719, 731). Therefore the old will is still with man when a new will has been given. The old will is then no longer allowed to express itself in its old evil ways, so the new will of good from the Lord and the old will of evil from man seem to exist side by side. This is a frightening concept, as the evil might at any moment rise up and destroy the good, but we are assured that this is not possible, for man is no longer able so to destroy himself (AC 927 quote above).

The will corresponds to the heart

168. This has been said so many times that it is only necessary to refer to earlier paragraphs (see nos. 87 and 92). But it brings us to a point where we wonder if the "as it were a new will" could have as it were a new heart to correspond to it. We now spend a few minutes on bodily anatomy rather than spiritual (though corresponding), and find that we have two hearts.

The heart drives two separate circulations as though there where two hearts related to the two wills

169. The diagram shown in Figure 2 will assist the visualization of the two circulations. In reality, the heart and neighboring arteries form a very compact unit making it difficult to follow the flow routes through them and to illustrate the routes in only two dimensions. But by ignoring sizes, shapes, and relative positions, it is possible to draw a simple plan, such as that shown. Figure 3 is a drawing of an actual heart, presented to keep the plan in perspective.

170. It is well known that the circulation of blood through the lungs via the pulmonary arteries is quite separate from the circulation to the rest of the body via the aorta; also that the pulmonary arteries are the only exits from the right side of the heart which side can therefore send blood to the lungs only. So although we are accustomed to speak of it as one heart, the separation of the circulations is so complete that it is reasonable to think of it as two. In placing emphasis on the circulation, we are in agreement with the Writings where the heart is considered to extend itself by means of arteries and veins, for example, "the heart and its extension into the body through arteries and veins" (DLW 399, similarly in 412). The view of the heart as two pumps is also to be found in modern research; Pierre Dejour writes "in...mammals there is a cardiac pump for the low pressure pulmonary circulation and a second cardiac pump for the high pressure systemic circulation."

171. It is clear from Figure 2 that the blood from every part of the body, other than the lungs, drains into the right side of the heart, and all of it is sent to the lungs whence it returns to the left side of the heart and so to the body. Thus the heart is unable to send any blood to the body other than blood received from the lungs. This arrangement might well correspond to man's now being unable to destroy himself by immersing his understanding in his lusts (AC 927).

172. The separation of the two circuits of the blood is extremely important in ensuring efficient oxygenation and removal of carbon dioxide, and in view of its extreme importance we would expect equally important correspondences. This being so, it is remarkable to find so little mention of it in the Writings. The following is the nearest I have observed: "After birth the heart discharges the blood from its right ventricle into the lungs; and, after passing through these, empties it into its left ventricle" (DLW 405). One can only assume that the facts were not widely enough known to be of use, as is said in DLW 405 at the end. On the other hand, the important doctrines were to be made known and the correspondences pointed out as far as possible. Hence we find occasional anatomical references which seem obscure until interpreted into modern modes of thought. This applies to the dual circulation of blood. We read:

> In the state together with the heart [the follicular substance of the lungs] is expanded and contracted through the pulmonary arteries and veins, which are from the heart alone; in the state almost separate from the heart, through the bronchial arteries and veins, which are from the vena cava and aorta; these last vessels are external to the heart. This is the case in the lungs because the understanding is able to be raised above the love-proprium, which corresponds to the heart... (DLW 413)

In view of what we now know, the important meaning of "from the heart alone" is not that the pulmonary arteries do not come from anywhere else, for this applies to the aorta and *vena cava* also, but that the pulmonary arteries come from the heart alone, i.e. they are alone as they come from the heart, i.e. they alone come from the right ventricle so that all its blood must go to the lungs. Perhaps this argument will seem to some like semantic hair splitting, but when we consider that this is what Swedenborg wrote in trying to express "Angelic Wisdom" in natural language, we can picture his struggle after seeing with the eyes of his spirit the flow and pulsation of the blood in the lungs and the marvelous inflation of the air follicles. This corresponds to the purification of the impulses of the will and the putting to use of the purified products (AC 3889). He must have seen the spiritual counterparts of physiological mechanisms more clearly than we can envisage the latter even now, and he would have been utterly lost for words without Divine guidance.

173. In thinking about the correspondences of the dual circulation it must not be forgotten that the lungs are nourished by blood supplied from the left side of the heart via the aorta and the bronchial arteries. Most of this blood drains back into the vena cava and so to the right side of the heart with the blood from the rest of the body. This route of blood supply is different from that needed for respiration and it is also the one by which the lungs are nourished during embryonic life. Presumably it could correspond to the affections of the old will when there was external innocence enough to excuse its evils and when its activities stimulated the growth of the understanding. It is perhaps the first conjunction which "comes through an affection for knowing" (DLW 404).

174. From all this it must now be clear that the heart is effectively two pumps and so is able to correspond to two wills, one being the old will or proprium, the other the new will given by the Lord in the understanding. It seems very strange to suggest that two such different wills as the old and new could be related to the two sides of one heart, but we have already observed (nos. 165-167) that good from the Lord and evil from man continue side by side. A very remarkable record, lending some conformation, occurs in AC 10808 where we find: "they showed me their idea about evil in man and good from the Lord: how they are kept separate. They set one quite near the other, but still separated, yet bound together in a remarkable way, so that good led evil and bridled it..." This is reminiscent of the two sides of the heart which are bound together firmly but still separated, and which beat in such manner that one part follows another. Each contraction of the heart is initiated in the sinuatrial node (or pacemaker) in the right atrium and spreads to the rest of the heart in an orderly way by means of special fibres so that the ventricular contractions follow the atrial contractions in proper sequence. Surely this corresponds to "bound together in a remarkable way, so that good led evil..."

175. Since it is the new (separated) will and the "new understanding from it" which introduce new purifying truths into the regenerated mind, and since such truths can correspond to oxygen (nos. 245-247), one might consider that perhaps the right side of the heart corresponds to the new will, and the lungs, opened at birth by the flow of blood through the pulmonary artery correspond to the new understanding from the new will. Fetal circulation and the heart of the fetus are illustrated in Figure 7 and Figure 8. It is not to be supposed, however, that one side of the heart necessarily corresponds to evil; it might more acceptably correspond to the good state of the MAC. Still, it is remarkable that one side receives partially vitiated blood, and the other the refreshed blood from the lungs.

176. Having seen that the bodily heart may well correspond to the double will of the spiritual being we now ask what can correspond to the single will of people who lived before the Flood. Is there a suitable man having a suitable heart of a different kind? Indeed there is! Every unborn child has but one heart and one circulation.

The possible correspondence of a single will

177. A hint of a possible correspondence between the heart of an unborn child and the will of the Most Ancient people was given just above. This might seem a strange idea at first but there are many considerations which make the examination of the concept a worthwhile exercise. It is not put forward as doctrine. It is just a view of some fragments of scientific knowledge to be examined in the light of

FIGURE 7

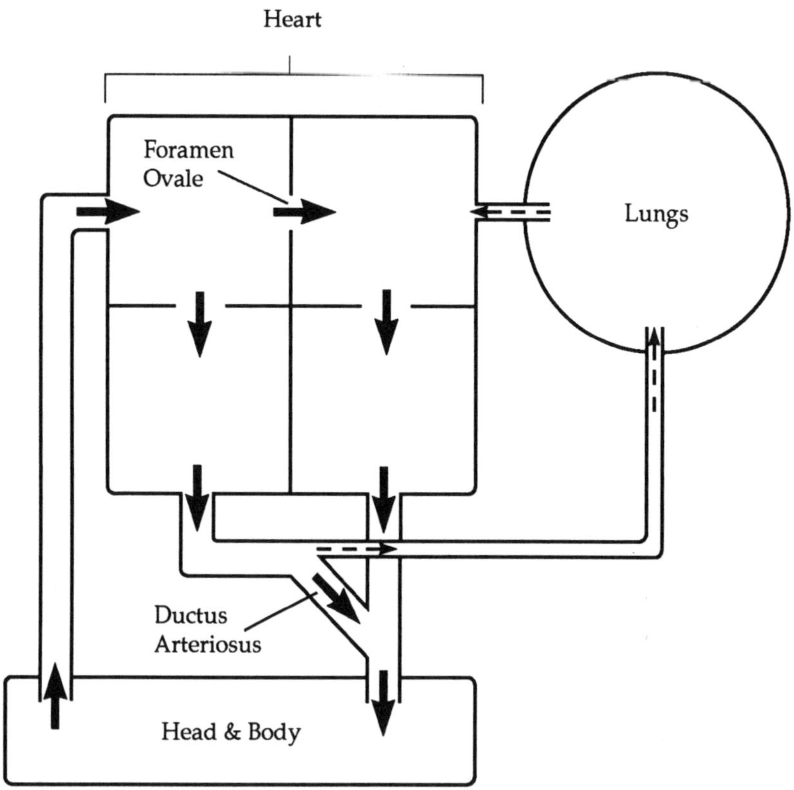

Figure 7: **Block Diagram of Fetal Circulation**

Block diagram of fetal circulation to show how most of the blood by-passes the lungs by means of the foramen ovale and the ductus arteriosus. To be compared with Figure 2. See also Figure 8.   Drawn by Richard Morris.

FIGURE 8

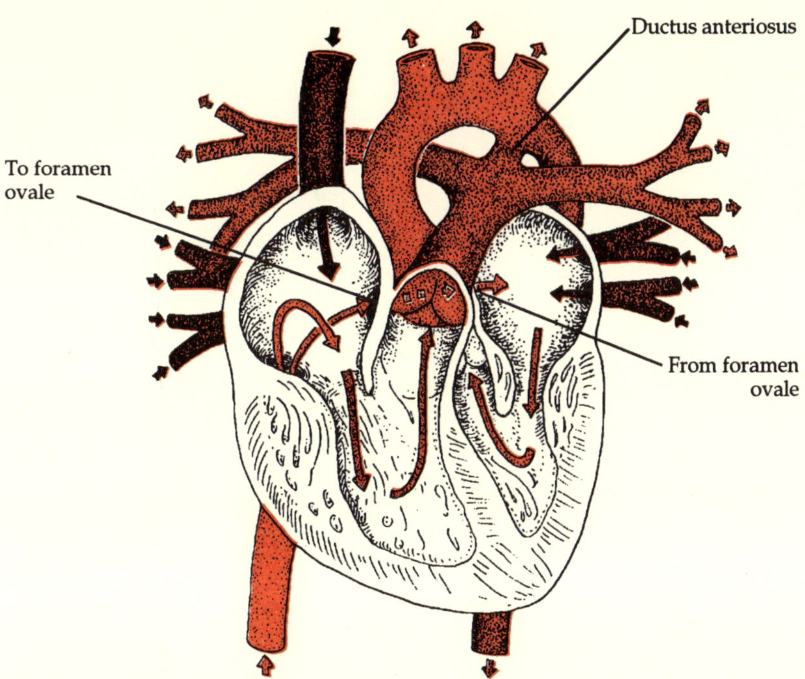

Figure 8: **Heart of the Fetus**

   A drawing prepared in the same way as Figure 3. Parts which are the same have not been labelled so that the ductus arteriosus and the foramen ovale can easily be picked out. Part of the left atrium cannot be shown behind the aorta and pulmonary trunk, but it is in contact with the right atrium; and the foramen ovale really is a hole not a tube.

Sources: Modified from Hamilton, et al., *Human Embryology*, fig. 190; Anthony and Kolthoff, *Textbook of Anatomy and Physiology*, figs. 13-15.

arcana revealed from heaven. We will therefore collect first those fragments concerning the anatomy of the fetal heart to see how it differs from that of a child after birth. Then we will review some of the parallels between the anatomy and physiology on one hand and the psychology of regeneration on the other.

178. There are two arrangements that make the four chambers of the heart of a fetus into one heart effectively. The first is merely a hole. The septum between the right and left atria is perforated so that the blood flowing into the heart can be divided between them. The second arrangement is a duct from the pulmonary trunk to the aorta. This enables blood to flow from the right ventricle to the aorta, thus joining the blood from the left ventricle. The hole between the atria is the *foramen ovale*, the duct connecting the pulmonary trunk and the aorta is the *ductus arteriosus* (see Figures 7 and 8).

179. Figure 7 has been prepared in the same way as Figure 2 to show diagrammatically how the *foramen ovale* allows blood to pass directly from one side of the heart to the other. Also how the *ductus arteriosus* sends most of the blood from the right ventricle to join that from the left in the aorta, instead of sending it to the lungs. A more realistic diagram is shown in Figure 4.

Although the embryo in its later stages possesses lungs and pulmonary arteries, the flow of blood through them is very small because of the effects of the *foramen ovale* and *ductus arteriosus*. Obviously, the small flow is all that is required as the lungs are not yet in use. Owing to the arrangement of the heart and arteries, even this small amount of blood can mix with the rest so that there is, in effect, only one circulation and one heart.

Occasionally the *foramen* or the *ductus* remain open after birth, causing congenital heart disease. There is, I think, no proof that such openings did not persist into adult life in the Most Ancient people, but without causing disease. One can imagine that arteries of a suitable size and type would enable such people to lead healthy and active lives in spite of having effectively only one heart corresponding to one mind. Now, however, these means of short-circuiting the lungs disappear at, or soon after birth.

At birth the baby receives, as it were, a new heart

180. When the baby is born, the *ductus arteriosus* becomes constricted and during subsequent weeks it gradually closes. The *foramen ovale* is closed also, and as inspection of Figure 7 will show, these changes effectively change the one heart into two. Now it is no longer possible for the right heart to send its blood anywhere except into the lungs. The left heart sends all its blood to the rest of the body. So the new baby has, as it were, a new heart. The lungs have not been used at all before the birth so they too are new.

181. Once we are accustomed to thinking of the heart as will and the lungs as understanding we cannot help comparing the condition after birth to the condition of the spiritual person after rebirth. Just as the heart after birth cannot avoid sending its blood through the lungs before sending it to the body, so the regenerate man is obliged to submit the wishes of his loves to the scrutiny of his intellect. This scrutiny is sometimes cursory, and sometimes he imagines he is acting spontaneously from love.

182. It may seem improbable that the changes at birth could correspond to the mental changes associated with Noah because the anatomy applies to all men, whether regenerate or not. But the mental change also applies to all men so that regeneration might be possible for each. The changes foreseen and provided by the Divine are already present with Him. The natural correspondences can begin or continue as the Lord may provide. It would seem that the spiritual aspect of any such process as the one we are looking at, might make it independent of time and perhaps of other limitations, rather like the spiritual sense of the Word. From AC 618 we learn that the internal sense of the Word "is more manifold than anyone could believe; and therefore it does not suffer itself to be limited by times and distinctions."

183. It might seem difficult to think that the baby's new heart corresponds to the new will of the spiritual man because the spiritual man receives his new will in his understanding (see quotation above; nos. 163, 164) and the baby's "new" heart is exactly where the old one was. However, it has already been established that the kingdom of the heart includes all the blood vessels, and even the blood itself (nos. 72 to 76). This means that the pulmonary and bronchial arteries and veins and the capillaries connecting them as well as the blood flowing through them would be a kingdom of the heart within the lungs. It may be satisfactory to think of this kingdom as of the heart itself, but there is another important consideration. In spiritual matters it is not correct to think spatially and "in" has a spiritual meaning independent of space as when we may be in heaven and heaven in us. This suggests that the new will which the Lord forms in the understanding does not necessarily have to be enclosed and surrounded by the understanding. It could correspond to a heart closely conjoined with the lungs—more closely than before but not necessarily inside them.

The circulation of the blood shows how the will and understanding can be conjoined in the spiritual man but not united as in the man of the Most Ancient Church

184. We have just said that the new will *in* the understanding would correspond to a heart closely conjoined with the lungs, and indeed, after birth the conjunction is closer because the flow through the pulmonary arteries is full and free. However, we now find a serious challenge, for we read that although the will and understanding of men of the MAC were united, in the spiritual man they are never united (AC 875). The corresponding heart and lungs work closely together; indeed many paragraphs in DLW are devoted to elucidating the steps towards union and their meaning. Moreover from AC 3887-9 we learn about "the influx of all things of the heart into those of the lungs," about "the influx of the will into the understanding, and of the understanding into the will"; and about "the union between the heart and the lungs." One reason for the difference may be that the will that is never united is the old will which is like that of the Most Ancient people and is set aside in the Spiritual Man when he is given the new will. But there are also additional points of interest in this part of the subject.

185. In DLW the relationship between the heart and lungs is described as conjunction and union and a marriage. In order to see what is meant in the Writings by marriage, we turn to Conjugial Love, where we find: "two married partners in heaven are not two but one angel" (CL 52), "two married partners are there called two when they are husband and wife, but one, when they are named angels" (CL 177), "the wife becomes the husband's and the husband the wife's; thus they both become one man" (CL 196), "The husband is in the bride-chamber of the understanding, and the wife in the bride-chamber of the will" (CL 270). These and many other passages show that although the union is very close, the husband and wife retain their individuality. So in marriage we find a conjunction and a distinction and these ideas can be further clarified by reference to the corresponding circulations.

186. In the embryo, as we have seen, the circulation is absolutely one unit—any particle can go anywhere from anywhere. The circulation is one unit, i.e. it is unit-ed. After birth it is not unit-ed as we have already seen, for the blood from the right side of the heart *must* go to the lungs before the left side can send it to the body. In this way the embryo shows how the will and understanding could really be one unit, and the adult circulation shows how the will and understanding can be distinct as well as being interdependent. However, the circulation is like will and understanding also in this respect: the separation is not 100% complete, for 1 or 2% of the blood finds its way through small connections between the bronchial and pulmonary systems. The amount may well vary between individuals. The connections are said to be more numerous in the very young. The understanding is also more easily swayed by the "old" will.

How is the change that led to the emergence of spiritual people like the change in the respiration of a baby at birth?

187. We have seen that many of the descendants of the MAC gradually lost the faculty of internal respiration and so suffocated themselves because they could not begin external respiration. The Ancient Church (Noah) which followed them consisted at first of the few who could respire in an external manner. Thus the change necessary for the establishment of the Ancient Church was the institution of external breathing because the internal respiration was no longer possible. In order to understand this change we need to examine internal respiration as well as the external that followed.

188. The internal respiration enjoyed by the MAC was not some miraculous way of causing the body to survive without oxygen, for, in AC 805 we read that the internal respiration was "similar to that of angels." This must mean that it was respiration of the soul or spirit. A fuller account of internal respiration is given in AC 1118-9, parts of which are here reproduced. As in many other passages, the Writings are inviting us to think carefully. The nature of internal respiration is expressed partly by the properties of the speech associated with it. Therefore we include below some of the statements from AC 1118 and 1119 concerning speech:

> 1118. There was shown me by a certain influx which I cannot describe, the nature of their speech when they lived in the world. It was not articulate, like the vocal speech of our time, but tacit, being produced not by external but by internal respiration. I was also permitted to perceive the nature of their internal

respiration—that it proceeds from the navel towards the heart, and so through the lips, without sound; and that it did not enter the ear of another and strike upon what is called the drum of the ear by an external way, but by a certain way within the mouth, in fact by a passage there which is now called the Eustachian tube. And it was shown me that, by such speech, they could much more fully express the sentiments of the mind and the ideas of thought than can possibly be done by articulate sounds, or vocal words, which likewise are directed by the respiration, but external. For there is nothing in any word that is not directed by means of the respiration. But with them this was done much more perfectly, because by internal respiration; which, because it is interior, is at once far more perfect, and more applicable and conformable to the very idea of thought. Besides, they also conversed by slight movements of the lips, and correspondent changes of the face; for being celestial men, whatever they thought shone forth from their faces and eyes, which were varied conformably. They could by no means put on an expression of countenance different from that which was in agreement with their thoughts. Simulation, and still more deceit, was to them a monstrous crime.

1119. It has been shown me to the life how the internal respiration of the most ancient people silently flowed into a kind of external and thus tacit speech, perceived by another in his internal man.

189. As the speech produced by internal breathing was tacit, i.e. silent, it would not affect the bodily ear no matter what route it took, whether through the external meatus or through the Eustachian tube. Possibly changes of air pressure from the breathing of one person into the mouth of another could relay meaningful symbols. Movements of the lips were used "besides" the speech of internal respiration, which shows they, the lips, were not used to produce the speech. It is worth emphasizing that the breathing "*silently* flowed into a *kind of* external and thus *tacit* speech perceived by another in his *interior* man" (emphasis added). One way of looking at these statements is to suppose that the silent speech was a transfer of ideas like that which occurs in heaven, as is actually said in AC 607. Thus the bodily organs mentioned in AC 1118 could refer to the spiritual body and not to the earthly body. Then it is easier to see why the speech from internal respiration is "far more perfect and more applicable and conformable to the very ideas of thought." Also the word "external" and especially "a kind of external" used above is perhaps being used in a comparative sense, as in AC 4286 (where all angels are distinguished into internal and external), and not in an absolute sense to mean physical things.

190. It is true that in AC 607 many details are mentioned concerning muscular fibres in the lips. Such details may incline the reader to think of the lips as of the earthly body. Nevertheless, the expression by the lips and face is here so closely linked with internal respiration that perhaps now, more than 200 years later, the transmission of ideas by facial expression is not so incredible to those who accept the Writings. For instance, how long would it take to describe in words what you receive in two seconds (let alone a whole minute) from the face of a loved one? How much more, and how much more clearly would you perceive if you had also the internal respiration for the transfer of ideas? Thus it might have been that the essential transfer was by the communication between souls and that the expression of the face was a confirmation in ultimates. It may, however, seem inconsistent to think of the ears as belonging to the spiritual body and the lips to the physical body. On the other hand, we all have both and obviously the people of the MAC were conscious of both. In view of all these things it seems reasonable to continue with the hypothesis that internal respiration was a drawing of the air of heaven (i.e. spirit, wind, breath, living truth) into the mind or spirit of the individual, i.e. into the interior man, as is said of the tacit speech in AC 1119.

Putting speech aside for the moment, one may look at the internal respiration itself from the same point of view. We read that it "proceeded from the navel towards the interior region of the breast" (AC 1120), and of the spirits of Mars it is said "that their respiration was interior, proceeding from the region of the chest towards the navel and thence rolling itself upwards through the breast..." The spirits of Mars "were of a celestial genius...not unlike...the Most Ancient Church on this Earth." In this second case it is made very clear that we are dealing with breathing of the mind or spirit, for not only is it said, "spirits of the planet Mars" but also, "for spirits and angels respire" (AC 7362).

191. We have seen earlier (AC 3887 and nos. 72-76 herein) how the lungs and heart are united in every extremity of the body because the blood caries oxygen from the lungs to every part. It is therefore quite logical to relate the proceeding of the respiration (as described just above) to the flow of blood. It then becomes almost obvious that it is the circulation of the fetus that is being described, for the blood that is to be refreshed in the placenta is pumped by the heart of the fetus through the aorta and umbilical arteries towards the navel, thence to the placenta and then back through the umbilical vein and vena cava (and the liver) to the breast where the heart is. In reality, the mother's lungs are providing air for the fetus since it is her lungs that introduce oxygen into her blood and it is her blood which carries the oxygen to the placenta where it can diffuse into the blood of the fetus. This blood is kept absolutely separate from that of the mother, yet the barriers to mixing are so marvelously designed that everything the fetus needs can get across.

192. The anatomy and physiology of the fetus and the womb have, like all other things, not been created out of nothing. Is it too great a stretch of the imagination to see the internal respiration of the angels, spirits of Mars and people of the MAC as represented by the respiration of the fetus? Or should not the great gentleness and beauty of the celestial heavens have some correspondence in material bodies even now?

193. When the later generations of those who descended from the MAC fell, internal respiration ceased, and in a few, as mentioned above, it was replaced by external respiration. From the internal sense of those parts of the Word it seems as though the external respiration was that of the mind and not of the body. Those people who perished were not literally drowned. If their bodily lungs did fail it was because their spirit failed. It is the failure of the spirit which is described in the internal sense, as one may deduce from AC 608 which is as follows:

> When internal respiration ceased, external respiration gradually succeeded, almost like that of the present day; and with external respiration a language of words, or of articulate sound, into which the ideas of thought were determined. Thus the state of man was entirely changed, and became such that he could no longer have similar perception, but instead of perception another kind of dictate which may be called conscience; for it was like conscience, though a kind of intermediate between perception and the conscience known to some at this day. And when such determination of the ideas of thought took place, that is to say, into spoken words, they could no longer be instructed, like the most ancient men, through the internal man, but through the external. And, therefore, in place of the revelations of the Most Ancient Church, doctrinal things succeeded, which could first be received by the external sense, and from them material ideas of the memory could be formed, and from these, ideas of thought, by which and according to which they were instructed. Hence it was that this church which followed had an entirely different genius from that of the Most Ancient Church, and if the Lord had not brought the human race into this genius, or into this state, no man could have been saved.

Reading this, one gradually becomes aware that, although external breathing and external senses are mentioned, the important change was in the mind or spirit, when perception was changed into "a kind of dictate which may be called conscience." Conscience needs knowledge, cognition and doctrine. It "is formed by means of the truths of faith, for that which a man has heard, acknowledged, and believed makes the conscience in him" (AC 1077). Later (AC 9112-9121) many more points of doctrine are shown concerning conscience. For example, conscience is really the new will given by the Lord, but it still needs the knowledge derived through the bodily senses, i.e. by the external way. Hence it was that instead of drawing in the truth of heaven, mankind had to draw in external ideas by means of the senses of the body. Under the influences of heaven, i.e. the Lord, the external ideas or "material ideas of the memory" could develop into ideas of thought which could serve for instruction. It was because they could no longer receive the ideas of heaven that the Lord gave them truths "dressed up" or disguised or encoded in words of earthly language. The essential change was the loss of internal instruction and the arising of external instruction.

It is worth emphasizing that "doctrinal things succeeded which could first be received by the external senses." It is clear from very many places in the Writings that these doctrinal things were vessels capable of receiving internal truths, thus even Divine Truths and life from the Lord. They were a new means whereby spiritual things could be received, as the heart, linked with the lungs, enables the body to receive oxygen. In several places we find wind or breath corresponding to spirit (AC 97, DLW 383), so that air flowing into the lungs could correspond to a Divine influx through an external means such as the learning of doctrine by hearing, reading or example. These things involve the use of the senses.

194. At this point it becomes of special interest to think about the relation between birth, rebirth, the womb and the change in respiration when a child is born. It is so well known in the New Church that birth and rebirth correspond to one another that extensive quotations are not necessary. Perhaps parts of AC 4918 and 9042 as follows will suffice:

and that "coming forth from the womb" denotes to be reborn or regenerated.

For when a man is being born anew, he is then first conceived, afterward carried as it were in the womb, and finally is born.

195. The change in respiration of a child as it is being born means, of course, that it no longer receives oxygen dissolved in blood through the womb but through its own lungs. To see what might be the spiritual things to which this could correspond, we look at the meaning of "womb" in the Word. The womb is where good and truth lie conceived (AC 4918) and, by derivation, often signifies the church. Most of the explanations found in the AC seem to refer to the regeneration of the spiritual man. The specifically celestial quality which one associates with the embryo appears only by implication. For example, we find that "in the genuine sense" the womb "signifies the inmost of conjugial love in which is innocence," and innocence and the inmost of conjugial love are surely the inmost of heaven, which, in its turn is the celestial. "Those things are called celestial which are in the inmost of heaven" (AC 8945). Now we associate the celestial especially with the fetus, for we find the following in AC 5052:

> The Lord instills marriage love through the inmost heaven the angels of which are in peace beyond all others. Peace in heaven may be compared to spring time in the world which renders all things joyous, for in its origin peace is essentially celestial. The angels of the inmost heaven are wisest of all, and their innocence gives them a childlike appearance, for they love infants much more than do their fathers and mothers. They are present with infants in the womb, and through them the Lord cares for the nutrition and development of the infants therein; thus they have charge over those with child.

It is clear then that a whole series of senses are signified by "womb." (This is not surprising because: (a) it is generally so with the Word and

(b) the regeneration which is meant by birth is a process which must be repeated often for each one of us.) But, as noted just above, in the genuine sense the womb means the celestial. The MAC was celestial. It had internal respiration, and the people were wiser than we are now (AC 6876) and had external knowledges by which their perceptions were confirmed. There is, however, something of similarity in the way the fetus receives all it needs through the womb, and the way the MAC received all it needed (for perception and love) through heaven; enough similarity, perhaps even of correspondence, to arouse our wonder and reverence as well as to confirm our belief in the revelation we have been given. There is also a link with Dr. Woofenden's feeling that some early part of the Bible must correspond to prenatal life (See New Philosophy LXXXIV, 1981, p. 7: see also the very useful letter by J. and J. Pendleton, *New Church Life*, October, 1982, p. 471).

CHAPTER VIII

THE LYMPHATIC SYSTEM

The correspondences of the lymphatic system are explained by reference to people in the next life whose work is like that of the lymphatics in the body

196. The lymphatic system is not one which receives much attention in elementary biology, as it is difficult to see without special techniques. Nevertheless it is an essential part of the body's make up. In the Writings its correspondences are explained by characteristics of people in the next life whose functions there are like the functions of the lymphatics in the body. Much of what is said in the Writings about the correspondences of certain organs is related in this way, and different classes of people are said to belong to different provinces named according to the corresponding organs. The activities and interrelations of these different classes follow so closely the activities and interrelations of the bodily organs that the people (or spirits) are often described as if they did actually belong to the organs themselves. Indeed every one in heaven and many in the spiritual world are part of one great human organization or, rather, organism.

197. To those who are not familiar with these things it must seem very strange that, on passing into the next life, human souls find themselves becoming members of one human organism. However, they continue to live amongst appearances like those of this world (HH 171), and it is not the appearances amongst which they live, but the genuine inner reality of their life and functions that corresponds to the human form. Here, by "human form" we wish to convey an idea not precisely limited, but one which begins with anatomy (which is a matter of shapes, sizes, and relations) and progresses to physiology

(which includes functions and dictates the anatomy), and thence climbs to psychology and spiritual doctrine which teach about the human form of heaven. For the human form of man exists only because the essentials of the human form of heaven flow into it. Similarly, heaven derives its human form from the Lord. Hence a study of the human form is an eminently rational way to comprehend the organization of heaven (and of every regenerate man who is a heaven in the least form). This can nowhere be seen more clearly than in AC 3624-3645, but it is of course a common thing in ordinary speech to mention parts of the body symbolically. We have heads of state, the brains of a society, the arm of the law, the eyes of the fleet, and so on. When heaven is regarded as to its human form it is called "The Grand Man."

198. When one has become accustomed to the assignment of various spirits (i.e.,people) to societies which correspond to the functions of particular organs, one is not surprised to read that there are some spirits that correspond to the lymphatic system, since it forms such an important part of the body's economy and defences. (But one cannot fail to be continually surprised and delighted at the opening of new ideas when the revelations of the Writings are applied to modern knowledge.) In the case of the lymphatic system, the result is all the more gratifying in view of the sparseness of references to it in the Writings. A brief study of the lymphatic system as it is now known is, of course, a necessary preliminary to the appreciation of its correspondences.

The lymphatics constitute a system of ducts and nodes, including the receptacle and ducts of the chyle

199. Throughout most parts of the body there are many microscopic tubes which begin blindly in spaces between cells and form a network analogous to that of the blood capillaries. These are the lymph capillaries. In their course through the tissues they join together and become larger and easier to see, but still they are thin-walled and their contents are colourless so that only a few of the largest can be seen without the use of special techniques (e.g., the injection of dyes). The large vessels also join one another in their turn and most of the main trunks thus formed lead to the thoracic duct which pours its contents into the jugular vein at the base of the neck. See Figure 9.

200. It is assumed that the receptacle and ducts of the chyle mentioned in AC 5180 are approximately equivalent to the lymphatic system. This is because they are part of it, the only difference being that the ducts happen to run in the mesentery near the intestines and even into the intestinal walls themselves so that they are able to absorb fat-globules from the digested food. The fat acts as it does in milk, making the fluid in the ducts white and milky and causing these ducts to be more easily visible than others. (Hence they were classed separately as lacteals.) The connection between the lacteals and the other lymphatics is seen in AC 5181, which notes the movement of spirits who belong to the province of the lymphatics. We find that they "are afterwards conveyed into places which, they said, have reference to the *mesentery*, and where I was told that there are as it were labyrinths, and that they are afterwards taken away to various places in the Grand Man to serve for use, as is done with chyle in the body."

The first and most general function of the lymphatic system is to return tissue fluid to the blood

201. The origin of tissue fluid by seepage through the walls of blood capillaries was described above (No. 76). Most of this fluid drains back into the blood stream at sites where the pressure inside the capillaries is lower. (These are the capillary sections distal to the arteries and nearer to the veins.) There remains, however, a residue of fluid to which are added any substances produced by the activities and breakdown of the tissues. The resulting mixture is the lymph which is collected by the system of ducts described above.

FIGURE 9

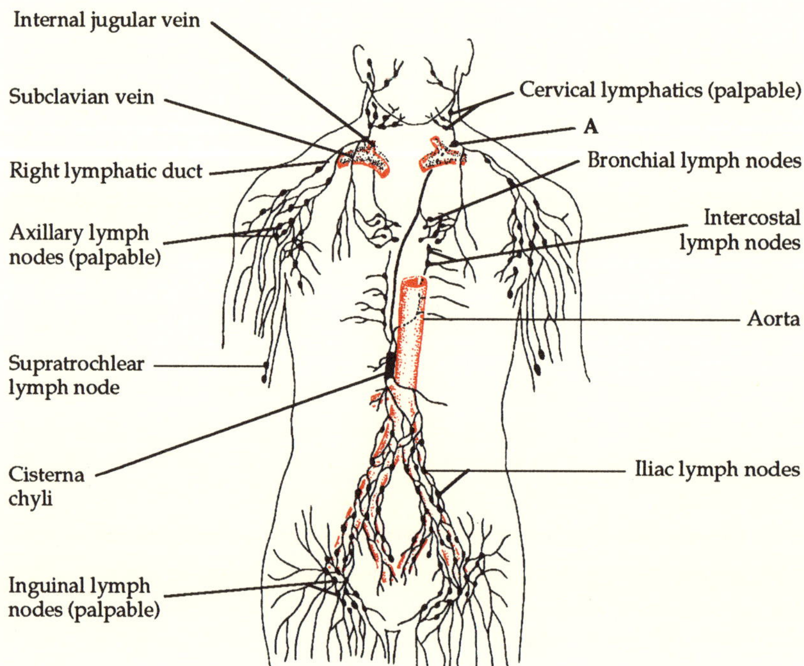

Figure 9: **Lymphatic System**

A simplified diagram showing the larger ducts and some of the lymph nodes. Some of those that are near the surface and can easily be felt are labelled "palpable". The letter **A** points to the site where the thoracic lymph duct empties its stream into the blood system. There is a similar junction on the right side, but details vary.

Sources: Based on D. B. Wilson, *Human Anatomy*, fig. 10-1;
Clemente, *Gray's Anatomy*, figs. 10-18, 10-20, 10-22, 10-23, 10-24, 10-3; Anthony and Kolthoff, *Textbook of Anatomy and Physiology*, figs. 13-38, 13-40.

202. There is no pump to cause a flow of lymph, and its movement is quite slow (in contrast to that of the blood). Movement does occur because all muscular activity produces fluctuations of pressure in the tissues. Moreover the squeezing effect causes flow only in the required direction because the ducts contain many valves which prevent the reverse flow. In places, the effect is augmented by the pulsation of nearby arteries, and everywhere the pressure of fluid in the tissues (derived from the pressure of the blood) is higher than the blood pressure at the point where the lymph ducts open into the blood stream. An example of this is in the veins of the neck where the blood is, as it were, merely falling towards the heart. Thus there are several factors which ensure that the flow of lymph, though slow and gentle, is certain. The gentle flow is linked with the state of souls who belong to the province of the lymphatics. In the words of the Writings their "gyres...are slight and rapid like gently flowing water so that scarcely any gyrating can be perceived" (AC 5181).

The tissue fluid or lymph contains many kinds of particles

203. Lymph vessels differ from blood vessels in being able to admit particles through their walls. Such particles are only microscopic but still millions of times larger than the molecules which normally pass through the walls of blood capillaries. There is a wide range of particles which can be found in lymph, but the most important are: (1) debris from the decomposition of worn-out cells in the tissues, (2) bacteria and other micro-organisms which invade the body from time to time, and (3) various wandering cells which have important functions in the blood and other tissues. All these particles drift into the lymph ducts with the stream of tissue fluid. From this it can be seen that the lymphatic system works like a slow motion vacuum cleaner "sucking up" all kinds of materials, good and bad, from almost every site in the body.

Lymph is cleaned before being returned to the blood

204. There is no use in collecting waste unless its disposal can also be arranged. This is done efficiently in the lymphatic system. At frequent intervals in the network of ducts there are nodes. These are small bodies containing spongy material through which the lymph must flow. The spongy substance is made of microscopic threads and these are partially covered with scavenger cells which, acting like amoebae, swallow any particles that come to them. Hence they are known as phagocytes (also as macrophages). They remove from the lymph all kinds of microscopic particles, even scraps of carbon or metal, if present, but normally such materials as residues from effete body cells and bacteria. There are also some phagocytes that leave their filamentous supports and are swept along with the lymph into the blood where they continue their function. Figure 10 illustrates in detail the structure and organization of the lymph node.

205. Some of the phagocytes have a special ability to penetrate the walls of capillary blood vessels, by which means they reach tissues that would otherwise remain uncleansed. They are particularly important in the lungs, from which they remove dust particles drawn in during respiration. (Dust particles act as vehicles for many bacteria, which, unless they were killed, would choke the lungs with harmful growth.) Phagocytes digest many of the particles they take in, but this is not always possible, and in such a case the cells provide a degree of protection by isolating the particles. Carbon, for example, is indigestible, so that even if absorbed by phagocytes it remains, and the lungs of people who live in smoky districts change from the pink colour of childhood to grey in old age. When the protection by isolation is inadequate, serious consequences ensue, as in cancer of the lungs caused by smoking, silicosis, and so on. If they are not poisoned by the particles they ingest, the phagocytes find their way back into the blood stream through the lymphatic system.

FIGURE 10

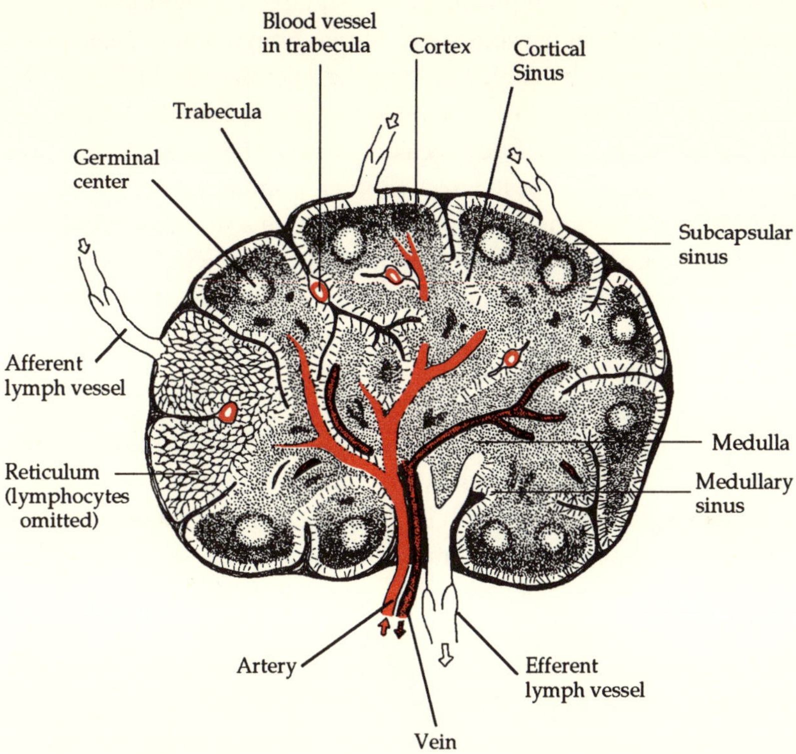

Figure 10: **Lymph Node**
    Section of lymph node showing internal structures, blood and lymph vessels. Germinal centers contain rapidly dividing lymph cells.

Source: Clemente, *Gray's Anatomy*, figs. 10-6, 10-7.

The lymphatic system produces immunity

206. Although we regard the lymphatic system as the source of immunity, the protection immunity provides occurs in all parts of the body. This is due to the activity of yet other kinds of cells which float in great numbers in lymph and blood. These cells or lymphocytes are produced largely in the spleen, but also in lymph nodes. They spend part of their time entangled among the microscopic threads of the nodes but eventually they break free and travel with the lymph into the blood stream. Chemically speaking, their activities are as varied as the diseases and poisons to which the man is immune, and the subject of immunity has many complexities. Although a summary cannot do justice to such a subject, a brief account will suffice to indicate possible new ways of looking at the correspondences. Immunity is an ability to cover foreign molecules in the body with a coating like the veils mentioned in AC 963 and 964.

207. When foreign substances enter the body (i.e., when they gain access to the tissues, not when they are merely in the stomach or intestines), they are dealt with in a variety of ways. Those that have large molecules (or that become attached to large molecules) often stimulate the production of immunity. They are called anti*gens* which name merely indicates that they normally cause the immune reaction. Many of them are produced by bacteria or other microscopic organisms which may grow in or on the body. The immune reaction itself consists in the production by the body of new substances with molecular shapes which enable them to "lock on" to the antigen and form a blanket, thus sealing off each antigen molecule so that it cannot exert any harmful action. The substances with these new molecular shapes are anti*bodies*. They can be isolated from the blood of immune individuals and their "blanketing" activities can be demonstrated in the laboratory. Because the action between antibody and antigen depends on the molecule of one fitting onto the molecule of the other, each antibody is very specific; it will combine only with its "own"

antigen. Hence immunity to each toxin or disease must be developed separately.

208. Immunity to disease caused by bacteria is often acquired by becoming immune to substances which form the coat of the bacterial cell. Then the particular specific antibody covers the bacteria so that they have a different surface. This can have a number of consequences: The disease-producing or toxic properties may be neutralized, the growth of the bacteria may be interfered with, they may be unable to disperse or spread, and they may become easier for the phagocytes to swallow. This last is a specially important consequence, for there are some bacteria which resist the phagocytes, but after immunity has developed, such bacteria may be covered with antibodies and they are then readily devoured.

209. Diseases correspond to evils and falsities, that is, to people in the spiritual world who are evil and false and especially to those in hell (AC 5172). Quite a large group of diseases appear to be caused by bacteria and viruses, so that in considering the spiritual causes behind these natural phenomena we readily identify evil spirits as correspondences of disease-producing bacteria, and we do not have to search far to find a correspondence of the immune reaction. The blanketing part of the immune process, seen from the molecular level, is irresistibly similar to the veiling of evil spirits described in AC 963 and 964 where we read that the veil "is like a closely clinging cloud that increases in density in proportion to the phantasy." This is just like the antibody molecules clustering round a bacterium, attaching themselves in greatest numbers where the antigen molecules are most numerous.

The characteristics of some of the spirits in the lymphatic province are like those of lymphocytes and phagocytes

210. The kind of immunity we have been discussing is acquired after exposure to an antigen, and it is well known that the range of possible immune reactions is very wide. Why is it that complete immunity to one disease, say, whooping cough, in no way diminishes an individual's ability to become immune to some other toxin or microbe, such as tetanus, for example? The answer to this very puzzling question lies with the lymphocytes.

211. Lymphocytes do not manufacture antibodies until they meet a foreign protein, carbohydrate, or other antigen. They then elaborate a certain antibody and become so committed to this particular process that they are unable to make any other antibody. Their activities will, however, in due course remove all that particular antigen so that new lymphocytes (which are continually being produced in the spleen and nodes) will remain uncommitted until another antigen appears. Thus it is that in health the body always has a good stock of uncommitted lymphocytes to meet any new invasion, but many of those circulating in the blood and lymph will be already committed.

212. The inability of lymphocytes to change reminds us of the persistence of certain spirits of this province who are also said to be impudent and of a wandering kind. In AC 5180:2 we read that they never give way, further that they "keep the others as it were in bonds and under their control," which is like the effect of antibodies on foreign cells. The phrase, "being privy to their evils," reminds us of the ability of lymphocytes and phagocytes to detect any kind of irregularity which would label a cell or a substance as foreign. The impudence of some of the spirits is matched by the readiness of the phagocytes to swallow any foreign particles that come their way, an impudence which is their undoing when the particles happen to be poisonous.

Like the lymphatic system itself, the spirits corresponding to it are, in part, of a wandering kind

213. The lymphatic system must, of course, include the phagocytes and lymphocytes, for they are living cells in the system. Their motion in the lymph and subsequently in the blood stream means that they wander into all parts of the body. Of the two kinds of spirits that belong to the receptacle and ducts of the chyle, only the impudent ones are of the wandering type. We regard the receptacle and ducts of the chyle as equivalent to the lymphatic system (No. 200), but it is difficult to say how far we may go in relating bodily phenomena with spiritual activities. Can we think that spirits of a wandering kind correspond to cells that are mobile and only to such? The next number (AC 5181) suggests that here at least we may do so, for we read that "They who belong to the lymphatics are afterwards conveyed into places which they said have reference to the *mesentery* and where I was told there are as it were labyrinths, and that they are afterwards *taken away* to various places in the Grand Man to serve for use *as is done with the chyle in the body*" (emphasis added). If the movement of the spirits corresponds to the movement of the chyle, the wandering kinds of spirits would correspond to the living cells in the lymph. The spirits that do not wander would then correspond to the stationary parts of the lymphatic system, i.e., the ducts and nodes, for these also are living and must have spirits corresponding to them.

214. It is noteworthy that labyrinths are mentioned in the above quotation, and that the nodes which transmit lymph are in the form of microscopic networks, the pathways through which must necessarily be of labyrinthine form.

During health the cleansing effect of the lymphatic system is like the reaction of evil and falsity before they cause temptation

215. We have seen that the lymphatics act as a continuous cleaning system, and it is one which can respond to any increased demand, as in illness, by intensifying its activities. This it does by a great increase in the number of phagocytes and lymphocytes. The action of these cells is as it was before. There are merely more of them, especially of lymphocytes, which will become committed when they meet the antigens associated with the illness. It is clear then that the activities of the cells themselves are the same in health as in recovery from illness. Immunity may even be acquired without an illness intervening, and the body is continually destroying invaders of many kinds before they can do any harm.

216. The possibility of fighting successfully against many toxins and diseases so early that one does not suffer from them suggests that a similar process operates spiritually. In this case, illnesses would correspond to temptations, and immunity without illness supervening would correspond to other means of overcoming falsity and evil. The overcoming of evils and falsities by means which do not include temptation is described in AC 8910. Although it is not said there that the rejection of evils and falsities from the thought before they enter the will is the same as overcoming them without temptation, this must be implied; for if they do not contaminate the will to some extent, the man will not really be suffering temptation. From *Divine Providence* no. 25, we learn that spiritual fermentations are an alternative to temptations as a means of purification but (lest we should think that temptations are unnecessary) AC 7906 puts the two together, saying that temptations are fermentations in the spiritual sense. The correspondences show that no contradiction is involved, for, as we have said, the normal cleaning process in the body and the recovery from illness are the same, one being merely an intensification of the other[11]

217. Although it seems that fermentations by yeast are the correspondences indicated in DP 25, it is entertaining to observe how closely the language of the Writings about spiritual fermentations

---

[11] In an earlier contribution (*N. C. Magazine*, Jan-Mar 1979, p. 79) it was suggested that fermentation could include all the enzyme activities in the body because this is in agreement with a strict definition of fermentation used in the early days of biochemistry. However, this wide meaning of fermentation does not constitute an essential step in the argument, and it seems likely that only fermentations by yeast are meant in DP 25, i.e., that the reference is limited to correspondences in the second degree which are the vegetable kingdom (HH 104).

describes the defensive actions of the body. We note that "spiritual combats or temptations are fermentations in the spiritual sense, for falsities then desire to conjoin themselves to truths; but truths reject them and at length cast them down as it were..." The activity of the falsities is like that of invading micro-organisms, for these join to themselves (as their own food) various substances in the body. But the organisms are rejected and as it were cast down when the lymphocytes cover them with antibodies. In many cases the process can be watched in a test tube, and the organisms do actually fall to the bottom after the antibody has been added.

When the normal cleansing processes are inadequate illness or temptation ensues

218. If the response to an invasion of the body is too slow, the invaders multiply and life is threatened. Such is temptation. Later the defenses may gain the upper hand and immunity may be achieved. Then the invading micro-organisms are inactivated and they are disposed of by the cleaning-up processes. Similarly is a man purified from evil and falsity by temptations which, after he has recovered, leave him immune to attacks of the same kind. These changes cannot but correspond to the agitations and corrections mentioned in AC 5173. (The resemblance between agitations, infestations, and temptations can be deduced from Swedenborg's *Index to the Arcana*, for AC 7122 appears under *Temptations* (The Use of Temptations) in the following entry: "Infestations or the temptations of the upright in the other life, take place that evils and falsities, and filthy things, may be removed; and before this they cannot be elevated into heaven, 7122.") The common state of a man passing into the next life with impurities and defilements from his life in the world is very much like the all-too frequent state of the body which is continually harbouring many harmful bacteria (e.g., in the skin, tonsils, nose, throat, gut). The body wages continual warfare against these bacteria without becoming thoroughly immune and casting them out. The agitations in the next life would then correspond to a flare-up during which proper immunity would be achieved.

219. The development of immunity helps one also to realize in part how it can be that the Lord, having overcome the hells by victories in His temptations, should subsequently be in complete control of them. They can no longer assault His Divine Humanity because it is immune. The real reason is because it is Divine, yet the Divine does not work without means, and it may well be that some of the means correspond to the immune reaction.

220. The purification of the blood mentioned in AC 5173 is, of course, done in many ways. The kidneys remove water and many other small molecules. Others that are toxic are modified in the liver, as, for example, alcohol. But the purifications we have in mind in this section deal with infections and toxins that have large molecules. This work is done by the lymph, which flows into the blood stream carrying the lymphocytes which provide the means.

The importance of wisdom in spiritual purifications is represented in the colourlessness of lymph

221. This proposition requires elucidating in three steps as follows: (1) Colour is important when it is a characteristic property of a useful substance and not merely adventitious; (2) Haemoglobin is a useful substance, the colour of which indicates important states of the molecule; and (3) The colourlessness of lymph suggests a predominance of wisdom in the functions to which it corresponds, but not of truth only, because it contains many of the constituents of blood.

222. (1.) Colour is important when it is a characteristic property of a useful substance and not merely adventitious.

It might be thought that the colours of natural objects are merely accidental and could have but little importance correspondentially.

For example, there is no particular reason why vertebrate blood is red and crustacean blood is blue and plants are green. Often, indeed, colour seems to be no more than a label, as in the warning colours of wasps and in flowers (though it is hard to believe that flowers bloom just for insects). In spite of these things, however, it is a merely superficial assessment to conclude that colours are always accidental. If they were it would be difficult to account for the importance given to them in the Writings, as for example in the following from DLW 380: "Moreover the blood is red from the correspondence of the heart and the blood with love and its affections." Scientists may find it difficult to reconcile all the remarks in the Writings about colour with our knowledge of the spectrum, but it will surely be done in due course. For the present, it is sufficient to observe that care is taken in DLW 380 to point out that it is red in the spiritual world that corresponds to love. So blood is red there as well as here, but whether all natural red things have corresponding spiritual red things is another question. The definition of colour is also a question: whether it is an experience of seeing, or a light of a certain range of wave lengths. The importance of this latter objective kind of colour is seen from the fact that it depends on molecular structure. A great deal of knowledge about the relationship between colours and molecular structure has been collected. It is now possible to derive important information about the structure and state and behaviour of the molecules and atoms of many substances by studying the way light is modified or filtered when it passes through them.

223. (2.) Haemoglobin is a useful substance, the colour of which indicates important states of the molecule.

Blood itself provides a particularly interesting example of the importance of colour. The red colour is due to haemoglobin with oxygen inside its molecules, for haemoglobin is the carrier of oxygen. As the bright red blood from the arteries passes through the various parts of the body, the oxygen is removed from inside the molecules of the haemoglobin carrier, and as a result their shape changes. The change in shape causes a change in colour, which then becomes bluish, as is easily seen in veins near the skin. Immediately venous blood is shed, it absorbs oxygen and becomes bright red again. If the oxygen is replaced by carbon monoxide as in carbon monoxide poisoning, the blood is an even brighter red than normal (this is a diagnostic feature). From these things it is clear that in certain instances colour shows the character or state of a substance, and it must therefore correspond to spiritual qualities as closely as any other characteristic of the substance. We are therefore justified in considering the spiritual reasons for the colourlessness of lymph.

224. (3.) The colourlessness of lymph suggests a predominance of wisdom in the functions to which it corresponds, but not of truth only, because it contains many of the constituents of blood.

We have seen already that lymph is tissue fluid and contains water and soluble substances of blood that can ooze out through the capillary walls. Because the haemoglobin is contained in corpuscles larger than the pores of capillary walls, it cannot soak out, and this is why lymph is colourless; even single molecules of haemoglobin are probably too large to get out. For our present purposes we can consider white and colourless as the same. The first reflects all the light that falls on it, the second transmits all the light. Remembering that red corresponds to love and white to wisdom (DLW 380), we feel that lymph corresponds to wisdom rather than love, but here the detailed composition of lymph illustrates a truth frequently re-iterated throughout the Writings: there can be no wisdom without love. Lymph may look like water. If it were really water it might correspond to truth, but it contains many of the things that are in blood. So, correspondentially, there are *some* constituents from love that enable the truth to live as wisdom and to be active in protecting the man from evil and falsity. It almost seems as though the removal of *other* constituents of love (red corpuscles) were necessary for the efficiency of the wisdom (lymph).

This may indeed be so, for in the body the lymph reaches places (microscopic ones but important) that the blood cannot bathe and carries away particles the blood cannot touch. These things could not be done in a system that must retain red corpuscles. And in times of temptation, love does seem to withdraw. But we must consider the man as a whole. The lymph is only temporarily separated from the blood. It is moving all the time and the two fluids are soon re-united. Wisdom and love make one.

CHAPTER IX

THE SPLEEN

There is something of love in the correspondences of the spleen

225. The spleen is the subject to be considered immediately after the previous chapter because of its close connection with the lymphatics. As will become apparent, much of what has been said about the lymphatic system applies also to the spleen, but there are additional functions to be taken into account.

226. The spleen contains a red pulp which is rich in red blood corpuscles (i.e., erythrocytes) and a white pulp in which lymphocytes predominate. This mixture of colours suggests a correspondence with more of love than is the case with the lymphatic system.

The spleen stores, processes, and produces several different kinds of cells for the blood

227. The spleen is a remarkable organ because the blood therein is not entirely confined to arteries, capillaries, and veins as in many other organs. There is a spongy network of fibres through which the small arteries run, but when they have divided into capillaries they expand again into little capsules formed from special cells which can move apart enough to allow the erythrocytes (or red cells) to spread between them. This is quite exceptional, for, as mentioned above (No. 224), the erythrocytes are much too large to leak out of capillaries in the ordinary way, and the haemoglobin (see No. 223) they contain is kept safely in the blood. It is not known whether the system in the spleen is quite open, i.e., whether the erythrocytes get out because the blood as a whole is allowed out, or because the linings of the little

capsules allow erythrocytes only to pass through them. But whatever the mechanism, the production and storage of many of the different kinds of cells that circulate in the blood is well established. It is clear that the spleen is like a giant lymph node, but with the addition of the special blood system and means of storing red cells that have been described. See Figure 11.

228. Although, in the embryo, the spleen produces erythrocytes, in the adult it seems only to store them and to break down some of them. This is done by the white cells, i.e., phagocytes or macrophages, which appear to be of the same group that fights infections. It would seem that from the point of view of a phagocyte, some of the erythrocytes are foreign material, to be swallowed up as part of the normal cleaning operations.

The destructive activities of the spleen are a necessary part of the body's economy

229. It is the digestion of red cells that is a particularly striking function of the spleen (although the liver also has this as one of its many activities). To destroy such important and precious components of the blood seems a dreadful action. Bad qualities also appear in the reference to the spleen in the *Spiritual Diary*, where we read that those who pertain to the province of the spleen commit the abomination of mixing holy things with profane (SD 1005). No good thing is subsequently said of them,[12] in spite of the fact that the spleen itself has its uses, as is also pointed out (SD 1007). These things are considered in

---

[12] Concerning the frequency with which Swedenborg encountered evil spirits, John Worcester makes the following interesting comment: "It seems strange to think of spirits so perverse as having access to so interior a province of the heavens. Probably it would be impossible now; but before the Last Judgment there were many evil persons penetrating even to the higher parts of the Christian heaven, and causing much disturbance. In the higher heavens, and probably in the Christian heaven now, instead of such evil spirits we might find angels who have some morbidness or sluggishness to get rid of, and are there subjected to some purifying processes corresponding to those by which evil spirits were separated" (Worcester, 1889, p. 405).

FIGURE 11

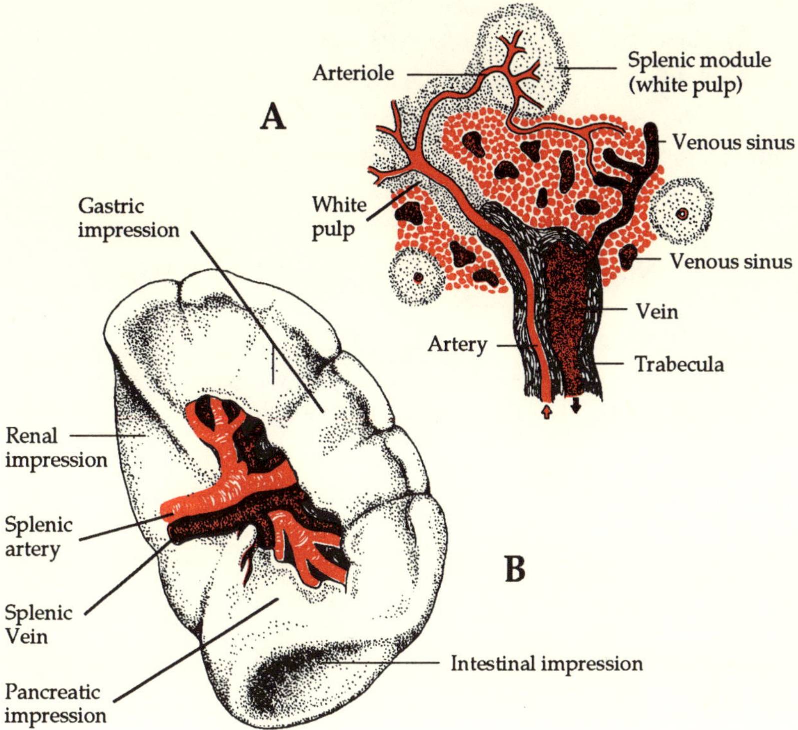

Figure 11: **The Spleen**

A: Diagram of a small particle of splenic tissue showing the pathway of blood through the spleen, starting with the trabecular artery and proceeding to the artery ensheathed in white pulp,* the splenic nodule, and the red pulp, ending in the venous sinuses which send the blood to the trabecular vein.~

B: The visceral surface of the spleen showing the main blood vessels, and indicating where it contacts various digestive organs. See the figure on digestion for the spleen's location in the abdomen.

* A collection of white lymphatic cells massed around the artery. ~ A result of erythrocytes being allowed to escape from the blood system by means of the special capsules of stave cells. The supporting network is not shown.

Sources: A: Modified from Ham, A. W., *Histology*, 7th ed., J. B. Lippincott, Phila., 1974; Clemente, *Gray's Anatomy*, fig. 10-45.
B: *Ibid.*, fig. 10-41; Anthony and Kolthoff, *Textbook of Anatomy and Physiology*, fig. 13-43.

more detail below (Nos. 248-250). The digestion of erythrocytes by the spleen can be put into perspective by a glance at the life history of the erythrocytes. These corpuscles are the remains of the cells in which the haemoglobin is made. The haemoglobin is retained in them, and they become thin and delicate so that they pass easily through the finest capillaries of the blood system. Being delicate they do not last long. After about 100 days they begin to wear out, their surface changes, and they must be replaced. (One can imagine the serious consequences of permanent adhesion between erythrocytes or between them and the walls of the blood vessels.) New erythrocytes are being made continually in the bone marrow, and the old ones must be reprocessed to obviate toxic decomposition and to avoid wastage of the materials, especially the iron, that went into them during their growth. (Perhaps not every reader will know that iron is an essential part of haemoglobin and that the body's economy is arranged as though iron were scarce.) The short life of the erythrocytes, their destruction, and the continued production of new ones leads us to wonder what can possibly be the correspondence of these minute organs.

The functions of erythrocytes are like those of good thoughts

230. The purpose of erythrocytes is to convey oxygen and it was assumed earlier that air, and therefore oxygen also, correspond to the Divine Spirit or Truth. This supposition is further examined below (Nos. 245-247). Nothing loves truth more than good or love, so the affinity of haemoglobin for oxygen, as well as its red colour, indicates a correspondence to love. Now, as we have seen, haemoglobin is contained in very many minute, discrete vessels which, however, are not themselves red. (They form colourless "ghosts" if they lose their haemoglobin.) So the correspondence of the envelopes is probably not love, but could well be a form of truth other than that which corresponds to air.

231. If we liken the corpuscles to truths which may contain good, we look next for forms of truth which are very small and numerous.

One such form is that of words. Although the possible number of words is unlimited, the number in use for one man is much less than the number of erythrocytes in one man, and it seems unnecessary to imagine that one word might correspond to one corpuscle. So, although smallness and number have provided a hint, they cannot be used as logical points in an argument. In order to see whether words could correspond to erythrocytes, we need to think about them one at a time to see whether they could:

    a. contain love which could mediate truth,

    b. be raised to an internal level of understanding to absorb truth,

    c. convey such truth for use elsewhere, and

    d. become worn out or useless and be discarded.

Clearly a word as printed or spoken is too low or ultimate. Possibly the idea a word produces may meet these criteria.

232. The first ideas produced from words are usually simple matters of knowledge which reside in the external memory. We will call them *Knowledges of the External Memory* or *KEM*, but in the Writings they are called scientifics (Swedenborg Society translation). Although KEM are matters of the external or natural memory, they can become of the internal or spiritual memory when they are about doctrine and life and are put into practice. They can therefore contain either truth or good, but if they contain truth, the truth should also contain good. This means that both kinds of KEM are really vessels which should contain good. If they do not contain it they are useless (except as potential containers). These things however are explained more clearly in AC 9918 and 9922, from which the following are taken:

233. From AC 9918:

Scientifics of good and truth are doctrinals from the Word in the external memory. When man lives according to them they enter the memory of the internal or spiritual man. Then the doctrinals which concern the truth become matters of faith and those which concern good become subjects of charity. When this is the case they almost vanish out of the external memory and appear as if they were inborn, like things which have become natural as it were by daily use. Matters of knowledge remain underneath intelligence and wisdom until they have become subjects of faith and charity in the internal man. Then they ascend, i.e., enter into the life.

And from AC 9922, scientifics are,

the recipients and as it were the vessels of truth and of good...All things of the external, that is, the natural memory, are called scientifics; for there is the external memory, which is that of objects in the natural world, and there is the internal memory, which is that of the objects in the spiritual world...The things which are inscribed on the internal memory are not called scientifics, because they are subjects of a man's life; but they are called truths...and goods...These are the things which ought to be interiorly in the scientifics...there are scientifics of good and scientifics of truth, and...the truths in them are again vessels receptive of good, for the truths of faith are vessels of the good of love.

234. It is, perhaps, not profitable to attempt to see which anatomical objects correspond to KEM of good and which to KEM of truth, for so many of the bodily organelles are structures within structures. We are already concerned with at least two kinds of vessels, the blood vessels (arteries, capillaries, veins) and the corpuscles (erythrocytes); good is never very far from genuine truth, for they are always striving to come together. So it is probably sufficient for the present to notice several ways in which erythrocytes are like KEM of good (but see also Nos. 238 et. seq.).

235. The erythrocytes (KEM) contain haemoglobin which is red (good or love). They can enter into the lungs (understanding) and receive oxygen (Divine Truth) which they convey to other parts of the body (the Truth is made use of in daily life). They eventually wear out (KEM are no longer useful when their good becomes habitual), and are replaced by new erythrocytes (fresh KEM are learned).

236. If our assumption of a correspondence between KEM and erythrocytes is correct, we obtain an impression that KEM are continually of use. Although erythrocytes become worn out and disappear, fresh ones are continually provided. Similarly, particular KEM may be retained and obeyed until they become habitual and disappear from the external memory, but fresh KEM are continually being learned. Thus there are always plenty of KEM as there are always plenty of erythrocytes. The process by which Divine Truth is relayed to all parts of the personality is not interrupted.

237. With regard to the destruction of erythrocytes, it is clear that if the old ones were not destroyed, new ones which are more useful could not take their place. So it is with KEM. Even with the Lord there was grief "that the scientifics which He had learned with pleasure and delight should be thus destroyed" (AC 1492).

238. It must now be admitted that a limitation begins to be apparent, for the vanishing of KEM out of the external memory when they are put into practice indicates progress. Fresh KEM are learned to prepare for further progress, and every KEM is different from the next, whereas the erythrocytes are all the same until they begin to wear out. We must therefore examine the question from a slightly different point of view.

239. KEM are related to bones (AC 8005) and to muscles (AC 9394:5). The latter reference points out ways in which a muscle is like KEM but without actually saying they correspond. The point of interest is that KEM are general objects, each one of which contains particulars and singulars as a muscle contains fibres, blood vessels, nerves, etc.. Thus although it is not actually spelled out, it is highly probable that muscles and KEM correspond in some way. The reason why it is not a simple correspondence (and hence is not stated to be such) is found in the following: "All things which are learned and stored up in the memory, and which can be called forth from it for the use of the sight of the mind, are called scientifics" (KEM) (AC 9394:1). This statement and the expansion of it which follows in the same number makes it clear that in the Writings the term "scientifics" covers a vast range of different things. The correspondences must therefore also be various. We cannot say that erythrocytes do not correspond because they are not muscles; rather that they correspond because they serve muscles (as well as other organs). As they are simple things compared with other cells (though far more than mere envelopes containing haemoglobin), and much simpler than muscles, we may think of their correspondence as something like, but less than KEM, such as certain kinds of thoughts. For, there are innumerable thoughts that play an essential part in the activities of KEM by conveying life from the Lord down to that particular level where those KEM are, transforming them from mere records in the ultimate brain to living spiritual entities. But we already have some instruction concerning thoughts.

240. The minute alveoli of the lungs correspond to thoughts because they act in conjunction with the thought by correspondence (DLW 413). Their function is to facilitate the transfer of oxygen to haemoglobin of the blood. What then can the haemoglobin correspond to but the next link in the chain? We can deduce from correspondences that there is at least some kind of chain that is agreeable to what the Writings teach.

241. Air corresponds to the life of Divine Truth accommodated to man (see Nos. 245-247). To the uninitiated, the breathing of air is a simple necessity of life. To the physiologist it is the first link in a long chain of transactions which enable the oxygen to perform its energy-releasing function in every part of the body. To us, uninitiated as we are in spiritual things, the reception of Divine Truth is a simple necessity of spiritual life, but we can see from the correspondences that many links must be connected in due order if we are to receive the intended benefit of that life. We may not as yet be able to define each link, but the Writings provide us with several words which might be arranged as a series. We have, for example, ruling love, affections, perception, conscience, internal dictate, doctrine, doctrinals, scientifics, spiritual truth, rational truth, natural truth, scientific truth, and sensual truth. But this may not be the right order. Sometimes some of these terms seem like synonyms, but the choice of words in the Writings was the Lord's and no word is used in place of another except in accommodation to the reader's limitations.

242. Many of the things indicated by the terms above have thoughts composing them, causing them, or being caused by them. Therefore thoughts are of many different kinds. Some, like alveoli, are expandable to take in the Divine Breath or Spirit. Some, like erythrocytes, can absorb their own quota of this Spirit and convey it to every other part of the mind, returning over and over again to the source of inspiration, but eventually being replaced by newer, better, more serviceable thoughts. Such thoughts might well correspond to the red cells of the blood.

243. This concept suggests that in order to be active and useful, the KEM in our minds need the services of innumerable thoughts which must all be full of the love of Divine Truth as the erythrocytes are full of haemoglobin.

There is a correspondence between the air and the life that flows from the Lord

244. Much of the discussion above has been based on an assumption that life from the Divine corresponds to oxygen or air. This belief was dealt with briefly above (see footnote 9) and it is now desirable to confirm it.

245. In AC 9987:1 we read that the breath of the mouth of Jehovah is life from the Divine Truth proceeding from the Lord. AE 419 shows that wind in reference to the Lord denotes the proceeding Divine, and that wind and breath in reference to man signify the life of truth because respiration corresponds to that life. But, since wind is air in motion, and exhaled breath is air modified in the lungs, further confirmation is welcome if we wish to appreciate the correspondence between ordinary air and life from the Divine. An interesting suggestion for a different approach is found in AE 419. In an explanation about winds in the spiritual world it is said that separations of the good from the evil and castings out of the evil are effected by modifications of the Divine which proceeds from the Lord as a Sun, as though that proceeding Divine were itself the wind, or caused the wind. It is therefore interesting to study the Divine Sun and its connection with spiritual air.

246. We begin with TCR 39 where the following words occur:

> From the Sun of the spiritual world proceeds heat, which in its essence is love, and light, which in its essence is wisdom;…and with men they enter into the will and understanding which were created to be the receptacles of this influx, the will to be the receptacle of love and the understanding to be the receptacle of wisdom.

Something similar is found in TCR 641 where we also read that the Lord adapts the light and heat "to the capacity and nature of every recipient angel and man." The same is found in more detail in the following beautiful passage from AC 7270:

As the truth which proceeds immediately from the Lord is from the Infinite Divine itself, it cannot possibly be received by any living substance which is finite, thus not by any angel; wherefore the Lord created successive [degrees or substances], through which as media the Divine Truth proceeding immediately might be communicated. But the first successive [substance] from this is still too full of the Divine to be received by any living substance which is finite, thus by any angel; wherefore the Lord created another successive [degree or substance], through which the Divine Truth proceeding immediately might be capable of being received as to some portion: this successive [degree] is the truth Divine which is in heaven. The first two [degrees] are above the heavens, and are as it were radiant belts from a flaming [substance], and encompass the Sun, which is the Lord. Such is the successive order even to the heaven nearest to the Lord, which is the third heaven, where are those who are innocent and wise. From this they are continued successively even to the last heaven, and from the last heaven to the sensual and corporeal [degree] of man, which receives the influx last. From these considerations it appears that there are continual successions from the First, that is, from the Lord, even to the last things which are with man, yea, to the last things which are in nature. The last things which are with man, as well as those in nature, are relatively inert, and thus cold, and they are relatively general, and thus obscure. From this it is also evident, that by means of those successions there is a continuous nexus of all things with the First Esse. Influx is circumstanced according to those successions, for the Divine Truth which proceeds immediately from the Divine Good flows in successively; and in the way, or around each new successive [degree], it becomes more general, and thus grosser and more obscure, and it becomes slower, and thus more inert, and colder. From these considerations it appears what is the character of the Divine order of successive [degrees], and consequently of influxes. But it must be well borne in mind that the Truth Divine, which inflows into the third heaven that is nearest the Lord, at the same time flows in, without any successive formation, into the ultimates of order, and there also governs and provides all things in general and in particular immediately from the First.

We find that air is linked with the spiritual Sun by mention or implication in several places. First, in TCR 641 (quoted in part above) the adaptations are said to take place "by means of spiritual airs or atmospheres," and in TCR 661 near the beginning, it is said that the heat (which in its essence is love) and the light (which in its essence is wisdom) "are breathed into" those who are being instructed. A connection between spiritual light and spiritual air is mentioned in AC 1621 which states, "the atmospheres in which the blessed live...are of the light because from that light..." It is not actually said that such spiritual airs correspond to the air of the earth, but the suggestion is there. It is, however, the implication of the whole that encourages one to believe that air corresponds to Divine Truth. For, as we have just seen, spiritual light, which in its essence is wisdom, enters the understanding which is the receptacle of wisdom. We have also seen in great detail that the lungs correspond to the understanding (Chap V), and as the lungs are receptacles for the air which flows in, the air must correspond to the wisdom (or to the essential activating part of it).

247. The above argument leaves out natural light and the natural eye, which also correspond, and it is an interesting exercise to fit them into the scheme. A few comments on the similarity between the correspondence of the eyes and the lungs were made in an earlier essay (Berridge, 1980 C, p. 119). For the present it seems that the air cannot but correspond to one of the ways the Lord's life is available to be drawn into our understandings, and to be conveyed thence even to the most external limits of the soul. In this same way, oxygen penetrates to the furthest extremities of the body by means of the haemoglobin (affection) in the erythrocytes (thoughts), which are swept along by the beating of the heart (love, or the will).

The abominations of certain spirits in the province of the spleen may correspond to useful activities

248. Of the few references to the spleen in the Writings, one in SD is most puzzling for it seems to contradict itself. It reads as follows: "The spirits of the spleen are those who commingle profane with holy things and separate them" (SD 1011). Earlier numbers (SD 1005, 1006) enlarge on the mingling but ignore the separation.

249. Since there are always plenty of bad kinds of people in the spiritual world awaiting their own particular judgement, it may be enough to think that there are wicked spirits of the spleen who mingle profane with holy things and good spirits who separate them. But the corresponding things of the body suggest that the matter is much less simple than that. Some of the most important functions of the spleen are carried out by the lymphocytes and phagocytes which it produces and retains in large numbers (for at least a part of their lives). These cells account for the activities of the spleen that are mentioned in SD 1005-1011. As we have seen above, the phagocytes avidly seize any foreign particles they meet and destroy them if they can. In this way they purify the blood. In the language of SD 1007 the spleen "twists and tears asunder the filthy blood—not the serum—and delivers it thus sundered to the veins…In this way it also relieves the liver." It is doubtful whether this could have been confirmed in Swedenborg's time but it is easy to understand and confirm it now. "The filthy blood—not the serum" can only mean foreign particles in the blood, for the serum is the whole of the fluid part in which are suspended the many kinds of cells and particles that go to make up clean whole blood and that are not attacked by the phagocytes. "Twists and tears asunder" is a lively expression for the molecular disruption we usually call digestion, whether it goes on in the stomach of a whole animal or in the cell of a microscopic phagocyte. "It relieves the liver" refers to a fact of physiology, now confirmed by countless studies, namely that the liver is the chief organ by which poisonous substances are modified to render them harmless and to enable them to be excreted. (Many substances that are more or less poisonous but not usually lethal, may get into the blood—for example, alcohol. They are dealt with by the liver, which, indeed, sometimes suffers harm in the process.) Those that are seized and degraded by the phagocytes of the spleen will obviously not have to be de-toxified by the liver. Both organs also process effete erythrocytes, so that in this also the spleen relieves the liver.

250. Returning now to correspondences and to the question of mixing profane and holy things, it would seem that the avidity with which the phagocytes seize foreign materials could correspond to a love of evil things—things that are foreign to the Grand Man. The holy things with which they are mingled could correspond to the genuine substances of the phagocyte which is as truly a part of the body as any cell in other tissues. But as the digestion which ensues takes place within the phagocyte rather than outside it by the secretion of enzymes as in the stomach and intestines, the digestion in the phagocyte might be considered as a commingling.[13] When the phagocyte has digested the foreign material, the resulting harmless products can be allowed to leak out into the serum. Hence, after commingling, there is again a separation of the holy things. The profane things no longer exist.

---

[13] The difference is that digestion in the stomach and intestines is due to enzymes which are active but dead, and which are secreted by the living cells of those organs. Hence digestion takes place outside the living tissues of the body. In digestion by phagocytes the particles are taken into the living cell itself.

CHAPTER X

THE THYMUS GLAND

The thymus has strong celestial associations

251. The relatively large size of the thymus in the very young and its importance to them suggests that its correspondences are specially celestial, for the spirits of infants are with celestial angels (AC 5342:2). The celestial associations of the thymus are confirmed in AC 5172 which is short enough to quote in full:

> There are certain upright spirits who think without reflection, and who therefore rapidly and as it were without premeditation utter whatever occurs to their thought. They have an interior perception, which does not become so visual by means of reflection and thought as is the case with others; for in the course of their lives they have been as it were self-instructed about the goodness of things, but not so much about their truth. I have been told that such persons belong to the province of the thymus gland; for the thymus is a gland especially serviceable to infants, and during infancy is soft. In such spirits likewise there remains a soft infantile quality, into which flows the perception of good, and from this perception truth shines forth in a general manner. These spirits can be in great turmoils without being disturbed, as is also the case with the gland in question.

It will be seen that there are several phrases that indicate a leaning more towards the celestial than the spiritual. Celestial quality is suggested by "interior perception," "the goodness of things," "soft infantile quality," and "perception of good." Less concern with the spiritual (except as derived from the celestial) is shown by "does not become so visual," "not so much so about their truth," and "from this perception truth shines forth in a general manner." After a few points of anatomy and physiology, the implications of an organ with celestial correspondences having such functions as the thymus will be considered.

The thymus is the principal organ of the lymphoid system

252. This will become clear when the activities of the thymus have been described, but first some anatomical background may be useful. A more complete account is to be found in *Gray's Anatomy* (Williams, 1980). Advances are now so rapid that the most recent edition should be consulted. In infants, the thymus is a sizeable gland situated in the upper part of the chest and extending into the base of the neck. It diminishes in size after puberty reaching, in adults, an average weight of only 12-15g; nevertheless it is still important for adults. See Figure 12. The thymus is in some ways similar to the spleen or a lymph node in being a spongy structure in the interstices of which numerous lymphocytes are stored. In one respect, however, it is in direct contrast with the spleen; whereas particles as large as erythrocytes are allowed to escape from blood vessels into the spleen (No. 227), in the thymus even some very small molecules are denied access. This applies, for example, to the molecules of antigens. The experimental finding that antigens cannot get into the thymus is linked with microscopic observations which show that the whole gland is surrounded by a membrane which also covers all the blood vessels, including capillaries inside the gland. There is thus a barrier between the blood and the gland itself. However the barrier is not absolute. Waste products, products of metabolism, and some lymphocytes escape, and nutrients also get in, as do stem cells (see below, No. 255). See Figure 13.

253. In the new-born, the thymus is essential for the development of peripheral lymphoid tissues such as lymphocytes, lymph nodes, tonsils, etc. This statement, however, only indicates what happens if a young animal is deprived of its thymus gland. As the lymphoid

FIGURE 12

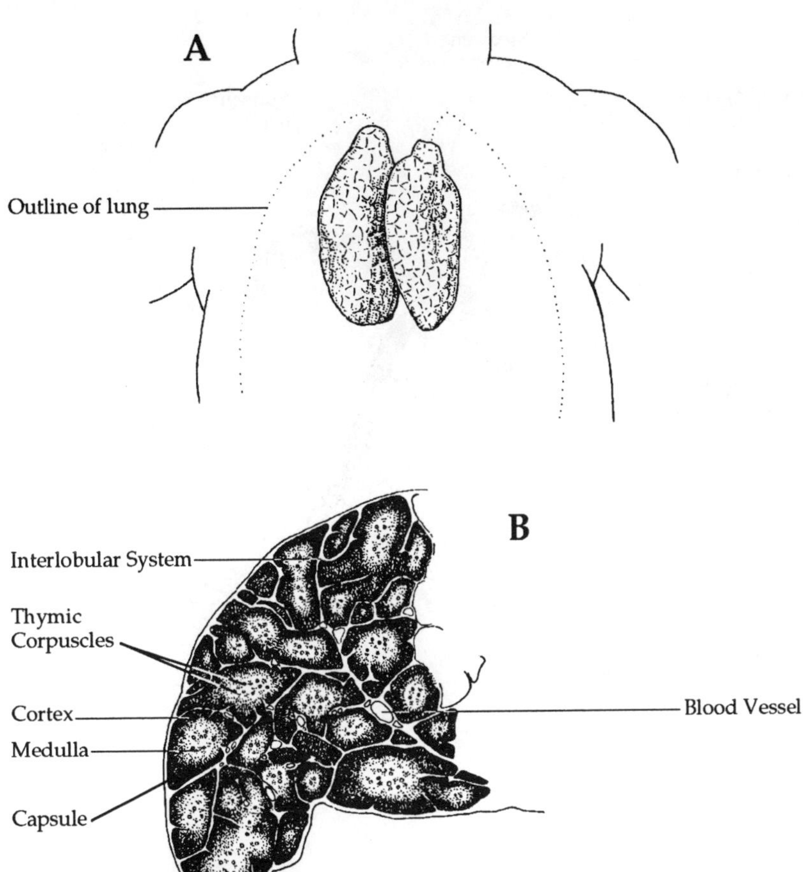

Figure 12: **The Thymus**

A: Appearance of thymus in newborn. The thymus gland is located in the ventral part of the mediastinum behind the sternum. It reaches its largest relative size at two years of age, and its largest absolute size in adolescence.

B: Section of the thymus showing internal structure. Although the section seems to show some lobules completely enclosed, they are not so in fact (in a different plane), but are continuous in the central parts of the lobe.

Sources: A: Modified from Clemente, *Gray's Anatomy*, fig. 10-46. B: Based on Wilson, *Human Anatomy*, fig. 10-2; Clemente, *Gray's Anatomy*, fig. 10-48.

FIGURE 13

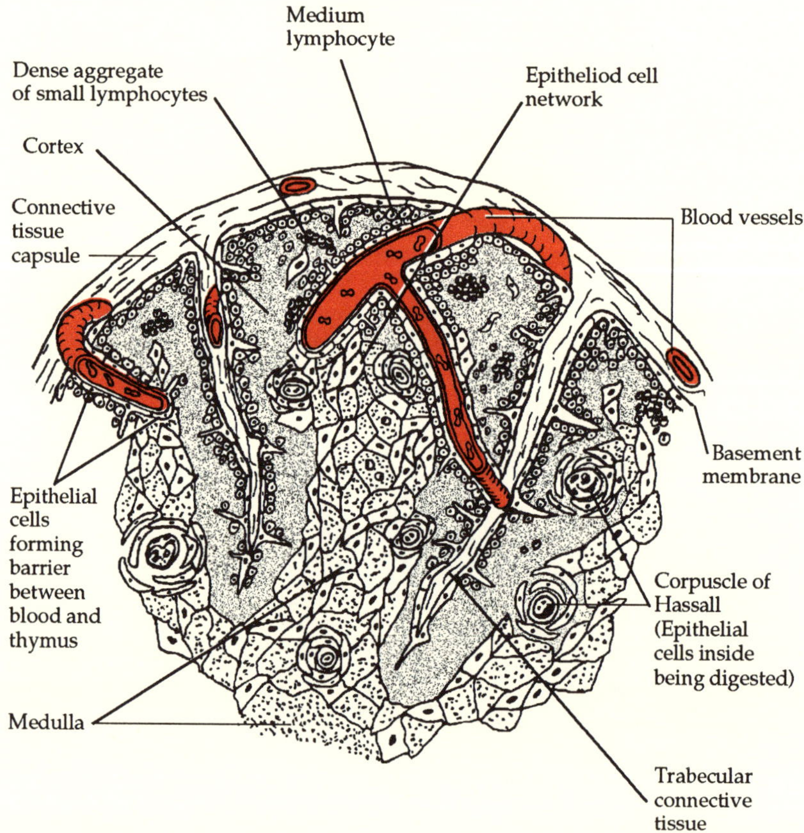

Figure 13: **Tissues of the Thymus Gland**

A representation at the cellular level of the special tissues and arrangements in the thymus gland. Bone marrow stem cells in the blood stream enter the cortex of the thymus gland, there proliferate greatly, then move to the medulla during maturation, where some of them become immunocompetent and then migrate to secondary lymphoid organs including lymph nodes and spleen.

Sources: Redrawn by ThomasRose from Norman Berridge's sketch and from William and Warwick, *Gray's Anatomy*, ed. 37, 1980, p. 835; redrawn, partly by computer, by Alan Laidlaw and Charles Cole from Rose's and Berridge's drawings plus the following: Roitt, Brostoff and Male, *Immunology*, 1985, Fig 14.3; Rubenstein and Federman, *Scientific American Medicine*, 1990, Fig. 2, p. 6:I:4.

tissues do not develop, the deprived animal dies fairly soon, because it cannot develop immunity to any infection. In an older animal, the loss of the thymus takes longer to make itself felt, as the lymphatic system is already fully developed and the animal is already immune to the commoner infections of its surroundings. It is, however, unable to respond effectively to new antigens.

254. The thymus is necessary for growth of peripheral lymphoid tissues. In addition to this, it is thought that its central part, or medulla, secretes a hormone-like substance, lymphopoietin, which stimulates production of lymphocytes in those tissues as well as in the outer part or cortex of the thymus itself. Newly produced lymphocytes do not react against antigens. They are said to be incompetent. Lymphopoietin, or perhaps another substance secreted by the thymus, acts as a competence-inducing factor, effecting a transformation of the new lymphocytes to a mature state in which they are competent to produce new antibodies to new antigens. Those lymphocytes that are stored in the thymus do not react against antigens while they are there for, as we have seen, antigens are kept out of the thymus; but the lymphocytes are competent. In due course they leave the thymus and join the general pool of circulating lymphocytes, of which, however, they form only a small proportion.

255. The origin of the lymphocytes of the thymus has been traced to the stem cells mentioned above (No. 252). These come from the bone marrow and when they reach the thymus (presumably via the blood stream) they settle there and multiply. Part of their progeny becomes modified into lymphocytes and the rest continue the function of the parent cells, producing partly lymphocytes in the next generation. In this way a very large number of lymphocytes is produced, but most of them (over nine tenths) die within 3-5 days and are consumed by phagocytes still within the thymus. The phagocytes migrate into certain microscopic structures known as corpuscles of Hassall in the medulla where they in turn disintegrate. Thus there are many short-lived lymphocytes in the thymus and it is thought that some of them are auto-allergic, i.e., that they would produce antibodies against the tissues of their own parent organism. Possibly this property causes the lymphocytes to be recognized as "foreign" by the phagocytes which engulf them. Failure on the part of phagocytes to remove efficiently all auto-allergic cells is considered to be the cause of auto-immune diseases. The lymphocytes referred to as "stored" in No. 254 are longer lived. They are the five percent or so that are not destroyed and that eventually leave the thymus in small numbers. They are competent but uncommitted.

The tranquility of the thymus is readily explained in terms of anatomy and physiology

256. How can a gland be in great turmoils without being disturbed, as is said in AC 5172? The barrier between the thymus and the blood was mentioned in No. 252 just above. It is clearly the structure responsible for "as is also the case with the gland in question." When the body all around the thymus is in great turmoils, owing perhaps to some disease, the gland itself is protected by its barrier from the toxins. It can remain undisturbed so as to be able to direct, as it were, the operations of defence, despite the many germs pouring into the body. What seemed to be a puzzling phrase is easily understood when the facts are known.

Correspondences of the lymphatics show that the defence of good is derived from the interiors of knowledge

257. At first it seems very strange that the stem cells which are essential for the functioning of the thymus should come from the bone marrow, because we find that in the Writings bones are often considered as relatively inert, or as having but little life. How then should they produce such important lively reproductive cells? Some comments on the life in bones were made earlier (Berridge, 1980 A, p. 22)

where their correspondences with scientifics (KEM) were discussed. The gentle love which forms KEM and the knowledge and use which harden them like bones were mentioned, but to that must be added the specific teaching quoted above (No. 232) to the effect that KEM should contain goods (which are of love, thus soft and living).[14] Regarded in this light, the correspondences all go nicely together, but still there must be many more repercussions of this strange process. We have cells from one environment making, as it were, a journey to a strange new environment in which they become highly productive. One is reminded of the sojourn of Jacob with Laban. In psychological terms we may say that we have thoughts of good leaving an environment of truth to enter another of innocence and love. There they form a whole army of quite inoffensive but extremely effective defensive thoughts, without which the kingdom of the soul cannot survive the onslaughts of hell. Such a theme might well suffice for a whole volume of sermons, could we but see the details clearly.

The activity of the thymus shows how the celestial operates upon the natural

258. An interesting aspect of the central control exerted by the thymus on the peripheral lymphoid tissues is that, although the thymus is essential for the defence of the body against all kinds of antigens, it cannot itself produce any effective defensive action. The small number of lymphocytes that leave it would presumably be inadequate. The thymus thus represents in a striking manner the activity of the celestial internal of man which cannot operate into the natural without a means of communication. Concerning this we read that "by the interior man the internal man communicates with the external; without this medium, no communication at all is possible.

---

[14] Such goods could well correspond to the bone marrow, which, in the young, is soft and full of blood vessels and living cells. It is to be emphasized that this kind of marrow is quite a different tissue from the spinal marrow (medulla) of AC 5717 and 8593.

The celestial is distinct from the natural…and unless there is a medium by which there is communication, the celestial cannot operate at all into the natural…" (AC 1702:2). The thymus cannot operate into the body without the medium of the peripheral lymphoid tissues. We read further in the same passage that "it is the interior man which is called the rational man; and this man, because it is intermediate, communicates with the internal man, where there is good itself and truth itself; and it also communicates with the exterior man, where there are evil and falsity." The exterior man, where there are evil and falsity, may be thought of as corresponding to the body, where there is disease. The internal which is celestial is, like the thymus, too infantile and gentle to fight, but it can mount an effective defence through the intermediate or rational corresponding to the lymphatics.

There is a correspondence between remains and lymphocytes

259. Having suggested that the lymphatics correspond to the interior man, we notice next that remains are stored in the interior man.

There are a number of terms for the various kinds of white cells that populate the lymph and the blood. Strictly, lymphocytes should include all that are to be found in the lymph, but it is often convenient to distinguish between phagocytes which means cells that eat (like amoebae) and the round cells that produce antibodies. These have often been called lymphocytes in contrast to phagocytes, but here by lymphocytes both kinds are meant. There are so many kinds of cells that the more one begins to be precise the more different kinds there appear to be, as distinguished, for example, by function and staining properties. Lymphocytes are stored in the lymphatics i.e., in the nodes, spleen, etc. Hence it is worth while to compare lymphocytes with remains. Remains are goods and truths stored up by the Lord in the interior man (AC 5342:3, 5897:11). Everything of spiritual life is from remains (AC 5898). It is therefore difficult to see how the interior man, where they are stored, could correspond to such a limited system as the lymphatics, or how the things through which all spiritual life comes could correspond to such specialized single cells as lymphocytes. On the other hand, in the very next number (AC 5899), deliverance from damnation is said to be effected by means of remains, which may therefore be termed a means of defence. In a sense the natural and the spiritual are parallel. In the disease-ridden environment we are used to, there would be no life for us without a good defence by the lymphatics. Spiritually, we are surrounded by evils and falsities against which the Lord continually fights by means of the remains He has stored within us. Otherwise there would be no life for us. Is this what is meant by "everything of spiritual life is from remains"? It seems more probable that there are many kinds of remains, of which some are more militant than others. (See no. 261.) Similarly, though the thymus may correspond to the celestial, it might be difficult to find all the celestial qualities clearly represented therein. Nevertheless, correspondence is the means by which life from the spiritual world can flow into and cause the natural, however limited the latter may appear to be. As is widely known, each individual's unique DNA is replicated in every ordinary cell, and this provides another representation of the truth that in spiritual things the part is an image of the whole. Therefore the correspondence of the lymphatic organs, both central and peripheral, can provide an image of the whole man. The limitations that have been mentioned need not hinder a fuller exploration of the possible correspondences.

There is also a correspondence between remains and antibodies

260. When immunity was considered earlier (No. 207) it was described as a blanketing reaction by an antibody whose molecules would fit only those of the intruding antigen. This means that each antibody is unique, but many antibodies are formed from the same series of units (20 or so amino acids and a few sugars). By linking the units into one specific sequence a lymphocyte is able to make one specific antibody. Another lymphocyte, "programmed" differently, will make a different antibody. An uncommitted lymphocyte is induced to make an antibody by the presence of an antigen. This seems to be an automatic process. Nevertheless it is a kind of information which the lymphocyte receives and upon which it acts: namely, information about the molecular "shape" of the antigen. Correct information is truth, so that we may think of the whole process as the qualifying of good by truth (AC 5342:3), the amino acids and sugars being the good, and the order according to which they are put together being the truth. Thus once again we see that truth is the form of good, and as "Remains" in the proper sense (AC 5342:3) are "truths adjoined to good," we may think of the antibodies themselves as corresponding to remains, or perhaps to a particular kind of remains.

261. It has now been indicated that both lymphocytes and antibodies correspond to remains. The two former are certainly related but they are not the same. It has also been suggested that there are many kinds of remains. Even in AC 5342 we find signs of three. First, there are the goods of innocence and charity which are later withdrawn and stored up. These are called remains in AC 661. Then there are truths "conjoined with good"; and finally, "it is these truths adjoined to good that in the proper sense are called 'remains'" (assuming that "conjoined" is not the same as "adjoined"). The statement about remains in AC 661 might be summarized by saying that remains are all things of innocence, of charity, of mercy, and of truth. "All things" must embrace quite a variety. The wording of AC 5342 leads one to think that the goods of innocence and charity might not be "remains" in the proper sense because they are not withdrawn from store for use as are the "remains" proper. They are like the stem cells and other tissues of the thymus that remain in that gland behind the protection of its special membrane, whence they exert their so important influence.

262. Having established that there is a variety of remains, we explore next the close relationship between lymphocytes and antibodies. It is not only that one is the producer and the other the product, but also that the lymphocyte contains within its cell a molecular shape

(DNA). This controls the sequence according to which the amino acids are linked together to make the antibody. Thus in regard to essentials there is a point of great similarity.

263. We may take the correspondences a step further and compare a lymphocyte to an angel. Both are living units. The lymphocyte fights against a disease by putting together molecules provided by the body, doing this according to "information" or "skill" which only the lymphocyte has. An angel combats evil in a man by taking his good (i.e., the Lord's good in the man) and qualifying it with his truth so as to make it effective, doing this from the Lord with a skill which only angels possess. The conjunction of love and truth and protection by angels as described in AC 5893 seems to be in harmony with the activities of lymphocytes. Hence possibly angels correspond to remains, which correspond to lymphocytes; but also, of course, all societies in heaven correspond to societies of spirits, which correspond to the body.

264. A fascinating account of how a lymphocyte is changed (i.e., committed) by meeting an antigen and "remembering the experience" is given by Martin M. Echols as part of an article about analogies between mental processes and the biochemical behavior of cells (Echols, 1980 A, p. 18). The events he describes are remarkable enough to make it easy to accept a correspondence with remains and angelic influences.

The development of man's soul can be seen as in a mirror in the growth and use of the lymphatic system

265. Concerning the beginning of man's life we read that "from earliest infancy to the beginning of childhood, man is being introduced by the Lord into heaven, and indeed among celestial angels, by whom he is kept in a state of innocence" (AC 5342:2). This is the state in which the thymus is a relatively large organ, and the peripheral lymphoid tissues are not yet adequately developed. At least two causes operate to preserve the very young who cannot easily become immune. The first is that they are usually in a protected environment with the mother; the second (and more important) is that they do have some immunity derived from breast milk. Both of these seem to be correspondences of being among celestial angels. It is worth noting also that, as the influence of the thymus is necessary for the growth of the peripheral lymphoid tissues, so also the remains from the early celestial period are necessary for future regeneration. This has its correspondence at an intermediate level also, for, as is well known, depriving an infant of maternal love in its earliest life can have serious consequences.

266. "When the age of childhood begins, the child gradually puts off the state of innocence...and meanwhile he is among spiritual angels" (AC 5342:2). This state includes the development, or at least the beginning, of the rational; and the corresponding state of the body would be that in which the peripheral lymphoid tissues are growing. Both spiritually and naturally, preparations are being made for resistance to harmful forces.

267. When the youth begins to think from himself and to be led by evils, the goods of charity and innocence "are withdrawn by the Lord towards the interiors and there stored up" (AC 5342:2). Here it is difficult to see an exactly parallel correspondence, but there may well be some connection with the storage of lymphocytes which takes place in the peripheral lymphoid tissues (nodes, spleen, etc.). Also, the "inherited evils by which he suffers himself to be led" could correspond to inherited weaknesses which commonly allow infectious diseases to reach serious proportions.

268. The youth we are following through AC 5342 has the goods of innocence and charity, but these goods "have not yet been qualified, for truths give quality to good, and good gives essence to truths;

wherefore from this age he assimilates truths by instruction, and especially by means of his own thoughts and confirmations therefrom." The goods which have not been qualified by truths are like new lymphocytes which are not committed to making any antibodies, and probably not even competent to react against any antigens. So it is that we find next a correspondence of the competence-inducing factor from the thymus, for we read, "in so far, therefore, as he is then in the affection of good." An affection of good is derived from the celestial, just as the competence-inducing factor is derived from the thymus, which we have suggested corresponds to the celestial. Later, our youth has his truths adjoined to good, which remains are available for use in regeneration, that is, for defence in temptations, as competent lymphocytes defend during disease, and in due course confer immunity.

Immunity provides an example of "cometh of evil"

269. Foreign substances in the body, especially antigens produced by invading micro-organisms, are regarded as correspondences of evil. The production of antibodies suggests that good is qualified by truths only in response to evil—even that the form into which the good is qualified is related (as an opposite) to the evil that is to be overcome, and that the truth is available only for this purpose. Obviously, not all truth is for the sake of fighting against evil. There is much that is sheer delight and life to those who are in good. There is also much that is only for combat; hence the Lord said "whatsoever is more than these cometh of evil" (Matt. v. 37). Perhaps not much reliance should be placed on the choice of a preposition, especially in a translation, but it is interesting that we find "cometh of evil" and not "from evil." This suggests that the faith of truth (see DLW 427, 428) is made necessary because of evil, as antibodies are necessary because of disease. They are of the disease but not from the infecting organisms.

CHAPTER XI

THE BRAIN—PART 1

The brain of man is the most wonderful mechanism created by the Lord in ultimate nature

270. When we look at the brain from the scientific point of view, the huge number of its nerve cells and the complexity of the links between them are sufficient to arouse wonder. Estimates suggest a total of 2,600,000,000 to 14,000,000,000 nerve cells in the cerebral cortex, each of which is connected to about 600 other nerve cells.

271. The nerve cells are known as neurons. For further information about cells in general and neurons in particular see Martin M. Echols, "The Cortical Gland and its Relationship to the Modern Neuron" (Echols, 1980 B, p. 104). The neuron is the essential living cell out of which nerves are made. An orderly massing together of millions of neurons and their supporting cells, called glial cells, makes the brain. Glial cells are also known as neuroglia. They are very important for maintaining the proper conditions for the functioning of the neurons. Each neuron can receive electrical impulses from other neurons and pass impulses to still others (few or many in each case). The impulses are not like an electric current but only localized changes in electrical status. They pass from neuron to neuron along very fine threads. Some neurons are shaped like whole trees; the trunk being the cell body, the branches being sending threads (called axons), and the roots being receiving threads (called dendrites). There are many other shapes and most have only one axon but it is often branched. Some neurons excite those in communication with them; others inhibit. Thus there are complex networks of turning on and turning off. There are tracts

which can be rendered specially quiet, as though for the receipt of faint signals. Figure 14 illustrates the structure of neurons and the passage of nerve impulses.

272. We have mentioned above only a few of the interesting things that have been discovered in this century about the brain, but the smallness of the units and their complex linkings are almost beyond apprehension. What is the result of fourteen thousand million units connected each one to six hundred others? Very much more than 600 x 14,000,000,000 for there is a complexity which requires its own type of mathematics or language or symbolism. In addition there is the cerebellum in which the neurons are even more numerous. The cerebral medulla also contains groups of neuron bodies besides the fibres of which it is usually said to consist. These marvelous results of prodigious scientific labor leave us still absolutely ignorant of the soul. All we have are fantastic weavings of minute electrical changes. Obviously life itself eludes the instruments of science.

Is it difficult to believe in spiritual things? It is terribly difficult to believe that nature and material things are all there is. The brain is wonderful but it is still material. Our chief interest lies in its correspondences.

The brain is formed in accordance with the form of the flow of heaven

273. Of course, it almost goes without saying that the brain is unimaginably complex, since all the complexities of human behavior originate in, or are mediated and directed by, that organ. These however are familiar wonders. Less familiar, and therefore more apt to arouse astonishment, is the knowledge that the brain communicates with heaven. For this reason, it is the pinnacle of creation (Berridge, 1979 A, p. 61). The fact, however, ought not to be unfamiliar. It is well known that love is heavenly, and that it is experienced in the brain as love and expressed in the natural world of earthly things by means of the brain acting through the body (See, for example, Nos. 5-10 above).

FIGURE 14

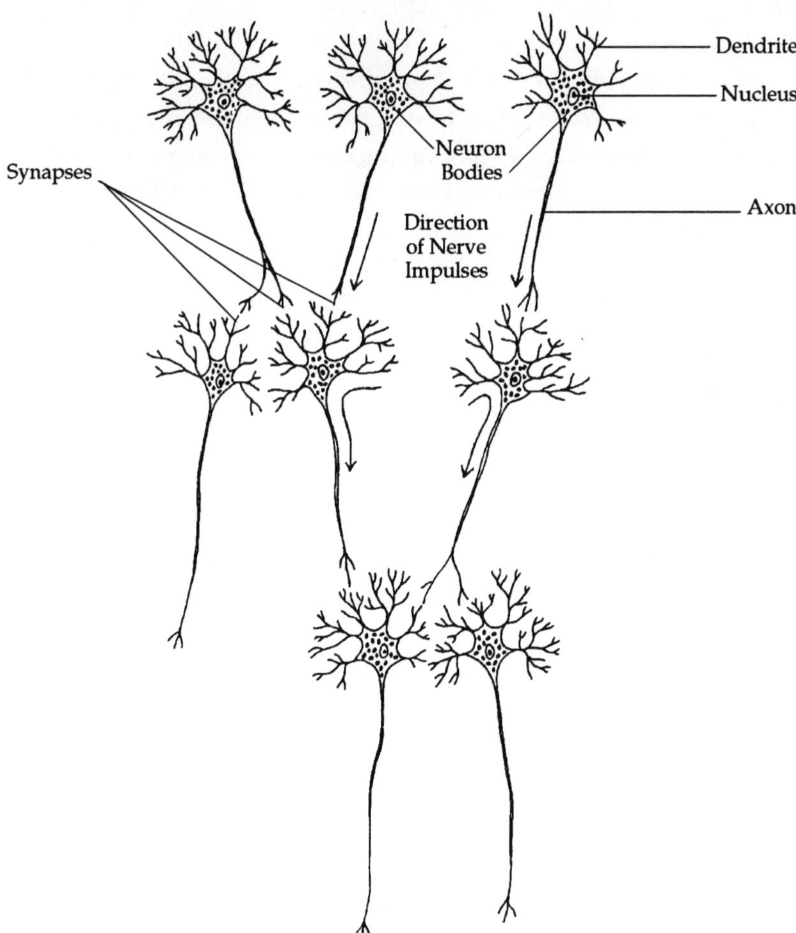

Figure 14: **Neurons**

Diagram of eight neurons, showing the passage of nerve impulses from one to another, or several others. Most of the dendrites, which are normally in contact with axons from other neurons, have been left vacant for simplicity. Similarly, only two of the cells show contacts with two others through branched axons. The junctions between dendrites and axons (synapses) have been left open as they are difficult to represent on this scale. There are many complicated multiple contacts between neurons. This diagram presents only the simplest and most general idea. See text for details.

Source: Wilson, *Human Anatomy*, fig. 12-2.

The experience is familiar; nay, it is more; it is a continuous necessity of life. "Love is the life of man" (DLW 1). It is, however, the Word of the Lord that unites heaven and earth. Clearly it is the Word in the mind of man, living and full of goodness and truth, which it can be only when it is in his brain. In order that the brain may be able to receive such heavenly goodness and truth, it has been made "in exact accordance with the heavenly form" (AC 4040). (This includes also the orderly rule of the body by the brain.)

274. In AC 4041 we are told that "the heavenly form is amazing and quite surpasses all human intelligence." Thus, not unexpectedly, puzzling things follow: gyrations, circumvolutions "seen in the human brains," and a flow (i.e., gyrations) which assured Swedenborg that the brain is formed "in accordance with the form of the flow of heaven." This is enigmatical, but the angels informed him "that man is a little heaven in the least form." We feel this is more understandable (until we begin to analyze it) and it seems possible that the abstruse quality of the description of flows and gyrations was due at least in part to the limitations of natural knowledge and language at that time. As has been pointed out (Alden, 1979, p. 356), we think now of brain function in terms that fit our observations better, namely, electrical potentials, computers, holograms, and so on. But still, this is really nothing to do with the question. This is merely the mechanics. The question really concerns the heavenly form; and possibly the natural terms describing shapes and flows act as cherubim of the literal sense of the Word (AC 308). This description deflects the merely curious or potentially profane into idle speculations about whether the angels go round and round as does the earth, and into imagining scenes like some of the paintings of William Blake. But the heavenly form is not a geometrical matter. It is a form in which every one is in the centre of all and receives from and gives to all. Such a form can be found nowhere in the natural world except in the body (which includes the brain) and similar organizations such as various communities corresponding more or less with the heavenly form.

In AC 4225:3 we find: "And every one when in his own heaven is in his life, and receives influx from the universal heaven, each person there being the centre of all the influxes and, therefore, in the most perfect equilibrium; and this according to the wonderful form of heaven, which is from the Lord alone; thus with all variety." In paragraph No. 65 above this was likened to each cell in the body receiving from every other cell by means of the blood, but the heavenly form is seen even more clearly in the brain.

It is the heavenly form which makes it possible for each person to love his neighbor more than himself. Similarly in the individual brain it is this form which causes each neuron to be connected to all the rest. Although there may be only 600 primary connectors, each of these will have 600 more connected to them, giving 360,000 connections at one remove, and correspondingly more after the second relay (ignoring reciprocal connections). This is one way in which we can see a correspondence between the anatomy of the brain and the form of heaven.

Correspondences of the brain enable us to form useful ideas concerning the otherwise incomprehensible form of heaven

275. It is a characteristic of human development that a beginning has to be made with sense experiences of concrete things (No. 42). From these we can move gradually to spiritual things. There is always a higher level to which we can hope to climb. There is always a lower level to which we can look for representations and correspondences and thereby confirmations. So it is that, although the interior things of the brain, which are in accordance with the interior forms of heaven (AC 4041), are quite incomprehensible, there are lower corresponding things through which useful ideas may be obtained (AC 4043). This we have already seen in a small way just above (No. 274).

276. The representation of spiritual things by the bodily acts they cause was mentioned earlier, and it is obvious that the brain, although part of the body, is the link between the spirit and the body. The action of nerves on muscle was used as an example to show how two things so different as to appear to have nothing in common can yet correspond so well that one controls the other (No. 7). As the brain is nothing but nerves and their supporting tissues, the correspondence between the brain and the body is like that between nerves and muscles. The correspondence is perfect; the difference is enormous. That thing in the brain (i.e., love?) that makes the mother smile bears no resemblance to a smile. Its physical form is merely a storm of tiny electrical impulses (Sir Charles Sherrington, quoted by Allen, 1982, p. 138). In this example we have climbed, as it were, from one physical form (the smile) to a more interior one which corresponds (the nerve impulses), but they are still both physical. Hence we have taken but a very small step on the ladder of Jacob, but the Writings teach us to take further steps. It is said that the subsistence of one thing is from another, this one from still another, till all subsist finally from the First, "and this by a connection of correspondences." Thereby we may know "that there is a correspondence between man and heaven; and further between heaven and the Lord who is the First" (AC 4044).

277. These preliminary considerations are specially important in a study of the brain because the brain is the home of man's spirit, the form of heaven, a house of heaven on earth where the man may dwell, and the place where even the Lord may come to be with him. As it is in the form of heaven, we cannot appreciate its form and beauty without bearing in mind something of what has been revealed about heaven.

Some of the correspondences of the first membrane lining the skull are clarified by modern anatomy

278. The most important and interesting parts of the brain are the neurons or nerve cells, those highly specialized units which all affect each other, and which seem to be responsible for remembering, thinking, and controlling the body (No. 271). These are delicate cells which need special protection and care besides the merely mechanical pro-

tection of the skull. There are, therefore, in the skull, a number of accessory structures that may be considered part of the brain, inasmuch as they are essential for its welfare and maintenance. Figure 15 provides an illustration of these accessory structures, or meninges, discussed in the numbers following this. The first and most external of these is the Dura Mater. It is a thick, dense membrane which encloses the whole of the brain and spinal chord.

279. It seems strange that in an account of the brain we are told of external kinds of spirits who relate to a part of the dura mater and who "wend their way more and more outward, even to *the outer skin* of the head, which they represent" (AC 4046, emphasis added). It is strange, because the dura mater lines the inside of the skull and is not the outer skin. Nevertheless, "wend their way outward" can be explained very simply. It is apparent to the reader of AC 4046 that the dura mater consists of two layers, and we are here concerned with the outer one. This is applied closely to the inside of the skull, for it serves to supply nourishment to the growing bone. The dura mater extends even over the edges of the plates of bone that form the skull, and before they knit together the dura is continuous with the membrane that covers the outside of the skull. So we have a neat representation of the way those external spirits can move away from the internal things corresponding to the brain. As a man ages, the bones of the skull knit together, and the outer layers of membrane become more isolated. So such spirits may move further away until they represent merely the outer skin.

280. Those who relate to the inner layer of the dura mater are slightly less dense, but still they had been unable to penetrate further than natural things. As they had been good citizens, had worshipped the Divine and "said their prayers," they belonged to the Grand Man (as do even those who relate to the outer skin).

281. The quality of this whole group is easily seen as represented in the dura mater, for even the inner layer is relatively external, sending

FIGURE 15

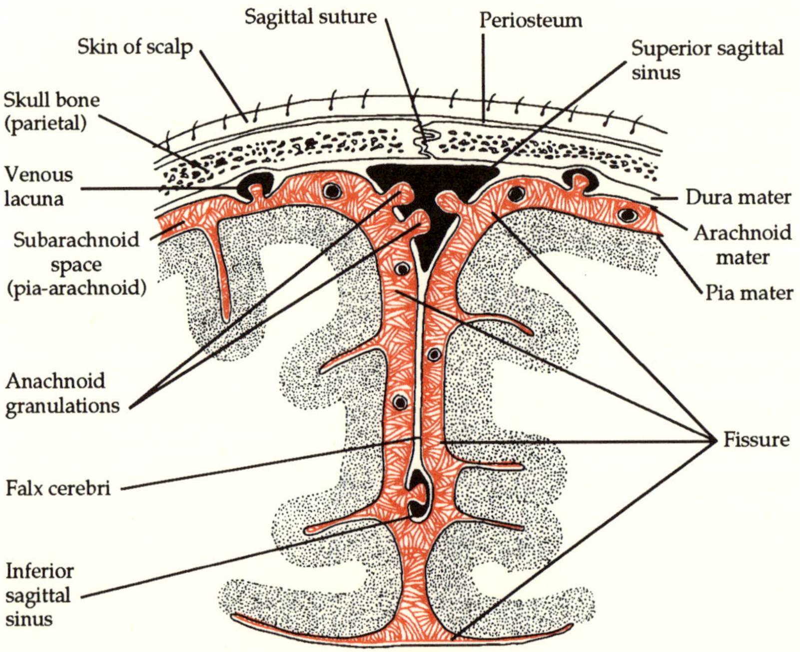

Figure 15: **Meninges of the Brain**

The upper central portion of a coronal section of the skull and brain, including the cleft between the cerebral hemispheres. As shown, the cleft and the space between the skull and the brain are occupied by several membranes. The width of the cleft between the hemispheres has been exaggerated for clarity. It is considerably narrower than shown. (Compare Figure 16)

The cut has been made downwards at right angles to the sagittal sinus which runs from the front to the back of the head just beneath the skull. (There are several such sinuses in the head. They serve as veins.) Hence the sagittal sinus is cut and appears as a triangular shape with dents made by the arachnoid granulations. Note that the dura mater (left - white) is fairly thick. The space between the arachnoid and pia mater is occupied by cerebrospinal fluid and very fine threads, indicated by red lines. Several blood vessels are shown in section. The venous lacuna is connected with the sagittal sinus, but not in the plane of the section.

Sources: Gardner, Gray and O'Rahilly, *Anatomy: A Regional Study of Human Structure,* fig. 53-15; Wilson, *Human Anatomy,* fig. 12-5; Anthony and Kolthoff, *Textbook of Anatomy and Physiology,* fig. 8-1; Gardner, Ernest, *Fundamentals of Neurology,* fig. 7-2.

no fibres into the brain, and being separated from it by the pia-arachnoid (see No. 284) and cerebrospinal fluid. The dura mater supports and protects. It is dense and thick. Its use is as important as the tissues it protects, and the people who correspond to it are similarly important.

282. Having seen how easily "wend their way more and more outward" is explained in anatomical terms, we are hopeful that it will not be too long before we are also able to understand the references to pulsations and undulations and various lights. We cannot yet easily explain all these things, but hints of solutions are already extant. Why, for example, was there a light "gross but not yet luminous," "dim and yet flaming, not bright"? Perhaps the anatomy of the optic nerve provides the answer. The dura mater extends as a sheath around this nerve and blends in front with the sclera or outer coat of the eyeball. Other nerves are said "to pierce" the dura mater as they pass from the brain through the skull (but it is more correct to say that the inner layer of the dura mater becomes continuous with the ordinary nerve sheath, which is obviously a different structure). It has been explained in a previous essay, that the retina is to be regarded as part of the brain (Berridge, 1980 B, p. 68) (see also Chap XV), and that even the coating of the brain extends as far as the eye. This special relationship was indicated by the light Swedenborg saw, and its dimness showed that it was only the outer layer of the eye to which those spirits corresponded.

283. It is important to add here that the nerves which "pierce" the dura mater do not include the olfactory nerve. This has a special anatomy of its own, which is reflected in comments about it in the Writings. The agreement between the Writings and modern ideas is more than might be gathered from a mere consideration of excretion of brain fluid into the nose. We return to this theme below (Nos. 295-298).

The pia mater illustrates the services that can be carried out by those who lack self-confidence in spiritual matters

284. Beneath, i.e., inwards from, the dura mater is the arachnoid mater, which is a delicate membrane lining, as it were, the whole of the dura mater. Below the arachnoid is a space filled with cerebrospinal fluid[15] and bridged by fine threads (hence the term 'arachnoid'). Next is the pia mater. This also is a delicate membrane and it is very important as it carries many blood vessels and dips with them into the clefts of the brain. This is noted in AC 4047, where the pia is said to communicate with the cerebrum and cerebellum by emitted threads. We read here also that the pia "is the second integument more closely investing" the brain; whereby a first integument more closely investing is implied. This is clearly the arachnoid, for the dura does not so closely invest. The arachnoid is mentioned in Inv. 49 as one of three tunics which cover the brain. Here, in AC 4047, it is not mentioned separately, and this need not surprise us, as it is closely related to the pia both phylogenetically and embryologically (though one imagines this was not known in the 18th century). The two membranes are now often classed together as pia-arachnoid and the space between them is regarded as part of the single structure. The same membranes extend round the spinal cord but there are differences in detail.

285. The spirits of this region were they who did not trust much to their own thought but depended on the belief of others (AC 4047). Thus they lacked self-confidence in spiritual matters. Such people can be useful in heaven where they receive a good influx, though at risk elsewhere. (The pia-arachnoid would not be serviceable except to the

---

[15] The cerebrospinal fluid bathes the whole outer surface of the brain and spinal cord and fills all the cavities (i.e., ventricles) inside the brain. It is produced almost (or perhaps quite) entirely by the choroid plexuses. These are frilly types of structure inside the ventricles and they seem to have no other purpose than the production of cerebrospinal fluid. The fluid itself has its own characteristic composition by which it is easily distinguished from serum and lymph.

brain and when protected by the dura and the skull). Their ideas were readily opened, they easily received influx, and they were modest and peaceful. As the pia-arachnoid is serviceable to the brain, keeping it in a healthy and active state, so are these spirits to the angels of heaven. Their peace and modesty also agrees with the delicate nature of the pia. We are told that they could serve the angels as mediums, and although it is not categorically stated that they are intermediate spirits through whom communication between the heavens takes place, we are led to think that communication is one of their functions. (See AC 9670 regarding conjunction between the celestial and spiritual heavens.) These ideas lead one to ask what corresponding communication there can be by means of the pia-arachnoid? The answer shows how precisely the Writings are worded, for there are other communications besides those between the celestial and spiritual heavens.

286. When one thinks of communication in the brain, one's thoughts immediately fly to axons and dendrites through which the neurons and groups of neurons communicate with each other (No. 271). This does not happen in the pia mater. A hasty reader of the AC might think he has found an error, but there is no error. The communications that take place via the pia-arachnoid are those that depend on the blood, for most of the blood vessels supplying the brain divide in the pia before sending vertical branches down into the cortex. Thus all the nourishment and any hormonal influences come through this route. Another communication is that of the sympathetic nervous system which has fibres extending to the branches of the arteries in the pia. These fibres presumably control the arterial tension and hence the blood supply through the various branches, but even now the innervation of these arteries is not well understood. These, then, are the kinds of communication that correspond to those of the spirits of the province of the pia mater. It is credible that such relatively simple spirits, with no confirmed opinions of their own, should aid in a general type of communication and provide simple services. These things are easily seen to correspond to the way the pia-arachnoid provides services for the brain.

287. The spirit who is described in the next number of the *Arcana* (AC 4048) was, like those of the pia mater, in a peaceful state, and, like them, he could accept and bring forth what the angels said. (Here, however, "interior" angels; in AC 4047, "angels.") No connection with the pia-arachnoid is mentioned, in spite of the similarity. There is, however, a close connection. Spirits like the one in question relate to the longitudinal sinus (now called saggital); a long, wide blood vessel like a vein, but bigger, and running above and partly within the cleft that is between the cerebral hemispheres. Now called the superior sagittal sinus, it is one of a number of large vessels into which the venous blood from the brain (i.e., the `used' blood) is collected on its way to the internal jugular veins and hence to the heart. Like several other sinuses, this one is between the two layers of the dura mater, but its connection with the pia arachnoid is through the arachnoid granulations. These appear, in a dissected specimen, as small nodules on the inner surface of the longitudinal sinus, so that they project into the blood itself during life. A sketch of them is to be seen in a communication by Pacchioni,[16] but it is to modern works that we turn for details of their structure and function. They are found to be stalk-like outgrowths of the arachnoid which push through the inner layer of the dura mater and into the venous sinus where they expand into knob-like projections. Since the arachnoid is mostly space containing cerebrospinal fluid, it will be seen that these projections bring the cerebrospinal fluid into close proximity with the blood in the sinus, and it is here that the fluid finds its way back into the blood. Observations with the electron microscope (on sheep) indicate that fine tubes

---

[16] In *The Cerebrum* (See Footnote 18 in No. 312), Swedenborg described Pacchioni's findings (Swedenborg, 1938). His sketch is reproduced in the companion volume of anatomical plates. From Nos. 232d and 232e of *The Cerebrum*, it is clear that Pacchioni observed the connections between the granulations and the pia mater, but he seems to have been alone in this. The granulations were thought to be glands.

perforate the granulations, allowing the fluid to escape, as if they were valves. This is reminiscent of that spirit's statement that if anything not good and true flows in, he does not admit it or utter it. In a parallel passage (AC 7744), he is said to admit it but not to utter it.

The course of the cerebrospinal fluid is like the flows of spirits belonging to the province of the pia mater

288. We have seen that the pia-arachnoid forms a layer containing spaces filled with cerebrospinal fluid. This same fluid also fills the hollow parts inside the brain, i.e., the ventricles. See Figure 18. All the ventricles communicate with one another, but the communication with the pia-arachnoid space is through the last, or fourth, ventricle only. The cerebrospinal fluid is secreted into the ventricles, whence it can pass into the pia-arachnoid by way of openings in the roof of the fourth ventricle. Some of the structures which produce the fluid (i.e., the choroid plexuses) are in the lateral ventricles and these ventricles extend some way forwards into the cerebrum so that the fluid secreted by them must flow "from the front backwards" (as in AC 4047) in order to find its way out. After this, the cerebrospinal fluid flows upwards and then forwards and sideways beneath the cerebrum. Finally, it climbs over the outer surfaces of the cerebrum and then over their upper surfaces to the middle line where is the longitudinal sinus, through which it returns to the blood stream as mentioned above (No. 287). This last flow is "from each temple towards the middle of the brain" (as in AC 4047), and it is therefore like the inflowing action of those who belong to the province where this flow occurs. Since Swedenborg thought that the cerebrospinal fluid is absorbed by the choroid plexuses and did not seem to know that it returns to the blood through the arachnoid granulations, these statements about flows are remarkable.

289. The flow of cerebrospinal fluid takes place partly because it is produced in the ventricles and passes into the blood stream in the longitudinal sinus. It is also moved partly by the cilia (waving fibres) on the surface of the cells that line the ventricles. Thus we need not think of the spirits of this region as if they were themselves flowing like fluid and we may prefer to regard them as corresponding to the living cells that contribute to the movement. Thus it is not said "they flowed" but "whose common action...flowed" and "whose inflowing action was" This might seem to contradict the reference in AC 4049 to "the nature of the better kind of lymph"; on the other hand, in literature, the tool is often mentioned in place of the user—a hammer for the smith, a sword for the soldier, and it is ordinary usage to speak of the violins of an orchestra. These examples are similar to the naming of a vessel to signify the contents. The point is that cerebrospinal fluid is a relatively simple liquid, devoid of living cells, whereas the flowing action refers to living spirits.

The "lymph" which returns into the brain is, as yet, not identifiable

290. A consideration of the spirits that relate to the ventricles (AC 4049) leads us into a difficult area when we try to understand what is meant by "the better kind of lymph which is there." It is clear from AC 4050 that, in the terminology of the Writings, there can be a number of lymphs. Because "lymph" now has a specific meaning, perhaps we should think of them merely as liquids, or perhaps several "lymphs" could be together as constituents of one fluid. This was suggested in an earlier article (Berridge, 1979 A, p. 61), because there is only one fluid in the brain cavities. In the same article, an attempt was made to explain the meaning of "it is the nature of the better kind of lymph which is there to return into the brain" (AC 4049). This was done by pointing out that diffusion, i.e., the random motion of molecules, causes constituents which are disappearing at any point (being used, for example) to seem on the whole to move towards that point, because there are none to move away (Balls in random motion on a billiard table would all finish in the pockets). Similarly, molecules which are being produced at any point will diffuse away from it toward a point at which they are being consumed. This could explain why the better kinds, or those of use, would move into the brain and the worse kinds would move out. However, it is generally accepted that the nutrition of the brain is through the blood stream and that its waste products are carried away in the blood. There is no lymphatic system in the brain. The waste products which are too large, molecularly speaking, to pass through the walls of the capillaries, are dealt with by the glial cells, whose functions are the maintenance of the neurons in a healthy condition. There are practically no large molecules in the cerebrospinal fluid, which does not act as a means of disposing of them (contrary to what was suggested in the earlier article (Berridge, 1979 A, p. 61)).

291. The function usually ascribed to the cerebrospinal fluid is that of supporting the brain tissues by reducing their weight, since they almost float in it. Other functions, however, are possible. It is said that certain cells are associated with secretion into and uptake from cerebrospinal fluid but no facts about this are reported. It has also been shown that quite large molecules injected into the ventricles can diffuse through the brain tissue right across to the pia mater (but not into the blood capillaries of the brain). Thus there is some experimental support for the suggestion that diffusion would account for substances getting into the brain if they were being used up. Such a movement would occur unless the fluids inside and outside were exactly the same.[17] The fluid inside is produced by seepage through the capillary walls (but see No. 300 concerning the blood-brain barrier), and it is

---

[17] It was thought at one time that the spaces between the cells of the brain were too small to allow diffusion to be significant. This opinion arose when studies of fine structure, as opposed to ordinary microscopic observations, were made. It has since been shown that when the tissues are deprived of oxygen in the course of ordinary methods of preparation, most of the intercellular fluid is absorbed by the cells themselves which therefore expand into all the available space. It is now thought that this space is much more than the early estimate of five percent of the total volume and nearer the still earlier figure of twenty percent. With spaces like this, diffusion is likely to be important if the fluids are not identical.

modified in its composition by activities of the glial cells (No. 271). On the other hand, the fluid outside is the cerebrospinal fluid (See no. 284). It is produced largely by the choroid plexuses, and its composition is different from a filtrate such as that which seeps through the capillary walls (No. 76). Thus it is likely that the fluids are different, and there will be an ebb and flow of ions and small molecules, depending on a number of factors such as blood flow rate and activity of glial cells.

292. The structure of the brain would allow fluids to move between it and the fluids contained in its cavities or ventricles. We are as yet unable to identify any component whose nature it is to return into the brain. However, there is another way of looking at the problem.

293. We are often told (e.g. in AC 4043) that the things of heaven are incomprehensible and unutterable. In order that Swedenborg might be able to comprehend them and utter them, i.e., write about them, they had to be expressed in representatives "by means of forms to which the forms seen in the world bear some resemblance" (AC 4043). These forms were necessarily the mental concepts that Swedenborg had in his own mind. As already argued above, such forms were also those of his contemporaries, in order that the Writings could be understood (even if only by a few). We believe that the wisdom of the angels with whom Swedenborg conversed, and the truths revealed to him by the Lord, correspond to natural things as they really are, so that the truths are in agreement with modern science (except when science is in error). There are changes taking place between heaven and the world of spirits which correspond to the ebb and flow of molecules between the cerebrospinal fluid and the brain fluids. How, then, could Swedenborg have understood this process better than to speak of a lymph whose nature it is to return into the brain? There was not enough knowledge available to him. But his notes include other parallels with current science, two of which can now be mentioned.

294. There are many passages in the SD that are difficult to understand from the scientific point of view, and perhaps this is why the Lord delayed their publication. On the other hand, we find comments which are highly interesting. We read, for example, (SD 830) that the fluids in the ventricles flow from between the fibres of the brain "and from elsewhere." We now know that "elsewhere" are the choroid plexuses, which are largely responsible for the production of cerebrospinal fluid. In SD 831, part of this fluid is said to be absorbed by the choroid plexus. This is remarkable, because the fine structure of part of the choroid plexus is like that part of the kidney that absorbs water from the very dilute urine produced in the renal corpuscles. (As a first approximation we may say that urine is produced by filtration from blood followed by re-absorption of much water and other useful substances.) Further, the fluid produced by the choroid plexuses is not merely a filtrate. This is deduced from its composition. Thus, it seems at least possible that some of the liquid produced by one part of a choroid plexus is re-absorbed by another part, and that in this sense it is operating like a kidney although no excretory function has been ascribed to it. Nevertheless in view of the limitations of science in Swedenborg's time, a description of the ventricles as urinary bladders of the brain "as it were" suggests a bias derived from angelic knowledge. A similar bias can be noted in Swedenborg's opinion that the olfactory "nerves" are organs of excretion. This we now proceed to examine.

It is incorrect to ascribe an excretory function to the olfactory "nerves" but to do so shows a bias towards correct anatomy

295. We turn to this subject here because its relationship to the brain led Kenneth J. Alden to include it in his study of the brain (Alden, 1979, p. 358). In that very useful work, he shows that Swedenborg was limited to the science of his time. This is an important concept that we have already had occasion to emphasize. Alden's contribution encourages one to think around that limitation and to realize the chaos that could have followed if it had not been observed. The interest has always been in showing the miraculous nature of the revelation granted through Swedenborg, and it is characteristic of enthusiasm that it tends to blur distinctions and overstep boundaries. We know that Swedenborg himself was anxious that he should not be worshipped, almost as though he foresaw that men might regard him as infallible. So we are able to detect "errors" in the Writings, and having accepted that they were inevitable, we can marvel at how few they are, and turn again to the remarkable evidences of special enlightenment even in matters of science. This enlightenment appears to have taken the form of a bias towards the less incorrect notions of that time. The ascribing of an excretory function to the mammillary processes is a case in point (AC 5386).

296. Alden "discovered" that mammillary processes used to mean olfactory nerves (or, more precisely, the olfactory tracts, as pointed out in his more detailed but unpublished notes on the subject (Brown, 1979, p. 356)). This proves to be particularly helpful because what are now known as mammillary bodies are quite different structures of the brain some distance away. The term "mammillary processes" is not now used. Thus it seemed, before Alden pointed out the contrary, that the two terms might mean the same. This made the beginning of AC 5386 impossible to understand. Now, however, one can at least see the origin of the comments there.

297. As Alden has also demonstrated, Swedenborg formed his own opinions, although he was obliged to rely largely on the anatomists of his time. Now, however, their methods have no special claim to our respect. Some of the experiments quoted in The *Cerebrum* (Swedenborg, 1938) now seem crude and sometimes self-defeating. We have no qualms about differing from Vieussens as Swedenborg also did on occasion (Brown, 1979, p. 356).

298. According to the account given in *Gray's Anatomy* (Williams, 1973), there is continuity of tissue spaces between the nasal mucous membrane below and the pia-arachnoid round the brain above, and so, even to the ventricles, as explained above (No. 288). In cases of injury this allows access of infection to the brain, and it has been thought that the germs of meningitis can spread along this route, but this has not been conclusively demonstrated. It is clear, however, that cerebrospinal fluid can move into the tissues of the nose, and if there is injury it escapes. When one remembers how common bleeding from the nose is, one realizes that a slight escape of cerebrospinal fluid may also be quite common. We return to the subject in more detail in a later chapter. Meanwhile, it seems possible that the spiritual anatomy known to the angels would bias Swedenborg towards the thought of fluids in the nose descending from the brain. Phlegm is another thing!

Phlegm in the brain is the "abomination of desolation"

299. It is a horrible matter to contemplate the presence of phlegm in the beautiful and delicate structures of the brain. The very horror of it suggests equally horrible spiritual things. Hence we are grateful to Alden for having endured the horror and for making his conclusions available (Brown, 1979, p. 356). He points out that in those days, unhealthy cadavers were often used for dissection, and that hygienic conditions seldom prevailed (if ever?), so that pus and other viscid substances might have been mistaken for phlegm, or merely have received that name. These comments are essential knowledge for translators; indeed for all who would understand the AC rightly. Such comments lead us to remember that the experiences we read about in the *Arcana* took place before the Last Judgement, as also noted by Worcester (1899, pp. 403 and 405). At that time hellish spirits abounded. Disorderly conditions prevailed. This is most clearly brought out in AC 5717 and 5718, from which it is permissible to conclude that "viscid substances of the brain" and "thick phlegm of the brain" refer to diseased conditions. It is not so clear from AC 5386, but still, this number is in a series which leads the thought towards hell. We conclude that phlegmy substances in the brain are the direct opposite of "the brain is heaven," and of "the better kind of lymph which is there" (AC 4049). The question that now arises is, why did the Lord cause Swedenborg to observe phlegmy matters in the brain so often, or at least to become so familiar with their occurrence? Clearly because it was the last time of the Church, the state of which, in the absence of love and charity, or at its end, is denoted by "the abomination of desolation" (AC 2454:4, 3562). It appears that the Lord made use of the unhealthy state of men's bodies so that through the anatomists we might see representations of the abominable things that had to be overcome in the world of mind and spirit. There was confusion among the anatomists of the time because some of them seemed unable to distinguish between viscous fluids which were normal (protoplasm for example) and those that were due to disease (such as pituita or phlegm). At least this seems to be the cause of the opinion that merely an excess of viscous material was a cause of disease.

The nourishment of the brain by blood from the body illustrates a spiritual process which could not previously be described to the apprehension

300. Perhaps the reader will enjoy this "discovery" in the order in which it occurred. The question arose in connection with the blood-brain barrier. This barrier is an important property of the circulatory system in the brain that we have as yet mentioned only in passing. Experiments show that large molecules do not pass out of the blood stream into the brain as readily as they do into other tissues. It seems that the lining of the capillaries is different. It is interesting to note that the other organ that has celestial associations as the brain has, namely the thymus gland (Chap X), also possesses a barrier to protect it from too free an influx of large molecules from the blood.

301. In seeking for a correspondence of the blood-brain barrier, one thinks at first of barriers in the Word, such as cherubim, and especially the veil in the tabernacle, since this was a barrier between the Holy and the Holy of Holies. However, we learn that the correspondence of the blood-brain barrier is with the intermediate angelic societies through whom communication is made; and their correspondence in man is with "the cardiac and pulmonary plexuses" and with the medulla oblongata, these being the means of communication between the heart and lungs and between the cerebellum and cerebrum, respectively (AC 9670). This would seem to make the veil a representative of communication rather than of a barrier. Nevertheless upon the veil were cherubim, which signify a guard, to prevent the mingling of spiritual and celestial goods; and even in the intermediate societies these goods are not conjoined (AC 9673). Thus the societies act as guards also. It is the same in the body. The heart is united with the lungs in an orderly way and not mingled; the cerebellum is connected with the cerebrum by nerve fibres running between well differentiated centres to produce a well coordinated whole. Thus in both cases there are barriers and limits as well as communication, but these things seem to be too specific. We need something lower and more general—a little more like the communication ascribed to the pia mater (Nos. 284-287).

302. When we look at the question of correspondences in a more general way, from a distance, as it were, we observe the head as the celestial, the body as the spiritual, and the feet as the natural. It is specifically stated (AC 9913:2) "that *in general*, the head corresponds to celestial things" (emphasis added), and consequently it is the neck "that by virtue of correspondences…signifies the influx, the communication, and the conjunction of celestial with spiritual things." Next we find, like the cherubim of the veil, a binding or boundary (AC 9914) which is required to be very strong (AC 9916). This was the binding round the opening of Aaron's robe which would rest upon the neck during wear. Therefore it has the same signification as the neck. It is emphasized (AC 9914) that "it is bounded and closed on all sides." These things describe the mode of influx of celestial into spiritual good, which is thus limited or bounded as the neck is strengthened by sinews and bones.

303. It seems that we are, as yet, a long way from the blood-brain barrier, but these things provide a direction for our enquiries. In the first place, the strength and completeness of the limitation or binding is reminiscent of the physiological strength and completeness of the blood-brain barrier. We next realize that, if the outward flow of the celestial is to be so controlled, how much more must the reverse flow be kept in order, exactly as with the thymus. Now the reverse flow is extremely important. It is essential for continuing the life of the body; the blood supplies to the brain food, water, and oxygen, and removes carbon dioxide and other wastes. The barrier there presumably prevents the brain from being poisoned by many other substances that find their way into the blood (such as break-down products due to wear and tear of muscles, decomposition of food in the intestines, unwholesome substances in food, and so on). Can these things apply also to the Grand Man? We must first remember that there can be no influx of what is lower into what is higher, but there is reciprocal flow (DLW 410). Indeed, the nourishment of the brain by the blood, and the limiting of the exchange by the barrier in the brain, helps us to understand, to a slight degree, a process which could not be described to the apprehension when the Writings were given. Concerning this we read "let not any one wonder that the things which are here contained in the internal sense cannot be described to the apprehension, and that what are described transcend it" (AC 3085). We are now permitted to look at the process a little more closely.

304. The transcendent operations we are now attempting to grasp are thus described: "there is a continual Divine influx through the internal man into the external, that is, an influx of celestial and spiritual things through the rational man into the natural, or, what is the

same, into the natural things which are of the external man; and…by this influx, truths are continually called forth out of the natural man, elevated, and implanted in the good which is in the rational man" (AC 3085). This is similar to the activation of all parts of the body by the descent of commands from the brain through the nerves. These commands cause the body to eat, drink, and do many other things, by which a great variety of useful substances are procured or prepared and transferred to the blood stream, in which they are conveyed towards the brain. That is, they are "elevated." Now the blood-brain barrier comes into operation. It is a product of the brain corresponding to the celestial, as the binding round the neck of Aaron's robe represented a production by the celestial (AC 9915). As, in the body, the barrier prevents access to the brain by deleterious substances so, we deduce, the things that are "elevated and implanted in the good which is in the rational man" are strictly sorted, purified, and separated from the many harmful things that may be in the natural man. Thus the science of physiology now is such that by means of it we can apprehend the process of AC 3085. However, it still remains that we are seeing it only in a general way from correspondences, for "it is of such great wisdom because it is from the Divine" and "it can in no wise be explored as to a ten thousandth part of it."

305. It would not be surprising to find such an important process described in other parts of the Writings. In DLW, we find, for example: "Out of these [star-like forms in the cineritious, i.e., grey matter] go forth fibres…into the body. These proceed to the ultimates of the body, and from ultimates return to their firsts. The return of fibres to their firsts is made through the blood vessels" (DLW 316). The first mental image this statement produces is of a fluid flowing through the nerves and returning via the blood stream, as though the nerves could feed their contents into the blood vessels. But this does not happen. Prior to Harvey (1578-1657) it was the authoritative view amongst anatomists that the arteries terminated in nerves. The capillaries were not seen until 1661. Even in those places where nerves have been

shown to secrete substances into the blood, a general flow has not been found. In the case of the infundibulum and pituitary gland, only minute particles or droplets are transferred, and this is done in a controlled manner across barriers that prevent mixing, which would be chaotic and disorderly. The ultimates of the body to which the nerves descend are an expression of "thousands and myriads of forces [that], operating in act, appear as a one" (DLW 16) and the return to the firsts in the brain is quite different in character from that which was sent out as a cause. This return is far more wonderful than a mere return flow (such as that of electricity along the neutral wire). The return that is made through the blood consists in chemical activation, protection, nourishment, and cleansing. These take place when the nerves, activated by the brain, stimulate the body to its normal healthy functions. It is easy to see how this corresponds to the "progression of love though wisdom into uses," or ultimates, and to the return "out of these, by means of the enjoyment of uses…to their firsts." That is to say, there is a return of uses to the brain in the form of various chemical and physical services. This physiological circle of flow and return is particularly instructive as an example of correspondences, for we have here a process in brain and body corresponding to mental processes that we can observe by introspection. These are also out-lined in DLW 316.

306. The circle that has just been discussed is put forward in DLW as an image of creation. There is also another path of return to the brain and that is via the nerves connecting the various sense organs to the brain. This opens a vast new field of correspondences into which we will not now enter except to say that it forms part of a circle that is quite different. Although the nerves of the senses are connected to the brain, they conduct only information to it. They provide no material sustenance. They are, as it were, in a discretely different degree. Dealing with information only, they seem to be a step nearer the spiritual, though still actually material. It is almost as though they do not quite descend to the ultimates in the sense of food, drink, and cleansing. We must not, however, imagine either creation or the body to be as simple as two circles. There is yet another return via the blood that would appear also to be an image of creation. For there are nerves from the brain that go only to the pituitary gland. They secrete hormones into the blood and thereby exert profound effects upon the body, as will be seen in the chapter following.

307. The circles comprising outflow from the brain and return via the blood are, as we have said, images of creation. From these circles, it is clear that the return is in an altogether different form from the outflow. As a created subject, man receives life from the Lord, and makes a return to the Lord whenever he engages in some use (from love, charity, obedience, fear, etc.), but it is not a return of life. Life flows out from the Lord and ultimates are created. They produce returns in great variety, whereby heaven is nourished.

CHAPTER XII

THE BRAIN—PART 2
THE INFUNDIBULUM AND THE HYPOPHYSIS CEREBRI

The control of the body through the infundibulum and hypophysis cerebri is like the mediate presence of the Lord

308. The infundibulum and hypophysis cerebri or pituitary gland are small organs of great interest. They are attached to the base of the brain, the infundibulum being part of the brain itself for it contains many neurons and the axons of neurons (see No. 271) whose cell bodies are higher in the brain. The axons convey both nerve impulses and hormones (chemical messengers) to the hypophysis cerebri or pituitary gland which is like a small knob at the narrow end of the funnel-shaped infundibulum. See Figures 18 and 16. When the hormones reach the hypophysis they are either released into the blood or they control the synthesis and release of other hormones. The picture is further complicated by the observation that some of the messenger hormones travel with the blood in a special system of vessels that runs only between the brain and the hypophysis cerebri. This latter is perhaps the most important gland in the whole body in spite of its small size (It weighs only about 0.5 grams). Hypophysis cerebri is a better name than pituitary because pituitary is associated with phlegm (Latin pituita) owing to the misconceptions of the early anatomists. Kenneth J. Alden has considered this subject in detail in his notes referred to earlier (No. 296). The hypophysis is so important because its hormones which are secreted into the blood affect a number of other so-called endocrine glands (for example the thyroid; the adrenals). These glands, in their turn, control many of the physiological activities of the body. Thus there is a descent of influence from the

FIGURE 16

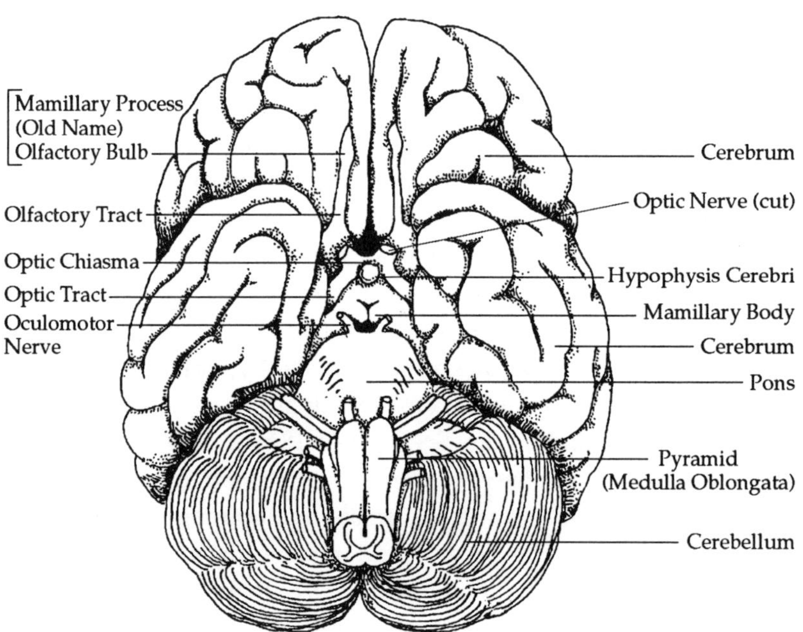

Figure 16: **Brain Seen from Below**

Somewhat simplified: the hypophysis cerebri is shown, as are also major structures and some nerves for comparison with the other figures, *eg.* olfactory bulbs, optic chiasma (which is a good "landmark"), mamillary bodies, medulla oblongata, cerebrum. (See Dr. Berridge's legend, Figure 20). The spinal cord is cut off just below the medulla oblongata.

Sources: Gardner, *Fundamentals of Neurology*, figs. 7-5, 7-6; Anthony and Kolthoff, *Textbook of Anatomy and Physiology*, fig. 8-9.

brain through the hypophysis, then through the other endocrine glands, and so to the body as a whole. The hypophysis cerebri is shown in detail in Figure 17.

309. For a time it was uncertain whether genuine nerves could actually produce hormones, but it has now been settled. The nerves are real nerve fibres composed of neuron bodies and axons and dendrites. They produce volleys of electrical impulses in the typical fashion. Those we are concerned with also synthesize hormones in the main cell body. The passage of such hormones along the axons to the hypophysis has been demonstrated. There are still many questions about what follows, but the general picture of activity in the brain is now accepted: this activity is conducted to the hypophysis which then affects other glands, which then affect the body. However there are quite a number of these hormones, and some of them exert their effect directly instead of affecting other glands. An example is somatotropin which controls growth in childhood. As already mentioned (No. 308) some of the hormones that are produced in the brain exert their effect by controlling the production and release of other hormones by the hypophysis; some pass directly into the blood stream. An example of the latter is the anti-diuretic hormone vasopressin, which, among other activities, prevents excessive excretion of water by the kidneys. Somatotropin belongs to a group that is synthesized in the hypophysis but controlled by other hormones from the brain.

310. This is the shortest account that can be given of a very complicated physiological unit. It is fascinating in its ramifications and any one who finds it interesting is urged to study it in more detail in the many works that are available. It is particularly interesting at the moment to notice the dual nature of the influx of the brain into the body. On the one hand we have the instantaneous impulses of the nerves; on the other the slow but persistent effects of the hormones. Without the latter the body would not be in a fit condition to respond to the nerve impulses; for although we read that "the whole, that is,

FIGURE 17

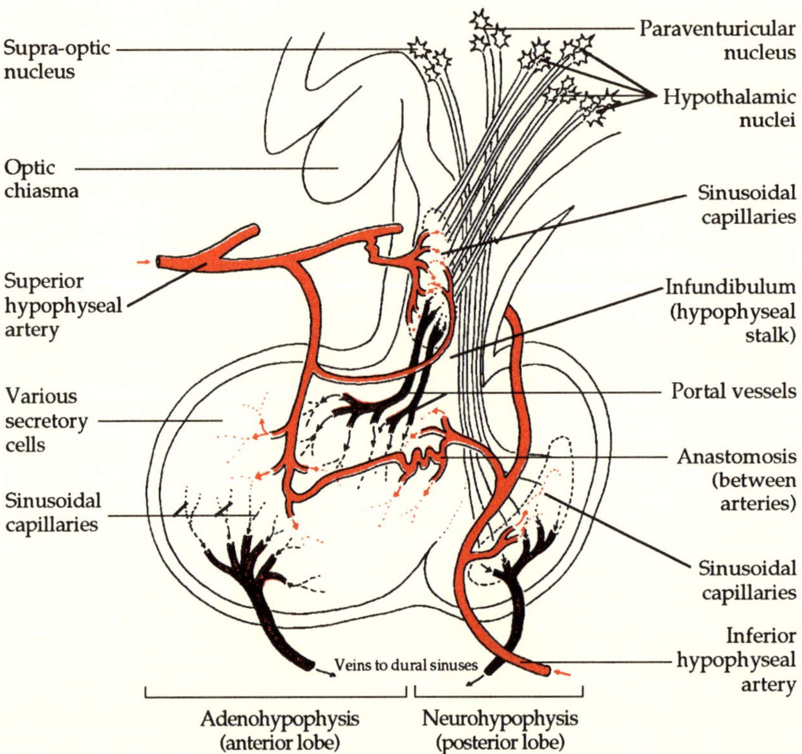

Figure 17: **Hypophysis Cerebri**

Diagram of the hypophysis cerebri in median section showing major blood vessels and neural connections thereto. The superior hypophyseal artery breaks up into sinusoidal capillaries in the infundibulum, where hormones from the hypothalamic nuclei are secreted into the blood, then portal vessels carry these hormones to the adenohypophysis, where they act on the "various secretory cells" and trigger the release of other hormones. The neurohypophysis, in contrast, is innervated directly by the supra-optic and paraventricular nuclei, and thus receives other hormones from them. The various nuclei named at the top of the drawing are each symbolized by three neurons much larger than to scale. A "nucleus" in this context is a small specialized region of the brain consisting nevertheless of a great number of neurons.

Sources: Clemente, *Gray's Anatomy*, English edition, 1973, fig. 11-91; Gardner, Gray and O'Rahilly, *Anatomy: A Regional Study of Human Structure*, fig. 53-9; Gardner, *Fundamentals of Neurology*, figs. 15-8 and 15-9. (Based on Guillemin, R. and Burgus, R. in *Scientific American* 227: 24-33, 1972, by permission of authors and publisher.)

the brain and body together, by its origin, exists only from the fibres which proceed from their beginnings in the brains," we also find "that they are fixed by means of such substances and matters as are in the earths…and that this is effected by means of the blood" (DLW 367 and 370). It is perhaps worth more thought than we can give it at present to consider whether this is a correspondence of the immediate and mediate presence of the Lord (AC 9682e). For the brain is present everywhere in the body immediately through the nerves and mediately by means of the hormones of the hypophysis cerebri.

Even angels may be in error, and Swedenborg himself suffered from the misconceptions of his contemporaries

311. Reference was made above to the need for Swedenborg to write according to the idiom of his time (No. 293). Incidental to our study of the infundibulum, we find an example of the burdensomeness of this limitation. In the *Diary* he writes that it is "so tedious to describe" (SD 914e). Such a comment about a short paragraph made by one who has written so many long volumes makes us pause. Why was it tedious? Was it because Swedenborg could not really understand what the angels were trying to tell him? Is this why he got some parts of it wrong? Is it why he repeated it all over again in the second half of the paragraph? We notice next that it "was said by angels to other angels" when in the beginning he says, "I was told." Precision is not to be expected in private notes probably written in haste. The important thing is that it was said by angels. The fact that all these things were done under the Lord's auspices does not mean that every word or idea is Divinely perfect; these ideas seem not to be the things Swedenborg had from the Lord alone. It seems more likely that the effect of being under the Lord's auspices more than usual was that every one's freedom was expanded and thus their individuality was not overruled. From this, errors were certain to arise, for angels are not omniscient. If they were they would be Divine. We can therefore be as critical as we wish about what the angels said. We must not be at all surprised that they were sometimes in error. We can still be filled with delighted wonder at the prescience of so many of the statements that they made, especially when we contrast them with the general level of futile speculation in the medical world of the time, as shown, for example, in TCR 665:5. It is, of course, possible to ignore those things that look to us like errors, but it is better to examine them, lest, unobserved, they assume a false importance and obscure the perspective. Now, therefore, we consider a few errors before passing on to greater things.

312. The infundibulum was so named because it is funnel-shaped. It was assumed at the time (and Swedenborg seems to have accepted it) that this organ funneled the cerebrospinal fluid into the hypophysis cerebri where it was processed in various ways. It was a reasonable assumption by men who had no conception of a hormone, especially as the cavity of the brain (the third ventricle) extends right down into the hypophysis in some animals (for example the cat, though not in man, except at an early stage of the fetus). In his notes already referred to (No. 296), Kenneth Alden shows that Swedenborg probably thought that considerable volumes of fluid were processed in, or through, the infundibulum (from *Swedenborg's work The Cerebrum*[18]). In SD 831, however, he only says that a part of the fluid passes into the third ventricle and through the infundibulum to the pituitary (hypophysis) where it is separated "in a 3-fold manner." "A part" is too indefinite to have much meaning, but in SD 1798-1800 we find three humours mentioned, the third of which "is collected in the lateral ventricles of the brain and is discharged through the infundibulum and so on." This we now know not to be the case. Even the anatomy seems inaccurate. The lateral ventricles are said to communicate with the third ventricle through a foramen beneath the pineal gland (stated in

---

[18] This work by Swedenborg (1938) is in 2 vol. Vol. I contains 3 transactions. Vol. 2 contains anatomical drawings from authors quoted in Vol. I. Obtainable from the General Church Book Center, Bryn Athyn.

SD 914, implied in SD 831). This, however, is not quite right. Communication is through two other openings at the anterior end of the third ventricle. The pineal gland is at the posterior end, and the opening beneath it is the cerebral aqueduct which leads into the fourth ventricle. There may be a few other points at variance with present knowledge but it is those that seem to forecast later discoveries that are of special interest. Figure 18 offers a more modern view of the cerebral ventricles.

This criticism is based on the assumption that the large ventricles of SD 914 are the lateral ventricles. This interpretation is reasonable because (1) they are the largest cavities in the brain, (2) the next larger is the 4th ventricle, of which there is only one, and (3) it is the lateral ventricles that are said in SD 1800 to discharge their contents through the infundibulum.

Most of the outline in SD 831 and 914 agrees with modern concepts

313. These entries in the *Spiritual Diary* are similar to one another; they both deal with the infundibulum and hypophysis cerebri. They are reproduced in part herewith.

314. From the *Spiritual Diary*, No. 831:

Thus when the heterogeneous parts have been cast out from them they return again into heaven, exactly as is the case with the serosity in the ventricles, of which a part, as being the part that is cast off, is absorbed by the choroid plexus, a part transpires elsewhere, a part passes into the third ventricle beneath the pineal gland, and thus through the infundibulum toward the pituitary gland, where it is separated in a three fold manner, and the parts are afterwards carried by various passages, channels and sinuses toward the jugular vein, so that they may be at hand to meet the chyle coming up through the thoracic duct. There the two are consociated and carried toward the heart,

    The Natural Basis of Spiritual Reality

FIGURE 18

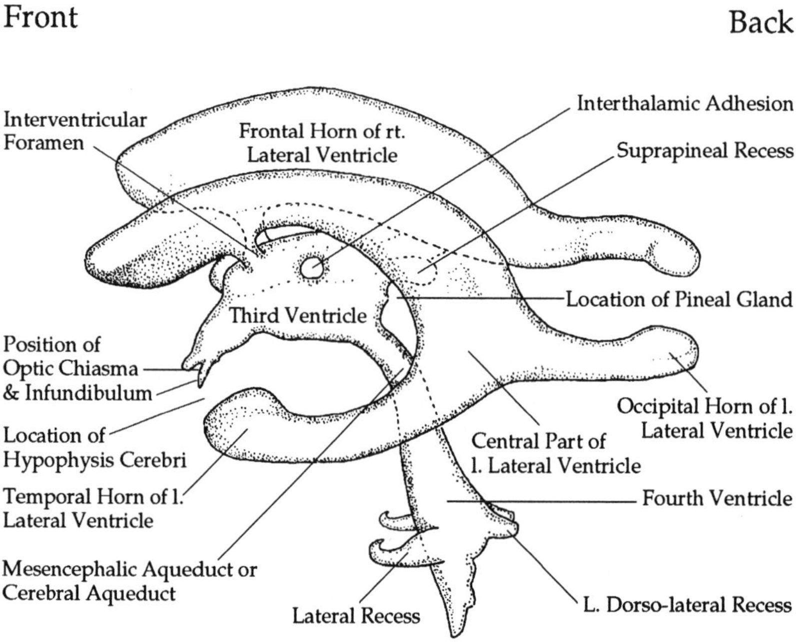

Front   Back

Figure 18: **Cerebral Ventricles**

The hollow parts of the brain (ventricles) as they would appear if filled with some solid substance, (*eg.* a resin) and then "cleaned" by digesting away the soft parts. Viewed from the left and slightly above. The interventricular foramen is the sole communication between the lateral and third ventricles, (one lateral each side).

Sources: Clemente, *Gray's Anatomy*, figs. 11-107, 11-158, 11-159; Gardner, *Fundamentals of Neurology*, fig. 7-12.

thence into the lungs, and so back again into the left ventricle [of the heart], and so on; part is carried towards the head through the carotid arteries; part goes downward towards all the viscera of the body. All of this is to the end that the purer blood or animal spirit may be formed, and thus the red blood; namely, that material things united with spiritual things may effectuate their living a unanimous life. 1748, Feb. 18.

315. From *the Spiritual Diary* No. 914:

I was told that such is the representative of the infundibulum of the brain, the nature of which is evident from its description: namely, that it receives spirits resolved from the blood, and besprinkled on the way with a suitable serum lest they exhale through the pores. They are then carried off through very many paths into the large ventricles, and thence through their own foramen under the pineal gland to the third cleft or ventricle, and from there to the infundibulum and so to the pituitary gland. There they are separated, and by determinate paths they are carried down through their fibres into the ventricles, and then through the infundibulum to the blood, that they may vivify the dry and lifeless blood in the extremities of the sinuses. After this they are born along to the chyle, fresh from the body, and being conjoined therewith in the heart, thus vivify the mass of the blood in the heart. All this, together with the process so tedious to describe, was said by angels to other angels in a moment, almost in a second.

316. In thinking about SD 914 we need to understand "spirits resolved from the blood [globules]" and "new spirituous essences." In those days, when proper chemistry was in its infancy and serious scientists could postulate a substance of negative weight (phlogiston), some general term for the mysterious effects of unstable agents was needed: they seemed to evaporate like alcohol or spirits of wine. They certainly disappeared; the chemists could not get hold of them; they could not even condense them as they could spirits of wine. What was more natural than to call them spirituous essences, or just spirits? We still use the word in a variety of ways; there are thirteen meanings for the noun "spirit" given in *The Concise Oxford Dictionary*. One of these is "animating principle." This is probably the one most frequently applied in discussions of this kind, but it may not always be correct and the chemical meaning should also be remembered. All these considerations apply also to stable substances which eluded chemical recognition either because they were present in amounts too small to be detected by the methods then available, or because it was not known how to test for them. The vitamins provide examples of both. For the present we will equate "spirits" and "spirituous essences" to the elusive chemicals. "Lest they exhale through the pores" strongly suggests some kinds of evanescent chemical substance. "Animal spirit" carries a different aura (see below, No. 320).

317. When one allows for the impossibility of expressing present knowledge in 18th century terms, one sees that "besprinkled on the way with a suitable serum" describes clearly enough what the neurons do with at least some of the hormones they produce. For example, vasopressin, mentioned above (No. 309) is combined with a much larger molecule of protein and sugar together, from which it is released when it arrives in the blood stream. Similar molecules proper to the blood then protect it until it reaches its spheres of use in the kidney and elsewhere.

318. The phrase "dry and lifeless blood" is an example of semantic difficulty. The meaning is fairly obvious though blood is not dry and it is no less living than arterial blood. As far as we can tell, it is just ordinary venous blood; and the blood sinuses are to the head what the large veins are to the body. Since the hormones in the blood stimulate so many organs to their proper activity, it is easy to conceive of the blood as life-giving in a restricted sense when it has its complement of hormones. In this sense, the hormones may be said to vivify it.

319. At this point it is worth enduring a little repetition to see how closely the account in SD 914 (slightly rearranged) follows a modern account. The two can be interlined as follows.

S.D. 914:   (The) spirits
Modern: a variety of important substances (unknown in earlier times)

S.D. 914:   resolved from the blood globules
Modern: pass by diffusion out of the blood stream

S.D. 914:   come to the cortical beginnings
Modern: to the neurons where they are

S.D. 914:   and being there conjoined with new spiritous essences
Modern: built into minute quantities of very active chemicals (hormones)

S.D. 914:   are carried down through their fibres
Modern: which pass down the axons

(S.D. 914:   into the ventricles)
(Modern: not confirmed)

S.D. 914:   and then through the infundibulum
Modern: which are in the infundibulum

S.D. 914:   and so into the pituitary gland
Modern: to the pituitary gland

S.D. 914:   There they are separated and
Modern: Some pass directly into the blood, some control the release of other hormones

S.D. 914:   by determinate paths they are carried…to the sinuses
Modern: The hormones travel with the blood through the veins to the sinuses

The rest is as we think of it today.

"Animal spirit" has a wider meaning than hormones

320. In No. 316 just above, we have interpreted "spirits resolved from the blood" and "new spirituous essences" as elusive chemicals. Alden, however, seems to equate them to "animal spirits," which, he says, are "agents of the soul in the body which provide and sustain life in the body" (notes for the SSA Brain Research Project (Brown, 1979, p. 356)). Animal spirits would thus differ from hormones, each of which has a more limited function. Nevertheless the numerous processes that go on in the body which are much more complicated and interwoven than could have been imagined a short time ago, have but one objective: "namely, that material things united with spiritual things may effectuate their living a unanimous life" (SD 831). It seems reasonable to call this life "animal spirit" or "purer blood," for it appears to be the result of a general influx from the spiritual world, which influx we share with animals. It is true that SD 831 does not define "animal spirit" as the "unanimous life" of "material things united with spiritual things." But in searching for a term to cover this wide general living force or unanimous life from the influx of spiritual things into material things, we could hardly find a better expression than "animal spirit," that is to say, the spiritual life of the body as distinct from the life of the soul. As it is also called a purer blood we must not expect to find one substance to answer to it. Rather it is the integral of many activities; an entity which comes into existence when all the material parts work harmoniously, and vanishes when they fall apart (unlike the soul of man). In *The Cerebrum* (See footnote 18) we have an indication of a difference between animal spirit and spirituous juice. Various fluids are put in order after the soul "in respect to perfection and presence," namely "the animal spirit; then the spirituous juice; then the red blood; afterwards the nervous juice; and lastly the grosser pituita" (Swedenborg, 1938, no. 650). Clearly there is great scope for studies of this kind, but for the present it is hoped that the small samples of the *Spiritual Diary* and *The Cerebrum* that have been looked at will provide a sufficient background for the more important study of the *Arcana* to which we now return.

The representation of the infundibulum by things shown to Swedenborg constitutes an important revelation which is full of meaning

321. The infundibulum, together with the hypophysis cerebri into which it flows, is a supremely important link between the brain and the body (Nos. 308-310). These are the organs through which the brain produces a body in which it can exercise its uses. These organs are therefore a link between the spiritual matters of the brain and the corresponding ultimates of the body. They are a means whereby the brain is ultimated in the body so that later uses can come about on the same ultimate plane. Moreover the spiritual forces in the individual which are received in the brain (in part unconsciously), make for themselves ultimate forms in the body. This process is an image of the way heaven makes for itself a church on earth; or, rather, the way the Lord produces the human race. Secrets of creation here await the wiser Church to come. Thus the infundibulum is of such fundamental importance that its description in the Writings merited the utmost angelic wisdom. Probably such wisdom could be expressed and communicated only in pictorial forms, although we must not fall into the error of imagining them as mere pictures. It is to be understood that they are appearances and that such appearances are more real than things we see in this world (HH 175). A description of appearances is necessarily less adequate than the experience of seeing them, but we can at least supplement the words by a knowledge of representatives. The things that were seen are described as follows.

322. From *Arcana Coelestia*, No. 4050:

A certain face was first seen by me above an azure window, but presently withdrew itself within. I then saw a little star near the region of the left eye, and afterwards a number of ruddy little stars that sparkled with white. Afterwards I saw the walls of a house, but no roof, the walls being only on the left side; and lastly I saw as it were the starry heaven. As these things were seen in a place where there were evil ones, I supposed that some hideous sight would be presented to me. But the wall soon disappeared, together with the starry heaven, and then there appeared a well, out of which came forth as it were a great white cloud or vapour; and something also seemed to be pumped up out of the well. I asked what these things signified and represented, and was told that it was a representation of the infundibulum in the brain above which is the brain itself, which was signified by the starry heaven; and that what was next seen was that vessel, signified by the well and called the infundibulum; and that the cloud or vapor rising from it was the lymph that passes through and is pumped out of it; and that this lymph is of two kinds, namely, that mixed with the animal spirits, which is among the useful lymphs; and that mixed with serosities, which is among the excrementitious lymphs. I was next shown the quality of those who belong to this province, but only those of the viler sort, whom I also saw running about hither and thither, applying themselves to those whom they saw, paying attention to everything, and reporting to others what they heard; and being prone to suspicions, impatient and restless, in close resemblance to the lymph which is therein, and is born hither and thither; their reasonings being the fluids there which they represent. But these are of the middle sort. But those who have relation to the excrementitious lymphs, are those who drag down spiritual truths to natural things, and there defile them, as for example, those who when they hear anything about conjugial love apply it to whoredoms and adulteries, and thus drag down the things of conjugial love to these; and the same with everything else. These appeared in front at some distance to the right. But those who are of the good sort are similar to those described just above in no. 4049.

323. A few general remarks may now be inserted before the details of representation are considered. First, it is important to notice that the pituitary gland (i.e., hypophysis cerebri) is not mentioned here, although it is included in the parallel passage in the *Spiritual Diary*. Differences between the *Spiritual Diary* and *Arcana Coelestia* provoke thought. They show, possibly, that Swedenborg was better informed when *Arcana Coelestia* was written, but more especially that Providence was more concerned over the choice of words that were soon to be published. This is not to say that Providence was not over the writing of the *Diary*, but that there may well have been more of permission for Swedenborg to express himself freely. In the passages now under discussion we note a very important difference. AC 4050 is almost certainly an account of the same experience as that detailed in SD 913 and 914. In the SD account we have "to the infundibulum and so to the pituitary gland." The pituitary gland is very important but it is omitted from AC 4050. Why? Perhaps because of its association at that time with phlegm which association was completely erroneous and would not have the correct correspondences. Angelic influences would therefore bias Swedenborg against the use of a word which would suggest phlegm to his contemporaries. It is not, however, merely a matter of terms. Another, and quite important reason resulting from the anatomy as we now know it to be, is that nerves of the brain tissue reach right down into parts of the hypophysis cerebri. Also, the glandular tissue belonging to other parts of the hypophysis extends upwards over the outer layers of the infundibulum. There is, therefore, much to be said for the use of a single name and it is clear that both structures could be included in the term "infundibulum" as used in AC 4050. In the discussions below both organs will be considered as one unit.

324. We next consider a peculiarity of AC 4050. As Alden pointed out, it seems strange that a bodily organ and its fluids should be the subject of such a vision. Again following Alden, we observe that

Swedenborg "asked" and "was told that it was a representation of the infundibulum." According to SD 914, it would appear that he was told this by angels. In this connection one cannot avoid recalling AE 1061 where an angel explains seven heads of the scarlet beast as meaning seven mountains and seven kings. This is described as "an explanation in a sense merely natural in which the spiritual sense lies concealed which is to be unfolded." The reason for such an explanation was that "the Word in the letter must be natural, in every particular of which the spiritual sense must be stored up." AC 4050 seems similar, for what is more natural than the infundibulum, the brain, and their fluids? This being so, it becomes a useful exercise to find out whether a spiritual sense can be deduced from the particulars given. As we are writing, printing, and reading, it will still be a natural sense, but perhaps it can be what is called in AE 1061 "the natural sense from the spiritual." It is a simple task to collect correspondences from Swedenborg's Index to the Arcana, though a little selection has to be exercised. We obtain the following result:

Object seen	**Signification(s) Correspondence(c) Representation(r) What is denoted (d)**
Face	Interiors (c,d,s) with the Ancients and Angels
Face (of Jehovah)	The Lord; whatsoever is of the Divine; mercy, peace, every good (d,s)
Azure (=blue)	External of good of celestial kingdom
	Internal good of spiritual kingdom (s)
Window	Intellectual or internal sight (d,s)
Stars	goods and truths (s) (or opposite); cognitions of good and truth; cognitions of faith; therefore the spiritual (d)

Left hand	good of spiritual love (d); parts on the left relate to truth by means of what is good
Eye (sight)	Understanding and truths (c); Sight of left eye c. to truths of faith
Red	Good of love (d)
White	Truth (r); truth of faith (d)
Bright	Truth (d) because from light of heaven
Wall	Truths of faith which defend (d)
Wall of house (= a portion)	Interior or middle things (d)
Roof	Inmost (d); (same as head)
Heaven (sky?)	The angelic heaven & the internal man (d)
Well	Word as to literal sense (d); falsities; doctrine; truth less pure (d)
White	Truth of faith (d)
Thin bright white clouds	When angels' thought descends to lower planes (r)

325. We are now in a position to see how the narrative may signify spiritual things and what those things may be. The withdrawal of the face from the window suggests the departure of interior things from the intellect. Previously, the face above the window must have represented the interiors within the good of the celestial heaven because it was a blue window. We wonder why it was a certain face. Whose? Perhaps it was even the Lord. The stars near the left eye show that, although interior things had withdrawn, truth was nevertheless still from good. This is confirmed by the red and white. The appearance of walls with no roof indicates again the absence (or perhaps remoteness) of inmost things from the intermediates. This is similar to the withdrawal of the face; possibly a correspondence of that withdrawal at this next lower, i.e., intermediate level. As before, these walls being only on the left suggest a continuing trend towards truth and away from good. The starry heaven that was seen last is prefaced by "as it were," as though it were a mere substitute for the genuine angelic heaven. The wall (now only one) and the heaven disappeared presumably because of the presence of evil ones. Clearly the trend away from internal good is continuing. However, instead of the expected hideous sight there appeared a well with a bright white cloud. At this point, therefore, the trend toward evil is halted by the Word in which angelic thoughts are presented at the lower level acceptable to men. Something other than the bright white cloud is pumped out of the well. The later parts of AC 4050 suggest that it may have been something not very nice.

326. This account can now be put together into a sort of historical internal sense which agrees with other parts of the Writings. We are reminded of the decline of the Churches, and it will be clear that the particulars of the vision represent the various states of that decline as described in more detail elsewhere. Thus when the MAC lost internal perception there were still means by which truths could be procured from the remnants of good (the ruddy stars were little ones). Then the intermediate truths lacked good (walls on left only) and the inmost goods (the roof) were missing. Next, as evil states grew, even apparent truths from good (the "as it were" starry heaven) disappeared. The disastrous result of this (a hideous sight) was anticipated, i.e. prevented, by the giving of the Word (a well). The literal sense of the Word is as a cloud, which can be truth accommodated to reception (with some) or obscurity (with others). Since it is a bright white cloud we are led to think that the truth is illuminated from heaven but not very greatly, for it is said "as it were."

327. It is noteworthy that both a well and clouds denote the literal sense of the Word, but in this case it was a bright cloud. In the *Spiritual Diary* (SD 913) it is said to be like smoke which is hardly seen. These things agree with experience, for there are different levels of the literal sense, some more, some less remote from the spiritual sense.

328. Since bright clouds appear when angelic thoughts descend to a lower level (AC 6614, 6615), we can see that there is here a representation of the flowing of angelic ideas through the ultimates of the Word. The bright cloud seems to come forth of itself, for such is the case when the Word is read by the innocent. That which is pumped up out of the well could be the laborious thought that we sometimes engage in when evils and falsities impede a clear understanding.

The pictorial representation of the infundibulum encourages further contemplation of the importance of this organ and of its spiritual counterparts

329. The above interpretation of the things that represented the infundibulum and the brain begins, so it seems, a second part of the account. An earlier passage (AC 3889) describes also an anatomical representation when the angels formed a similitude of the heart and lungs by following freely the flow of heaven. The reasons why anatomical details are given such prominence in the Writings could be: (1) because Swedenborg was specially interested in anatomy and the things seen in heaven depend on the state of the observer (HH 156), (2) because heaven is in the human form, (3) because the human form partakes, to some extent, of the Divine. These three reasons, however, are only part of the truth. The whole truth is that it is the Lord's human that is Divine and that from it descends Love-and-Wisdom which carries every truly human quality in its bosom. Hence there come into existence very many things, for example mutual love, mutual service, love of the community, and an indefinitely great number of activities of use at many different levels, all expressing nearly or remotely a love to the Lord. The interplay of all these uses cannot easily be grasped by human thought, and it can be seen only in a limited degree by angelic thought. But something approaching a natural understanding of it can be obtained from its correspondence with the human body (and the bodies of animals). Indeed these bodies exist only because they are in correspondence with those transcendent realities. This seems to be a valid general conclusion from the several examples of angels being involved in representations of parts of the body. What they were really representing were spiritual entities to which those parts of the body correspond. When the angels presented semblances of the heart and lungs and their union, they did so in order that Swedenborg might know how the case is with the correspondences (AC 3889). These things were done and the records written for our instruction. We ought, therefore, to see whether the Lord will permit us to contemplate the vast riches of revealed spiritual knowledge with the aid of anatomy and related sciences. So we come to reconsider the infundibulum with the help of the representations.

330. We have already seen that several details of the vision denote the withdrawal or removal of interior things. This includes the starry heaven which signified the brain itself. This obviously represents the withdrawing of brain-function from the infundibulum, although it still remains a part of the brain. Thus, unlike the cerebral cortex, it does not "think" or relay messages, or balance opposing influences, or command muscles, or receive sense impressions. The typical electrical impulses that have been observed in the nerves of the infundibulum serve, perhaps, to control the release of hormones into the adjacent blood systems. (However, a direct relationship has not been observed.) So instead of typical brain function the infundibulum is busy making or conducting a variety of hormones for the chemical control of the body below. It is even responsible for producing the

body, since somatotropin, which controls growth rate in the young, is one of the most important secretions of the gland. These considerations show the infundibulum as the essential link ensuring the production of a system in ultimates which will correspond to the brain, and hence also to the spiritual entities residing in the brain. In other words, the infundibulum is the means whereby the brain forms the body. It seems likely, therefore, that it embodies the means used by the Lord through heaven for the formation of man in the sphere of nature.

331. We notice next that the well signified that vessel "called the infundibulum" and we have found that a well signifies the Word. Now that the functions of the infundibulum are known, it is possible to see that these meanings are the same. The Word enabled the highest spiritual things to be represented in the lowest natural objects and actions of the Jewish Church. The production of the letter of the Word was like the production of the body through the infundibulum. So spiritually there was heaven, like the brain, and beneath it the world of spirits through whose less heavenly offices the ultimates could be suitably arranged, and finally even the disorderly spirits who corresponded to "excrementitious lymphs." This, of course, was not a "once for all" production. Like the human race it is on-going. Whenever the Word is read, the spiritual infundibulum supplies spiritual hormones to strengthen the spiritual-natural man on the earth who must continue to fight his battles in ultimates, "as of himself."

332. From the well which represented the infundibulum, a cloud arose. This was the lymph "that passes through and is pumped out." In attempting to relate this account to modern concepts it is suggested, as before, that a lymph could be some constituent of a fluid. This is the only way that so many different lymphs could be together. The things which pass through the infundibulum and are pumped out are hormones. (Blood passes through, of course, but so it does through all other organs.) Since only hormones are pumped out, the lymphs cannot be other than hormones of the hypophysis cerebri. The adjective "excrementitious" can be interpreted according to usage in the Writings, which usage is connected with adultery and other foul evils. Then an excrementitious lymph would be a hormone that stimulates sexual activity, for hormones have no concern for right or wrong. They run "about hither and thither" in the blood stream throughout the whole body and stimulate an appetite which can be the ultimate of a most noble and heavenly love; but if this appetite is left to the hormonal influence alone it is foul, destructive and deceitful, like the spirits who have relation to the excrementitious lymphs.

333. The spirits related to excrementitious lymphs are not actually said to be deceitful, but the defiling of the truths of conjugial love with whoredoms and adulteries is a form of deceit. It so often includes a suggestion that the appetite stimulated by the hormone is conjugial love whereas it is only love of the sex (e.g., see CL 48). Sometimes it is even only self love. How often when a man says, "I love you" does it really mean "I want you to love me"?

334. The fact that Swedenborg's contemporaries, and perhaps Swedenborg himself, thought of the infundibulum as an organ of excretion has really nothing to do with the case. In His Providence, the Lord ensured that truth descended into the best terms then available. He also provided a multitude of clues by which coming generations would be able to follow His lead to an ever clearer understanding.

CHAPTER XIII

THE BRAIN—PART 3: DECUSSATIONS

Some of the nerves that descend from the brain cross over on their way to the body

335. In the foregoing two chapters we have made a slight acquaintance with the anatomy and functions of some few parts of the brain. A little more knowledge will enable us to think from correspondences about good and truth and the way these are represented by the right and left sides of the body and brain. Although we are given correspondences of parts of the body on the right and on the left, the chief concern is with the brain and nerves since life descends to the body through them. Some parts of the brain are more obviously separated into right and left halves than are others. In particular, the cerebrum is very deeply divided and the cerebellum has well marked right and left sides. The brain-stem, to which these parts are joined, is not so clearly divided. The cerebrum and cerebellum both have bands of fibres which connect one side to the other, besides the fibres that run down towards the body. The fibres that run down into the body are often in bands that are decussate (which means X-shaped or intersecting). In anatomy, the word is used to describe the crossing-over of nerves or tracts of nerves from one side of the head or body to the other at a lower level. The most outstanding example is entitled "The Decussation of the Pyramids" and has no reference whatsoever to Egypt! (The pyramids are tracts of nerves in the medulla oblongata. They are wider at one end than at the other and this is the only way they resemble pyramids.) See Figure 19 which shows the decussation of the pyramids.

336. The decussation of the pyramids is responsible for the commonly observed fact that injuries to one side of the head often cause

FIGURE 19

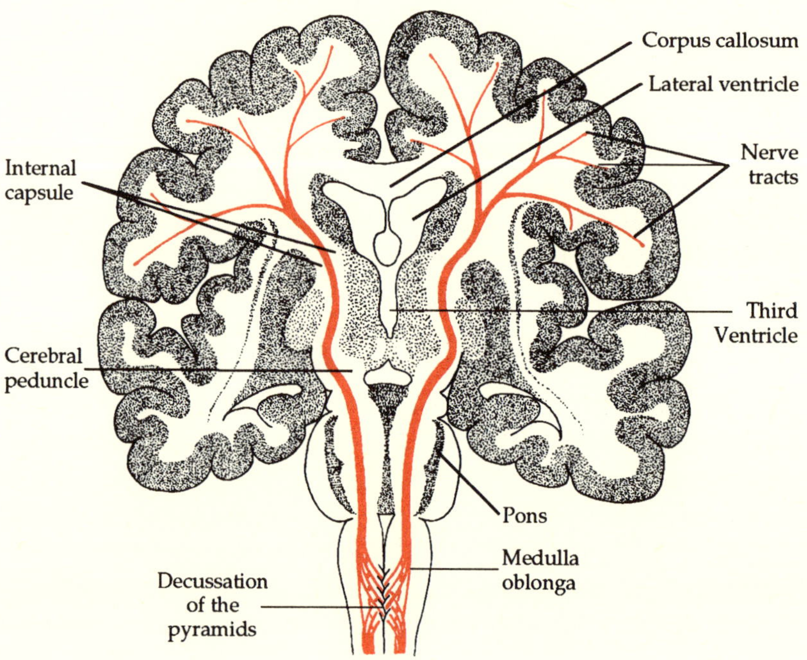

Figure 19: **The Decussations**

Decussation of the Pyramids. Scheme of the brain in coronal section at the level of the brain stem and major cortex, showing the crossover of nerve fibres in the medulla oblongata. The cut passes from the front backwards. Hence the intercerebral cleft can be seen. The section is not quite horizontal, being higher at the front. The fibers descend from the cortex through the internal capsule, the cerebral peduncle, and the pons. The pyramids are medullary structures composed of bundles of these fibers, of which the majority (70-90%) cross over before the junction of the medulla and spinal cord.

Sources: Gardner, *Fundamentals of Neurology*, figs. 10-6, 7-15;
Anthony and Kolthoff, *Textbook of Anatomy and Physiology*, fig. 8-22; Clemente, *Gray's Anatomy*, Classic Collectors Edition, fig. 369.

paralysis on the opposite side of the body. The connections have been known for a considerable time. Swedenborg refers to them in the *Spiritual Diary*.

An observation on decussation was made with the help of spirits

337. We read in the *Spiritual Diary*, "The contents of the left side of the brain correspond to the right portion of the body." We also read that when spirits acted on the left side of the brain Swedenborg felt sensations as if from the right nostril and the palm of the right hand (SD 1666). This is specially interesting because, although nerves to the arms and hands pass through the medulla oblongata where they usually cross over, the nerves to the nostrils (not the olfactory nerves) follow a direct route through the base of the skull. The neuron bodies of the sensory nerves are outside the brain and they send their axons (see No. 271) to groups of other neurons in the brain. These groups have fibres that connect them to the cerebral cortex (where consciousness is thought to reside). The connection is usually with the cerebral hemisphere of the opposite side, that is to say, the connecting fibres within the brain are decussate. The mapping of nerve tracts within the brain to produce this kind of information is comparatively recent.

As Swedenborg also moved his hand "from some unknown cause," we presume that both afferent and efferent nerve tracts, or rather their terminals in the brain, were activated. Although there are relays in the spinal cord and plexuses where nerve tracts branch and rejoin, none of these structures causes a crossing over from left to right.

A brief entry in the Spiritual Diary may lead to a misunderstanding of the correspondences

338. From AC 5725 we learn that an inundation of lusts "belongs to the will part, and is on the right side of the brain; but that of falsities belongs to the intellectual part and is on the left side of the brain." We also find, "the left side of the brain corresponds to rational or intellectual things, but the right to the affections or things of the will" (AC 3884). Thus, clearly, the right side of the brain is the home not, be it noted, of the will per se but of "things of the will" or affections. It will be well to adopt this as a general but quite firm statement of primary importance.

339. It had been thought (Berridge, 1981, p. 35; Worcester, 1889, p. 422) that the entry in SD 1667 (quoted below) is at variance with this teaching from the *Arcana (quoted just above)*. It is necessary to examine the supposed discrepancy. Spirits from Jupiter said that the intellectual principle was on the right side of the cerebrum, etc. This is not stating that the right cerebral hemisphere is the home of the intellect, but merely that there is an "intellectual principle" there. As will be seen below (No. 352), principles of good, which are dominant in the right hemisphere, do not preclude truth and understanding. Indeed it is made clear in many places that celestial angels understand truth very well. However, the entry in the *Spiritual Diary* (n. 1667) continues, "[From this it is to be inferred] that the right part of the brain is the seat of the intellectuals, and the left of affections." The square brackets indicate a suggestion by the translator which gives the impression that Swedenborg was still in the process of learning. An earlier passage (SD 1027) is similar, but includes the words, "I was told." One may thus incline to the belief that these ideas were tentatively held, but further study will show that it is not really necessary to adopt such an opinion. Indeed, these sources differ only when we misunderstand them by instituting a divorce between intellect and will or between faith and love.

Decussation is accepted in the Spiritual Diary but ignored in parts of Arcana Coelestia

340. The passages in the SD considered just above include a reference to a decussation of the optic nerves and suggest from that a similar crossing over between the brain and the whole body. The eyes, however, constitute a special case which will be considered in a later chapter (Nos. 368 and 369). For the present we note that a general decussation is assumed or deduced in SD but it appears to be denied in parts of AC. We have noted above that the right side of the brain corresponds to things of the will and we find (AC 9556) that "by the things which are in the right side of the body are signified goods" (which are of course things of the will). Also "those things which are on the right side of the man correspond to celestial good" (AC 9511) which must be of love or the will. Thus a crossing over between the brain and the rest of the body including the eyes is envisaged in the *Diary* but not in these parts of AC. In AC 1270, however, a decussation is clearly indicated, for antediluvian spirits were allowed to flow into the right side of Swedenborg's head, "and from the right side of the head into the left side of the chest." We have, therefore, some passages for, and some against decussation; but we know that it does occur and it is instructive to find out why it is sometimes ignored. To do this we consider first what some other parts of the Writings say about the right and left hands and sides of the body.

The correspondences of right and left sides are complex

341. For the sake of clarity we begin with the right side only and select simple statements. One such statement is that the right hand or right side denotes good. For example, "by the right is signified good" (AE 600:8). Similarly, the right hand signifies everything pertaining to the will and affection thence. Even the right eye has connections with good, as explained here (AE 600:8), although the eye signifies everything pertaining to the understanding and thought therefrom. However, if good is to be anything, it requires truth as a means to its ends; thus it produces, or finds, or gives life to truth. It follows that the good which is denoted by the right or the right hand is good from which is truth, as follows: "All those things in man which belong to his right side have reference to good from which is truth" (AE 1120:2, similarly AC 9604, 10061).

342. These meanings are in obvious agreement, but as one continues the study, apparent discrepancies occur. For example, we read in AE 336:6 that the right hand signifies the truth of good (rather than good from which is truth). Many other examples are given in AE 600 where one may find also the explanations that are necessary to harmonize truths that look different at first sight. But in spite of the explanations some readers might feel that the significations are distressingly different. We find, for example, that only just over half the references given in AE 600 are in obvious agreement with what we have already learned, i.e., that the right signifies good from which is truth.

343. Some of the other meanings of right are as follows:

1. the south in the spiritual world (from which other meanings are derived),
2. the clear light of truth from good (AE 600:9) (this is notable because the left often corresponds to truth from good),
3. truth in light,
4. the good of charity and of faith therefrom (rather than good of charity from which is faith),
5. truth of the understanding (because in this case it is "the eye of his right side"), and
6. Divine Truth in light, intelligence, and thence power.

344. In AE 600 there is clearly a majority of references where right signifies good, usually good from which is truth. But correspondences and the significations of passages in the Word may not be counted in natural numbers, nor balanced one against another for they form a harmonious whole. So if disagreements appear, though they be only apparent and few in number they are like discords in music. One cannot enjoy them until they are resolved.

345. It will be clear from a perusal of the whole of AE 600 that each individual item that appears at first to be in discord is reconciled with the main theme by means of suitable related truths; thereby, the rational mind can assent to them and enjoy a great increase in enlightenment. However, although the rational might be convinced, the mind as a whole might still not see the subject clearly and be able to confirm it to the extent of faith. Such a mental state has been mentioned in DLW 405, where confirmation is given by thinking from correspondences; in that case, correspondences with the heart and lungs. Here we will make bold to consider a few more details about the central nervous system in the hope of enabling the mind to see the spiritual teaching more clearly.

The anatomy of the brain illustrates the relationship between the right and left sides and shows how complex it is

346. A little information about brain cells, especially neurons, has already been given (no. 271). To this we now add the following. The neuron bodies are massed on the outer surfaces of the cerebrum and cerebellum forming the grey (or cineritious) matter, and most of the axons and dendrites are within, forming the white matter. This, however, is only a very general description. There are, in addition, various other neurons that are organized into groups or nuclei with specific purposes, often connected with the control of the body. These groups are also part of the grey matter. Between them is white matter consisting of their own very numerous fibres, forming a communication system between different nuclei and between nuclei and the cortex. There are also regions where grey and white matter, that is, neuron bodies and connecting fibres, are mixed in what seems to be a random fashion. The complexity of the system has already been mentioned but it is especially noticeable when the decussations are studied.

347. If the student of anatomy wishes to know whether the right eye communicates with the left hemisphere as indicated in SD 1667, or with the right as deducible from AC 9511 and 9556, he finds that it communicates with both (see no. 369). If he turns his attention to the

ear he finds at least four sites in the brain where nerve impulses may be passed on to either or both sides. When he comes to consider the body, the right hand, for example, he finds a massive crossing-over of nerves from the left cerebrum to the right side of the spinal chord (the decussation of the pyramids). But when he looks at the detail he finds that in most individuals more than thirty percent of the nerves do not cross over (but in some cases the proportion may sink to ten percent). Still he has problems because, throughout the spinal chord itself there are bands of nerves which provide communication between opposite sides. Nor has he finished yet, because in the brain there are, as already mentioned, many regions consisting of a more diffusely ordered mixture of white and grey matter having the appearance of a network. It is hence called the reticular formation. This formation is closely associated functionally with the more distinct parts and its interest for us at present is that within it the nerve pathways form many junctions. These include ascending (i.e., towards the cerebrum) and descending components, some of which cross over to the opposite side (decussate) while others make connections on the same side. The reticular formation receives convergent information from all principal parts of the nervous system and projects directly or indirectly back to all these regions including the cerebral cortex.

348. There are also various other nerve tracts in the brain which connect one side with the other. An example is the *Corpus Callosum* which connects the cerebral hemispheres, although this is not a decussation but a connection at the same level.

349. These facts of anatomy indicate that what happens on one side of the brain can usually only be partially separated from the other side. Though one side may be dominant, it is still one brain, for a vast number of parts of one hemisphere are connected to parts of the other. So many parts of one hemisphere are in mediate or immediate connection with one another that it is difficult to think that any significant portion of the brain cannot be reciprocally connected with a part on the opposite side. Thus, although what is on the right is certainly

different and distinguishable from what is on the left, the connections are so multifarious that an activation of parts on the right may in some cases lead to greater activity on the left, and what is really right may seem like left. The situation is not actually confused; the brain works wonderfully well, but it is so complex that the student may become confused.

The unity in diversity of the brain illustrates the marriage of love and wisdom or of good and truth

350. The anatomy of the brain suggests by correspondence that there is no type or kind of genuine good which cannot be reciprocally connected with a suitable truth; nor can such good avoid activating truth. The anatomical facts thus emphasize the closeness of the union between truth and good. We have seen how nerve impulses occurring on one side of the body or brain may be radiated to the other side, or perhaps even pass from side to side and back on their journeys between various centres of the brain, and on their way from the brain to the body. Retaining the simple notion of the right side being good and the left truth we can now see how, in the living soul, and in Heaven or the Grand Man, good or love radiates itself to innumerable connected truths. These truths, in turn, can reflect back into good at the same or at a lower or even a higher level. We can also see that all the living truths and goods are more or less directly connected with each other and organized into a whole by means of these connections. So it is that whether you start from good, (the right) or truth (the left), the whole man is activated as to both. So it is also that a rigid mechanical division between good and truth is no more possible than a complete dissociation of each side of the body-brain unit.

The apparently variable correspondences of right and left reflect the true situation

351. Looking back upon the significations of right and left mentioned earlier, one may perhaps feel that their apparently contradic-

tory nature is dispelled by their true internal harmony, so much so that the following thoughts occur: How could any man of Swedenborg's standing have had the audacity to present such an apparently variable and inconsistent interpretation had he not been instructed by the Lord by means of experience? And further, how privileged we are now to have confirmation by scientific knowledge. We can now see that it is only the apparently inconsistent interpretation that corresponds to the facts of anatomy.

Correspondences of the brain suggest four angelic categories related to two ways of receiving good and two ways of receiving truth

352. Having studied the correspondences so far we now return to the Writings and find the following in AC 4052:

> that those [in the Grand Man] who are in the first principles or beginnings of good have relation to those things in the brain that are the beginnings and are called the glands or cortical substances; whereas they who are in the first principles of truth relate to those things in the brains that flow out from these beginnings and are called fibres; and yet with this difference— that those who correspond to the right side of the brain are those who are in the will of good and thereby in the will of truth; whereas those who correspond to the left side of the brain are those who are in the understanding of good and truth and thereby in the affection of them.

Since there are cortical substances and fibres on both sides, we have four categories. Two of them are easy to understand, namely:

1. cortical substances on the right corresponding to first principles of good and the will of good, and
2. fibres on the left corresponding to first principles of truth and the understanding of good and truth.

The other two are less obvious, namely:

3. cortical substances on the left, corresponding to the first principles of good and the understanding of good and truth, and
4. fibres on the right corresponding to first principles of truth and the will of good.

It follows that first principles of good do not preclude understanding, and first principles of truth do not preclude will. This must be so even though spiritual space is non-Euclidean and even if ordinary mathematics do not apply in heaven.

The anatomy of the brain shows that angels who are in good rely on those in truths for confirmation

353. It is worth emphasizing here that every fibre is a living outgrowth from a neuron body. The cortical substances are either neuron bodies or those parts where the cell bodies of the neurons are most numerous, but as "glands" are also mentioned we tend to equate them with individual cell bodies of neurons. This, of course, is all in agreement with the clear teaching that there is really no such thing as genuine truth without good; indeed it indicates that it is the good which produces the truth as a means of communication. It would also seem reasonable to believe that no category in which truth or good is predominant is actually exclusive. But this belief is unimportant because we are considering the Grand Man, or Heaven, and there is full communication between all in Heaven. This is reflected in the anatomy of the brain, in which it appears that all neurons receive communicating fibres from other neurons (see above). If translated into spiritual terms, this means that all those who are in the first principles of good are in communication with each other through those in the first principles of truth.

354. These considerations also show that the distinction between right and left and between good and truth is not a simple exclusive one; though they are distinct, yet they are one.

355. For a final word we read from DLW:

The right of these [various organs] relate to the goodness belonging to truth, and the left to the truth belonging to goodness; or what is the same, the right has relation to the goodness of love from which comes the truth of wisdom, and the left to the truth of wisdom which comes from the good of love. And because the union of good and truth is reciprocal, and by means of that union they become as it were one, the effect in man is that these pairs act together and jointly in their functions, movements, and sensations. (DLW 384)

CHAPTER XIV

CORRESPONDENCES OF THE EYE

356. Sight is such a remarkable faculty that whole volumes would
be needed to do it justice. The more one learns about it, the better one
sees how well it corresponds to the understanding. Knowing, understanding, and being wise are such a large part of life that we are not
surprised to find that eighty percent of all learning involves the organs
that correspond to the understanding. This is among the many things
that we have been told in Dr. Allen's papers on "Sight, the Visual
Process and Doctrine" (*The New Philosophy*, 1981, pp. 26-35 and 1982,
pp. 138-147. See also 1980, pp. 72-74.). These papers have been included as an appendix by the kind permission of Dr. Allen. The reader is
urged to study them. He will be amazed, and delighted by the wide
extent of the correspondences presented, including those parts of the
brain concerned with sight. Between those contributions and this one
there is no significant overlap. Neither is there any disagreement. It is
my hope that they may be considered complementary.

Correspondences of sight or the eye are specially beautiful

357. Some of the most delightful and joyous passages of the Writings are devoted to descriptions of the correspondences of the eye. In
order to appreciate their quality one needs to read them in full, but for
our present purposes a few brief extracts must suffice. The province of
the eye includes the heaven of little children where there are delightful
gardens (HH 332, 333, and 337). Those who relate to the coats of the
eye communicate with the heavens where truths and goods are represented by a paradise and a city. There are, as Dr. Allen also points out,
three coats of the eye. The outer coat is continuous with the dura
mater, the spirits of which are in relative obscurity (see Nos. 278-282

above) but, as we see, they communicate with the heavens. Those who belong to the provinces of the inner layers will obviously communicate more nearly. Such may have been the person mentioned in AC 4412, who presented beautiful and delightful representatives related to the eye. We are told that "the more interior things of the eye have more beautiful and more delightful correspondences" (AC 4411), and also that "the eye, or rather its sight, corresponds primarily to those societies in the other life that are in the paradisiacal regions...where gardens are clearly presented to view" (AC 4528). The regions are representatives of the beauty and pleasantness of angelic discourse in a higher heaven. The lower heaven, where the representatives are, is distinguished into many heavens corresponding to various things in the chambers of the eye (AC 4528). The splendid colours seen in the other life that derive their origin from the truth of intelligence and the good of wisdom belong to the provinces of the eyes (AC 4530). It is instructive to place these statements in perspective by comparing them with what is said about some other senses.

Correspondences of senses other than sight are less delightful

358. Here we consider briefly smell, hearing, and taste. In trying to understand what is said about the sense of smell, it is important to bear in mind that it is related to perception. The scene depicted in relation to those who correspond to the exteriors of the nostrils is not particularly attractive. The societies there need protection by angelic choirs from dull and stupid spirits who are represented by mucus (AC 4627). Nevertheless a comparison of AC 4624 and AC 4627 shows that the persons in this province are in the Grand Man and that, although they are said to correspond to the exteriors of the nostrils (by which one might have understood only the visible part of the nose), they also correspond to the sense of smell.

359. More pleasant things are related of those who correspond to the interiors and internals of the nostrils, such as bright and variegated lights and a warm atmosphere like that of early summer. But they are mentioned only very briefly and one is left with a feeling that the state here is less glorious than that in the province of the eyes. However, the brief description and the resulting feeling may well be due to the state in the province of the nostrils being relatively remote from our present style of thought, since we now use the understanding more and perception less than did the MAC. We may therefore be unwilling to think of the state of those in the province of the interiors of the nostrils as being inferior and merely note that it is different. Correspondences of the sense of smell are examined further in a later chapter.

360. On turning to the sense of hearing we find that we are told but little concerning those who correspond to the external ear. Perhaps this is because they are simple and merely obedient, a state in which there is little life (AC 4656) and therefore little of interest.

361. As matters related to the ear become more internal, the mental sight (or understanding) becomes involved. Certain parts of the *Arcana* (AC 4653-4658) seem to show that as the spiritual relationships of the ear tend towards internal things they tend towards sight. By correspondence, this would mean that if obedience is to have a genuine internal it must be from understanding. This is confirmed in AC 3869 and also where it is said "the things that enter by the sense of hearing enter into the understanding and at the same time into the will; therefore the hearing signifies perception and obedience" (AE 14). The understanding in this context must therefore be that special quality of enlightened understanding which is called perception, as we also read in several places (e.g., AR 87). Such enlightenment is a blessing enjoyed by celestial angels whose wisdom is beyond our grasp. There is, however, plenty for us to learn at the lower level where the province of the ear is constituted by those who are called obediences (AC 4653). A more detailed study will be undertaken in Chapter XV. Meanwhile, it is sufficient to note that in the accounts in AC we find little or no representation of heavenly things although the wisdom itself is clearly of heaven.

362. Concerning taste, we are shown very clearly the devastation that occurs when it is depraved, but comparatively little is said about its correspondence when it is in order; only that it corresponds to the perception and to the affection of spiritual food.

Correspondences of sight are glorious because of the special importance of faith and understanding

363. Faith is referred to in the story of Cain when a mark was set upon him to prevent anyone from killing him. The internal sense of this was that violence should not be done to faith because it was going to become the means of salvation. Faith at that time was acquired through hearing and was probably merely obeyed and not understood by most of those who received it. Yet, in time, understanding was to grow (just as hearing tends to sight as it gets more internal) (See n. 373 below). Thus the understanding also was to be inviolable, as we read in many places where it is pointed out that even with the evil the understanding can be elevated into heavenly light (e.g. DLW 416 et. seq., AC 9399). Here we see the special quality of faith and hence of the understanding where faith lives; it seems fitting that the representation of these things, i.e., the correspondences of sight, should be specially beautiful and glorious. These considerations, however, are only general and introductory. They require the infilling of many particulars to enable one to partake of the joy that an appreciation of the subject can give. Perhaps it will be possible by means of correspondences to provide some of those particulars. We begin by selecting a few points from the anatomy of the sense organs.

The unique quality of the eye is due to its being a part of the brain

364. We read in AC 4407, "The eye is the noblest organ of the face, and communicates more directly with the understanding than the rest of the organs of sense...the sight penetrates to the internal sensory, which is in the brain, by a shorter and more interior way than the speech perceived by the ear." This statement may seem difficult to understand, for the eye is at the front of the head, and that part of the cerebral cortex which deals with vision (presumably "the internal sensory") is at the back. So the eye and its internal sensory are as far apart as they can be. How can they communicate by a shorter way? What is "a more interior way"? An attempt to answer such questions could be made by considering all the anatomical and physiological qualities known to us that make the eye so special. See Figure 20. Obviously there are many of them, but there is one in particular which is the natural centre and cause of the rest. Knowledge that is now available enables us to go a step further than could safely have been indicated in the Writings, for we can now say that the eye is, as it were, the brain itself responding to light. The other senses serve the brain, but they are not themselves the brain. Certainly several parts of the eye are not the brain, but the retina, the optic nerve, and to some extent the vitreous body are more truly represented as a part of the brain than as any other tissue. Thus the eye shares with the brain a more exalted status than any other organ.

The eye is seen to be part of the brain when details of development and anatomy are known

365. Although it is not necessary to justify a view generally accepted by anatomists, some readers may be interested in the evidence, which is as follows:

1. The eye begins as a small pit or dent in the side of the brain of the embryo very early in its development. The pit is soon covered by another layer that forms the lens, and the brain cells lining the pit become the retina which is thus a part of the brain from its first moment of differentiation. The ensuing formation of the optic nerve is merely a lengthening of nerve cells in the retina still within their own milieu of the brain. The development of other sense organs follows a different course and they are linked to the

FIGURE 20

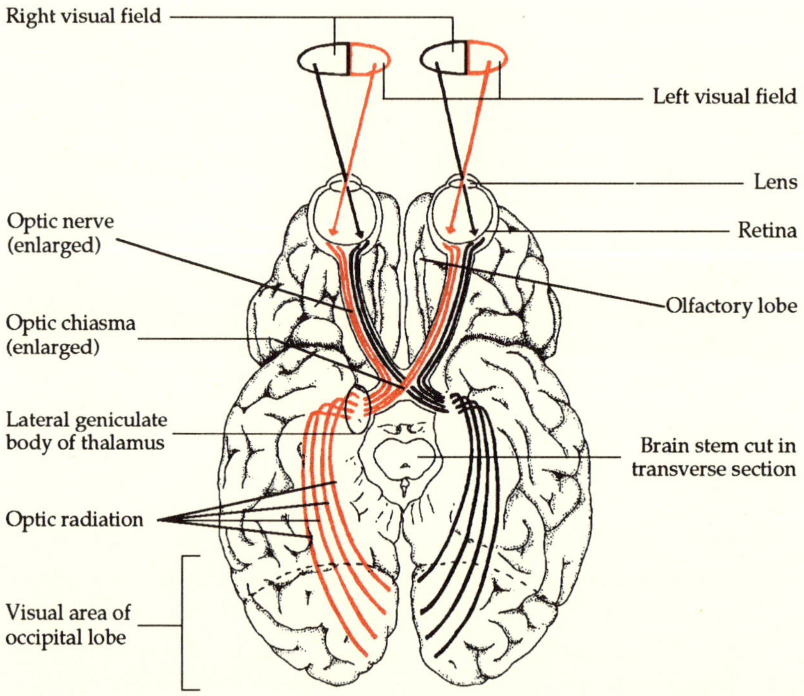

Figure 20: **The brain from below showing optic pathways**

A diagrammatic representation of the connections between the retinae and the visual cortex. The nerve fibres from half of each retina cross over to the opposite side so that each side of the brain sees through both eyes. As the brain is seen from below, its right side is on the left of the drawing. The optic chiasma is also shown in Figure 17, but here in Figure 20 the nerves are enlarged and spaced out for clarity. As is clear from Figure 17, the optic tract is quite a normal sized compact bundle of nerves. Since the lens of the eye reverses the image, the left fields of view (not quite identical for stereoscopic vision) are on the right side of each retina, and each right half-retina communicates with the right occipital lobe.

The lateral geniculate nucleus of each side is shown. It is a complex region including many neurons and synapses— (almost a small brain).

Sources: Anthony and Kolthoff, *Textbook of Anatomy and Physiology*, figs. 10-18; Gardner, *Fundamentals of Neurology*, fig. 7-17.

brain by the subsequent growth of nerve fibres. Figure 21 illustrates the stages in the development of the eye.

2. The membranous sheaths around the optic nerve can be recognized as dura mater, arachnoid mater, and pia mater. This applies also to the olfactory nerve but the other three points in this section do not. These are the membranes that enclose the brain and nerves arising from it, but in most if not all other cases they give place to a different kind of coat as the nerves leave the skull. It might be thought that there would be insufficient length of optic nerve outside the skull for a change in its coat to be easily observable, but this is not so. There is muscle and fat behind the eye and the length of nerve in the eye socket is 2.5 cm.

3. All nerve cells, whether in or out of the brain, require assistance, support and protection by other specialized cells which do not conduct nerve impulses. Those assisting cells within the brain, known as glial cells, are quite different from those associated with other nerves, known as Schwann cells. In the optic nerve, the assisting cells are glial. (Glial cells also accompany the acoustic nerve but only in its proximal part.) Even in the retina the assisting cells have many features in common with one of the types of glial cells.

4. The retina itself is also like a little brain. Even the rods and cones, which are the light sensitive elements, are modified nerve cells, but there are also several layers composed of many additional cells like the nerve cells of the brain. These make multiple contacts with one another and with the rods and cones like the multiple contacts in the brain.

366. Knowledge of the eye as part of the brain, or the retina as a little brain, lends special interest to the following statement from AC 4407:

Hence also it is that certain animals, being destitute of understanding, have, as it were, two subsidiary brains within the

FIGURE 21

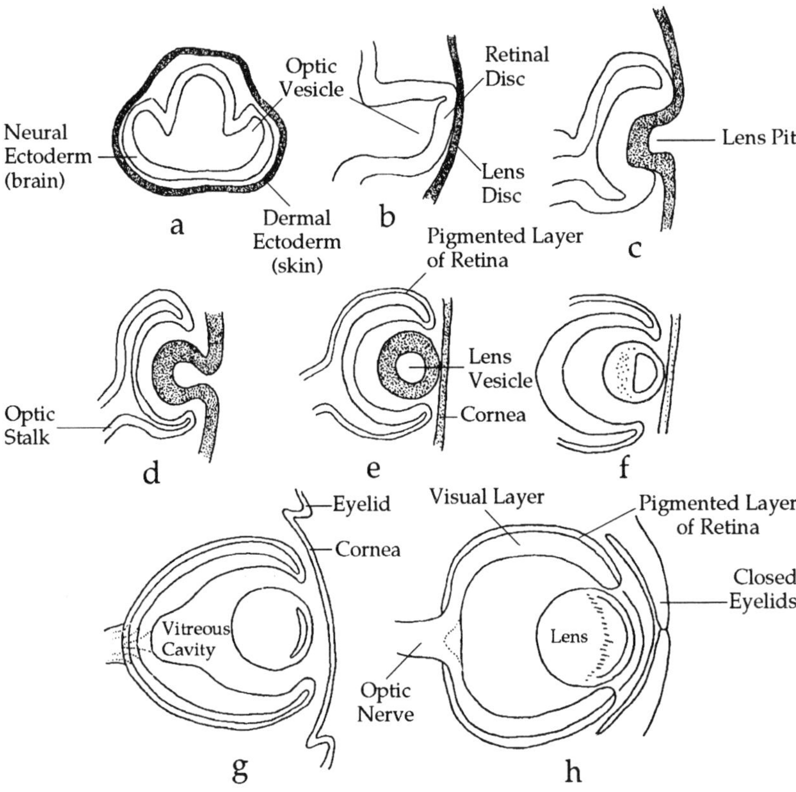

Figure 21: **Development of the Eye**

In the early stages of the embryo, when it is very small the brain is a hollow tube. At one spot on each side a circular area begins to appear. Figure 21*a* shows a section of the embryo across these two points from which it can be seen that the circular area is due to an outgrowth of the primitive brain resulting in a slight swelling or extension of the delicate skin or ectoderm. Subsequent stages are shown in diagrams *b* to *h*, drawn on a larger scale. In *c* the retina is beginning to take its hollowed shape and the ectoderm to form the lens pit. By *h*, the pigmented layer and the nervous layer of the retina have come together.

Sources: Modified from Gardner, *Fundamentals of Neurology*, fig. 12-13; Hamilton, et. al., *Human Embryology*, figs. 410, 411, 414, 418.

orbits of their eyes, for their intellectual depends on their sight. But with man this is not the case, for he enjoys the use of an ample brain.

As in innumerable other instances the structure of man's body has much in common with those of animals, and, as we have just seen, he also has subsidiary brains within his eyes. The phrase "with man this is not the case" means that his intellectual does not depend on his sight. But the little brains within the eyes must be of use to carry out some preliminary processing of sense impressions in order to leave the main brain more capacity and freedom for intellectual response and rule.

As the retina is already brain, the optic pathway is more interior than the pathways of other senses

367. Having shown that the eye, unlike other organs, is itself part of the brain, we can conclude that the image on the retina is already in the brain and therefore the pathway conducting information from the retina to the internal sensory must be more interior than others.

The optic pathway is more direct than the acoustic

368. None of the myriad nerves sending information from the head and body towards the cerebral cortex makes direct contact with the cortex. Every nerve ends in one or more relay stations in the spinal cord or in the brain. Here each fibre passes its impulses on to one or many other nerve cells. There are many relay stations and most of them have several (or many) other functions such as, for example, inhibition, excitation, integration and interaction between incoming impulses from sense organs and out-going (controlling) impulses from the central area or cerebral cortex. Some sense organs, e.g., those of touch, can even be instructed to respond to different stimuli, e.g., warmth instead of pressure (See also No. 346).

369. The pathway for sight may be described very briefly as follows. The optic nerves from both eyes come together in the optic chiasma near the centre of the base of the brain, and then diverge again. In the chiasma about half the fibres from each eye cross over to the opposite side. Since it is only about half, there is no difficulty in each eye having the same sort of correspondences as the same side of the brain. Moreover, each side of the brain sees through both eyes, the right side using the right halves of both retinae.[19] From the chiasma, nearly all the fibres continue to the lateral geniculate body which is the one relay station whence new nerve fibres radiate to the visual cortex. The few fibres which do not connect the retina with the lateral geniculate body send impulses via a different relay back to the iris for adjustment according to light intensity (a typical reflex).

370. The path of the nerves for hearing is more complicated. Some impulses reach the auditory part of the cerebral cortex through as few as three relay stations. Others may pass through as many as five, besides extra ones involved in several places where some (N.B. not all!) of the fibres cross from one side of the brain to the other.

371. These details confirm that, physiologically speaking, the pathway to the internal sensory involves fewer stages for sight than for hearing, and in this sense it is shorter.

372. The anatomical facts adduced above serve to show that, although some of the statements in AC 4407 might be difficult to accept at first, a quite brief excursion into the anatomy as now known shows them to be correct in a way that was not known, and could not have been understood or accepted when they were written.

---

[19] It is difficult to see the purpose of this decussation since the inputs from both retinae must be combined "higher up" in the brain for proper vision, but correspondential reasons of great interest have been put forward by Dr. Allen (1982, p. 138). See Appendix A530 ff.

Hearing often stimulates the sight of the mind

373. Words spoken to us are often translated first into visual memories before being submitted to the understanding. Thus, on receipt of a command, e.g., "Thou shalt not eat of it," we first make a picture of the things mentioned, e.g., a fruit tree. This explains the use of the phrase "sight of the interior hearing" (AC 4653:2). It is confirmed in other places, e.g., "what is heard passes into the internal sight which is that of the understanding." (AC 83611, and 9311). These things do not detract from the neurological correspondences. They are part of the same phenomenon.

Correspondences of the eye enrich our ideas of heaven

374. The eminent quality of the eye has now been sufficiently established, and the relationship between the anatomical facts and the beauty of the representations seen in the province of the eye will now be clear. The eye is brain. The brain is heaven. When we discussed the heavenly form of the brain (Nos. 273-277) we saw how fugacious is knowledge of the heavenly form. Here, however, where correspondences of the eye are the subject, we have delightful things that we can even now appreciate. Such correspondences are not related of the brain itself. This is perhaps because, as we are repeatedly told, its inner form is beyond our comprehension. The eye provides an eminent substitute, being still of the brain, but a little removed.

CHAPTER XV

CORRESPONDENCES OF THE EARS
AND THE ORGANS OF BALANCE OR ORIENTATION

People who obey without question are in the province of the ears

375. The spirits who correspond to the hearing constitute the province of the ear in the Grand Man. They are in simple obedience. They do not reason about things, but believe and do what others tell them. Hence they may be called "obediences." There are many differences among them from the most external to the most internal. They are intimately conjoined with those who belong to the internal sight, but differ from them in having less discernment, and giving as it were a passive assent to them (AC 4653). This second part of AC 4653 appears to indicate a wide range of correspondence from the mere external ear or auricle to the spirit itself, for it is said, "and finally to those that are in the spirit." Thus we have certain ones who correspond to the hearing of the spirit. This is in agreement with what we learn elsewhere of the correspondence between the world of spirits and heaven. Although the spirits indicated as belonging to the province of the ear extend internally as far as the spirit itself, they all follow the introductory indication of being obediences. But No. 4654 suggests that those in simple obedience belong to the auricles. On the other hand, 4655 states that spirits within the ear were "as it were," simple and obedient.

The importance of the ears for balance is implied in a discussion about dancing

376. The efficient functioning of every organ in the body is the lowest, most mechanical form of obedience, corresponding, presum-

ably, to the higher forms of obedience. There is also a particularly important and beautiful form of bodily obedience which, like hearing, belongs to the province of the ears. To this we are introduced by a conversation with Aristotle. It is clearly a perfectly orderly matter that Aristotle, being in the province of the ear (because he was obedient to his spirit), should be mentioned while Swedenborg is describing the correspondence of the ear. It is to be expected that two such men would discuss philosophical matters of mutual interest. This is sufficient reason for the inclusion of a paragraph (4658:3) about philosophy, analytical science, and the foolishness of trying to think from mere terms instead of from use and "from within." But one may ask, "Why is it that when Swedenborg wished to exemplify the futility of thinking artificially from terms, he chose to mention the impossibility of a person being able to dance by means of a knowledge of motor fibres and muscles throughout the entire body?" It is a matter of faith to accept the wisdom of the choice, but it becomes a matter of sight when the physiology is known, because the connection with the inner ear is very close. The importance of the semicircular canals of the inner ear for balance is now well known. For those to whom the physiology is not known, the wisdom of the Lord's choice is hidden. It is in keeping with its arcane quality that no mention of the semicircular canals seems to be made in the Writings, except as a mere item in the list given in AC 4653:2. (The Latin is translated "cylinders" in my edition (Swedenborg Society 1922), but "canals" in another.) I can find nothing more about them and no reference to them in other indices of the Writings that are readily available to me, nor in *Potts' Concordance* (Potts, 1888). Yet their importance for normal bodily life, and especially for dancing, cannot be exaggerated. Their connections through the cerebellum and brain stem with the rest of the body are like a fantastically complex, speedy, accurate computer system whereby a dancer is able to execute marvelous rapid complicated evolutions with perfect bodily control. (The eyes help and the cerebrum is certainly concerned when the dance is complicated; but the routine of balance and coping with starting and stopping and changing direction must be largely the responsibility of the cerebellum and its sense organs in the semicircular canals.) This is the reason for the inclusion of such an example in a section of the Writings devoted to the correspondences of the ear. If I add that this again shows that there is much more in the Writings than we think when we first read them, I hope those who had already seen the connection will still share the joy of confirmation. But we must consider a few more details.

377. Aristotle was in the province of the ears because he was obedient. Since the obedience normally mentioned in the Word is obedience to commands we usually assume that the connection with the ears is through the hearing of speech. Thus it might be thought that Aristotle, as an obedient spirit, need not have any connection with the apparatus of balance which is in the inner ear but has nothing to do with hearing. This would mean that the relation to the semicircular canals would be only that of contiguity and not of function. On the other hand, it is obvious that the maintenance of balance is often essential for the preservation of bodily life. Immediate, unquestioning obedience to the sensations derived from the apparatus of balance is often vital. Now the signals that travel along the nerves from the canals are not of a different kind from those that come from the organs of hearing; they merely go to a different part of the brain. Moreover, unlike speech, they require no activity of the understanding. They can be obeyed more promptly. They are never questioned. Therefore, the whole system by which balance is maintained provides a perfect example of complete, unthinking obedience. Since the system comprises several stages, including some in the cerebellum, it could correspond to many societies of spirits in the province of the ears, for this province is very extensive, as we have already observed (No. 375). However, these societies would all be simple obediences, in contrast to others corresponding to different parts of the body. Perhaps it is because of the essential quality of prompt unquestioning obedience that the ultimate organs of balance (i.e., the vestibule and semicircular canals) are placed in the ear. However, it is not the semicircular canals that are obedient, but the rest of the body that is obedient to them. It is the same with the organ of hearing. Hearing is only the beginning of obedience. The sensation of movement and position is only the beginning of balance. The similarities and differences between the organs of hearing and balance will become clearer when we enter into a little more detail of the anatomy (see No. 383) and return later to an analysis of what constitutes obedience (Nos. 389-392).

378. Senses other than those of the ear are not so firmly wedded to mere obedience. Sight demands much of the understanding. There are, it is true, rapid, thought-free reactions to other senses, such as taste, smell, and touch. There are also reflex actions, but these are usually merely a shrinking from pain or unpleasantness, and not a well-coordinated obedience like that required for balance.

Obedience to the spoken word is not due to connections between the ears and the cerebellum

379. With regard to the relation between hearing and obedience, two statements by John Worcester in *Physiological Correspondences* (1889) are of special interest. On page 284 we find:

But an important part of the auditory nerve goes directly to the cerebellum, which is the seat of the affections of the life, and of involuntary motion, and there has a tendency to produce immediate impulsive action in response to its impulses.

And later (p. 393):

In studying the sense of hearing, we have seen that it has relation to obedience; and it is interesting to remember that the nerves of the ears, besides their extension to their special convolutions of the cerebrum, send large branches directly to the cerebellum, having thus a tendency to produce prompt and involuntary obedience, as well as voluntary.

380. It is interesting to consider a possible line of thought which may have led to these statements. Apparently, they follow from the relation between the sense of hearing and obedience, and it is possible to develop the ideas as follows: there are a few phrases in the Writings that, taken out of context, might lead one to think that sounds flowing into the ear affect the will immediately. For example, we read "whatever they [celestial angels] hear of Divine things they receive in the will" (AE 14); and "What the angels of the third heaven hear from preachings enters directly into their perception and will" (loc. cit.). Sometimes it seems that perception has very little to do with understanding. For example, "the correspondence of the variations of tone which derive very little from the understanding is with perception" (DW X 5), also "the sounds enter the will and thence the affection" (AE 588e). This is often the case with music, but for our present purposes we are mainly concerned with speech. Therefore a fuller quotation from AE 588 is added:

> The reason why to hear, signifies perception from the will of good, and thence obedience, is, that speech enters the ear together with sound, and the truths of speech enter the understanding and thence the thought, and the sounds enter the will and thence the affection.

381. It is taught throughout the Writings that there is a correspondence between hearing or hearkening and obeying, e.g., "they who are obedient and submissive belong to the province of the ear and indeed correspond to the hearing itself" (AC 2542). Since obedience is often a matter of submission of the will, the idea that hearing and the will are closely connected is further strengthened. It is also said (DLW 384) that the cerebellum exists chiefly for the sake of the will.

382. As hearkening means the will must acquiesce in obedience and as the cerebellum is for the sake of the will, it would be of special interest if the ears really were directly connected to the cerebellum. However, such a connection is not supported in a recent edition of *Gray's Anatomy*. From it we learn that it is not the auditory nerve that leads to the cerebellum but its close companion, the vestibular nerve which leads from a different part of the inner ear. In view of this, the second statement in Worcester about the nerves of the ear is also misleading, though in itself it is correct because the ear as a whole includes the vestibule.[20] A brief outline of the appropriate anatomy will clarify the matter.

It is not the organ of hearing that is connected to the cerebellum but the organ of orientation in the inner ear

383. The inner ear consists of two distinct parts, the cochlea and the vestibule with its semicircular canals. The former, shaped like the spiral of a snail shell, is the organ of hearing, and the latter are organs of balance which are sensitive to position and acceleration. See Figure 22 showing the inner ear. In each ear, there are three semicircular canals in three planes approximately perpendicular to one another. In spite of their name, each forms about two thirds of a circle, and the ends come together in the vestibule. This gives its name to the nerve which conveys impulses from the canals and the vestibule towards the brain. Thus it is known as the vestibular nerve. It originates in the vestibular ganglion which occupies an adjacent cavity in the bone of the skull. The cochlear or auditory nerve has a quite separate origin in the cochlear ganglion which occupies a hollow space in the central pillar of the spiral bone of the cochlea. After leaving their special

---

[20] In spite of this criticism, I think Worcester's book is in many ways an admirable general introduction for the New Church reader. It is, of course, limited to knowledge of its time (1889), but for gross anatomy this is probably adequate. The book contains little of what we now call physiology, most of the descriptions of the body being anatomical. This is, of course, because physiology has developed mostly in this century.

FIGURE 22

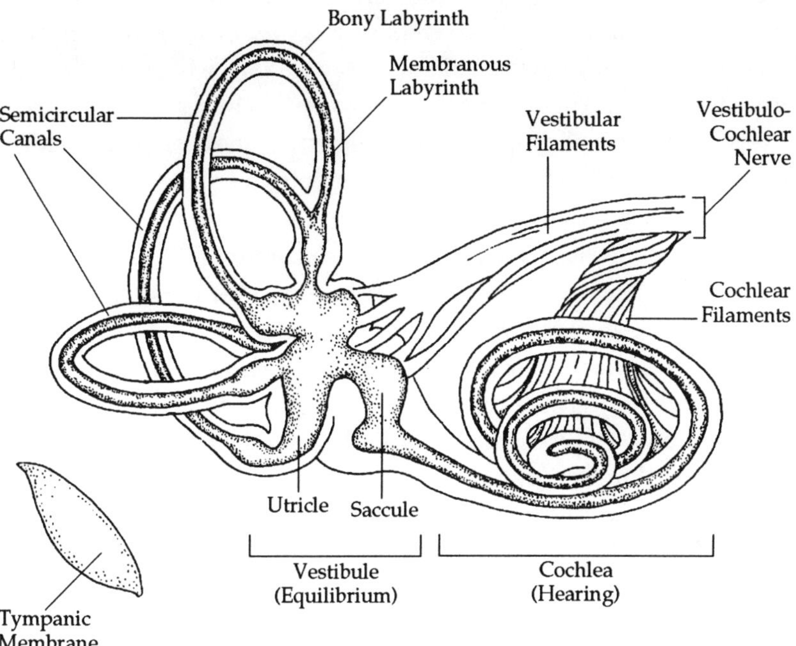

Figure 22: **The Inner Ear**

View from the front showing separate fibers from the vestibule, which is involved with balance, and the cochlea, the organ of hearing, combining into the vestibulocochlear nerve. The tympanic membrane (eardrum) is shown, but the ossicles, (bones which transmit vibrations from the eardrum to the cochlea), are not. Although the cavities of the vestibule and cochlea communicate as shown, the nerves from them do not (see text). The shapes outlined in the diagram do not exist independently of the skull, but are cavities in the bones at the side of the head, and they are very small. Within the cavities is the membranous labyrinth which appears as though it might be a sort of lining to the bony labyrinth, but it is much narrower and it contains a fluid which is different from that outside it in the bony labyrinth.

Sources: Redrawn from Wilson, *Human Anatomy*, fig. 12-42; Anthony and Kolthoff, *Textbook of Anatomy and Physiology*, figs. 10-19, 10-20, 10-21.

organs, the vestibular and cochlear nerves travel so closely together through one passage in the skull towards the brain that they have become known by one name: the vestibulocochlear nerve. On arrival at the brain, they separate again and end in different relay stations (see No. 368 for the meaning and function of relay stations). Impulses from the vestibule pass along the vestibular nerve, most of the fibres of which end in one or another of four relay stations which are different from those of the cochlear nerve (see No. 370). The rest of the fibres of the vestibular nerve do actually lead directly to the cerebellum (unlike those of the cochlear nerve). Controlling fibres also pass in the reverse direction to the vestibular relay stations. In response to signals from the vestibular system, the cerebellum sends impulses to many nerve centres which activate muscles in various parts of the body. Besides this, some of the relay stations on the vestibular route directly activate other centres which control muscles of the eyes, neck, and other parts of the body so that the total effect enables one to keep his balance automatically. These are the reflex mechanisms by which we maintain bodily equilibrium through instantaneous adjustments without thought. It must be added, however, that the eyes also help in maintaining balance.

Obedience to speech cannot take place without the understanding

384. We have seen (No. 383) that the immediate connection between the ears and the cerebellum does produce "prompt and involuntary obedience" to the impulses from the vestibular system, though not to those from the organ of hearing. Besides the lack of direct connection, there is another reason why involuntary obedience to spoken words could not normally take place. It is because the meaning of the words of the command must first be understood. One would expect such a complex activity of the intelligence to require participation of a considerable area of the cerebral cortex. Indeed various cortical areas are believed to be involved in the numerous activities related to language, including speaking and listening. Clearly obedience is by no means an automatic response of the cerebellum, nor is it usually a mere response of the will independently of the intellect. The Writings make it clear that the understanding is often involved. For example, in AE 14, besides the phrases already quoted we read, "things which enter by hearing enter directly *by the understanding* into the will" (emphasis added). The wording is notable. Perhaps it means not directly into the will but through the understanding. However, we are not accustomed to finding "by" in the Writings if "through" is meant. Moreover, from the way the brain is constructed, it could mean that the cerebrum is able to influence the cerebellum causing it to respond in an appropriate way to nerve impulses from the ears; or that the understanding can influence the will in its response to sounds. (The love perceived in a tone of voice may be genuine or feigned.)

385. In view of other statements the word "directly" is probably used to mean that the information is not first filed away in a long-term memory. Apart from a few phrases, such as those mentioned above, none of the many passages relating hearing to obedience indicates that it is by a direct influence on the will. Understanding or perception is always a prerequisite, except for the most external kinds of spirit who correspond to the external ear or to skins. These do what other spirits tell them (AC 4654), and some do not even reflect upon the meaning of things that are told them (AC 4656, and SD 2667). Perhaps, since spiritual language is "thought speaking," such obedient spirits do not even need to "translate" words into ideas but merely accept the ideas and act upon them.

Speech stimulates the internal sight

386. An example of the translation of speech into visual memories was given above (No. 373). Except for the most external kinds of spirit mentioned just above (No. 385), it is clear that hearing requires the attention of the understanding. For example, we find: "natural hearing [is] from a spiritual hearing which is attention of the understanding and at the same time accommodation of the will" (CL 220). So hearing involves the following: receiving in the memory, being instructed, receiving with the understanding and believing, and finally receiving in obedience and doing (AC 9311). We also read that "to hear" signifies to perceive, understand, and have faith, and "to do" signifies to live according thereto. "But where hearing is spoken of, and not at the same time doing, then 'hearing' signifies faith in will and act, thus obedience." The reason is that *what is heard passes into the internal sight, which is that of the understanding,* and is there received by the will, and passes as by a circle into act" (AC 8361, emphasis added).

Spiritually considered, the translation of speech into images is a simple matter

387. We draw this conclusion from what is said about spirits whose rational faculty leaves something to be desired. Of some we read (AC 4658) that they had studied logic and metaphysics solely for the sake of reputation and money and were therefore miserable. It is at first surprising to find that they belong to the interiors of the ear and "have the sight of the interior hearing...who obey the things that its spirit there dictates and give fit utterance to its dictates." But as there is a spirit whom they must obey it seems possible that they are merely servants and "belong" to the interiors in no other way than a servant belongs to a household. However, it is also worth remembering again that, as Worcester points out, "these descriptions seem all to be taken from the Christian heaven before the Last Judgment, thus during the process of its formation and purification from evil spirits. The Ancient heavens would be described very differently, and likewise the Christian heaven now that it is in order" (p. 403).

388. In acquiring learning merely for honours and wealth, the spirits we are considering had not perfected their Rational, and it is interesting to notice how easily these few hints about their character enable us to understand their role. Having no genuine Rational (which

is the faculty of perceiving truth), the best such learned men could achieve was to be obedient to the truth that was told them (perhaps even forced upon them?). One assumes that as educated men they were able, once they had submitted, to understand the truth more clearly than the less learned, and that by virtue of this understanding they had some relationship to sight. Since they were unable to discern the truth for themselves, however, the best they could do was to obey, hence their connection with hearing as well as sight, and hence their possession of "the sight of the interior hearing" and their ability to serve its spirit.

The province of the ears is very extensive because obedience involves the whole personality

389. The symbolic representation of obedience by the hearing is easy to understand, for it is largely by the aid of the ears that children first learn what orders and obedience mean. Experience shows that the disobedient are often unwilling to hear. We have seen that the vestibular system (including the cerebellum) induces obedience of the rest of the body to its demands (Nos. 377, 383), and that the hearing is different, so that the living, correspondential and causative relation between obedience and the ears is not so readily apprehended. It is here that AC 4653:2 provides a lead, for, as we have noted, it indicates an extension of the province of the ear in a long series from the most external to the most internal part, suggesting the following train of thought.

390. The ear itself is not obedient, except in faithfully rendering the sounds that impinge upon it into corresponding nerve impulses. It appears that the faithful performance of duty or function is not the meaning of obedience, because many parts of the body that do not correspond to obedience perform their functions efficiently. The drum of the ear is not more obedient than the cornea of the eye, nor the stirrup and anvil than the taste buds of the tongue. The nerves from the ear and those parts of the brain with which they communicate are not obedient either, except in faithfully interpreting the trains of nerve impulses into words. A still more internal part has the sight of the understanding and this also is limited in its response. It can only present the meaning of the words. When the will sees this meaning in the understanding, it perceives, with the aid of the understanding how its own love or its love for the speaker can be furthered. Only then can obedience to the spoken words follow.

Obedience from fear is similarly produced; the love may be self love or love for another. Thus it is not the efficient performance of duty that constitutes true obedience, but the loving acceptance of the will of another. This must be the reason why the province of the ear which corresponds to obedience extends so far inwards.

391. These thoughts show that obedience is a function of will and understanding together, that is, of the whole man. Yet we gather that there are simple spirits who merely do what they are told, and certain ones who correspond to the different little organs of which the inner ear is made. Of these we have said that they cannot be truly obedient, but merely efficient. Perhaps the simple spirits who do as they are told are not capable of more than an automatic response, being 'obedient' in that very limited sense. This, however, would seem to be going too far and making them not really human. It is, perhaps, more acceptable to remember that even these simple spirits have their own complete personality and free will. Because of their obedient nature, that is, their willingness to serve from love, they find their own particular place somewhere in the great extent of the province of the ear. It is important to bear in mind the living nature of the Grand Man, and hence the life derived into the body. The ear is not like a microphone at all. The drum, for example, is skin, but not mere skin. It is a sheet of several layers containing living cells. Each cell has a full complement of DNA and thus, theoretically has the potential required for developing into a complete human body. So, in the Grand Man, the life of the Lord is fully present in His own special way in every angel.

392. From these things we see how important it is to respect the obedient. After the glorious things related of the correspondence of the eye it seems strange that the province of the ear should be "in the axis of heaven" (AE 14). We see how far internally the province extends; we realize that the life of the Lord is fully present in each individual of that province, and remember that true obedience is from love. Then we can respect, admire, and possibly emulate those of this province.

CHAPTER XVI

PERCEPTIONS, DELIGHTS, ODOURS
AND THE SENSE OF SMELL

Delights correspond to odours, and the perception of them corresponds to the sense of smell

[393.] Every particular delight corresponds to an odour, and in the spiritual world can be converted into it, and then the general delight in heaven is sensibly perceived as the odour of a garden, with variety according to the fragrances there from the flowers and fruits. (DP 304)

The correspondences extend, of course, to the organ and sense of smell and to their part in the Grand Man. (The subject is dealt with in AC 4622-4633, and to avoid unduly lengthy quotations, familiarity with these passages is assumed.) The particulars about affection begin with No. 4624 where it is said that those persons who are in general perception belong to the province of the nostrils in the Grand Man. The sense of smell and its organ correspond to these persons who may therefore be called perceptions. The subsequent numbers continue the theme of the correspondence between the sense or organ of smell and perception, so that it seems necessary to begin by studying perception.

All people have some form of perception

394. The word "perception" is used in the Writings with a range of meanings from mere mental awareness to the Lord's experience of Divine influx during His life on earth.

395. The lowest perception is what every man has, for

there is with every man a capacity of perceiving whether a thing is so or is not so. The capacity of drawing a conclusion within himself, or in his own mind, causes a thing to be perceived. This capacity is quite impossible unless there is influx from the spiritual world…the perception which exists with every man is of worldly things but not at the present day with any one of spiritual things. (AC 5937)

Even the perception of those who belong to the spiritual church is only of this lower kind, for we read:

all the good with those who are of the spiritual church is acquired by means of truth, since without truth which is of faith they do not know what spiritual truth is, nor what spiritual good is. They are capable indeed of knowing civil truth, also moral truth, and their goods, because these harmonize with things which are in the world, *from which also they have their perception.* (AC 7977) (emphasis added)

We also read that the perception of what is honorable, just, and fair in moral and civil life is possessed by those who are rational, although they have no perception of the good and truth of faith (AC 2831). In TCR 603 this level of perception is called "an interior thought" such as that of a judge who decides the merits of a case in his higher mind and then descends to a lower level to give details and pronounce sentence.

396. In the next life, even the evil have perception through communication with heaven by means of cognitions of truth and good, but only until these knowledges have been taken away by the processes of vastation.

With spiritual people perception takes the form of conscience

397. Although lacking the higher forms of perception, spiritual men are not devoid of assistance, for they have conscience (AC 104):

> which is also a kind of perception...but not from the good which flows in but from the truth which, according to the holy quality of man's worship, has been implanted in the Rational from infancy, and afterwards confirmed; this alone in such a case they suppose to be good. Hence conscience is a species of perception, but...arising from truth of such a nature. (AC 2144)

With the spiritual it is through conscience that good and truth are dictated by the Lord (AC 2515). It is of course in the next life that perception is fully enjoyed, and men who become angels have perception even while they remain spiritual rather than celestial; for we find "spiritual angels who likewise have perception although not such as the celestial have" (AC 1384).

With celestial people perception is more excellent than can be described

398. The perception of celestial people was of an entirely different nature from the conscience that exists with the spiritual. It is difficult for us to understand celestial perception because it perished from this world when the Most Ancient Church was consummated. However, the Lord clearly expects us to know something about it, for many passages in the Writings comment upon it. Perhaps one of the most useful for our present purposes is AC 521 where we read:

> To those who learn by perception the Lord grants to know what is good and true by an inward way; but to those who learn from doctrine, knowledge is given by an external way, or that of the bodily senses; and the difference is like that between light and

darkness. Consider also that the perceptions of the celestial man are such as to admit of no description, for they enter into the most minute and particular things, with all variety according to states and circumstances.

Of this perception it is said that it "is the very Celestial itself given by the Lord to those who are in the faith of love" (AC 536). This is especially the case with celestial angels, "for through love they have a perception from the Lord of what is good and true" (AC 202). This extends to the source and quality of their thoughts, words, and actions when these are from themselves. They also perceive what is from the Lord and what from self (AC 1383). The Writings sometimes refer to perception as if the only real perception is celestial perception. Other ways of becoming aware of things are described in different words. This appears clearly in AE 307 as follows:

> The angels of the third or inmost heaven have perception; the angels of the second and the ultimate heaven have enlighten-ment of the understanding: they are distinguished by this, that perception is full confirmation from influx from the Lord, but enlightenment of the understanding is spiritual sight. Those have the latter who are in charity towards the neighbor and thence in faith; but those have perception who are in love to the Lord. (What perception is may be further seen in the *Doctrine of the New Jerusalem*, n. 135-140.)

There is another kind of perception that belongs to all in the spiritual world

399. Three kinds of awareness, which could be called three kinds of perception, have been noted. These are only the most general kinds, for the varieties in heaven are innumerable. In the next life there is yet another kind that belongs to all, "to angels in the highest perfection, and to spirits according to their respective qualities" (AC 1383, see also AC 1388). This form of perception is the ability to know the quality of another on his first approach. It is a result of the particular and characteristic sphere which emanates from each spirit or angel. The ability to become aware of and to assess this sphere enables one to know the quality of another who is approaching. The presence of spheres makes this kind of perception not only possible, but perhaps even inevitable, making spheres an important part of future life. AC 1504 shows that information about spheres may be deduced from the occurrence of this form of perception. It is explained as follows:

> It has already been said that it is known in the other life what another is on his first approach, even though he does not speak. From this it may be known that a man's interiors are in a kind of unconscious activity, and that from this the quality of the spirit is perceived. That it is so has been evidenced by the fact that this sphere of the activity not only extends itself to a distance, but that sometimes also, when the Lord permits, it is in various ways made perceptible to the senses.

We note: (1) that the quality of the spirit is said to be "perceived," (2) that the product of the unconscious activity is called "this sphere," (3) that it is sometimes made perceptible to the senses "in various ways."

The perception of personal qualities in the other life is often an awareness of odour

400. Having been informed about the generation of personal spheres by spirits and angels we learn next that such spheres are "made susceptible to sense by odours, which spirits smell," for "odours correspond to spheres" (AC 1514). When it pleases the Lord (which is often (AC 5621)), the spheres of approaching spirits are turned into odours (AC 4626). Even the way the references are listed in this number shows the relationship between spheres, perceptions and odours, for we have the sequence "concerning spheres…concerning perception...and concerning the consequent odours." This indicates that odours are the result of the perception of the spheres of approaching spirits. However, it is probably wise not to subscribe too exclusively to this view, for although it is said very definitely that the sense of smell corresponds to perception, it does not appear to be stated categorically that it corresponds only to the perception of personal spheres, rather than to the other kind, namely, angelic perception. The general delight in heaven referred to above (No. 393; DP 304) may correspond to fragrance produced by the harmonious spheres of the angels, but it can also be a perception of blessings flowing in from the Lord. Indeed, when we read that fragrance corresponds to a pleasing perception like that of truth from good (AC 4748:2), we realize that there may be factors common to both kinds of perception. For example, when the ability to recognize genuine truth is the result of being turned towards the Lord and loving Him. The angel with this ability will surely be keenly aware of the truth "reflected" by another and he will know the extent to which such truth is joined with good (as well as many other details). These considerations, however, do not diminish the distinction between the two kinds of perception, and it is clear that there is often considerable difference between the two. It is thus with spirits who have the second but not the first of the two kinds of perception mentioned in AC 1383, that is, angelic perception and common perception, respectively.

Awareness of odour reflects the condition of the observer

401. We have just seen that spheres are turned into odours when it pleases the Lord. This seems, at first, like an interference in the normal processes by which spheres manifest themselves, for one tends to imagine that the sphere would have an appropriate odour all the time. We often think in this way about earthly odours, confusing our own sensation with the objective reality. The objective things which I have been rash enough to call reality are various molecules floating about in the air. They can be recognized and measured by chemical and/or physical tests and instruments that give reproducible results which are independent of the sensitivity of the human who observes the instrument. But it cannot be said that there is an odour unless someone can smell it. Thus odour is the response of the living subject. This concept is explained particularly clearly in DLW 41. These ideas make it easy to understand how spheres can be changed into odours without the sphere itself being changed. It is a matter related to the condition and awareness of the observer (a contingency that often occurs in this life).

402. The dependence of the perception of natural odours on the state of the individual extends even to the effect on the ambient level of the odours. Everyone can confirm for himself that his sense of smell very quickly becomes exhausted, or accustomed to the prevailing level; providing irritation is not also present and providing the level is not being changed by the movement of the air. How long can you continue to sniff a rose and enjoy its scent? When you come home to a house that has been closed you can probably notice an odour if you think about it at the time, but your awareness of it will vanish probably in a few seconds. Thus it is easy to accept that evil spirits are not sensibly aware of the foul odours corresponding to their evil delights until a change due to the approach of a heavenly sphere is noticed. Even those in heaven are not aware of the odours corresponding to their delights, as we read in DP 304:

> These delights, because they constitute the life of every one in particular, and of all in general, are not sensibly perceived by those who are in them, but their opposites are sensibly perceived when they come near, especially when they are turned into odours, for every particular delight corresponds to an odour, and in the spiritual world can be converted into it; and then the general delight in heaven is sensibly perceived as the odour of a garden, with variety according to the fragrances there from the flowers and fruits.

This seems to mean that the angels are not aware of the odour, being, as it were, in it all the time. When the Lord pleases, the delight in heaven is perceived in the spiritual below as an odour. We may conclude that, in the spiritual world, as in the natural, it is changes in odour that are observed rather than any particular level.

Different types of perception are illustrated by correspondences of the nose and of the bronchia

403. We are now in a position to consider what would earlier have appeared as an anomaly: Having read that the organ of the sense of smell corresponds to perception, we next remember that "the branches of the bronchia of the lungs [correspond] to perceptions and thoughts" (DLW 405). Nasal passages and bronchia both belong to the same continuous air ducts and may therefore be regarded as belonging to the same general province. But the perception of an odour is a very different matter from merely inhaling air. The latter is the more essential for the continuance of bodily life. We may therefore think the bronchia correspond to the first, i.e., celestial, type of perception, or to conscience, or to the residues that serve as conscience with the natural man, for these are all means whereby life is received from the Lord. Some details of how the bronchia could be related to perception or conscience or the inflow of life from the Lord were presented above (Nos. 139-141). In these numbers, it was suggested that this kind of perception is the drawing-in of Divine Truth or life from the Lord as the atmosphere is drawn into the lungs through the bronchia.

404. Such an interpretation leaves us with the nose as corresponding to the perception of the quality of other spirits and angels. This does not exclude a perception of general or composite spheres from many spirits together, nor does it exclude the perception by scent of blessings flowing from the Lord. We may think either of the similarity of breathing and smelling, since it is not too easy to separate them, or of the difference, since they have such different functions. Looking at the question from one point of view and then from the other helps one to appreciate the variety of perceptions (AC 483) and confirms the link between them. The odour of the sphere of a spirit may then be thought of as due to the contamination by the proprium of the inflowing life from the Lord. (A contamination is more or less objectionable as the spirit is less or more regenerated, and not objectionable at all in the case of angels, but still a contamination in the strict sense of the addition of something less pure.)

With respect to contamination, it is interesting to observe that some of the best scents contain minute traces of substances that smell horrible in larger quantities. It is now some years since it was found that the flavor of good butter is due in part to minute quantities of mercaptans (organic sulphides, smelling like bad eggs, or worse). Mercaptans also contribute to the flavor of cheese.

Correspondences indicate an equivalence between interiors of the nostrils and parts of the brain

405. Those who belong to the province of the sense of smell and of the nostrils are in general perception (AC 4624). "General" can mean "obscure," for in another place we find "conscience is a kind of general dictate, and thus an obscure one" (AC 1919). This suggests that the spirits in question had only an obscure perception. This would agree with their being in the province of the olfactory organ itself which, of course, cannot smell without interpretation by the brain above it. Although these persons relate to the exteriors of the nostrils (AC 4627), the relationship cannot be limited to the skins and cartilage of the nose, for "to these [people] correspond the sense of smell and its organ" (AC 4624). This organ, strictly speaking, is the olfactory mucosa in the nose. See Figure 23. It is interior with respect to the visible nose but it is clearly excluded from "the interiors of the nostrils" treated of in AC 4627:1 and 4627:4.

FIGURE 23

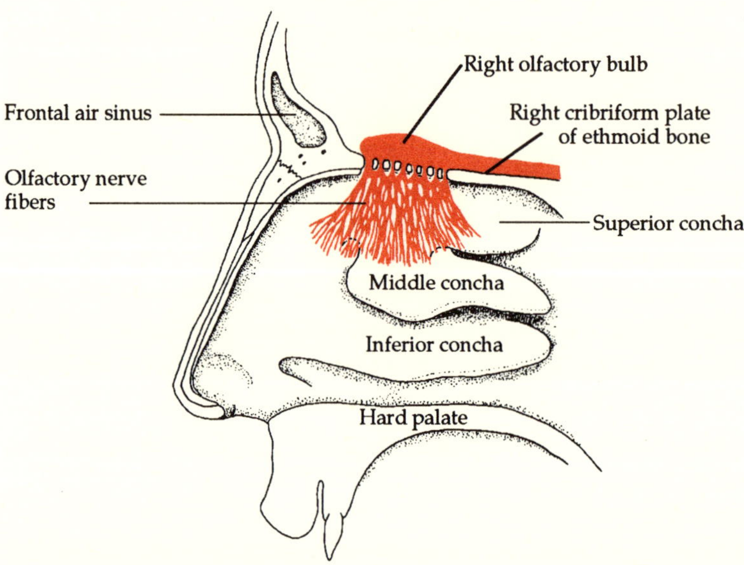

Figure 23: **Olfactory Mucosa (1)**

A sagittal section through the nose just to the right of the median plane and showing the right wall of the right side of the nasal cavity. The superior, middle, and inferior conchae are elevations or protrusions covered with mucous membrane. The conchae are arranged in such a way that the inspired air of breath passes under, over, and between them. The olfactory part of the mucous membrane extends only as far as the superior concha and the opposing surface of the (central) nasal septum. The right olfactory bulb (which is part of the brain, see Figure 16), sends its fibres to the regions just mentioned, and the left bulb to the corresponding structures on its own side. The ethmoid bone is part of the base of the skull, and the plate is called "cribriform" because of its perforations through which the bundles of nerves pass as shown. However, there are about twenty bundles each containing many nerve fibres. They join and re-divide as shown, and it is supposed that interactions can occur. Each bundle is surrounded by extensions of the brain meninges and cerebrospinal fluid.

With reference to paragraph 417, the olfactory bulb is part of the brain itself, as may be clear from several other figures (eg. Figure 16), and it is within the dura mater and pia mater. These membranes descend around the nerves into the tissues of the nose, though they cannot be conveniently shown here. Obviously the membranes must be much finer here than they are in Figure 15.

Sources: Redrawn from Gardner, *Fundamentals of Neurology*, fig. 12-5; Clemente, *Gray's Anatomy*, (CCE) fig. 439; Gardner, Gray and O'Rahilly, *Anatomy: A Regional Study of Human Structure*, fig. 63-4.

[406.] Those however who relate to the interiors of the nostrils are in a more perfect state of perception than those...who relate to their exteriors. Concerning the former I may give the following account. I saw as it were a bath, with long seats or benches, and from it heat exhaled. A woman appeared there who soon vanished into a blackish cloud; and I heard little children saying that they did not desire to be there. Soon afterwards, I observed some angelic choirs, who were sent to me for the purpose of averting the endeavors of certain evil spirits; and then, suddenly, above the front there appeared little apertures, greater or less, through which a beautiful yellow light was shining; and in this light within the apertures I saw some women in a snowy radiance. There afterwards appeared little apertures in a different arrangement, through which the women within were looking out; and again other little apertures through which the light did not so freely pass. (AC 4627)

In this number, those who relate to the "interiors of the nostrils" are contrasted with those who relate to the "sense of smell and its organ." Hence there must be another meaning for "interiors."

407. In searching for another meaning for "interiors" we turn again to AC 4627. The female angels were accompanied by little children. Thus three things show that those who related to the interior things of the nostrils were in heaven: (1) a more perfect perception, (2) they were angels and (3) there were little children with them (HH 329, 332). As, therefore, the province of the interior nostrils is in heaven, and as there is a specially close correspondence between heaven and the brain (see Nos. 273-277), we expect correlations between the heavenly province of the interior nostrils and certain parts of the brain.

408. The correspondences of most beauty and interest were not seen until the endeavors of evil spirits had been frustrated. Then little apertures appeared (AC 4627). They remind one irresistibly of the little apertures in the ethmoid bone at the base of the skull. This bone is pierced in about twenty places for the passage of nerve bundles from the olfactory epithelium of the nose. Through them, the brain becomes aware of whatever spheres of odour are drawn into the nostrils. See Figure 24 in which these structures are shown on a much larger scale than in Figure 23. This is like the women looking out of the apertures. However, one cannot be certain of their interpretation, for several other sets of apertures appeared and they are said to be representative rather than correspondential. An aperture is a place where the substance of a wall or partition has been removed to allow something to go through. Hence an aperture may represent communication; the partition, separation and protection. The female angels referred to in this section are accompanied by little children and remind us of the angels who care for little children (HH 332), although those were in the province of the eyes (HH 333). (We return to this question in a later section.) Protection would be needed for such a community, but not isolation. The two needs can be represented by some kind of partition, with apertures. We are not told what the partitions were like and this may be because there is, or seems to be, no corresponding partition in the physical body. There are indeed other sets of apertures in those structures in the brain that have some connection with the sense of smell, namely, in the anterior and posterior "perforated substances," but in this case the perforations are for the passage of blood vessels and not for nerves.

409. If we think that the representative apertures mean communication, we have a possible interpretation. The nerves from the nose pass through the ethmoid bone, as already mentioned, to end in the olfactory lobe which lies just above. Here the incoming nerve impulses are modified and relayed in a complex way before passing along a band of nerves, the olfactory tract, towards higher centres in the brain (see No. 426). We have three additional sets of apertures to account for and it so happens that the olfactory tract splits into three bands just before making connection with other structures. If a single nerve could corre-

FIGURE 24

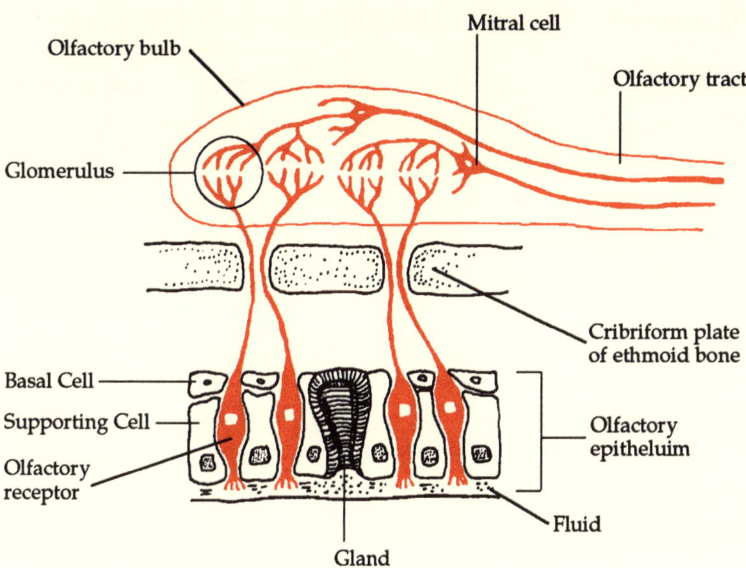

Figure 24: **Olfactory Mucosa (2)**

Schema of olfactory mucosa (on a much larger scale than Figure 23), together with simplified nerve connections in the olfactory bulb. The olfactory receptors are parts of neurons; their axons pass through the perforations in the ethmoid bone as shown on a different scale in the previous figure. Since the axon bundles are each surrounded by the several maters of the brain (see Figure 15), it is easy to understand how the cerebrospinal fluid can reach the tissue spaces of the nasal mucosa. Only two axons are shown in each perforation but they represent bundles containing a large number of axons. Of the several neuron types present in the olfactory lobe, only the mitral cells are shown. All the nerve tissues are in color. The glomerulus is a region mainly of synapses, as indicated in the drawing. Above the olfactory bulbs are the frontal lobes of the cerebrum (not shown).

Source: Gardner, op. cit., figs. 12-24, *Anatomy Coloring Book*, plate 142.

spond with the communication represented by an aperture then an arrangement of apertures could relate to a band of nerves. In the natural brain, the different bands are unequal. One of them is sometimes indistinguishable and sometimes seen as fine striae. This could be the set of apertures through which the light did not so freely pass. Figure 25 shows the olfactory lobes and the associated nerve tissue.

410. It should also be mentioned that we are not concerned with the correspondence of the number three (or four), because we are told only that apertures appeared, then others and others.

A spiritual meaning can be deduced from the representatives related to the interiors of the nostrils

411. We have been shown representatives that can be related to anatomical structures, probably in order that we may know that everything human, even down to the body, lives through correspondence with the Grand Man. The system of correspondences is so well ordered that the causes of the representatives can also be deduced. These causes are the spiritual matters that produced the representatives. Although it is but little that we can see, the impression persists that there would be much more if we had a little more wisdom. The representatives we now wish to interpret are seen from AC 4627 quoted above (n. 406).

412. We cannot help wondering why such strange things were seen (AC 4627) before the correspondences of the interiors of the nostrils were revealed, but a view of the collected significances leads to a possible explanation. The blackish cloud signifies falsities of evil; the little children (signifying innocence) are unwilling to remain; and there is a need for an angelic choir to avert endeavors of evil spirits. All of these things indicate that we are looking for significances of the evil and false in those cases where a heavenly or an opposite meaning would each be possible.

FIGURE 25

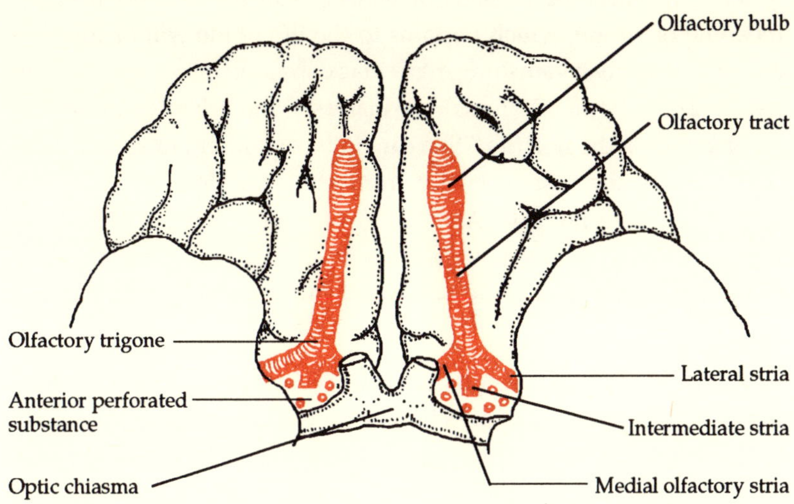

Figure 25: **Olfactory lobes and associated nerve tissue**

Anterior parts of the base of the brain (compare Figure 15). They are viewed from below and are drawn to show the olfactory bulbs and tracts in color and to emphasize the olfactory trigone and its striae. The latter are not easily seen in photographs of intact brains, being mere surface marks or slight furrows, but it has been shown that the nerves of the olfactory tract do indeed split into medial and lateral bands. (The band in the center, ie. the intermediate stria, is less clear, although shown plainly in the diagram; perhaps it varies.) On the other hand, the Anterior Perforated Substance, (APS), can easily be seen. It contains neurons which make synaptic connections with those fibres from the olfactory bulb which reach the APS through the lateral stria. The medial stria leads to other parts. The APS is hence part of the primary olfactory cortex which, in turn, is part of the limbic system. (See paragraph 406 and 425 end.)

Sources: Gardner, *Fundamentals of Neurology*, fig. 7-8; Clemente, *Gray's Anatomy*, (CCE), fig. 350.

413. A bath from which heat exhaled is mentioned in TCR 834 in respect to some Mohammedans, the heat of whose polygamous love was like the heat in baths after bathing. In CL 344 it is said to be "like the foul heat of a bath."

414. The meaning of seats or benches can be deduced from the meaning of sitting, which pertains to the life of the will or love (AE 687:6). The woman vanishing into a blackish cloud (as we are told later (AC 4627:3)) signified "female ensnarers" who relate to the mucus "which infests the nostrils." She can only correspond to an evil affection such as the lust of falsity from evil (AE 555:17). Black(ness) indicates what is not true (AE 372:1) (or falsity of evil; AE 412:30) and dense and dark clouds, falsities of evil (AE 594:19). Children signify innocence and this meaning is given to "little ones" in AE 624:6 and AC 5608.

415. These meanings suggest the following interpretation. The disorderly conjunction of affections with falsities led to a state of will or love in which the lust of falsity from evil drove away innocence so that perception from heaven could no more occur than a nose blocked with mucus from disease can smell. This vision may well have been given as an indication of the state of mankind at that time. It seems, from many other signs, that Swedenborg himself suffered from the sphere of spirits in that state. Because of this, he could not see the angelic spirits corresponding to the sense of smell and to the interiors of the nostrils until angelic choirs had been sent to disperse the evil spirits. This sad state of affairs leads us to an even more dreary consideration, namely, the possibility that thick mucus of the nose could be derived from the brain. Anatomically this seems to be almost possible, but the subject is presented in some detail below.

There is continuity of fluid spaces between the brain and the nose but it is not a route for excretion

416. The continuity of fluid spaces between the brain and the olfactory epithelium, as well as the possibility of leakage from brain cavities into the nose, has been discussed in a former chapter (Nos. 295-298). In the present context some statements from the *Spiritual Diary* and *Arcana Coelestia* should be quoted. In the *Diary* we read:

> There are spirits who relate to the phlegmy or viscous excre-
> tions, namely those which are excreted from the brain through
> the meninges and the fasciculated fibres into the nostrils, as well
> as through the little glands of the nostrils. (SD 1267)

And under the heading "Concerning those who Constitute the Nasal Mucus in the Brain" we find:

> I was instructed that these are they who constitute the pituitary
> mucus of the brain which is wont to obstruct...whence arise
> dullnesses and similar insanities. (SD 1793)

417. As explained more briefly above (No. 298), these ideas are closely related to the anatomy of the nose and brain. As Swedenborg's note suggests, the meninges are extended to provide sheaths for the whole length of the nerves connecting the olfactory organ to the brain. The outer membrane of the brain, which is the dura mater, descends into the nose and is continued into the periosteum which is the membrane that covers and helps to nourish the bones. The inner membrane, which is the pia-arachnoid, contains the cerebrospinal fluid in which the brain "floats." This membrane and its fluid descend also round the nerves into the nose and make connection with the tissue spaces of the mucous membrane, as shown in Figure 23. One can therefore understand the anatomists of the 18th century assuming that a continuous passage from the brain into the nose, however microscopic, must allow fluid to escape. However, a connection with tissue spaces does not imply a leak to the surface. Most tissues have spaces between some of the cells and these spaces are filled with a watery lymph. Some of this fluid is collected by the lymphatic system and returned to the blood from which it originally came (No. 201). Although the membranes of the nose are delicate, they will not leak fluid to the surface any more than any other membrane unless they are injured. Nevertheless the direct connection with the brain has been thought by some to permit access by organisms that cause meningitis. (The evidence for this is not free of doubt.) An additional point to note is that the nasal mucus has a different chemical composition from that of the cerebrospinal fluid which bathes the brain. For these reasons one is loth to believe that any part of the nasal mucus is normally derived from the brain.

418. The reference to pituitary mucus needs separate consideration. In the *Arcana Index* "phlegm" is given for "pituita," and the reference is AC 5386, the subject being the correspondence of the pituitary glands of the brain. However, there is no mention of what we now call the pituitary gland or hypophysis cerebri, and it would seem a fair supposition from the subject matter of AC 5386 that in those days pituitary meant merely excretory, or producing phlegm. Although mention is made of phlegmy substances being removed from the brain (in AC 5386), when viscid matters are referred to as being present (AC 5717, 5718 and 5724), the corresponding spirits have relation to disease or anxieties and as we have seen (in SD 1793), "pituitary mucus" in the brain causes "dullness and similar insanities." The natural evidence for this may well have been derived from anatomists of the time who may have found thickened cerebrospinal fluid when they examined diseased brains. A possible connection between those observations and a diseased state of the Church at the time of the Last Judgement was discussed above (No. 299). It is clear that a viscous fluid in the brain is disorderly, as the above numbers of the *Arcana* also indicate. Neither here, nor in any other part of the *Arcana* have I so far been able to find any statement that nasal mucus is derived from the brain. It would appear that there is a difference between the private notes which constitute the *Spiritual Diary* and the works published by Swedenborg himself. Although we would like to think that the private notes are correct in all respects we must accept that the differences are "of the Lord's Divine Mercy." If some of the statements in the *Diary* are really incorrect we may be pleased to find them omitted from the works published during Swedenborg's lifetime.

The protecting and cleaning effects of mucus may correspond to spiritual refreshment

419. Even the evil have their uses, and this is illustrated by the functions of mucus. The evil spirits mentioned above (411-414) were presumably those who were cast down and who related to the mucus of the nostrils (AC 4627:3). Mucus itself is merely a secretion, and as such is dead. However, it is here said to "infest" the nostrils. This indicates a disease such as a cold, in which mucus production is increased and many harmful microorganisms are entrapped in the mucus. Such germ-laden mucus would fittingly represent dull and stupid spirits who were also devoid of conscience. As is well known, in a healthy individual the mucus is a useful secretion which serves to moisten the inhaled air, to trap dust, and to keep the linings of the air passages and sinuses moist and healthy. Without it the organs of smell would become parched and useless, hence mucus is essential to the body's economy. In the days before bacteriology it may have been difficult to distinguish between mucus, phlegm, and pus. It may well be that any of the terms used in those days would cover the whole range of secretions from the gentle, bland moisture to the acrid, foul, irritating, germ laden product of dying tissues. If so, the correspondences of mucus could be equally varied, and might include many spirits who, not knowing what conscience is, are nevertheless harmless. At the other extreme would be those who ensnare for evil purposes. The ability to ensnare (AC 4627:3) relates obviously to the properties of mucus in entrapping and removing all kinds of particulate matter, especially dust and germs. How can this function relate to spiritual health? Consider how refreshed one sometimes feels after engaging in some perfectly useless activity that has no connection with conscience.

Are not many unhealthy impulses such as aggression or self-pity tangled up with such activities and neutralized, eventually to be removed? Recreation has a similar effect, though different in many respects; it is limited to certain times, for example, whereas protection by mucus is continuous. The unbalanced states corresponding to excessive production or inadequate production consequent upon various diseases might deserve further discussion but need not now detain us.

The development of the sense of smell illustrates the Lord's mercy and power in drawing the animal man upwards to heaven

420. Phlegm in the brain seems to represent the lowest state of man's decline. (It would also be the death of his body.) But from this nadir we may at last begin to ascend, starting again with the strange relationship between the olfactory epithelium and the brain. The continuity of fluid spaces already mentioned (No. 416) is especially interesting because the olfactory nerves do not grow down from the brain, but begin in their own place in the embryo and send their filaments towards the brain. What guides them is not known, but the tiny spaces in their sheaths must become continuous with those of the brain during this development. What can it mean correspondentially?

421. In many animals the sense of smell is much more important than it is in man, so that the ability to smell reminds one of man's animal nature. The growth of the nerves from the nasal organ towards the brain suggests the Lord's power of drawing this animal upwards towards Himself. The subsequent connection of the spaces with those of the brain suggests the subsequent descent of Divine influence. We are reminded that ascent came first in the dream of Jacob's ladder.

422. There is another descent from the higher parts of the brain in the form of nerves which control the olfactory lobe, but this type of control happens with other (all other perhaps) organs too so that the nose is not unique in this respect.

423. We have implied that smelling is closer to our animal nature than (say) seeing. We also know that "to smell" corresponds to "to perceive," and that perception was the characteristic of the Most Ancient Church. Dare we follow the argument as far as to suggest that the men of the MAC were more like animals than we are? Perhaps we dare, for the Writings often point out that animals live in the order in which they were created, whereas man has destroyed the order of his life. Moreover, the permission of the fall cannot have been forced on the Lord by man, and the Lord's coming cannot have been a mere rescue operation to remedy a desperate and unforeseen situation. It was all hidden in the Divine Wisdom for the sake of an end more glorious than the beginning. Thus the wisdom and understanding (sight) of the men of the future church may become more blessed than the perception (smell) of the men of the MAC; for the indications of our present study suggest that such wisdom would not preclude celestial perception, as sight does not preclude scent.

Correspondences show the kind of relationship there is between perception and understanding

424. We have seen the consanguinity there is between perception and celestial qualities (No. 398), and hence the dependence of perception upon love. There is also the relationship between understanding and wisdom. Now since love and wisdom ought to be united as in a marriage, so perception (related to love) should be joined with understanding (related to wisdom). Correspondences give a clear indication of such a joining, for not only does sight not preclude scent, but it lends it more meaning. When we notice a perfume we usually look for the source. The desire to see suggests that perception leads to a desire to understand. Indeed the perception of the angels relating to olfaction has a close connection with sight, for the apertures that were seen in the world of spirits represented the *clearsightedness* of the angels who relate to the interiors of the nostrils. We note also that although the apertures were said to be representative, suggesting that they were not really apertures (as a television system would not be an aperture), nevertheless they were a real means by which the angels could see. The rest of the paragraph (AC 4627:3) contains much about what they saw. The close connection with sight is further shown by the presence of little children, all of whom are in the province of the eyes in the Grand Man (HH 333). Besides this, we are shown (AC 4625) that at least some of those who relate to the nostrils were not of that province as a whole in the Grand Man but of a sub-province "in the society to which I was sent." We later learn (AC 4627:2) that this society was of the province of the eye, for every society of heaven is an image of the whole. The society relating to the eye must therefore include a smaller society relating to the nose, and vice versa.

425. Celestial angels who are in perception are averse to discussing matters of faith. There is so much in the Writings about this that it may come as a surprise to realize the close connection between perception and understanding. We are often told that perception is superior to knowledge derived by an external way. The latter is often called faith, and faith is of the understanding. Thus arises the notion that perception has no need of understanding. However, there are innumerable varieties of perception, and possibly some are more closely related to understanding than others. It may be said that there are some that need very little of the understanding. Some aspects of these subjects elude the natural mind. Many things relating to the celestial are of this class and so appear either incomprehensible or contradictory. The fourth posterity of the MAC (AC 283), for example, had become celestial and thus wise and intelligent (AC 298). Nevertheless, they were not allowed to be instructed in the mysteries of faith. Such apparently contradictory matters can sometimes be resolved with the help of correspondences which point the way for us who need to visualize. In this instance it is appropriate to introduce something about the limbic system, as it includes parts of the brain that are active in responding to odours. It is also the home of primitive emotions and it generates bodily responses which sometimes contradict the main personality. More realistically, we would say that it is more liable than other parts to the influx of those less noble spirits whose uses are close to the body and who include some that are only too ready to sweep a man off his feet.

The interplay between the limbic system and the cerebrum underlines the conflict in man

426. The anatomy of the limbic system is helpful since it gives a physical basis for many human peculiarities, including the constant struggle to behave as human rather than as animal. The region of the brain that gives the name "limbic" to this system was so called because it forms a sort of border (limbus) to the cerebral cortex where this overlies the brain stem in the region of the temporal lobes. The limbic lobe merges with the cerebral cortex in such a way that it is difficult to define it precisely. There are close links with other brain structures of comparatively primitive type, to produce the limbic system as a whole. Altogether the system has a wide range of responsibilities for maintaining the functions of the body that we usually think of as automatic. These include many movements and bodily responses to fear and anger and pleasure and even possibly something of the emotions themselves. (This need not surprise us because in AC 4947 we find a reference to desire being of the body; it is called "external desire.") The nerves of the olfactory tract (called mammillary processes in earlier times, see No. 296) lead into this border region, which is therefore the part of the brain most closely concerned with the sense of smell, and it forms part of the higher centres mentioned above (No. 408).

427. The limbic system is complicated and its actions are only partly understood. It is closely associated with the cerebral cortex but not entirely dependent upon it, so that experimental animals that have been deprived of the cortex continue many of their instinctive activities by means of the limbic system. From this we may be able to understand in a slight degree how it may be possible to live and feel, and perhaps be conscious with very little activity of the understanding. Perhaps this region predominated with the primitive men "who lived like wild creatures but at length became spiritual men" (AC 286), and with, for example, the fourth posterity of the MAC who were on their way back to the ground from which they were taken.

428. The union between the limbic system and the cortex depends upon whether dendrites from certain groups of neurons make contact with groups in the cortex, and to what degree their activities are enhanced or inhibited. The union is therefore flexible, and capable of being modified. If we accept the usual view that the limbic system is more primitive than the cerebral cortex, and note its great importance in the life of animals, we can imagine that in primitive man it may well have been more important than it is to us. The emotional predominance resulting from activities of the limbic system may not then have been subject to so much cerebral (or intellectual) control as it is in man today. In a state of innocence the emotions would have been of love and joy; with fear and hatred of natural hazards and suffering playing their protective part. As ages passed, the influx from the growing cerebrum (memories and imagination) would arouse intense desires that it might hope to control, but if the cerebrum were not yet dominant it would submit to the influence of the limbus and the man would relapse into an animal nature no longer innocent.

429. Such a process could have occurred as a result of the fall of the Most Ancient Church, and looking at these ultimates helps us to understand those unhappy beings. For it is astounding that they declined from such a blessed state when they knew the quality of the celestial with them (AC 146). As has been pointed out earlier, these changes were not unforeseen, and there can be no doubt that the Lord intended harmony between the limbic system and the cerebrum. In their freedom, men destroyed the harmony and themselves, but Noah was saved in spite of it all.

430. These changes are relatively recent and even today the situation is not all that different. There are often occasions when the limbic system is powerful, though not necessarily disorderly. These occur for example when certain odours arouse tender memories, delightful emotions, or powerful disgust; the last often in spite of knowing that the odour itself is perfectly harmless. In the last case the understanding (sight) often remains in abeyance, and the feelings (smell) drive one to avoidance. Similar neural mechanisms operate with the opposite result in the attraction of the sexes. These kinds of behavior, which correspond to perception having little relation to understanding, have their counterpart in brain structures which were mentioned above. Thus the correspondences help us to understand a little about the quality of celestial man as well as to recognize the vestiges of that quality remaining in us by heredity.

CHAPTER XVII

EATING AND DIGESTION—PART 1
A BRIEF ACCOUNT OF BODILY DIGESTION

Digestion is the breaking down of large molecules into smaller ones, a change that is sometimes dramatic

431. Everyone who is not familiar with chemistry is surprised to realize that there is a limit to the smallness of any piece of a substance. Although the limit is far below visibility it is so real that if this smallest possible particle or molecule is further divided or broken, two or more different substances are produced. The differences can be small or great. For example, a house is no longer a house if it is cut into two, but the pieces are still obviously pieces of a house. The great differences are no less amazing than it would be if a spade, being deprived of its handle, immediately modified itself into a foot-ball and a flower pot. Thus common salt, if separated into its two constituents, becomes sodium (a soft, shiny metal which tarnishes in a few minutes in air and decomposes water) and chlorine (a faintly greenish, very poisonous gas). On the other hand, common sugar, being split into two, forms two other sugars different, but not remarkably different, from their parent. Such analogies and particular examples can be quite misleading, but these may suffice for a first general idea.

Most of the constituents of food are molecules with a much more complicated make-up than common salt, and many of them are very large, as molecules go, and much too large to be accepted into the body (except fat, some of which enters in spite of its large molecules). These large food molecules must be broken down into specific units of a suitable size and quality by an orderly process. This is digestion.

Digestion in living subjects is carried out by enzymes which, however, are not themselves alive

432. In the whole of the animal and plant kingdoms the break down or digestion of large molecules is conducted by specialized agents known as enzymes. Other enzymes serve in the building-up processes. Most of the activities inside living cells are carried out by enzymes, and often the activities outside the cells by means of enzymes also, but different ones. All enzymes are produced by living tissues. There are very many different kinds of enzymes, each capable of one particular function. Many processes other than digestion are carried out by them; the digestive enzymes are a relatively small group out of a vast array. The digestive enzymes are wonderfully designed for their particular use. For example, they are produced in the inside of living cells but they do not digest the cell that produces them. This is usually because they are produced in an inactive form, the essential parts being tied up or blocked off. (Imagine a key wrapped in plastic.) After leaving the producing cell, they meet different conditions which remove the blocking agent. It is difficult to understand how enzymes work. It used to be thought that some special vital quality existed in them because they were produced by living tissues, but now their activities can be well explained in terms of chemistry and physics. They work equally well outside the body providing the conditions are correct (temperature, acidity, etc.).

433. The fundamental changes going on during digestion are best understood if the three main constituents of food are treated separately. We deal first with carbohydrates (i.e., sugars, starch, etc.), then with proteins (in meat, fish, cheese, and in some vegetable foods), and finally with fats and oils (as butter, margarine, etc., but plentiful in many foods and present as traces in most).

The digestion of large carbohydrate molecules produces sugars like glucose, the molecules of which are small enough to be absorbed

434. The digestion of carbohydrates is fairly easy to grasp. They form a large class and include the smaller class of sugars. There is a considerable number of sugars, ordinary sugar, i.e., cane or beet sugar being only one. Other common sugars are fructose (present in fruit) and glucose (the sugar that circulates in the blood and is fuel for bodily activities). Thus when glucose is taken no digestion is needed. It passes directly through the fine walls of the minute blood vessels in the inner surface of the small intestines. Cane sugar, on the other hand, must be digested before we can use it. It is fairly small as food molecules go, and is composed of only two other sugars, glucose and fructose. It is split into these after it has been absorbed by cells in the wall of the intestine.

435. The story with starch is different. It consists of a very long chain, more or less branched, the links of which are mostly glucose units. Several different enzymes can liberate the glucose; some can only break the chain into shorter lengths, and the glucose molecules are then chopped off the ends one at a time. Other enzymes act differently. For example, when barley grain is germinated, i.e. , made into malt, the stored starch is made available to the growing plant embryo by an enzyme that breaks off the glucose units in pairs. These two molecules of glucose joined together are called maltose. In the human, the digestion of starch begins in the mouth by means of an enzyme which is more efficient in breaking the long chain into shorter pieces than in liberating individual glucose or maltose units. The rest of the digestion is carried out by the juices from the pancreas. The glucose then passes through the intestinal walls into the blood stream and is carried to all parts of the body as a source of energy, that is, as a fuel.

Proteins need digestion with several enzymes in order to liberate amino acids

436. Proteins are the structural units used by the body to build muscle, skin, hair, tendons, and many other tissues. Edible parts of meat and fish are thus mostly protein (apart from the water). Useful quantities are also found in peas, beans, wheat, etc. Every living organism, plant or animal, contains some protein. Enzymes are also proteins. In order to produce his own enzymes and muscles and most other parts of his body, a man must absorb the small molecules from which protein molecules are built. Most of these small molecules belong to the class called amino acids. They are liberated by the digestion of the proteins present in the food.

437. Proteins are more complex than starch. Their very large molecules are built up from twenty or so different kinds of amino acids. Protein molecules vary in kind and in size. Some are built up from only about a hundred amino acids. Others require several thousands. Sugars also are combined in some proteins. The formation of such a variety of huge and complicated molecules from only twenty different kinds of units is sometimes compared to the formation of words, sentences, and long printed pages from only twenty-six letters of the alphabet. In this analogy, a small protein would be like one sentence, and a larger one like a page of print. Many proteins contain all the amino acids required by man. Some proteins contain a super-abundance of one or two amino acids, but in general a balanced diet gives an average mixture of amino acids regardless of which proteins are eaten.

438. The amino acids are tightly bound together in proteins, and their liberation is perhaps the main burden of digestion, which, in the case of proteins, takes place in three stages: one in the stomach and two in the intestines. The digestion in the stomach begins with hydrochloric acid which has an instantaneous effect on some proteins; it causes the chain of amino acids to extend into a more open structure, facilitating the attack by enzymes. The strength of the hydrochloric acid is remarkable as everyone knows who has suffered from regurgitation. Nothing can live in an acid of this strength, and many of the micro-organisms present in the food are killed; though some survive if they are protected inside resistant particles of food. The stomach itself is protected by copious layers of mucus.

439. The enzyme of the stomach (pepsin) can attack relatively few links in the chain of amino acids. Hence it breaks each protein molecule into only a few pieces, each piece still containing a number of amino acids. Nevertheless, the specific properties peculiar to each individual kind of protein are lost. The fragments produced by the action of the pepsin are further broken down in the intestine. Here, the stomach acid is neutralized, and powerful enzymes from the pancreas attack the amino acid chains at many points, liberating fragments containing only a few amino acids. As the partly digested food is moved along the intestine, it becomes mixed with a third group of enzymes which finally liberate the separate amino acids. These can then enter the blood, and be distributed for growth and maintenance, which require the linking together again, of the amino acids into proteins, but now into the characteristic order that is unique to the tissue being produced or repaired.

Fats are partly digested and partly absorbed as minute globules with the aid of the lymphatic system

440. The digestion of fats is carried out by an enzyme, or group of enzymes, known as lipase, but is assisted by bile from the liver. The bile acts as a detergent, breaking up the fat into minute globules. This is essential for adequate digestion because the lipase can act only on the surface of the fat, and the large drops of fat or oil would take a very long time to digest. Lipases are produced in a number of sites, but the most important is probably the pancreas. As mentioned above, some of the fat can be absorbed without digestion. That which is digested is resynthesized as soon as it has passed into the wall of the intestine. The result in either case is an emulsion of very fine fat droplets, and although they are very small they cannot pass through the walls of the capillaries into the blood stream. Instead they are absorbed by the lymphatic system which is adapted to receive particles that are too large to enter the blood (See Chapter VIII, Nos. 196-224).

441. In this part of the body, then, the lymph is rich in fat globules, giving it a milky appearance, so that the network of tiny transparent tubes is clearly seen. Since they look as though they contain milk, these vessels are known as lacteals, and the contents form the chyle which is mentioned in the Writings. As the chyle and the lacteals are easily seen *post-mortem*, they were known to the anatomists long before more advanced methods revealed many other lymphatic ducts. As related in Chapter VIII, the chyle flows into the venous blood system and then to the heart. So the fat is mixed with all the blood and is carried to sites where it may be stored for use in case of starvation; or to the tissues where it may be converted into simpler substances for energy production if required. This conversion is a more complex process than liberating glucose from starch.

There are important constituents of food that need no digestion

442. These constituents include vitamins and minerals, which form an essential part of our diet although the quantities are so small. Glucose is imbibed in much larger quantities (from grapes, raisins, and some drinks, for example) and needs no digestion. Many other substances are absorbed without digestion, but may be changed afterwards (e.g., fructose, alcohol, some medicines).

Many animals make use of bacteria to digest food that would otherwise be useless to them

443. It was mentioned above that nothing could live in the acid conditions of the stomach. As soon, however, as the acidity of the digesta is neutralized in the duodenum, the micro-organisms already there and others that have survived the acid either as spores or inside particles, grow under the new conditions and reach very high numbers. In the human they probably do not aid digestion significantly, but in the vegetarian animals that rely on cellulose for much of their energy, micro-organisms digest plant materials which otherwise would not become available. Such animals have a means of delaying the passage of food so as to give time for the micro-organism to effect digestion. In the cow, for example, the delay is in the first stomach or rumen; in the rabbit it is in the caecum and appendix; and in the horse it is in the colon. In such animals these structures are relatively large. In the human the caecum is quite short and it terminates in the appendix, which is only a narrow tube with no outlet. The micro-organisms that live in the rumen or in the caecum and colon are essential for the nutrition of mammalian herbivores which are themselves unable to digest cellulose. Without the aid of the micro-organisms they would need a richer diet than grass or hay. (Cows do receive a richer diet to increase milk production, but if they have too little fibre the amount of cream in the milk is reduced. This is because most of the milk fat is produced from the products of the action of bacteria in the rumen.) Some of the micro-organisms are also digested.

444. As we are studying the correspondence of the Grand Man with the human body, mention of digestion in animals might seem out of place. However, we know that the whole of nature is a theatre representative of the Lord's kingdom. Moreover, "the external man…separated from the internal, is in itself no other than a wild animal, having a similar nature, desires, appetites, phantasies, and sensations, and also similar organic forms" (AC 272). It seems reasonable, therefore, to assume that the organs in animals correspond to spiritual things, as do those in man. It is, of course, from spiritual influx that "rumination" has come to mean "thinking things over." Indeed we read in AE 242:4 that man's memory corresponds to the ruminant stomachs of animals and birds.

CHAPTER XVIII

EATING AND DIGESTION—PART 2
THE CORRESPONDENCE OF DIGESTION

The correspondences of eating and digestion teach many things about the spiritual progress of man

445. Eating is often mentioned in the Hebrew Word, and the Lord Himself said, "I am the living bread which came down from heaven; if any man eat of this bread he shall live for ever; and the bread that I will give is my flesh, which I will give for the life of the world." When the Jews heard this they were puzzled (John 6, 51, 52). Since that time Christians have been happy to treat these sayings as metaphorical and to enjoy the benefit of the truth they enshrine. In the New Church the doctrine of correspondences enables this truth to be perceived more clearly; it opens the way to an infinite series of truths relating to our life in the Lord, and the Lord dwelling in us.

446. The significance of eating is not, however, restricted to the holy supper. Students of New Church doctrine know that the signification of eating is appropriating, that is, making something one's own. Thus they will understand how the reception of newly arrived spirits in the other life can be represented by eating. The better ones among novitiates are taken into heaven, made heaven's own, and become part of that wonderful organization which is in such harmony that it is really one man.

447. However, many of those who will eventually reach heaven need first to be liberated from contaminating evils and falsities. Such spirits are said to be agitated and purified, like food in the stomach. Such agitation can be slight or severe, according to necessity (AC

5174). A study of digestion in the body gives hints as to how severe such agitation may be. It is clear, however, that those whose ruling loves are fixedly evil cannot be changed into their opposites by any degree of agitation. They are excreted into hell.

448. These general statements (AC 5174, 5175) will be sufficient for many, but the Writings always encourage us to think further if we can. It will be a useful exercise to try and discover a little more about what is involved in the correspondence of the digestive system with the Grand Man. Much that is now known about what happens to food during digestion was unknown in Swedenborg's time. By means of this more recent knowledge, together with correspondences and doctrines, we can form opinions about the preparation of souls for heaven. Such a study can be of practical value for, as death is a continuation of life, so the processes occurring after death have their beginning in this life.

Digestion corresponds to the preparation of souls for entrance into heaven or hell

449. Digestion corresponds to the preparation of souls in the other life, hopefully, for entrance into heaven. We read, "For when a man dies and enters the other life, his life resembles food which is...passed...into the stomach." (AC 5175). A reading of AC 5174 conveys the impression that not only acquired beliefs, habits and ideas are subjected to "digestion" in the spiritual world, but the man himself. Concerning this, we read:

> food in the stomach is agitated in many ways in order that its inner elements may be extracted...it is further agitated in the intestines. Such agitations are represented by the first agitations of spirits...therefore it may be said of souls or spirits that, shortly after death or release from the body they come first as it were into the region of the stomach...They in whom evils have

gained the ascendancy…are conveyed…into the intestines…the colon and rectum, and…into the privy, that is, into hell. But they in whom goods have had the ascendancy…become chyle and pass into the blood…so long as spirits are in a state resembling food in the stomach, so long they are not in the Grand Man but are being introduced into it; but when they are representatively in the blood, then they are in the Grand Man. (AC 5176) (No. 197 above explains "Grand Man.")

450. We note the use of "resembles" (AC 5175) and "as it were" (AC 5174), and think perhaps this case is one of similarity and not of actual correspondence. But against this idea we find "the correcting and purifying of the…food in the stomach correspond to such things in the spiritual world" (i.e., to spirits undergoing "very many methods of agitation" (AC 5173:1)). The same number continues to explain that unless there were "an inward active force from the spiritual world…nothing whatever in the natural world could act as cause and effect, and consequently nothing could be produced." We conclude that none of the ideas about the correspondences of digestion that we find in the Writings can be dismissed as mere metaphor or simile. Nor are they in the same category as the representations of things good and true by persons evil and false in the Jewish Church.

451. As, therefore, the digestive system is in genuine correspondence with the Grand Man, it is worth attempting to see in more details *how* it corresponds.

As in the body, the end of digestion is resynthesis, but in heaven there is endless variety within each tissue

452. Before digestion is described in AC 5173:1, mention is made of "agitations," and it is highly significant that the first mention of "agitations" is closely linked with "initiation into gyres." We learn later that the agitations correspond to digestion, and as digestion is a breaking down, so initiation into gyres must correspond to a building up or resynthesis. Most of the food by which the body grows or is renewed is first broken down by digestion, and after absorption via the blood, it is resynthesized into bodily tissues. This means that a study only of digestion provides no picture of reality. Such a study gives the oils, the pigments, the canvas. The real picture comes only with the synthesis. When re-synthesis occurs, the individual food constituents are not re-created. It follows that reformed souls in the next life are not reborn into their original imperfection. Thus, the Grand Man is not to be thought of as suffering limitations like those of the natural body. No particular new tissue in the body retains any trace of a link with any particular food (excluding isotope labelling for the moment); whereas in the spiritual world some residue of the proprium (duly modified) is retained. Therefore, any particular organ or tiny part of an organ must include a much greater variety than the corresponding tissue in the body. This is merely spiritual common sense, but we read also, "There are more things contained within a single idea of [spirits'] thought than in a thousand of the ideas they had possessed in this world" (AC 322).

453. The natural variations to which the variety in the Grand Man could possibly correspond include variations in the proportions of different isotopes of the elements present. Providing the isotopes are stable, such variations make no practical difference, but they are detectable by physics. If all the theoretically possible variations in the proportions of different isotopes were included, an enormous number of permutations could be imagined. However, this seems rather artificial. Carbon thirteen is still carbon. Nevertheless, we must bear in mind the presence of isotopes as a natural phenomenon with a spiritual cause that we do not know about, and it could certainly correspond to a kind of individuality. This is clearly an avenue which ought not to be neglected, but for the time being we will see where we can get to with the aid of biochemistry alone. We reiterate, then, that the smallest part of a tissue in the Grand Man must contain indefinitely more variety than the corresponding tissue in the natural body (and this may well still be true if isotopic variations in the natural body are included).

454. Further consideration of the re-synthesis of digested food into bodily tissues is too great a subject for the present, and we must limit ourselves to thinking of digestion. But it is of the greatest importance to bear in mind throughout that the purpose of digestion is constantly that re-synthesis may follow. In a similar way, the purpose of Providence is to bring good out of all the evil that is permitted, for digestion sometimes appears like a permission of evil. We proceed, then, to discuss the breaking down of food, which is digestion, and the agitation of spirits, which is their last judgement; from this we hope to see how the complete digestion of food can correspond with a judgement that is not totally destructive. This problem, however, scarcely arises with the first class of foods which consists of those which need little or no digestion.

Foods needing little or no digestion correspond to people who enter heaven easily

455. Examples of food constituents that require no digestion were given in Chapter XVII (Nos. 434, 442). Concerning these we read, "Food that is soft and contains what is sweet, oily, and spirituous is at once absorbed by the veins, and carried into the circulation" (AC 5175). We can be more precise about this category now. It appears that "spirituous" means substances like alcohol and the aromatic esters in fruit. Alcohol can be absorbed from the mouth as can also the esters given to relieve angina pectoris, for example. It seems that the food substances that can be so absorbed are relatively few. For the rest, we must interpret "at once" to mean without going through any preparatory stages of breakdown. We make this interpretation because the sweet and oily substances are absorbed, like the products of digestion, from the intestines, but without requiring digestion first.

456. It is interesting that some sweet substances like grape sugar (glucose) and fruit sugar (fructose) and some of the oils or fats are not only absorbed without digestion, but go through the digestive tract without being affected. In the section on natural digestion, the severe effect of hydrochloric acid in the stomach (and of pepsin) has been described, especially how the acid is able to kill many bacteria and destroy the native configuration of many proteins (No. 438); yet these sugars (presumably meant by "food juices" in AC 5174) are quite unaffected by it.

457. Turning now to people to whom these sweet and oily juices correspond, we note two classes who pass through the world of spirits, or stomach of the Grand Man, without significant change: (1) those who are so confirmed in evil that they cannot be purified, and (2) those who have already been sufficiently purified. This also agrees with experience in this life, for we know that there are wilfully evil men who will not repent however much they suffer. There are also good and patient people who seem to bear their trials as though they do not suffer, although they pass through vicissitudes of life that are very distressing to most of us. Thus in their entry into the Grand Man, these souls are not agitated like the rest, although they pass through the same spiritual environment.

458. As shown earlier, we include in this group of foods the minerals and vitamins, which are not mentioned in the Writings but which, as is now well known, are essential for the maintenance of the life of the body. They include, of course, water, a mineral corresponding to truth; without which all that is truly human expires. What special spiritual qualities do other minerals and vitamins correspond to? We can speculate about them from their known functions. Sight depends on vitamin A, and we know what sight corresponds to. Calcium and vitamin D are important in the growth of bones, the correspondence of which is also known. These are merely examples quoted in passing, this not being the place to enter into detail.

459. In regard to digestion, these foods have no interest. In regard to preparation for heaven, the corresponding people do not at present stimulate our interest either. This is odd because they are clearly the best and most useful. We conclude that the spheres where they are interesting are elsewhere, actually within the Grand Man. This agrees with biochemistry. The study of vitamins and their functions forms a major field in this discipline, and the minerals are no less important.

Foods needing digestion correspond to people whose mental associations must be loosened

460. It is here that we face the problem of relating the complete digestion of food to a judgement which does not destroy the individual.

461. It is tolerable to imagine a similarity between digestion and the fate of men in the next life, as long as one thinks that digestion is merely a liberation of the essential goodness of the food and forgets that even in the act of chewing much food is crushed out of recognition. One may think that the correspondence is with the essential goodness in a nutritional sense and that what corresponds to crushing will not affect those who correspond to such goodness. This seems satisfactory until one remembers that to get into heaven, i.e., the Grand Man, spirits must be "representatively in the blood" (AC 5176). This would relate spirits to those molecules which can pass into the blood, and this gives rise to some queries, for the digestion of the proteins and carbohydrates abolishes their individuality. Glucose from starch in, e.g., bread, is indistinguishable from glucose of honey which did not require any digestion at all (the bees having done it). It is similar with the amino acids. We have seen above that digestion destroys the characteristics of every digestible protein in the food and produces the same amino acids from all of them. (Notable differences in proportion remain only between special kinds of diet which we would probably regard as unbalanced.) Thus, the idea of relating novitiate souls to molecules on the basis of one person to one molecule would seem to be too restrictive.

462. Another reason why it does not seem possible to relate individual spirits to the units remaining after digestion is that some spirits seem to correspond to particular kinds of food. For example, "food that is still harder, more disagreeable, and non nutritious is thrust down into the intestines, and at last into the rectum, where first is hell...It is similar with the life of man after death" (AC 5175).

463. The problem may be expressed by saying that, as an understanding of chemical breakdown and recombination had scarcely begun in Swedenborg's time, nothing about the correspondence of it could be taught. We are left to deduce what we can. Clearly, the chemical, i.e., digestive, breakdown of foods which correspond to people in the next life cannot relate to the destruction of persons or loss of individuality (though this has gained credence in some religions). Although the destruction of food constituents is not "complete," or down to atoms, but an ordered taking to pieces, it still means a loss of individuality to any particular food. The apparent discrepancy indicates a more complex representation than appears at first sight, and therefore a more detailed examination is necessary.

464. We ask first whether an individual can be broken down spiritually, and if so, to what extent. First, in general terms, we have the well known quotation: "The Lord is nigh unto them that are of a broken heart and saveth such as be of a contrite spirit" (Ps. 34: 18). We know that the Lord does not break but bends a man's loves. Nevertheless, hearts get "broken," and if they rely on the Lord, the experience can be turned to good effect. But a more particular examination of the question may be facilitated by introducing the well known psychological concepts of association of ideas and formation of complexes. These may also be likened to items of food that may be more or less resistant to being broken down by digestion.

Revelation and current psychology both indicate that mental complexes have a life of their own which is often a mixture of good and evil

465. It is in agreement with the doctrines, with experience, and with the correspondence to food that each of us is a mixture of good and bad. Many of the souls which will be received into the next life will have goods and truths that will not be much affected by the agitations. These goods and truths are acceptable to the Grand Man as they are, and correspond to simple sugars, vitamins, minerals and water which are present in many foods and do not need digestion. In any individual there may well be other goods and truths the Lord has provided. But during his life on earth the man may have also imbibed falsities and evils and may have affixed some of them to these goods and truths (though not united them as in profanation). Thus the man has produced for himself ideas, opinions, beliefs, and convictions, clustering round various affections linked in various ways to his ruling love. Some of these things form associations which need to be loosened by the agitations. The Writings, in their references to the internal memory, to ruling loves, to affections being derivations of loves, and to loves collecting their supporting truths, revealed much that is in agreement with later discoveries of psychology. This science itself can therefore be of use to those of us who were not educated in the Church. It may help us to accept and understand the complexity of the mental (i.e., spiritual) life of each individual and the existence therein of complexes which can often rule in spite of the individual's attempts to dethrone them, indeed of complexes which even seem to take on a separate personality of their own. Presumably, this last is the ultimate of a close association with particular societies of spirits. Such complexes need not be bad; indeed they are often good; bad ones, being troublesome, merely come to notice more.

466. The idea of complexes having a life of their own receives support where "the creeping thing, the living soul" (Gen. 1: 20) is explained (AC 41).

> Every single expression, every single idea and every least thought in an angelic spirit is alive, containing in its minutest particulars an affection that proceeds from the Lord, who is life itself. And therefore whatsoever things are from the Lord, have life in them, because they contain faith toward Him, and are here signified by the "living soul": they have also a species of body, here signified by "what moves itself," or "creeps."

Hence all these things would appear to have some degree of autonomy or life of their own received from the Lord. Thus we move away from the simple idea of personality as a unit, towards the view that there is no difference in essence between an idea or a complex and the person in whom it exists. This is why angels can know a person's qualities from one of his ideas. The idea cannot occur without the person, and the person without an idea is not existing. Each idea takes a quality from the whole and so takes on a personality which mirrors the personality which gave birth to it. In this way we arrive at a concept which permeates the Writings, but seems not to be stated in so many words: namely that each man is not a unit but a population, as with Noah and the ark. We may summarize these ideas by saying that each individual entering the other life takes with him a unique synthesis of many different components, good and bad. Often the bad can be set aside only after more or less break-down has been induced.

Mixed complexes are not permitted in the next life

467. The occurrence of mixed complexes is according to the Divine Permission and their dissociation under Providence is inevitable (DP 16-18). Where this is not too difficult, it corresponds to digestion.

468. We have already seen that digestion is an orderly process of taking molecules to pieces. Although orderly, it is severely destructive as far as those molecules are concerned. Such a process would correspond to the agitations of AC 5174. These correspondences suggest that an early process in the next life is the taking to pieces of unacceptable complexes. From psychology we know that, even in this world, associations of ideas can be dispersed and replaced by others, and we would expect this to be done more skillfully and more extensively in the spiritual world.

469. As has been emphasized above, individual spirits cannot be destroyed as protein and carbohydrate molecules are destroyed, but they may be "taken to pieces," i.e. criticized with merciless severity. Psychoanalysts say they can change the personality of their patients by taking them or their complexes to pieces and rebuilding them in a more acceptable form. We have called digestion a breaking down of molecules and we can apply the same term to the ideas and loves of people, but the process can be distressing. We are here dealing with those who correspond to food that is "reduced with more difficulty" (AC 5175). This speaks of those who do not readily accept the means of reformation provided by the Lord or whose personalities are more resistant. The man as a whole is not destroyed; but even if not predominantly evil he may love his proprium too much; then many things that he holds dear may be broken down and he may feel as though he himself is being destroyed. Lest this should seem too drastic an experience for many to believe, let us recall some of the records in the Writings.

470. One of the most telling episodes is Swedenborg's descent to spirits who were for a long time crying out, "O God! O God! Take pity on us! Take pity on us!" They were in despair, saying that they believed their torment would be eternal. However, he was allowed to comfort them (AC 699), which suggests that perhaps they were eventually to be rescued. We observe that meanwhile they were in torment and despair. Similarly in AC 2130:2 we find reference to societies who were rescued after having been in despair; and in many places we are taught that temptations continue until a state of despair is reached (AC 6144). I suggest that, as a consequence, the personality can be to some degree disintegrated. Something like this is the experience of all who are regenerated in this life, but we must not allow our natural terms to lead us to forget that mental changes experienced in this life are often in a low key. Distractions of the world and the body produce a kind of anaesthesia. In the spiritual world similar changes are vivid and intense. The disintegration of the personality that I am here suggesting would be, to a spirit, the tearing apart of his body.

471. The amount of tearing to pieces which a spirit can suffer without being destroyed is made clear from the punishments endured in hell (see below). The simplest direct statement is found in the SD 515 to the effect that a man (i.e., presumably his body) cannot be torn asunder like a spirit. The suggestion then is that the tearing asunder of the large molecules of food constituents is not much more drastic than what some spirits have to undergo. In hell, this tearing is a punishment to enforce a certain degree of order. Above hell, something similar might be permitted to remove evil loves from the centre of the personality and to enable good loves to reorganize the personality into a useful and acceptable creature. Under these circumstances, the effect would not be induced as a deterrent and it might therefore be achieved without pain. All things of this world have their origin in the spiritual world and this must include the art and science of anaesthesia.

472. Another reason why preparation for heaven need not be very painful is because digestion, to which it corresponds, takes place by means of enzymes (see No. 432) produced in glands which are actually part of the body. These glands, therefore, have their correspondences in the Grand Man among angels. Orderly spiritual processes corresponding to digestion must take place under angelic control, which implies the maximum care and concern for the sufferer.

473. The drastic changes mentioned above (No. 469) were leading our thoughts towards the confines of hell. We were following the gut contents on their way down and were approaching the rectum "where first is hell," but we are not quite there yet. By the mercy of the Lord, many who we might think are not salvable are yet rescued in thousands of ways. Some of these ways are induced by means of the very evils and falsities that infest them. Such things may well correspond to digestion by micro-organisms.

The infernals who cause vastation probably correspond to bacteria that aid digestion in animals

474. We are now considering those who go to heaven after much difficulty, i.e., those who correspond to food that requires the maximum of digestion. Such people are to be found in the lower earth or in the pits beneath that earth. Of these two locations or spiritual states we read as follows:

[475.] That 'pits' are falsities is because men who have been in principles of falsity are, after death, kept awhile under the lower earth, until falsities have been removed from them, and, as it were, rejected to the sides. These places are called 'pits', and those who go into them are such as will undergo vastation. (AC 1106-1113, 2699, 2701, 2704)

It is for this reason that by 'pits', in the abstract sense, are signified falsities. The lower earth is proximately under the feet and the region roundabout for a short distance. Here are most persons after death, before they are taken up into heaven. This earth is also frequently mentioned in the Word. Beneath it are the places of vastation, called 'pits', and below them and round about for a considerable extent, are hells. (AC 4728)

476. As the pits here mentioned are places where falsities are removed, we may be sure that those who are there eventually become fit for heaven. Also, as "most persons" are in the lower earth before they are taken up into heaven, they are the ones who are capable of being adequately purified by the activities that correspond to digestion. We note also that the situation of the lower earth, the pits beneath, and the hells further below and round about, are similar to the course of the intestines into the colon and finally the rectum, toilet and sewage disposal corresponding to hell. We find further details in AC 7090 as follows:

[477.] At this day also, those who are of the Church, and have filled their ideas with worldly, and also with earthly things, and have caused the truths of faith to be adjoined to such things, are let down to the lower earth, and there also they are in combats, and this until those worldly and earthly things are separated from the truths of faith, and such things inserted that they can no more be conjoined. When this is accomplished, they are then elevated from there into heaven; for until such things are removed they cannot in any wise be with the angels, for those things are darkness and defilements which do not agree with the light and purity of heaven. Those worldly and earthly things cannot be separated and removed except by means of combats against falsities, which combats are effected in the following manner: those who are in the lower earth are infested by fallacies and consequent falsities, which are emitted from the infernals round about, but are repelled by the Lord through heaven; and at the same time truths are insinuated; and these truths appear as belonging to those who are in combats.

478. Here we have a factor not mentioned in the account of the correspondences of digestion, namely combat against falsities from the infernals round about. We saw above that the digestion that takes place by means of enzymes produced by glands of the body must correspond to angelic aid and correction (No. 472). There is an additional digestion in herbivores (No. 443) which takes place by means of bacteria within the contents of the gut, thus not caused by the tissues

of the body. We may assume that these bacteria correspond to the infernals who induce falsities.

479. Possibly bacteria in the gut of man can have a purifying effect (for example, the harmless help to inhibit the harmful) but they are probably not important for digestion. However, as we have seen, digestion in animals is also relevant. In such as the horse we have an example clearly corresponding to the combats endured by those who have adjoined the truths of faith to worldly things. It is clear that this kind of spiritual digestion is very important in this life also for all who are being reformed. But the insertion of things to prevent such adjoining being repeated must be similar to initiation into gyres (AC 5173). Unless it is temporary, it must correspond to the resynthesis of digested food into tissues (which is not considered here).

The final stages of digestion include the disposal of sewage and correspond to the uses of hell

480. Some of the punishments in hell are a sort of tearing to pieces or discerption (AC 957). This is reminiscent of the tearing to pieces of food constituents by bacteria in the gut. We read that the only tearing in pieces in the spiritual world is that of good by evil and falsity. This was so when Israel said in reference to Joseph, "Surely tearing he is torn in pieces" (Gen. 44: 28; AC 5828). We are familiar, too, with the teaching that in the next life the evil are deprived of any good they may have. We conclude that the good with them is torn to pieces (or digested) by their evil and falsity or by those of their companions. Similar processes continue in sewage, becoming more and more destructive as they correspond more nearly to hell. As hell has its uses, so sewage has its corresponding uses as a fertilizer (SD 2660) or a source of energy. However, dung also corresponds to previous evils which one learns to abhor to such an extent that "a faculty of good may be inseminated."

Unpleasant representations are permitted for useful purposes

481. Some aspects of digestion are unpleasant. We prefer to dwell on the delightful things we are taught in the Writings about paradise. This is pleasant, but it would be unrealistic to do so exclusively. We know too well that unpleasant things exist, and the Writings give us no encouragement to imagine that they cease when life in the world is over. The doctrine of the Church would be unrealistic if this aspect of man's experience were ignored; the proprium is itself horrible, and it is obvious that whenever it is allowed to break out, horrible things will ensue. Representations of them will appear when the Lord permits. For example, when the sphere of an approaching evil spirit is changed into an odour, the experience must be disgusting. The most unpleasant representations are probably those that terrify. An example is the irresistible power represented by a bare arm (AC 4934-5) shown for a useful end under Providence. Another example of unpleasant representations is the occasion when Swedenborg saw a spirit changed into filthy intestines (SD 3087).

482. Obviously filthy things must not be ignored, as is clear from many passages in the Writings concerning the permission of evil. These things must receive sufficient attention to bring them under control. We need not be surprised that the Divine Revelation includes references to them. Representations of them are seen in the spiritual world according to *Divine Providence*, that good may come of them. The prospect of being broken down in spirit like food in the gut is so important that we ignore it at our peril. Also, it is so unpleasant that we do well to try, as of ourselves but really of the Lord, to become persons who need little or no digestion, or who at least do not bring distress upon themselves by their attempts to resist the process. However, the prospect is not necessarily terrifying, and there is another and brighter side to the question which we may now consider.

The more interior correspondences of eating and digestion are Full of heavenly delight

483. When a spirit has successfully endured the horrors and tribulation of the temptations corresponding to digestion, he can join those who have not needed such experiences and enter with them into a peaceful state made all the more delightful by contrast with his previous experience (DP 24). We, too, may now consider a delightful heavenly aspect of this same subject. In following the correspondences of food as it is digested during its movement down the alimentary canal, we have, as it were, drawn closer to hell, and our attention has been diverted from a question which is fundamental to this whole subject. It has appeared as though novitiate souls are food for the Grand Man. This correspondence, however, must not be understood in a materialistic manner. In the next chapter, we try to see how spiritual and material things differ and yet correspond. Meanwhile, we attempt to understand more clearly how it can be that in the spiritual world the life of new arrivals resembles food. Thus we ask whether there is any other food for the Grand Man.

484. Every angel is a heaven in particular, and so is like heaven in general. Thus "heaven is like itself in general and in particular, and…the human form is the form of the whole, of every society, and of every angel" (HH 460; see also HH 59-86). From this we deduce that what is food for individual angels is also food for the Grand Man. Concerning this food we read, "The nature of celestial and spiritual food can best be known in the other life. The life of angels and spirits is not sustained by any such food as there is in this world but by every word that proceedeth out of the mouth of the Lord, as the Lord teaches in Matthew 4,4" (AC 681). Also "the nourishment by which children grow up in heaven is intelligence and wisdom, for these are essential spiritual nourishment" (HH 340).

485. Sustenance by every word that proceedeth out of the mouth of the Lord is related to the Word made flesh. In John, the Lord says "Who so eateth my flesh and drinketh my blood hath eternal life" (John 6: 54); (TCR 703). This must also be related to the doctrine that every man is led and taught by the Lord alone (DP 155-174). Thus, although a man may receive truth from another man, if he is receiving genuine truth in a genuine manner, he is receiving it from the Lord. As the Lord's truth is also the Lord Himself, the man is receiving the Lord. So if he makes the truth his own, he appropriates it, and implied in receiving it genuinely, is the necessity of receiving good at the same time. Thus, he is appropriating good and truth in, from, and of the Lord. This is to eat His flesh and drink His blood. Furthermore, in order to make it his own, the man must understand it. He must chew it over, ruminate upon it, digest it, and absorb it. These operations are accepted metaphors for mental processes (because they are true correspondences from the spiritual world), and here they involve first taking the Lord's truth and good to bits. This chewing, ruminating, and digesting are necessary because we cannot deal with the whole. Understanding involves seeing how the various bits of truth are related to one another, or how general truth can be made of numerous particulars; but the main purpose of digestion is to make possible the absorption of the truth into life. This last must correspond to the synthesis of bodily tissues from the digested food. Its spiritual counterpart is the formation of a new will, or new man, during the process of regeneration. Thus, what is the Lord's is built into the man; but it is clear that it also remains the Lord's. The man is in the Lord and the Lord in him (John 6:56).

486. Now, in spite of regeneration, man remains imperfect. In making the Lord's truth his own he will link it with apparent truths, even with falsities. (This is done with no evil intent, thus not from hypocrisy with deceit such as causes profanation.) Besides such contamination, the man will inevitably link truths together in an imperfect way, so that they do not serve good as well as they might. For example, there may be two truths which can only be associated correctly with the aid of a third, but the man may force them together in a disorderly way. There may also be two other truths which cannot function if the influence of a certain third one is made too strong. (These fairly obvious suppositions are based upon what happens in the building up of proteins from amino acids by living organisms and in the laboratory.)

487. We can now see what may be understood by "his life resembles food." The all of a man's genuine life is from the Lord. This also is the life and the food for angels and the Grand Man. We have already seen how a man can eat the Lord's flesh as he receives instruction. We now see how the angels can do the same as they receive newcomers in the other life, since each newcomer will have something of the Lord which, of course, must be made useful in heaven. For this purpose it must be purified, as described above in AC 5174 through 5175. However, from our knowledge of digestion we can see that the general idea of purification can and should include particulars that correspond; these particulars include what we know of the taking to pieces of large molecules in order that other molecules better suited to the life of the man can be built up. It is suggested, then, that the digestion of individuals in the other life is a taking to pieces of all those things of the Lord that the individual himself has assembled in an imperfect order. This done, the pieces can be reassembled correctly for the optimum use, and the man in whom they are can find his place and joy in heaven where the use is.

CHAPTER XIX

THE INTERFACE BETWEEN THE SPIRITUAL
AND THE PHYSICAL

*There is a great difference between the form of a cause and the form of
its effect*

488. Throughout this work we have tried to see how strictly things natural correspond to things spiritual and to learn something from the correspondences. This has necessitated a degree of preoccupation with natural science. It is clear, however, that there are additional dimensions in spiritual things; and that a too rigid adherence to natural phenomena excludes those dimensions and inhibits the appreciation of love and wisdom. But what is too rigid? The study of digestion in its harsher aspects, as depicted above (Nos. 463-482) stimulates further inquiry. Obviously it is important to militate against all merely materialistic notions of correspondences. Such notions tend to arise when one tries to understand them strictly, as we have been doing all along. On the other hand, they ought not to be used in a loose and arbitrary fashion. When things are said "to correspond" and when it is said that "Nature is a theatre representative, etc." (AC 3518 [3]), it is not meant that our ideas of nature can be used as mere symbols, as in mathematics, but that the things in nature are caused by those in the spiritual world. Much remains hidden concerning the manner in which a spiritual cause produces an effect in the natural world, but a few points are made clear. First, it is important not to lose sight of the discrete difference in degree between the spiritual and the natural. It is not possible to translate directly from the natural to the spiritual, even with a compendium of correspondences; for the form of the spiritual cause is quite different from the form of the natural, or physical, effect. This has been mentioned several times before (e.g., Nos. 6, 7 and 276). Such an important general principle must pervade all studies of this kind, and a reexamination of it forms a fitting conclusion. As in all other cases, the clearest teaching is directly from the Writings. The following is found in AC 5173:3:

> The case herein is like that of the motion of the muscles from which comes action; unless there were in this motion an endeavour from man's thought and will it would cease in a moment;…this…endeavour…is the spiritual in the natural, for to think and will is spiritual and to act and be moved is natural…Nevertheless that in the will and thence in the thought, which produces, is not alike in form to the action that is produced; for the action merely represents that which the mind wills and thinks.

489. An example from common experience enables us to apply these ideas to the digestive process. It is well known that in certain types of individuals, anxiety will stimulate overactivity of the stomach tissues that produce acid, so that gastric or duodenal ulcers arise. The cause is in the mind and is thus spiritual. It is but a small step to believe that benign spirits can stimulate the controlled production of all the juices necessary for healthy digestion. It is only one more step to think that, therefore, similar means are adopted by Providence to cause the growth in the body of the requisite glands. Thus we see how the spiritual cause is entirely different from the natural effect.

490. This "law" of correspondence has many natural laws corresponding to it. For example, the base sequence in the DNA molecules that controls the colours of dear old Mendel's sweet peas has no beautiful colour itself, and the other genes that shape the flowers have nothing that would suggest a flower. It is even more striking in the human organism, as we have already seen. Love produces a smile, willing service, and joy. Yet what is the form of the love? What is the form of the swarming myriads of nerve impulses in the brain that the love excites? Perhaps merely a pattern of minute electrical discharges in a bewilderingly complex sequence. We know only a little of the form of the nerve tissues in the brain (speaking spatially and chemically) in which these discharges take place. It looks nothing like a smile or a willing pair of hands. Spiritual things are even further from the everyday experience of our senses. What is surprising is not their difference but that we can be instructed at all about them from things of sense in time and space.

A cause cannot operate without efficient executive means

491. It is really very striking, if one has not thought about it before, to observe that the causes mentioned above are so different from the effects that they seem to have nothing in common with them. One is amazed that the cause can operate at all, but we see that it does so. Furthermore, it succeeds by adopting executive means from the realm of the effect: "in order that the cause may produce the effect, it must also adopt from the region where the effect is, executive means, by which the cause may produce the effect. These executive means are what correspond; and because they correspond…the cause can be in the effect and can actuate the effect" (AC 5131:2). It is the necessity for the means to be efficient that controls their form and is responsible, in part, for their great difference in form from the cause. To return to digestion again, the chemistry and physiology of the body is such that it cannot use most of its food unless the large molecules are broken down. Although the cause may sometimes be a gentle agitation and purification of souls for heaven, the corresponding nourishment of the body requires, or necessitates, the harsh means of complete digestion (except for the few items that do not need digesting).

492. It is the difference in form between the cause and the effect that renders an executive means necessary. So are all the tools of a workman; so are all the enzymes of the body. The intermediate nature of the executive means suggests a consideration of them as a kind of interface (or surface-between). This would be similar to the interfaces used to connect a computer to the various machines that it must operate; or, to use a very simple example, like the connectors between a stereophonic record player and the system of loud speakers it must operate. The arrangements of membranes and enzymes at the ends of nerves which control muscles are also a kind of interface.

493. Calling the executive means an "interface" solves no problems. It merely underlines some similarities between those means and the interfaces that occur in the body or that man has developed for the application of computers.

494. It seems likely that there is not one interface between the spiritual and the natural, but many. Truth Divine flows into the ultimates of order by successive degrees, but also without the mediation of such degrees (AC 7270:4). What can be the nature of the interface used by the Lord for this immediate influx? It must be quite different from that used by (or through) the angels who are our companions. It was perfected, one may believe, by the Lord's Glorification.

495. Even if the nature of the interfaces eludes us, we need to remember their existence, for difficulties sometimes arise with them which make some people doubt the reality of spiritual things. Possibly some mental diseases are examples of faulty function of the interface. See for example the booklet by Wilson van Dusen, "The Presence of Spirits in Madness." We also have the case of the partially healed blind man who saw people as trees to which they might have corresponded.

Executive means are harsher than their causes

496. Because executive means are in the lower sphere where the effect is to be, they are further from the Divine, and therefore less benign. As Divine Truth (which includes Good) descends from the

Lord, it is expressed in less gentle, and eventually in harsh and crude forms; even until in hell it is changed into the opposite. Thus in Genesis 29:31 the literal sense says that Leah was hated, whereas the spiritual reality is that the affection she represented was loved less than that represented by Rachel; "the affection of external truth was not so dear" (AC 3855). Similarly in regard to Esau hating Jacob; the internal sense of which is aversion but without any idea of hatred (AC 3605). The same effect of descent is described in AC 8823:

For the case herein is as it is with sound in elevated regions where the atmosphere is purer, and the sound is tacit; but when it descends to lower regions where the atmosphere is denser, it becomes louder and more sonorous. So it is with Divine Truth and Divine Good, these in the highest (regions) are peaceful and cause no disturbance whatever; but when they flow down towards the regions beneath, they by degrees become unpeaceful, and at length tumultuous. These things were thus described by the Lord to Elijah when he was in Horeb, in the first book of the Kings:

Go forth, and stand on the mountain before Jehovah; behold Jehovah is passing by; so that there was a great and strong wind rending the mountains, and breaking in pieces the rocks before Jehovah; Jehovah was not in the wind: then after the wind an earthquake: yet Jehovah was not in the earthquake: after the earthquake a fire; Jehovah was not in the fire: lastly, after the fire, a tenuous voice of silence. (Kings xix:11, 12)

497. From these particulars we can see why nature is "red in tooth and claw" and why natural digestion can be completely destructive, but spiritual digestion preserves the soul's identity, even while modifying it.

The richness and variety of representations is a result of the quality of spiritual things

498. The closeness and regularity of correspondences might lead us to expect a one-to-one relationship between spiritual causes and natural effects, but it is not so. We have seen that spirits who, according to some passages must be correspondentially in the intestines, are also in the lower earth (AC 4728; 5174). This raises the question of how they can be in two such different "places," and emphasizes further the importance of understanding correspondences in a spiritual and not in a material way.

499. There are a number of other representations recorded in the Writings that seem to conflict with one another. However, this conflict is often the result of our tendency to apply the limitations of time and space to spiritual things which are actually not so limited. This applies in the present instance, but there may well be additional reasons which explain why various representations are seen. Spiritual things that seem simple to us (or single) are often not really so and thus they have many different representations. We know also that representations in the spiritual world are not seen all the time, and that they occur by the Lord's will, good pleasure, or permission and according to the use to be served. Thus, for example, the spheres of spirits are changed into odours "when the Lord pleases" (AC 4626). Thus while the correspondences relate permanently to the production of phenomena in nature, they produce spiritual representations only according to the uses required. (Clearly the laws of Divine permission and use apply also in the realm of nature, but with a difference.)

500. The problem of manifold representations is not really hard at all. We have only to remember human affections and the many corresponding bodily actions. There is no numerical ratio.

APPENDIX

SIGHT, THE VISUAL PROCESS, AND DOCTRINE[1]

Aubrey T. Allen

A501. It is stated that:

Faith, as to its existence in man, is spiritual sight. Now as spiritual sight which is sight of the understanding, and thus of the mind, and natural sight which is sight of the eye and thus of the body, mutually correspond, every state of faith may be compared with some state of the eye and its sight—a state of faith in what is true with every normal state of eyesight, and a state of faith in what is false with every perverted state of eyesight. (TCR 346)

A502. According to this there are two kinds of sight, natural and spiritual. That there is a natural world of reality we can confirm by all of our bodily senses. However, it is not so easy to confirm the reality of the other, or the world of the spirit. In *Arcana Coelestia* 3721:2 it is said:

It appears to man that the objects of the world enter through his bodily or external senses, and affect the interiors; and thus that there is entrance from the ultimate of order into what is within; but that this is a mere appearance and fallacy is manifest from the general rule that posterior things cannot flow into prior; or what is the same, lower things into higher; or what is the same, exterior things into interior; or what is still the same, the things which are of the world and of nature into those which are of heaven and of spirit.

---

[1] Aubrey T. Allen, "Sight, the Visual Process, and Doctrine," in *The New Philosophy*, 84:1&2:26-35, 1981.

Also, in *Arcana Coelestia* 3739:2.

> In man that which is inmost inflows in like manner into that
> which is lower; and this in like manner into that which is lowest
> or last. The natural and corporeal consists of such an influx and
> concourse into those things which are beneath, and finally into
> those which are last.

A503. Influx is from inmost to outmost, and to seek direct access to
the spiritual world by means of sense experience is to invert the laws
of order. We can, however, observe organic structure in the course of
its development, and gain insight into what is normal and what is not
normal; or that which is of order and that which is not of order. This,
not only as to structure, but also as to function of structure.

A504. Now, if every state of faith may be compared to some state of
the eye and its sight, we would think that in the course of our observation we could gain some insight into the doctrine of truth. The normal
development of the eye and its function would correspond to true
doctrine and enlightenment of the understanding, while abnormal
development of the eye as to structure and function would correspond
to false doctrine and obscurity of the understanding. As far as any
individual is concerned, we know that this is merely representative
and not necessarily correspondent. Nothing is reflected upon the
person, but upon the thing that is represented (AC 665, 2010, 4281).

A505. It will be the purpose of this paper to investigate sight as a
process, and to consider how the various states of sight of the external
degree relate to, and correspond to, the various states of sight of the
interior degree, both as to their normal and abnormal aspects, and to
relate this to the Word and doctrine.

A506. The brain and the eye-visual pathway represent 2% of our
body weight, but demand 25% of fuel input (nutrition). The eyes'

visual pathway requires more fuel than any of our body's organ systems. It uses 1/3 as much oxygen as the heart, though it would take 60 eyeballs to equal the weight of one heart. Forty percent of all nerve fiber going to the brain originates in the retina, though it is one millionth of our body weight.[2] Each eye can send a million impulses per millisecond to the brain. For the whole organism, including the eyes, there are as many as three million signals per millisecond.[3]

A507. However, we must understand that when we use the term vision we must include more than just eyes and eyesight per se. Reliable sources indicate that at least 80% of learning occurs through the visual pathway, so we must consider vision as a process that includes the retina as a sense receptor, the brain as a control center, and the muscles of the eyes and body as external mechanisms to express behavioral responses triggered by sensory stimulation. This increases our scope to include vision and vision problems as part of the complete person as he performs in his every day environment.[4] And, as Gesell says:

the organ of sight...is more than a dioptric lens and retinal film. It embraces an enormous area of the cerebrum; it is deeply involved in the autonomic nervous system; it is identified reflexively and directly with the musculature from head to foot. Vision is so pervasively bound up with past and present perfor-

---

[2] Morgan B. Raiford, *Vision and Health* (Atlanta, Georgia: Health Symposium, 1978), pp. 1-3.

[3] Arnold Gesell, Frances L. Ilg, Glenna E. Bullis, *Vision, Its Development in Infant and Child* (New York: Paul B. Hoeber, Inc., 1950), p. 4.

[4] Elliot B. Forrest, *Vision and the Visual Process* (Indianapolis, Indiana: Bobbs-Merrill Co., Inc., reprinted from *Education*, vol. 82, No. 5, January, 1962), p. 299.

mances of the organism that it must be interpreted in terms of a total, unitary, integrated action system.[5]

A508. This leads us to understand more clearly why the Writings say that the eyes correspond to understanding. If we look at *Arcana Coelestia* 4410, it is said relative to correspondences:

It has been made clear to me by much experience that the sight of the left eye corresponds to truths which are of the understanding, and the right eye to affections of truth which also are of the understanding. Hence the left eye corresponds to truths of faith, and the right eye to the good things of faith.

A509. This would lend itself to the thought that the left eye corresponds to what we clearly perceive to be true, and the right eye to what we clearly perceive to be good. Projecting this thought outward to things of creation, we can see so many things that are created with a dual nature, especially in the higher degree. Some reflect more of Divine Love, and others more of Divine Truth. From lowest forms to highest forms we have, successively by degrees, a revelation of the Divine Love and Wisdom until it culminates in the highest degree and the image of that love and wisdom revealed in the male and female form. Can we ever comprehend this reality? Man is, in the highest degree possible to express, the object of Divine Love and Wisdom. It is the object of this love to love others outside of itself, to desire to be one with them, and to make them happy from itself. It would appear, therefore, that the most important thing in life, and I cannot overemphasize this, would be to understand how we can better cooperate with this love, so that we may better be able to reciprocate with it. To do so we must understand more about it. It is said in John 1:1-4:

In the beginning was the Word, and the Word was God. The same was in the beginning with God. All things were made by

---

[5] Arnold Gesell, *et. al., loc. cit.*, p. 6.

Him; and without Him was not anything made that was made.
In Him was life; and this life was the light of men.

A510. Here it is said that there is life in the Word, and that it created all things. This would lead us to wonder what in reality life is. If we go to Divine Love and Wisdom No. 35, it is said:

there is such a union of love and wisdom and wisdom and love in God-Man...and since there is such a union of these, the Divine Life also is one. Divine Love and Divine Wisdom are one because the union is reciprocal, and reciprocal union causes oneness.

A511. Thus, we should remember, life is one because it is the result of the reciprocal union of Divine Love and Wisdom, and this in God-Man. In John 6:63, it is said "the words that I speak unto you, they are spirit and they are life." Therefore, that which goes forth from the Lord as a result of the reciprocal union of love and wisdom constitutes life, and it is spiritual. It is spiritual as to essence, but in its ultimate form it is natural. This is the reason why, to the people of the Most Ancient Church, the world of nature was the Word. Their interiors were in a state of order, and for this reason to them the natural forms of creation were living correspondences revealing there a union of love and wisdom. This union of love and wisdom has to be in all created forms for it to have continual existence (DLW 36).

A512. If we want to understand more about the truth concerning life, we have to consult the Word, because the Lord is Speech and the Word (AC 1642). We learn from this source that the origin of life became flesh and dwelt among us (John 1:14). He therefore, has arms, legs, hands, feet, and eyes, just as you and I have. In man as to details of structure they are numberless; however, in God-Man, they are infinite (DLW 18). We should remember that the Word, as to its letter, has a natural sense that corresponds to the natural heaven; but internally it has a spiritual and celestial sense corresponding to the spiritual and celestial heavens (SS 6). It was written in this way so that all states of life, both in the natural as well as the spiritual world, could receive life from it.

A513. If we are to receive life from the Word, it is very important that we understand rightly how to approach it. We cannot approach it just any way, but it must be approached from a good affection, and for the sake of understanding truth for its own sake. Very few at this day do this, for most who read the Word do not read it from affection of truth, but from the affection of confirming therefrom the doctrinal things of the Church in which they were born (AC 6047). If we are to understand true doctrine we must approach it for the sake of truth itself, and this for the sake of life (AC 7053).

A514. Because the eyes represent understanding, and through these organs and their visual pathway 80% of our learning occurs, and because one represents love, and the other truth or wisdom, we can say that their reciprocal union represents life, or the Word. So, in our approach to the Word, let us here relate it to the eyes, and to the process whereby we acquire understanding of the Word. To do so we will first relate the globe of the eye to the Word in its three degrees, and thence to the three heavens.

A515. The globe of the eye consists of three concentric coverings or tunics enclosing the various transparent media:

1. The outermost coat, 5/6ths of which is made up of a posterior part which is white and opaque and called the sclera, and the remainder of which is an anterior transparent part called the cornea. (Represents the letter of the Word, or the natural heaven.)
2. The middle part from behind forward is the choroid, ciliary body, and iris. (Represents the interior sense of the Word, or the spiritual heaven.)

3. The innermost tunic is the retina, or the true receptive portion for visual impressions.[6] (Represents the inmost sense of the Word, or the celestial heaven.)

A516. We are, therefore, in a position to relate what has been said to the Word; to relate the globe of the eye in its three degrees to the Word in its three degrees and to the correspondent heavens; and to view vision as a dynamic process whereby we acquire understanding of the Word.

A517. When light enters the eye it must enter through the pupil. The clear front surface of the eye, anterior to the pupil, is called the cornea and consists of a small portion of the outmost tunic. The outmost tunic of the eye represents the letter of the Word, or the natural heaven, and the small anterior transparent part of this tunic called the cornea would seem to represent those clear truths in the letter of the Word upon which our understanding must focus—such truths as "he that hath seen Me hath seen the Father" (John 14:9); also "for as the Father has life in Himself so hath He given the Son to have life in Himself" (John 5:26). The as-of-self effort to locate and find these truths from good affections, and for the sake of life, would seem to be represented by the extrinsic muscles. Once the as-of-self effort has located and found these truths they are positioned directly in front of the pupil. They then pass through the pupil and enter the crystalline lens capsule.

A518. The capsule encloses the lens of the eye through which light must travel. The accommodative power of the lens would seem to represent an intense desire to acquire understanding for the sake of life. This is part of the second tunic of the eye representing the interior sense of the Word, or the spiritual heaven. The desire to understand

---

[6] Eugene Wolff, *The Anatomy of the Eye and Orbit* (Philadelphia-Toronto: The Blakiston Co., 1948), p. 29.

bends light toward the retina, and it is brought to a focus on the macula.

A519. The retina is the third or inmost tunic of the eye and represents the inmost sense of the Word, or the celestial heaven. The macula is the most sensitive area of the retina. When light strikes this area, behold, a strange thing happens. Natural light is converted into spiritual light, and man views the letter of the Word not from himself, but from the Lord. This area of the retina represents the Writings, and in particular the fovea, its inmost part, would seem to represent the Doctrine of the Lord. When light is brought to focus in this area, there is clear confirmation of those truths that have gained admittance through the pupil, especially those concerning the Lord. The scleral part of the outmost tunic of the eyes would seem to represent the clouds of heaven; but the clouds become transparent when the as-of-self effort locates them, and they then gain admittance through the pupil because they are seen in the light of the Heavenly Doctrines, from the Lord. We then see the New Jerusalem, the Holy City, descending from God out of heaven, and it is marvelous in our eyes.

A520. It would be good at this time if we reviewed some of the basic anatomy and physiology of the eye. If we are to relate the eyes to the visual process, we have to go beyond the retina tracing the visual pathway to the occipital cortex of the cerebrum—for this is the pathway, as represented in the Word, whereby the Lord reforms and regenerates man; and if we are to understand this process as it relates to our as-of-self part in it, a review of the anatomy and physiology of it will help, and then we can relate it to the Word.

A521. Once light enters through the various media of the eye and impinges on the retina it is converted in the retina into neural energy. Light does not, and this is a very important point, enter into the organ of sight. We cannot think in terms of putting such and such a stimulus into or through the organism.[7] These nerve impulses arise within the organism as a result of firing by the organism's own cells. This energy is transmitted by the retina via the optic nerve to the optic chiasma. It is here that the nasal fibers of each retina cross over, or decussate, to join the temporal fibers on the other side of the opposite eye. Once they leave the chiasma, they constitute the optic tracts, and proceed backward and outward to pass around the peduncles of the cerebral hemispheres. As they wind around these each tract splits and forms two roots, a larger lateral external root, and a smaller medial internal root. Fibers of the larger root proceed to the external geniculate body, while the fibers of the smaller root proceed to the ciliary body. Therefore, on the left side, the fibers of the left external geniculate body receive fibers from the temporal fibers of the left retina, and nasal fibers of right retina; and the right external geniculate body receives fibers of the right temporal retina and nasal left retina. They proceed from thence in the form of optic radiations. They end up in area 17, known as the visuo-sensory area. In the calcarine cortex we have a visual center of a higher order. To establish single vision, the nerve impulses from both retinas must be unified. The right and left are united in such a way that we are entirely unconscious of any separation they have undergone. Other modifications of the impulses from the eyes take place here, and unified modified impulses are sent higher up into the nervous system.[8]

A522. Regarding this Duke-Elder says:

It is interesting that in animals stimulation of the striate area results in ocular deviations; in man, however, this does not occur, but only on stimulation of the peristriate ocular motor

---

[7] N. C. Kephart, *The Perceptual Process* (Duncan, Oklahoma: Optometric Extention Program, Series I, No. 6, 1957), pp. 21-24.

[8] W. D. Zoethout, *Physiological Optics* (Chicago: The Professional Press, Inc., 1947), p. 136.

area, a finding indicating that in him these reflex functions have been completely transferred to a region of higher association.[9]

A523. In regard to this transfer region Adler says:

Outside area 17, and closely following its contours, are two other areas which are concerned with visual reactions also. These have been termed the paristriate area or area 18 and the peristriate area or area 19...Area 18 has been considered the visuomotor field and area 19 the visuopsychic field...The anatomic boundaries of these areas are not exact, and not only their function, but also their location and extent have been disputed. This is due partly to differences in various species. In man, for example, area 18 plus area 19 is almost three times as large as area 17. In the orangutan, area 18 plus 19 is not even twice the size of area 17, and, in the monkey, area 18 plus area 19 is still somewhat smaller in relation to area 17.[10]

A524. The macula fibers form a separate group from the rest of the retina. They run directly from the fovea to the disc in a compact bundle...The macula fibers...lie on both sides of the perpendicular line through the fovea [and] are both crossed and uncrossed...[in their progression].[11] In lower mammals, large numbers of retinal fibers run to the superior colliculus and...provide an integrating mechanism of considerable complexity in relation to visual impulses.[12] [This is not true in man, so far as is known; all these fibers end in the lateral geniculate body.] In man, the lateral geniculate body is the exclusive

---

[9] Sir Stewart Duke-Elder, *System of Opthalmology* Vol. VI, *Ocular Motility and Strabismus* (London, England: Henry Kimpton Ltd., 1973), p. 70.

[10] Francis Heed Adler, *Physiology of the Eye*, 4th Edition (St. Louis: The C. V. Mosby Co., 1959), p. 683.

[11] *Ibid.*, p. 669.

[12] *Ibid.*, p. 675.

source of fibers in the optic radiation...[and] give rise to new fibers, forming the third neuron in the optic pathway. This proceeds through the optic radiation to the cells in the striate area of the calcarine cortex.[13] In man, all the visual fibers end in the so-called striate area of the cortex...In monkeys, much of area 17 [the striate area] is found on the lateral surface of the occipital lobes.[14]

A525. The message which is relayed to the visual sensory cortical area [area 17] enables one only to see. It does not enable a person to recognize what he sees nor to recall things which have been seen.[15] [In order to do this the message must be sent to the peristriate areas 18 and 19, and to the angular gyrus where information for visual symbols is found.]

A526. If the sensory system alone were involved, and it was not necessary to trace this stimulus any further than its representation in the cuneus, we would have no problem so long as the sensory receptor and the conducting sensory nerves were intact. However, the final and most important element of seeing is the effector system.[16] Goldstein says, "the efficacy of the outside stimulus is determined by the effector itself...in other words the effect is really caused by the effector."[17] This is also stated by Renshaw[18] when he says that seeing is motor. We will discuss this in greater detail later when we consider the perceptual act.

---

[13] *Ibid.*, p. 678.

[14] *Ibid.*, p. 680.

[15] *Ibid.*, p. 695.

[16] A. M. Skeffington, *Near Point Optometry* (Duncan, Oklahoma: Optometric Extention Program, Vol. 2, No. 4, 1947), p. 18.

[17] Kurt Goldstein, *The Organism* (New York-Chicago: American Book Company, 1939), p. 81.

[18] Samuel Renshaw, *Visual Psychology* (Duncan, Oklahoma: Optometric Extention Program, Series 21, No. 12, 1961), p. 44.

A527. In the seeing mechanism there are two types of effectors, visceral or autonomic, and skeletal or somatic. The visceral operates through smooth muscle, while the skeletal operates through striated or striped muscle. The visceral operates the muscles controlling the crystalline lens, the iris, etc.,[19] while the skeletal operates the extrinsic muscles that serve to move the eyes in their orbit. According to what has been said, if the effectors really cause the effect, and if reception is really determined by the condition of the effectors, then seeing is dependent upon the reciprocal relationship between these effectors. If, in the act of seeing, this dual effector system must work together as one in order to accomplish its use, which is vision, it would seem to represent a functional concept of conjugial love, relative to the visual process.

A528. Therefore, to recapitulate, the visual process involves three degrees, just as the globe of the eye involves its three degrees; both corresponding to the Word and the heavens in their degrees. The three degrees of the visual process are as follows:[20]

A. SKELETAL: The visual system seeks and holds an image. (Represents the letter of the Word, or the natural heaven.)

B. VISCERAL: The visual system discriminates and defines an image. (Represents the interior sense of the Word, or the spiritual heaven.)

C. CORTICAL: The visual system unifies and interprets an image. (Represents the inmost sense of the Word, or the celestial heaven.)

A529. In future papers we will trace the visual process from the retina to area 17—and relate it to the process whereby the Lord reforms and regenerates man. It seems to recapitulate the history of the human race; also the history of the churches on earth and in each individual; also the pathway that the Lord took in the glorification.

---

[19] A. M. Skeffington, *loc. cit.*, p. 18.

[20] Arnold Gesell, *et. al.*, *loc. cit.*, p. 163.

SIGHT, THE VISUAL PROCESS, AND DOCTRINE[1]

Aubrey T. Allen

II

Introduction

A530. We have studied[2] the globe of the eye and have related its three coats, or tunics, to the Word in its three degrees. Also, we have discussed vision as a process, and have related it to how we acquire understanding of the Word; likewise, we discussed the three degrees of the visual process, and its relationship to the Word. In so doing we traced the visual pathway to the cortical area of the brain. At this point I would like to share with you these beautiful words of Sir Charles Sherrington—where he describes vision.[3]

> But the chief wonder of all we have not touched on yet. Wonder of wonders, though familiar even to boredom. So much with us that we forget it all our time. The eye sends, as we saw, into the cell-and-fibre forest of the brain throughout the waking day continual rhythmic streams of tiny, individually evanescent, electrical potentials. This throbbing streaming crowd of electrified shifting points in the spongework of the brain bears no obvious semblance in space pattern, and even in temporal relation resembles but a little remotely the tiny two-dimensional upside-down picture of the outside world which the eyeball paints on the beginnings of its nerve fibers to the brain. But that little picture sets up an electrical storm. And that electrical

---

[1] Aubrey T. Allen, "Sight, the Visual Process, and Doctrine," in *The New Philosophy*, 85:4:138-147, 1982.

[2] Aubrey T. Allen, "Sight, the Visual Process and Doctrine," in *The New Philosophy* 84:1&2:26-35, 1981.

[3] Charles Sherrington, *Man on His Nature*, Cambridge Univ. Press, 1942, pp. 128, 129.

storm so set up is one which effects a whole population of brain cells. Electrical charges having in themselves not the faintest elements of the visual—having, for instance, nothing of "distance," "right-side-upness," nor "vertical," nor "horizontal," nor "colour," nor "brightness," nor "shadow," nor "roundness," nor "squareness," nor "contour," nor "transparency," nor "opacity," nor "near," nor "far," nor visual anything—yet conjure up all these. A shower of little electrical leaks conjures up for me, when I look, the landscape; the castle on the height, or, when I look at him approaching, my friend's face, and how distant he is from me they tell me. Taking their word for it, I go forward and my other senses confirm that he is there.

Conjugial Love and Regeneration

A531. In a previous paper[4] we discussed the right way to approach the Word. After these prerequisites have been fulfilled, and we "as-of-self" approach the Word, light is brought to a focus on the retina. The effort to understand brings it to focus on the most sensitive layer of the retina, the macula. This area, we suggest, represents the Writings; and, inmostly, the fovea the Doctrine of the Lord. Here, by means of the Writings, natural light is converted into spiritual light, and we view the Word as to its letter from the Lord. Man is then able to confess that the Writings are in essence spiritual, and that they constitute the interior life of the letter of the Word. This is the only way that there can be a progression of the church in conjugial partners, and in mankind as a whole.

A532. In reference to conjugial partners, they now begin to confess that they have understanding from the Lord, and that they live from the Lord. However, this confession is a little bit different in each of them. The male confesses primarily from the understanding that truth

---

[4] Aubrey T. Allen, *loc. cit.*

is from Him, and secondarily that he lives from the Lord. The female confesses primarily that she lives from the Lord, and secondarily that truth is from Him. This, because the form of their life is different, consequently their approach to the Word. The Lord, therefore, leads them differently, but always toward union or oneness of life. However, the quality of the reception of this life will be dependent upon their reciprocal relationship toward each other.

A533. We need, now, to describe the difference in the quality of the nerve fibers in the retina. It has already been noted that the right eye signifies the feminine nature of man, and the left eye the masculine nature. In each eye though, there will be that which corresponds to both good and truth, or in the opposite sense evil and falsity.

A534. In the female, affections rule, and she is the form of them, so the temporal or outside fibers of the right eye represent the love of good in her. The nasal or inner fibers would seem to represent her inward nature, or the tendency to love falsity. The masculine nature is a form of truth, so the outside retinal fibers would seem to represent the love of truth, while the inward or nasal fibers would seem to represent the love of self. As these fibers from both eyes leave the retina, and progress along the visual pathway, they approach chiasma, or the pathway where two ways meet. It is here the Lord will separate their inward nature from their outward nature, and use good qualities in each to regenerate the dead quality in the other. His direct approach to each will be used by Him to infill and fulfill in the other that quality of life that will be a blessing to them. To do this, at the chiasma, he crosses their inward, perverted loves over to the other side. In the process, in the male the loves of self, represented by the nasal fibers, cross over and are associated on the other side with the temporal fibers of the right eye, represented by the love of good. As a result the love of self is replaced in him by the love of good, and constitutes the love of his wife in him, or his inmost love. In the female, the nasal fibers which represent the love of falsity, cross over and are associated on the other side with temporal fibers of the left eye. These fibers represent the love of truth from the Lord. As a result, her inmost life becomes the love of her husband's understanding, in her. The temporal fibers on each side, because they represent good qualities in each, do not cross over, but proceed with this new association to the lateral geniculate body on each side. This would seem to represent the inner celestial heaven.

A535. As a result of this association—resulting in the reception of the love of good from his wife—the husband begins to confess that not only does he have understanding from the Lord, but also that he lives from the Lord. The female, in the process of receiving inwardly within herself the love of truth from her husband, begins to confess not only that the affection for good is from the Lord, but the truth also which now constitutes her inmost life, or the understanding of her husband in her. As a result of this, the husband rejects any idea of merit in the good that he does, but acknowledges that it is from the Lord. The wife, also, will take no merit in the understanding of truth as it relates to life, but confesses that this wisdom is from the Lord. Consequently, when the fibers from the retina on each side reach the geniculate bodies, they begin there as new fibers, and are projected toward the striate area of the cortex in the form of optic radiations.[5]

A536. Thus far our heavenly pair has progressed a long way on the regenerative path. The journey has been full of obstacles, but in overcoming they have gained new delights, and are beginning to really believe, not from the lips but from the heart, that they live from the Lord.

A537. Full conjunction, however, has not taken place. On the right side we have the association of the nasal fibers from the left eye, and

---

[5] In man, all of the visual fibers end in the striate area of the cortex, but in monkeys and lower mammals much of the striate area 17 is found on the lateral surface of the occipital lobes (See F. H. Adler, *Physiology of the Eye*, Mosby, 4th edition, 1965, p. 680). Herein lies a difference between man and beast on the physical plane.

the temporal fibers from the right eye. The masculine side of life is receiving love of good from the female. On the left side there is the association of nasal fibers from the right eye, and the temporal fibers of the left eye. The feminine nature of man is being illustrated in truths, and instantly relating it to good, which is the wisdom of life. As they, then, from this point on proceed in their journey of life, in each and all things they speak, will, and intend, they give and receive from the other. There is complete unanimity of life, and in this way they proceed—in their journey of life—toward area 17, the calcarine cortex. They know and confess that they are being led by the Lord. Their mental view in all things, inwardly and outwardly, is from the other, and from this perspective they have their sight. They have depth of vision, and fusion in inmost principles, just as, through fusion of the retinal image from each eye, there is depth of vision and one sight; and so this heavenly pair is seen at a distance as one angel. This is the way they enter area 17, and it is here that full conjunction with the Lord takes place; and it is from this inmost celestial heaven that the Holy City, New Jerusalem, descends from God.

A538. Here, and in our previous paper, we have suggested that the visual pathway represents the pathway of life with the regenerating man. If this is so, then there should be a relationship between the visual pathway and the Genesis account of the seven days of creation—which account does, in fact, describe the stages in the regeneration of man. The following is meant to be suggestive of such a possible relationship.

Days of Creation	*Visual Pathway*
1st	From the cornea to the crystalline lens.
2nd	From the crystalline lens to the retina.
3rd	From the retina to the optic chiasma.
4th	From the chiasma to the other side, or to the optic tract.

5th	From the optic tract to the external geniculate body.
6th	From the external geniculate body (optic radiations) to striate area #17.
7th	Rest—Striate area #17.

Perception

A539. Having discussed the visual process, we have thereby laid the groundwork for us to understand more clearly what we mean by perception.[6] This in turn may be an aid to us in understanding what is meant by "as-of-self." The ability to respond as-of-self to the Lord is what distinguishes man from beast. The accompanying diagram[7] by Kephart illustrates what takes place in the perceptual process. This diagram can be applied to concepts in engineering, communication, speech pathology, etc., and it can be used to illustrate thinking in a variety of ways.

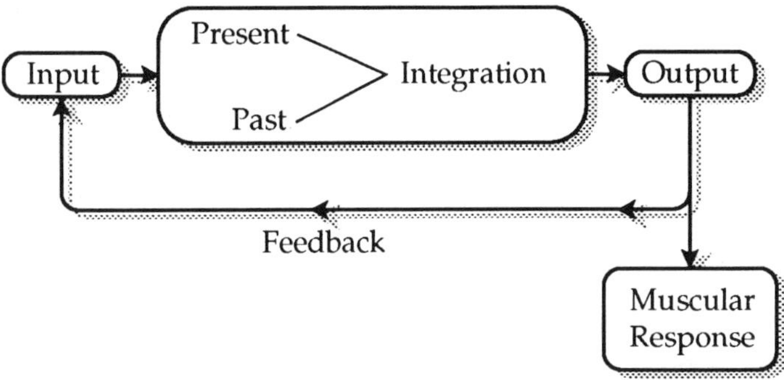

Diagram of feedback mechanisms in perception

---

[6] For my understanding of "perception," I am indebted to Newell C. Kephart, "The Perceptual Process," *Optometric Extention Program Paper*, Series 1, No. 6, March 1957, pp. 21-23.

[7] Newell C. Kephart, *The Slow Learner in the Classroom*, Merrill, 2nd edition, 1971, Figure 6, p. 108. Reproduced with the kind permission of the publisher.

A540. In the area marked input, he thinks of it as just being the organism's reaction to surface stimulation of the body, and by means of the five senses there is a reaction to it. He makes it clear that each organic part reacts in a different way, but in each case this outside energy does not enter into the organism, but the organism reacts to this energy. Whether from touch, taste, hearing, smell, or sight, sensitive cells within the organism react to the external stimulus in their way. These sensitive cells within the organism are then fired up and a simultaneous pattern of neural impulses is transmitted to the projection area of the cortex. There an analogous pattern of neural impulses is set up by means of the action of internuncial neurones. Kephart considers that it is this pattern of electrical impulses, in the sensory projection area of the cortex, which constitutes the input.

A541. Perceptions result from the activities of the organism itself, not from energy outside the body entering into or through the organism. All things being equal, it should correspond very closely to the energy impinging upon the organism, but he tells us we should remember that it is a translation of outside energy into patterns of neural response.

A542. Kephart considers that once these input patterns have been generated in the sensory projection area of the cortex, then by means of internuncial neurones its effects radiate out into surrounding associated areas. Integration takes place at this point.

A543. The integration process seems to be one of the mysteries of neurology. He indicates that although we do not know exactly how this takes place we must remember that this integrative process is concerned with all the sensory inputs operating in the organism at any given moment, and that there is hardly ever just one input present in the organism at any one time. In the integrative mechanism all these input patterns are organized and integrated so that the organismic response will consider all of them in one act.

A544. Kephart further considers that the integrative process is not only concerned with incoming stimuli at an given moment, but also with past experience and memory, and that a large part of the memory process is a more or less permanent alteration of the organism. He believes the organismic response takes into account the memory of past as well as present activities; therefore, that input patterns have been elaborated and synthesized.

A545. This elaborated pattern is translated into an output pattern, and it may be thought of as a scanning mechanism. He likens it to the television camera which has a scanning beam that translates the light in the studio into a series of electrical impulses. The picture on the television set is an accurate model of the light distribution in the studio. The scanning device in the integrative mechanism therefore acts to translate the afferent and association patterns into a motor pattern.

A546. He emphasizes the fact that we should remember the output process is a pattern of neural impulses that occurs within the organism. This time it is a pattern that can be sent down to muscle and will result in movement. He believes that consciousness first occurs at this point in the perceptual process and we are first conscious of the input patterns when an output pattern has been generated. Thus we cannot really "see" until associated areas have been consulted to attach meaning to this input. When it is fed down to muscle, that is, an output pattern is generated; it is only then we really understand or see. This is why seeing is considered to be motor.

A547. He brings out the point that on the way to muscle groups a portion of the output pattern may be drained off and fed back into the system, and that mind is conscious of muscle reaction at this point, and will monitor it. This feedback of the output pattern becomes in itself a part of the input. As it re-enters on the input end of the system it alters the input pattern and a new cycle of the perceptual process begins. This will continue until input exactly matches the output, or until muscle response is adequate to the organismic demand.

A548. The output pattern need not result in muscular response on every cycle of the process. We can generate an output, drain most of it off in feedback for control purposes, and permit none to go to muscle. Many solutions to a problem may be tried mentally before any activity is involved. Much of study and problem solving goes on in this manner.

A549. Before we relate this to the as-of-self, we need to review what has been said previously. It was stated[8] that in area 17—the visuosensory area—nerve impulses from both retinae are unified, and that these unified, modified impulses are sent higher up into the nervous system; also that in animals, stimulation of this area results in ocular deviations, but not so in man. Why is this so in the case of animals, and not man? It is because at this point in man volitional movement has been separated from the understanding, and transferred higher up into the nervous system. This is not so in the case of animals, and stimulation of this area will result in ocular deviations because motor fibers are connected with organismic parts on a lower level. This is the reason why animals have knowledge, it seems, already in the organic parts. Their maturation is much quicker than man's but the freedom that they enjoy is on a natural organic level, and not on a higher spiritual level.

A550. It was stated that in lower mammals the superior colliculus provides an integrating mechanism of considerable complexity in relation to visual impulses, and that in monkeys much of the striate area is found on the lateral surface of the occipital lobes. In man, however, all visual fibers end in striate area 17.

---

[8] Aubrey T. Allen, *loc. cit.*

A551. It was further stated in that same paper that in man parastriate area 18 is considered to be the visuomotor field, and peristriate area 19 is thought of as the visuopsychic field; also that in man area 18 plus 19 is about three times as large as area 17. In the orangutan, however, area 18 plus area 19 is not twice the size of area 17; and in the monkey area 18 plus area 19 is still smaller in relation to area 17.

A552. In man, therefore, these areas have been transferred higher up in the nervous system, and therein is the major organic difference between man and beast. The Lord has separated the will from the understanding. Everything that man knows he has to learn a different way. The understanding has to be consulted and pass judgment on it. A new will has to be built up in the understanding.

A553. Now we are in a position to relate what has been said to the as-of-self. We can see, according to the diagram, that there is a memory of past output patterns. There is also a memory of present activities, and a contemplation of future activities. There is elaboration and contemplation of present truths in anticipation of future action. As we learn new truths, those that agree with and reinforce past concepts of truth would seem to go out and return into the input process and consequently elaborate truths that have been in agreement with our understanding.

A554. This thought, and elaboration of concepts according to truth, is not from oneself but from the Lord. It is He who enables one to understand and see truths in a rational way. We see truths from him, because He is the Truth Itself. The proper approach to the Word, as explained previously, enables us to see these truths not from ourselves but from the Lord. This is why evangelistic activity in the New Church seems to bear such meager fruit. We cannot cause the world to view the Word as we do. This can only be done by the Lord from within, or from the spirit. This does not mean that we should not try to bring the truth to man, but internal sight, or spiritual sight, comes only from the Lord.

A555. We come to a point in time when truth must be grounded in good if our thought is to rise successively. Perception generally runs horizontally in truths that have been grounded in good. When these truths have been elaborated, through conscious thought and action, they can be raised up vertically or successively only by concepts drawn from previous elaboration. Truths illustrate and elaborate good, but if we do not apply them to life they cannot be retained in the memory.

A556. When, therefore, something comes into our conscious thought that does not agree with good, according to previous concepts of truth, we should not act on it. It is here that the as-of-self cycle starts. If it is something that we are prone to want to do, and we know that it is wrong, we must acknowledge to the Lord that it is a lie and that we want no part of it, we must ask for His strength to act, as-of-self, in resisting and overcoming this tendency toward disorder. This acknowledgment will return on the output cycle of the perceptual process, and be fed back into the input part of it; and will serve to reinforce previous concepts of good and truth. It is here that we can better understand what is meant by "influx is according to efflux."

A557. There is one thing that we must do at this point in the as-of-self cycle of the perceptual process. We must acknowledge, and really believe, that we do this from the Lord. How can we possibly do this? We can, simply because we know without any doubt whatsoever that we live from the Lord. Consequently, any good that we do as a result of His truth, really belongs to Him; it is not ours. By shunning evils as sins, we do good from the Lord, because we live from the Lord.

A558. No one in hell acknowledges that he lives from the Lord, but the whole of heaven does. Can we see what has been done by this as-of-self act, illustrated by the perceptual process? We have, from the Lord, turned ourselves away from hell, and toward heaven. We have confirmed ourself in good by acting according to truth. It will lead, in time, to the absolute rejection of any hint that the good that we do is our own.

A559. If we can act as-of-self in resisting evil, we can also do so to acknowledge truth. Because the Lord is Truth Itself, any understanding of the truth in us is His; it is not our own. This, because we live from him and not from ourselves. This as-of-self acknowledgment will go out of the output end of the process, and be fed back into the input end, where it will serve to reinforce previous concepts of good and truth. When the opportunity permits we will act on it; and this acknowledgment will go down into muscle. There it will serve to confirm in us good and truth from the Lord.

In Conclusion

A560. I hope, above all, that if there has been anything accomplished in writing these papers it has been to illustrate in a meaningful way that religion is of life. I have tried to relate doctrine from the Word to organic structure, and in turn show how structure and its functional processes, when properly understood, can be used to illustrate and confirm doctrine.

A561. Each of us, in whatever use we serve, should try to see doctrine in relationship to our use. This, because the Lord is Use itself, and He will let us see Him in use if we really desire to do so. There are knowledges particular to every use. They serve to illustrate this use, but one should not construe this to mean that our worldly occupation is necessarily our spiritual use. We should try, insofar as we can, to acquire worldly knowledges. They are first in time. However, spiritual goals should be primary in end; thus, in time, these worldly knowledges should be used to serve spiritual ends. I am reminded of what Dr. N. J. Berridge said:

Providing our method of seeing spiritual things reflected in natural things is sound, the wider and truer our natural knowledge, the better will be our vision of spiritual things. If we can make proper use of the current tremendous growth in scientific knowledge the church will have a better understanding of spiritual matters than ever before; whereby also its love will be strengthened.[9]

And in Isaiah 19:23-25 we read:

> In that day shall there be a highway out of Egypt to Assyria, and the Assyrian shall come into Egypt, and the Egyptian into Assyria, and the Egyptians shall serve with the Assyrians. In that day shall Israel be the third with Egypt and with Assyria, even a blessing in the midst of the land: Whom the Lord of hosts shall bless, saying Blessed be Egypt my people, and Assyria the work of my hands, and Israel mine inheritance.

Acknowledgment

A562. I would like to express my appreciation for the kind encouragement that the late Mr. Lennart Alfelt and Mr. Boyd Asplundh provided in getting me to write "something." Without this, most likely, these papers would never have been written.

COMMUNICATION[10]

To the Editor:

A563. I have been following with a great deal of pleasure the articles in *The New Philosophy* concerning "Thinking from Correspondences," by Dr. N. J. Berridge. In the January-March 1979 issue he discusses the importance of distinguishing between representatives,

---

[9] N. J. Berridge, "Thinking from Correspondences," *The New Philosophy*, 82:1:303, 1979.

[10] Aubrey T. Allen, *The New Philosophy*, April-June, 1980, pp. 72-74.

correspondences and significatives. He states that the information from which we think should be based as far as possible on true and accurate natural knowledges. By this I understand that he means that in determining the truth of any external or internal phenomena, in this case the bodily function of any organic part, we should understand as far as possible the process by which it operates. He states further that "the wider and truer our natural knowledge the better will be our understanding of spiritual things." He reemphasizes this in part VII, "Some Questions about the Eye," (April-June 1980 issue, *The New Philosophy*) and gives a very good explication of why the eye is part of the brain, and why the pathway from the eye to the internal sensory is shorter and more interior than that for sound perceived by the ear.

A564. There is no need for me to review in detail what Dr. Berridge has said concerning correspondence as it relates to the eye. The reader would gain much if he did this for himself; but I would like to comment on something that is part of the eye, yet is not the internal aspect of it. I am referring to the extrinsic muscles of the eye.

A565. We all know that we are not entirely comfortable when we look at someone who has crossed eyes, or when we converse with someone and that person will not look at us. Why is this so? It is because the eyes represent understanding, and in carrying on a conversation with anyone we get a better understanding of what is being said if we can see the expression of his eyes and face at the same time. Visual contact reinforces the auditory input, our memory of the conversation is better, and we just feel better about it.

A566. Past superstitions have been hard on cross-eyed people. Due to no fault of their own they have been labeled, expressly or not, as being a little loony, or not of sound mind. If we look a little closer we may see why the effects of this abnormality may bear such a representation.

A567. Let us review what is said in *Arcana Coelestia* 4410, relative to correspondences of the eyes: "It has been made clear to me by much experience that the sight of the left eye corresponds to truths which are of the understanding, and the right eye to affections of truth which also are of the understanding; hence the left eye corresponds to truths of faith, and the right eye to good things of faith."

A568. We can say, according to this, that the left eye corresponds to the understanding of things we clearly perceive to be true, and the right eye to the understanding of what is good.

A569. Now the eyes are controlled in their movement by the action of the extrinsic muscles. They serve to move them in their orbit so that incoming light will stimulate corresponding points in each retina. Control of this movement is a learned reflex, and under the auspices of the voluntary nervous system. This means that we should be able to direct the movement of our eyes through the conscious effort of our will.

A570. In the early stages of our life we do not have voluntary control over this system. Our first reaction to light merely serves to set off an awareness reflex. We seek to move our head and eyes in the direction of maximum light contrast, and through this endeavor we can gradually recognize shape and contour. Though this first recognition is very vague and ill defined, there is an effort to establish hand contact. Once this occurs sight is extended and refined under the tutelage of the active touch.

A571. As we learn to balance the body, first through crawling and then walking, the input patterns from both eyes are matched more precisely in the visual area of the brain. Ciliary muscles respond to more refined demand for focus, fusion is learned, and depth perception becomes a part of our experience.

A572. As a result of this sequence of events in our learning experience, and if there is no anomaly that would otherwise prevent it from happening, we have established in the act of seeing what is called a dual effector system. In this system the voluntary and involuntary components of the nervous system work together as a team. This they must do, and most precisely, if we are to meet the demands of information processing placed upon us by our modern present day environment.

A573. It would seem, according to *Arcana Coelestia* 1621 and 1623, that the crystalline lens and various media represent the first gathering of truth and its presentation to our understanding. What then do the extrinsic muscles of the eyes represent? It would seem that they represent our own efforts, as of self, to bring truth to the view of our understanding, our own as of self efforts to seek out the truth, to move and manipulate it so that we can see it from every angle, and thus see it in different perspective for the sake of regeneration and life.

A574. A cross-eyed person, on the other hand, would seem to bear the implication of someone who is not doing his part in the regenerative process; —not doing his part in the search for truth. This condition represents faith as an intellectual conceit, hatched up by a depraved will and forced on the understanding. Outwardly such "faith" may deviate in any direction, just as crossed eyes do. It has no corresponding points on the retina as truth does, so it cannot be raised up to interior principles. "Faith in any other than the true God, and among Christians in any but the Lord God the Savior, may be compared to the disease of the eye called strabismus" (TCR 346).

A575. As far as any individual is concerned we know that this is merely representative, and not necessarily correspondent. Nothing is reflected upon the person but upon the thing that is represented (AC

665, also AC 2010 and 4281). But it does reveal to some extent why, consciously or not, cross-eyed people have been looked upon with such uneasiness.

Aubrey T. Allen
1502 Dobbs Circle
Alexander City, Ala. 35010
1-(205)-234-2857

BIBLIOGRAPHY

Alden, Kenneth J. "The Philosophic Works, the Writings, and the Study of the Brain." *The New Philosophy* 82:2 (1979): 358-371.

Allen, Aubrey T. "Communication." *The New Philosophy* 83:2 (1980): 72-74.

__________ . "Sight, the Visual Process, and Doctrine." *The New Philosophy* 84:1&2 (1981): 26-35.

__________ . "Sight, the Visual Process, and Doctrine." *The New Philosophy* 85:4 (1982): 138-147.

Anthony, Jane Parker and Norma Jane Kolthoff *Textbook of Anatomy and Physiology*. 9th Ed. St. Louis: C. V. Mosby Co., 1975. (Illustrated by Ernest W. Beck).

Berridge, N. J. "The Brain." *New Church Magazine* 98:686 (1979): 61.

__________ . "Thinking From Correspondences: V. The Union of the Heart and Lungs." *The New Philosophy* 82:4 (1979): 443-446.

__________ . "Thinking From Correspondences: VI. The Role of Bone and Muscle in Breathing." *The New Philosophy* 83:1 (1980): 23-26.

__________ . "Thinking From Correspondences: VII. Some Questions About the Eye." *The New Philosophy* 83:2 (1980): 64-72.

__________ . "Thinking From Correspondences: VIII. Seeing and Understanding." *The New Philosophy* 83:3 (1980): 116-120.

__________ . 1981. Thinking From Correspondences: X. The Decussations." *The New Philosophy* 84:1&2 (1981): 35-42.

Brown, Michael A. "SSA Research Project on the Brain." *The New Philosophy* 82:2 (1979): 356-357.

Clemente , Carmine D., ed. *Gray's Anatomy*. 30th American Ed. Philadelphia: Lea and Febiger, 1985.

Cotes, J. E. *Recent Advances in Physiology*. 8th Ed. Edited by R. Creese. London: J. and A. Churchill, Ltd., 1963.

Curtis, Helena *Biology*. 2nd Ed. New York: Worth Publishers, Inc., 1975.

Dejours, P. *Principles of Comparative Respiratory Physiology*. Second. Ed. Amsterdam, Holland: Elsevier/Nort Holland Biomedical Press, 1981.

Echols, Martin M. "An Analogy Using the Cell." *The New Philosophy* 83:1 (1980): 18-20.

__________ . "The Cortical Gland and Its Relationship to the Modern Neuron." *The New Philosophy* 83:3 (1980): 104-115.

Gardener, Ermest *Fundamentals of Neurology*. 6th Ed. Philadelphia: W. B. Saunders Co., 1975.

Gardener, Ernest, Donald J. Gray and Ronan O'Rahilly *Anatomy: A Regional Study of Human Structure*. 6th Ed. Philadelphia: W. B. Saunders Co., 1975.

Ham, A. W. *Histology*. 7th Ed. Philadelphia: J. B. Lippincott, 1974.

Hamilton, William James, James Dixon Boyde and Harland W. Mossman. *Human Embryology*. 4th Ed. London: Macmillan Press, 1976.

Hole, Jr., John W. *Human Anatomy and Physiology*. 2nd Ed. Dubuque, Iowa: Wm. C. Brown Co., 1981.

Kapit, Wynn and Lawrence M. Elson *The Anatomy Coloring Book*. New York: Harper and Row, 1977.

Newton, Norman. "Communications." *The New Philosophy* 84:3&4 (1981): 128-131.

Pendleton, J. and J., letter in *New Church Life* 102:10 (1982): 471-473.

Potts, John F. *The Swedenborg Concordance*. London: Swedenborg Society, 1888.

Rubins, David K. *The Human Figure*. New York: Viking Press 1975.

Sigstedt, C. O. *The Swedenborg Epic:* New York: Bookman Associates, 1952.

Stanley, M. W. *Emanuel Swedenborg, Scientist, Philosopher, and Theologian*. Sidney: Swedenborg Lending Library and Inquiry Centre, 1977.

Swedenborg, Emanuel. *The Apocalypse Explained*. 6 vols. Translation revised by J. Whitehead. New York: Swedenborg Foundation, 1911-12.

____________ . *Arcana Coelestia*. 12 vols. Translation revised and edited by J. F. Potts. New York: Swedenborg Foundation, 1905-1910.

____________ . *The Cerebrum*. Translated by Alfred Acton. Philadelphia: Swedenborg Scientific Association, 1938.

____________ . *Conjugial Love*. Translated by S. Warren, translation revised by L. Tafel. New York: Swedenborg Foundation, 1915.

____________ . *Divine Love and Wisdom*. Translation revised by J. Ager. New York: Swedenborg Society, 1908.

____________ . *Divine Providence*. Translated by W. Wunsch. New York: Swedenborg Foundation, 1963.

____________ . *Heaven and Hell*. Translated by J. Ager, revised and edited by D. Harley. London: Swedenborg Society, 1958.

____________ . *Spiritual Diary*. A posthumous publication. Translated by G. Bush, J. Smithson, and J. Buss. 5 vols. London: James Speirs, 1883-1902.

____________ . *The True Christian Religion*. 2 vols. Translated by J. Ager. New York: Swedenborg Foundation, 1906.

Van Dusen, Wilson "Love in Understanding." *New Church Life* 95:9 (1979): 401-408.

Vickers, Paul V. *God-Talk and Man-Talk: A Study in Revelation and Dialogue*. London: The General Conference of the New Church, 1970.

Williams, Peter L. and Roger Warwick, eds. *Gray's Anatomy*. Edinburgh: Longman Group, Ltd., 1980.

Wilson, Doris Burda *Human Anatomy*. 2nd Ed. New York: Oxford University Press, 1983.

Woofenden, William Ross. *The New Philosophy* 84:1 and 2 (1981):7.

Worcester, John. *Physiological Correspondences*. Boston: Massachusetts New Church Union, 1931.

INDEX

Abbreviations:

c   corresponds, correspondence(s), corresponding

KEM   Knowledges of the External Memory

Fn   Footnote, with paragraph no. in brackets

Note: All numbers refer to paragraphs, none to the Writings unless preceded by the usual abbreviations (see finalpage).

AARON's robe, neck of 302, c of 304

ABIMELECH'S wife 42

ABRAHAM'S wife 42

ABSORPTION of food 452

ABSTRACT connection with natural 42

ACCOMMODATION of the Divine to man is beyond comprehension 27; of revelation to current errors, necessity of 107; of revelation to current errors, reticence due to 120

ACID of stomach 438

ACOUSTIC nerve 365

ACOUSTIC pathway 370

ADRENALS 308

AFFECTION(S) ruling influence in mind 79; that produce conjunction of will and understanding c to blood vessels of importance to lungs 116-119; that feed the understanding c to bronchial arteries 131; series of, in childhood 135; for truth 139; for understanding 139; for understanding c to desire for air 141; for seeing truth produces thought 142; for truth, for understanding, for seeing in bodily thought 146; on left side of brain 339; (see also WILL)

AGITATION(S) 449, 465; equivalent to temptations; c to acquirement of immunity 218; of new arrivals in the next life c to digestion 447; c of 452

AIR, saccules and thoughts 245; conjunction by c 118; c of 139, Fn 9 (139), 241-247; lack of, c of 141; c to wisdom because received by lungs which c to understanding 246, 247

AIR, spiritual, connection of with spiritual sun 246

ALCOHOL 220, 316; is removed by liver; causes liver damage if in excess 249; needs no digestion but is changed after absorption 442, 455

ALDEN, K. J. Ref. to article on Brain 295, 296, 297, 299, 308, 312, 320, 324

ALLEGORY, Divine, is the Word of God 15

ALLEN, A. T. (ref) 276; (ref) "Sight, Visual Process and Doctrine" 356, 357

ALVEOLAR phase 122E

ALVEOLI of the lungs 242; development of 122F; expanded in two ways 122K; c to thoughts 240; convey oxygen to haemoglobin 240

AMINO ACIDS from digestion of proteins 260, 262; molecules of, join to form proteins 436, 437; for growth and repair

AMOEBAE 204

ANAESTHESIA to sufferings of the spirit, from the body and world 470

ANASTOMOSES 122E

ANATOMIC representations in spiritual world, reasons for 329

ANATOMY in 18th Century, crudity of 297, 334; shown in TCR 311

ANCIENT CHURCH 163; formation of 161; external respiration 187

ANGEL(S), thinking with 45; c of 263; how like a lymphocyte 263; in error 311; communications of, by means of those in truth 353; female, in province of interior of nostrils 407; celestial 425; are concerned in spiritual dissociations 472

ANGELIC CHOIRS 411

ANGINA PECTORIS 455

ANGULAR GYRUS A525

ANIMAL nature of man in Most Ancient Church 423; man apart from internal is no other than an animal 444

ANIMAL(S), digestion in, an important c 479; relevant for c 444

ANIMAL SPIRIT, meaning of 320; perhaps the spiritual life of the body 320

ANTIBODIES 59, 209, 212, 217, 262, 262, 268; confer immunity 207; specificity of; blanketing effect on antigens 207; their effects on bacteria 208; c to remains; formed by lymphocytes; are goods formed specifically according to particular truths, unique 260

ANTIGENS 207, 209, 215, 268; stimulate production of immunity 207, 260; cannot get into the thymus 252; c to evils 269

ANXIETIES 418, 489

AORTA and its branches 124, 127, 136, 172; blood from, used in control system Fig. 6 and Fn 7 (124); perception 136

APERTURE(S) suggest communication and protection together 407; in parts of brain concerned with smell 407; represent clear-sighted- ness 424

APPEARANCES in spiritual world more real than in nature 321

APPEARANCE, FALLACY that natural objects enter through external senses and affect interiors A502, A503

APPENDIX 443

ARACHNOID granulations, early observation 281, 284; in
longitudinal sinus; their functions like those of associated
spirits 287

ARACHNOID MATER with pia mater as one unit 284; structure of 284

ARCANA COELESTIA and SPIRITUAL DIARY, differences provi- dential and important 323

AREOLAR tissue 122A

ARISTOTLE, conversation with; was in province of ears 376; obedi- ence of 376, 377, and organs of balance 377

AROMATIC ESTERS 455

ARTERIES as part of heart 75; nerves and; the early belief that
arteries terminated in nerves 305

ARTERIES, bronchial 120; function of 120, 122, 130; anatomical details 122A; c of 130; importance in embryo 130, 148; why said to be "almost separate from heart" 130; feed structures other than lungs, c of 131; use in adult life 133; lungs, etc., nourished by 148; c to collecting mere knowledge and thought from it 148; not from heart alone 172; c to affections of old will 173; c to first conjunction between will and understanding 173

ARTERIES, bronchial and pulmonary, connections between, c of 132

ARTERIES, carotid 125, 138

ARTERIES, pulmonary, 120; function of 120, 121; bring heart and
lungs into use 150; from heart alone, meaning; c to third
conjunction of will and understanding 150; c to full life of use
from the Lord 150; related to third conjunction (q.v.) 142

"AS-OF-SELF" approach to the Word A517-A520, A531; in resisting evil and looking to use A553-A561

ATMOSPHERES, spiritual, connection of, with spiritual light 246

AUDITORY or COCHLEAR nerve 382-383, Fig. 22 (383)

AUDITORY pathway, relay stations 370

AURICLE(S) of ear, c to simple spirits 375

AUTO-ALLERGIC 255
AXONS 271
AZYGOS VEIN 122A

BACTERIA 203, 204, 207, 209, 218; diseases caused by 208; resident
    and harmful, c evils remaining with man 218; large numbers of in
    the intestine 443; c of 474; in gut of man, relevance of 479; intestinal,
    that make poisons, c to hell 480
BALANCE, organs of 376; why in the ear 377
BARLEY, changes in, when made into malt 435
BARRIER(S) between thymus and blood 252; between brain and blood,
    as in thymus 300; in the Word; are an important part of communi-
    cation systems in heaven, and in the body 301-304
BATH, signification of, and polygamy 413
BENCHES pertain to the life of love or will 414
BETROTHAL of love and wisdom 114
BIBLE shows relation between spiritual and natural 8
BILE emulsifies fat to aid lipase 440
BIOCHEMISTRY 453
BIRTH c to regeneration 180; and the flood have similar c 183
BLAKE, William 274
BLOOD, c of chapter IV, esp. 61 ff.; representation of 61, 62, 63;
    signifies celestial things 62; functions of 64, 65; origins of, made in
    66, 67; spiritual appears to come from the Church Universal, but is
    really from the Lord 68, 70; constituents of, pass out of capillaries
    into tissues 76; belongs to kingdom of heart 83; pumped past
    carotid bodies 138; passage of whole stream through lungs c to
    treatment of all will's activities and invigoration of both will and
    understanding 151; refreshment of, control of, c to activity of the
    Lord through the conscience or perception 152; separation of the
    two circuits 169, 172; dual circulation of 172; only one circulation
    of, in embryo 176, 177; purification of 220; colors of depend on
    oxygen content 223; filthy - not serum, meaning of, is foreign
    particles 249; "dry and lifeless" vivified by hormones 318
BLOOD-BRAIN BARRIER 300, 303, 304; c of 301
BODIES, carotid, monitor aeration of blood 125, 138; carotid and
control system c to perception of truth 149; human and animal
exist only by correspondence 329

BODY, parts of, mentioned symbolically 197; c to realities of use
in next life, not to appearances of surroundings 197; as a source
of emotions (AC 4947) 426; A kind of body belongs to every
angelic thought 466
BODY-BRAIN UNIT 350
BONE, c to KEM and hardening by knowledge and use 257; life in 257;
    marrow origin of stem cells
BONE MARROW 67, 229, 257
BRAIN, the home of love 6; activates the face to smile from love 6, 10;
    complexity of 270, 272; consists of neurons and glial cells 271;
    connections between cells of 271; communicates with heaven, ex-
    periences love 273; heavenly form of 273, 276; why it is the pinnacle
    of creation 273; connections 274; functions within, differ greatly
    from effects through body 276; a link between spirit and body 276;
    c with body like that of nerves with muscles 276; the home where
    man live with the Lord 277; communication via bloodstream 286;
    of chemical and hormonal communication with 286; absence of
    lymphatic system from 290; spaces between the cells are significant
    Fn 17 (291); urinary bladder of 294; phlegm in, due to disease of
    decomposition; before Last Judgement; c to " the abomination of
    desolation" 299; barrier between, and blood 300; as between celes-
    tial and spiritual 303; nutrition and cleaning of 303, by bloodstream
    and glial cells 290; protection of, by blood-brain barrier c to binding
    round neck of Aaron's robe 304; fibres of, flow into ultimates and
    return to firsts through services 305; return of uses to, through
    nerves and hormones, an image of creation 306; outflow from and
    return 307; influx of into body is immediate by nerves and mediate
    by hormones 310; ventricles of, anatomy of Fig. 18 (312); right and
    left sides, connections between 335, 347, 348; right and left sides for
    will and intellect respectively 338; cortex of 346; cells, white and
    grey matter of 346; neuron bodies in, axons and dendrites of 346;
    nuclei of, are collections of neurons not in cortex 346; reticular
    formation of where neuron bodies and fibres are together 346, 347;
    hemispheres connected 349; unity of 349; unity of illustrates mar-
    riage of good and truth 350; fibres and glands of, on right and left c
    to four angelic types 352; anatomy of illustrates communications
    between angels 353; eye is part of 364; hence c with heaven 374;
    connection with nostrils 406; floats 417; not a source of mucus 417

BRAIN STEM 335, 376

BRAINS, subsidiary of certain animals in orbits of eyes 366

BREAD, the living, is the Lord 445

BREAKDOWN, of mental associations, c to digestion; is painful; a punishment; of use in reformation; might be done under anaesthesia 471; of people, hearts, complexes 464 (see also 466); of proprium, severity of 469, 471; severity of in the next life 470; is torment, despair, temptation 470; spiritual, c to digestion, avoided by regeneration 482

BREATH c to spirit 190; of Jehovah, is life from Divine Truth 245; of man is life of truth 245

BREATHING, control system of 123, 124, 125; use of various muscles for Fn 6 (123); c to conscience 138 or perception 139; is a conjunction of heart and lungs 139; c to reception of Divine Truth; as first link of a chain 241

BROKEN-HEARTED, the Lord is near them 464

BRONCHIA, 117; c to perceptions and thoughts 126, 139

BRONCHIAL arteries 122G, 127; different from pulmonary arteries 120; branches of 121; nourish 131; c of 131, 133; don't disappear after growth 133; in the embryo 148

BRONCHIAL system, leak with pulmonary system 132

BRONCHIAL tubes, c of 403

BROWN, M. A., ref. to article on Brain Project 296

CAECUM 443

CAIN, mark upon, signifies importance of faith 363

CALCARINE CORTEX A521

CANALICULAR phase 122G

CAPILLARIES, blood 76; lymphatic 199; permeability of, 203; not seen before 1661 305

CARBOHYDRATES 211, 433; digestion of 434, 469

CARBON DIOXIDE 4

CARBON MONOXIDE, poisoning 223

CARDIOVASCULAR system 83

CAROTID arteries 138

CAROTID bodies 124; operation 149

CAUSATIVE relationship 10

CAUSE 491; spiritual 5-10; form of 488

CAUSE AND EFFECT 5; discrete distinction 7; spiritual: many that are incomprehensible are well-known 10; relationship 450; difference in form of 488, 490, 491; to be efficient must have executive means from realm of effect 492

CELESTIAL, cannot operate into natural without an intermediate 258; is like thymus in needing an intermediate 258; states of infancy, c of 265; c to love 45

CELL(S), air, of lungs c to thoughts 144; stem, of bone marrow produce lymphocytes 255, 257; journey of, from bones 257; in thymus like Jacob with Laban 257; red, of blood, see erythrocytes; nerve, of cerebral cortex, large numbers of 270; nerve and glial 271; ciliated lining ventricles c to spirits of that region 289

CELLULOSE is digested by micro-organisms in herbivores 443

CENTRAL NERVOUS SYSTEM 126

CENTRES, respiratory of central nervous system 124, 125, 126

CEREBELLUM 272, 284, 335, 376; chiefly for the will 381; connected with vestibular not auditory nerve 382; important for balance 383; see BRAIN:

CEREBRAL aqueduct 312

CEREBRAL cortex 337, 368

CEREBRAL medulla 272

CEREBRI, in the *Spiritual Diary* 313

CEREBROSPINAL FLUID 284, 287, 288, 312, 417; produced by choroid plexuses Fn 15 (284); flow 289; function 291

CEREBRUM 284, 288, 335; see BRAIN:

CEREBRUM, THE,(ref) 3 transactions by Swedenborg and drawings 297, Fn 18 (312), 320

CHEMISTRY 316, 431

CHERUBIM, as barriers 301

CHILD, first breath 124

CHILDHOOD 266; series of affections in 135

CHILDREN signify innocence 414

CHORD, spinal, has nerve fibres which cross from one side to the other 347

CHOROID PLEXUSES 288, 291, 294

CHRISTIANS 1

CHURCH, function of, in relation to civil and moral good 71; the representative, evil in 52; the Lord's spiritual, is throughout the world; includes some ignorant 55; universal and specific 55, 56, 81;

specific, resembles heart and lungs 56, 57, 85; universal, resembles one man 56; universal and specific, related as heart and lungs are related to whole body and this via spiritual world 82; specific, rules as the servant of all 84

CHURCH SPECIFIC 55, 56; as a heart and lung 68; place of 81; rules 84

CHURCH UNIVERSAL 55, 56;

CHURCH(ES), Ancient from Most Ancient, ought to be seen by c of changes in body 158, 159; Ancient, establishment of, like regeneration of the spiritual man 157

CHYLE, receptacle and ducts of, are part of lymphatics 200; spirits of 213; is an emulsion of fat 441

CILIA 289

CIRCULATION of the blood, two separate routes 169, 172; unity of routes in embryo 176, 177

CIRCULATIONS of blood specially important for the lungs; there should be three such; the elusive third 120; a possible third 125; three listed 127

CLOUDS c to angelic thoughts through ultimates of the Word 328

COATS of eyeball represent 3 senses of Word, and 3 degrees of heaven A512-A519, A528-A531

COCHLEA, is organ of hearing 383

COCHLEAR NERVE 382, Fig. 22 (383)

COLON 443, 476

COLOUR(S), c of 45; importance of 221; of blood 222; as an indication of molecular structure 222; as a subjective experience 222

COLOURLESS is equivalent to white in some cases 224; beautiful belong to the province of eye 357

COMBATS in lower earth induced by falsities, remove worldly and earthly things; c to digestion by microbes 477, 478

COMMUNICATION, see NECK; between all body cells through the blood 65; with brain via blood vessels in pia 286; orderly, needs barriers 301; from body to brain, is controlled; is like reciprocal flow between spiritual and celestial 303

COMPLEXES, formation of 464; psychology of, revealed in the Writings 465, 466; that rule and take on a personality 465; the result of association with societies of spirits 465; life of explained in AC 41, 466; mixed, must be dissociated 467; dissociation of c to taking molecules to pieces by digestion 468

COMPUTERS 274

CONCEPTION, regeneration c to 180
CONES 365
CONFIRMATION 5, 112, 275, 345, 376
CONJUGIAL LOVE, represented by flowers 46; defilement of a form of deceit 333
CONJUGIAL RELATIONSHIPS represented by the visual system and process A533-A537
CONJUNCTION(S) of heart and lungs 115, 116; after birth, closer 122H; third, via pulmonary arteries 142; of will and understanding 115-118, 130, 137, 138, 140; of will and understanding, affections leading to 115-119, 130, 137, 138; of will and understanding, products of 146; three, of will and understanding seen by c 147
CONSCIENCE, and the celestial, and c with respiratory control 126, 138-140; formation of 161, 193; implanted in intellectual part 162, 164; is a kind of perception 241, 397
CONTAMINATION, minute for flavors and odors 404
CONTROL of breathing rate according to state of blood Fn 7, (124)
CORINTHIANS, Paul's epistle to 54
CORNEA, transparent part of outer layer of eye globe, may represent truths of the letter of the Word A517
CORPOREAL [degree] of man receives influx last 246
CORPUS CALLOSUM, connects cerebral hemispheres 348
CORPUSCLES of Hassall 255
CORRECTIONS c to acquirement of immunity 218
CORRESPONDENCE(S) the theory of 15; are actual, not symbolic listed 16; give ideas about spiritual things 27, 28, 86; as mirrors 42; essential for correct thought 42, 43, 114; unconsciously acknowledged 44, 48, 87; thinking from chap.II; is easy 44; emotional responses to 45, 48; thinking from for all 50; are between nature as it really is and the spiritual 51; meaning 52; nature exists from 54; are between numerous discrete levels 68, 69, 70; is with the use 100; is with the function of the organ 179; not restricted in time, show Divine intentions 194; between bodily organs and societies 196; connection of, causes subsistence of all things from the Lord 276; 324; not mere symbols, involve causation 488; law of 490; must be understood in a spiritual way 500
CORTEX, cerebral, communication with retina 19, and limbic system 428, 429; visual 364, 369
CORTICAL substances are probably neuron bodies 353

COTES, ref. to article in "Recent Advances in Physiology" 145

CREATION, a continual process 1; an image of 306; includes returns from man to the Lord 307

CROSS-EYEDNESS A565-A575

DAMNATION c to excretion 447

DECUSSATION, of the pyramids 335, 336; of nerve tracts from limbs 337; within the brain 337; observed with aid of spirits 337; of optic nerves 340; inferred in SD; in parts of AC it is ignored, denied 340; proportion of 347

DEGREE(S) 246; discrete, occur between many corresponding levels 68, 69; between cause and effect 488; (3) of visual process: skeletal, visceral, & cortical, c to 3 degrees of the Word and of the heavens A512-A519, A528, A530, A538

DeJOURS, Pierre, author of recent book on physiology (inc. ref.) 124, 170

DENDRITE(S) 428

DENOTE(D), what is 324

DESIRES, series of in a child 135

DESPAIR due to temptation 270, 470

DESTRUCTION of self by perversion of intellect no longer possible 163, nor by immersion in lusts 171

DIAPHRAGM, use of in breathing 122J, 123

DIFFERENCE, discrete between love and its effects, between nerves and muscle 7; between men and animals A522, A549-A552

DIGESTA 443

DIGESTION 249, Charts XVII, XVIII; in gut is not in living tissue Fn 13;250; in phagocytes is in living tissue Fn 13; 250; is splitting molecules into smaller ones 431; of carbohydrates 434; of proteins 436; of protein, three stages 438; of fats 440; none needed 442; use of bacteria 443; c of 449, 460, 472; c to preparation for heaven (from AC 5174-5) 449; natural, caused by c 450; purpose of 454, 485; spiritual, sometimes appears like evil, but its purpose is good, which is resynthesis 454; spiritual 460; individuality abolished 461; destruction of food by, does not c to destruction of people in the next life 461, 463; chemistry of, not known when Writings were given 463; by micro-organisms 473; final stages of 480; interior c of 483; healthy, caused through benign spirits 490; natural, is destructive, spiritual less so 499

DISCERPTION c to activities of bacteria in gut and in sewage 480

DISEASE(S) 263, 299, 418; and disorders 59; c to evils and falsities 209

DIVINE intentions seen in c beforehand 183

DIVINE mysteries 43

DIVINE TRUTH, flows into every thought (see also Chap II) 145; becomes less gentle as it descends 497, 498

DNA 259, 262, 391, 490

DOCTRINE ought to be seen from Divine Truths, i.e., the Word 42

DUAL CIRCULATION, c of 173

DUCTS, lymph, c to spirits that do not wander 213

DUCTUS ARTERIOSUS 122B, 122E, 175, 176, 177, 178; constricted, changes after birth 181

DUNG, c to previous evils 480

DUODENUM 443

DURA MATER 278, 357; outer layer and external connections 279; spirits representing, external nature of 279, 280; inner layer of 280; importance of 281; lights seen in province of, because it surrounds the optic nerve 282

EAR, external, c to simple obedience 360; internal, tends to involve sight 361; province of 375, 392; spirits in province of, linked with sight 375; balance, connection between, connection with dancing 376, 383; semi-circular canals of, importance for balance 376, 383; inner, parts of, 383; relation between obedience and ear 389; province is from most external to most internal 389, human quality of every part, each part c to angels in Grand Man 391; is in axis of heaven 392; quality of those who are therein 392

EARTH, lower, in the spiritual world. Spirits there c to food needing maximum digestion 474; contains most people before they ascend to heaven 475; c to intestines 476; is a place of combat 477; spirits there are also in province of intestines 500

EATING, signification of, appropriation is revealed by c 445, 446

ECHOLS, M. M. ref. to article on "Analogy Using the Cell" 264; ref. to article on cortical gland and neuron 271

EFFECT(S) 13; form of 488

EFFECTOR SYSTEMS A526-A527, A572; dual effector system represents conjugial love A527

EINSTEIN and the convertibility of matter into energy 28

ELIJAH 496

EMBRYO 122C; growth of lungs in 130; blood circulation in 175, unity of routes in effect 176, 177, 179; respiration of, is through placenta 179; single heart of, becomes two in new baby 181; circulation is one 186; of human race was Most Ancient Church 190

EMOTIONS can be of the body (AC 4947) 426

ENDOCRINE glands 308

ENERGY of the sun c to the Lord's DLW 28, 29; for vision 25% of total bodily requirements A506; light converted in retina into neural energy A521

ENLIGHTENMENT of the spiritual - its difference from perception 398

ENZYMES 250, 432, 436; starch digestion by 435; protein digestion by 439; fat digestion by 440; digestive, glands producing them c to heavenly societies 472, c to angelic control of spiritual dissociations 472

ERROR(S) permitted under the Lord's auspices; of angels 311

ERYTHROCYTES, storage of, in spleen 227; destruction of by spleen 228, role of phagocytes 228; life history of, and need for reprocessing 229; purpose 230; c of envelopes, i.e., cell walls, and haemoglobin 230; possible c to words discussed 231; (KEM) 235; destruction of 237; are like KEM (235-7) but with a difference 238

ESAU 496

ESKIMO 26

ESSENCE(S), spirituous, could be elusive substances 316

ETHMOID bone, apertures in, and apertures seen in spiritual world 407

EUSTACHIAN TUBE, used for respiration 189

EVIL(S) 419; evil men receive life from the Lord 59; inheritance of 163; from man, good from the Lord 174; and falsities c to diseases, bacteria, viruses 209, 258; remaining with man c to harmful resident bacteria which fail to produce a strong permanent immune reaction 218; not the source of "what cometh of evil" 269; c to antigens and other toxins 269; the faith needed to combat evil is "of" but not from it, 269; and falsities, liberation from 447

EVIL, hereditary, is not abolished 165; and falsities, uses of, c to digestion by micro-organisms 473

EXCRETION c to damnation 447

EXECUTIVE MEANS intermediate between cause and effect 491-6

EXERCISE 141; use; produces desire for air as use stimulates desire for truth 141

EXPERIENCE of man begins with externals 275

EXPRESSION, facial 190

EXTERIOR, if evil is like a diseased body 258

EXTERNALS form beginnings of experience, provide instructive c 275

EXTRINSIC EYE MUSCLES may represent as-of-self search for truths A517, A573

EYE(S) chapter II; 341, 347; means the ability to understand 9; "Eye for an eye" - interpretations of 9; is the sight of the spirit "led forth abroad" 20; function 22; spiritual 33; c of, similar to c of the lungs 247; c of are especially delightful 357; province of, includes heaven of little children 357; three coats, outer coat of, is continuous with dura mater 357, see also 278-282; is part of brain, communicates with understanding 364; development of, in embryo is from brain 365; heavenly form 374; c of with heaven because eye is brain 374; balance with aid of 383; and nostrils, provinces of, connection in spiritual world 424; c to understanding A501, A504, and esp re: c of left eye to perception of truth, of right eye to perception of good, and c of these and anatomical details of eyes to degrees of Divine Revelation in the Word A508-A519

EYE(SIGHT), state of, & correspondences A501ff; normal development of eye and its function c to true doctrine and enlightenment of the understanding A504

FACE, is material but smiles from love which is spiritual 10

FACT(S), discernible only by inflowing Divine Truth 30, 37

FAITH, that is needed to combat evil is "of" but not from evil 269; quality of 363; See intellect, understanding; ought not to suffer violence 363; in man, is spiritual sight A501, A504; state of faith in what is true, or false, compared with state of eye and eyesight A501, A504

FALL of man, MAC 156

FALLACY, APPEARANCE that natural objects enter through external senses and affect interiors A502, A503

FALSITIES of evil signified by black clouds; by a woman; by mucus that infests 414; are signified by pits, why 475

FAT(S) globules 200; in foods 433; digested by lipase and bile 440; digested, is re-synthesized in intestinal wall 440; digested droplets of, are collected by lymphatics and sent into the blood stream 440,

441; from food is stored or converted into energy (and heat) 441; of
milk is from cellulose and similar materials 443
FEMININE NATURE AND MASCULINE NATURE A533-A537
FERMENTATIONS and temptations ix, spiritual, c to immunity with-
out illness 216
FERTILIZER 480
FETUS, anatomy and physiology 192
FIBRES 239, 272, 281, 294, 305, 335, 337, 416; from brain, return to firsts
through blood, how this is done, not a flow of fluid 305; c of 352;
fibres and "glands" of brain on right and left 352
FILTHY things permitted for a good end 482
FIRST CONJUNCTION 116, product 134
FLAVOURS enhanced by foul substances 404
FLAMING red colour 45
FLESH, c of 62
FLOOD, the, and birth have similar c 183; spiritual changes shown
by it, expected to cause dramatic changes in the body 158, 159, 160
FLOW, reciprocal 303, and influx 304; flow of fluid not involved in
return of nerve fibres to firsts through blood vessels 305
FLOWERS represent conjugial love 46
FLUID(S), in tissues 201; nasal, relation to cerebrospinal fluid 297
FLUID, CEREBROSPINAL, production, differs from other fluids 284;
return of, into bloodstream 287; course of, over brain surfaces, like
the inflowing action of associated spirits; contrary to 18th Century
ideas 288; is moved by cells lining ventricles 289; contains no large
molecules 290; functions of; not a filtrate from blood; produced by
choroid plexus 294; relation to nasal fluid 297
FOOD(S), c of 47, Chapter XVII; constituents that need no digestion
442, 455, 459, 465; c of 455, 457, 459; unaffected by harsh digestive
juices 456, for angels is as for the Grand Man 484; celestial and
spiritual 484
FOOLISHNESS from reason and knowledge 42
FORAMEN OVALE 122B, 122E, 175, 177, 178; closure after birth 180,
181
FORCE(S), spiritual, in man 6
FORESIGHT, Divine, seen in c 194
FORM, THE HUMAN, of heavenly societies 85, 273-7; meanings of,
197; organic 444
FOURTH POSTERITY OF MAC 425, 427

of to other heavens shown by the heart 80; form of, surpasses human intelligence; is not geometrical; makes each angel the centre; is like multiple connections of neurons in brain 197, 274; many c to chambers of eye 357; entry into is like digested food entering the blood 461; preparation for need not be painful 472; preparation for, angelic control of 472; each part is as the whole 484

HEAVENLY things, c of agree with facts of nature; representatives of must agree with current opinions 293

HELL 209; light in, is from the Lord, as light of coal is from the sun 31, 32; punishment in 471; turns good into evil, c to bacteria that make poisons 480

HERBIVORES, digestion in c to combats in lower earth 478

HOLOGRAMS 274

HORMONES, of thymus 254; like affection of good 258; secretion of 308; production, effect 309; secretion of, sometimes in a protected form 317; production and secretion of, by infundibulum, as described in SD, is parallel to modern ideas 319; described as "lymphs" 332; like spirits of the region of the infundibulum 332

HUMAN FORM of heavenly societies 85; the human is the form of heaven 197; form of angels 484

HUMAN RACE, whole of is spiritually as one body 54; would instantly perish without a Church 56, 58

HYDROCHLORIC acid 438

HYPOPHYSIS CEREBRI, see INFUNDIBULUM; hormones from; is intermediate between brain and body 308, 309; described in SD 831 and SD 914; 313, 314, 315

IDEAS, abstracts begin from material experience 42; associations of 464; have personality 466; associations of can be dispersed 468

ILLNESS 215; c of 216

IMAGES, spiritual; when adequate 21, 33; are formed on the spiritual retina 33, include something of the Lord 34; of the whole, seen in every part of spiritual things 135

IMMUNE REACTION c to the veiling of evil spirits 209

IMMUNITY 208, 268; result of chemical activity of lymphocytes 206; c of 209; reaction 210; acquisition of one kind still allows acquisition of others 210; may be acquired without illness 215; spiritual, after temptations 218; like the Lord's power after incarnation 219

IMPONDERABLE, an 9

IN, spiritual meaning of, not spatial 184

INFANCY 265

INFLUX, accommodated 28; character of; mediate and immediate 246, 310; from inmosts to outmosts, A502, A503; according to efflux A556

INFUNDIBULUM, see HYPOPHYSIS CEREBRI; 305; neurons in 308, 309, 323; old ideas, faulty assumptions about 312 (but see 319); described in SD 831 and SD 914; 313, 314, 315; production of body by; spirit and matter linked by; image of creation; image of link between Lord and man 321, 330; representation by a vision, described in AC 4050, why needed 321; 322, 324; representation of, correspondences in 323, 324, 329; representation of, spiritual sense in 325; representation of, historical internal sense of 326; brain in, is brain without brain function 330; c to the Word, is signified by a well, how they are the same 330

INNER EAR 383

INNOCENCE, signified by children 414

INSANITY is from reason and knowledge 42

INTELLECT, things of, on left side of brain, principle of, on right 338, 339; and will, not to be divorced 339

INTELLECTUAL, left side of the brain 338

INTELLIGENCE things of, are spiritual objects 33; is from the Word 42

INTERFACE(S) 492, 493; between spiritual and natural 495; for immediate influx, possible nature of 495; effects of faulty function 495

INTERIOR sight 36

INTERNAL or celestial is like thymus 258

INTERNAL DICTATE 241

INTERNAL RESPIRATION 158; nature of 187, spirits of Mars 190

INTERNAL sight 30

INTESTINES 200, 250, 455, 476; province of, spirits there are also in lower earth 500

IRON, economy of, in body 229

ISOTOPES, a possible source of variation 453

ISRAEL 480

JACOB 257, 496; c show how to ascend ladder 276; ladder of 421

JEWISH CHURCH 450, 451

JOSEPH 480

JUGULAR vein 199
JUPITER 339

KEM, definition of: Knowledges of External Memory ("scientifics")
    232, 236, 238; as vessels of good 232-3; are like erythrocytes 235-7;
    many kinds of; they c to various organs 239, 257; muscles, bones
    239; relation of, to thoughts 239; conditions needed for use of 243
KIDNEY 220, 294, 309, 317
KINGDOM, the Lord's celestial, is like the heart; spiritual, is like the
    lungs 56
KNOWLEDGE(S) are useful in their proper place 42; external role of
    42; c to vessels 61; of nature and science, limitations of, at time
    Writings were given 107; of nature and science for confirming and
    exploring doctrine 112

LABAN 257
LABYRINTHS of AC 5181 200; c to lymph nodes 214
LACTEALS 200; are milky lymphatic ducts containing chyle 441
LANGUAGE, semantic difficulty 318
LAST JUDGEMENT 299, 387, 418
LEAH 496
LEAKAGE of blood between pulmonary and arterial systems 171
LEARNING through visual pathway 80% of total A507
LEFT, and right, distinction 354; c of 337
LEFT EYE c to perception of truths of understanding A508-A509,
    A567-A568; and signifies true masculine nature A533; whereas the
    right eye c to affections of truth of understanding and to perception
    of good A508-A509, A567-A568; and signifies the feminine nature
    of man A508, A509, A514, A532-A537, esp. A533
LENS, part of second tunic of eye, may represent desire to understand,
    to focus light upon macula A518, A573
LIBERATION from evils and falsities 447
LIFE of man, is the Lord's; eludes science 272; its reassembly in heaven
    487; origin and nature of, in relation to Divine Love & Wisdom, and
    to the role of vision in our understanding of the Word A509-A519
LIGHT c to truth which is from the Lord and is the Lord 9, 22; spiritual,
    is Divine Truth; without it no one can discern facts 35; which
    "lighteth every man that cometh into the world" 37; spiritual, is
    wisdom received by understanding, adjusted to capacity 246

LIMBIC SYSTEM is part of brain; anatomy and properties 425, 426; and the cerebrum 425; enables body to function without cerebral cortex 427; sometimes controls modern man 427; primitive 428; changes in control of, and the Fall 428, 429

LIPASES are the enzymes for digesting fat 440

LITTLE CHILDREN 407

LIVER 220, 229; how it is relieved by the spleen 249; removes harmful substances, may suffer damage 249

LONGITUDINAL SINUS 287; now superior sagittal sinus 281 and Figure 15

LORD the only One who lives and sees 18; is truth and light 27; His Love illustrated by the sun 29; flow of life from 82; Divine Truths and life from 193; how eating His flesh and drinking His blood may be understood 485

LOVE, see WILL; is a spiritual force which causes natural actions 6, 7; action of is accepted though the mechanism, is not understood 10; Divine together with Wisdom flows from the spiritual sun 27; conjugial, represented by flowers 46; love ruling influence in mind 79; works in the will as the heart in the body 91, 93; c to the heart itself 92 (see also HEART); is the life of the will 93; is the very life of man 102; experienced in, and expressed by brain 273; polygamous 413; love, or life of the will indicated by sitting 414; ruling loves 465

LOWER EARTH 474

LUNGS, see also heart; c to wisdom 57, and to understanding 87; rule throughout the body by means of respirations 73, 106-111; close association of, with heart 99, 109-111; swooning and suffocation 104; motion of, connection with rest of the body 107; refresh the whole of the blood 120; in embryo 122D; three phases in development 122E; opened by first breath 122I; chest and its muscles 122J; growth of, in embryo influenced by heart 130; nourishment 130

LYMPH, ducts and trunks of 199; capillaries 199; origin of 201; causes of flow of, gentle nature of flow 202; particles in, three kinds of 203; vessels differ from blood vessels 203; cleaned 204; nodes 204, 206, 214; carries lymphocytes 220; colourlessness of 221; why 224; c to wisdom because colourless or white but with some good because it includes many constituents of blood 224; absence of haemoglobin from, c to withdrawal of love during temptation - a temporary state 224; ref. in A.C. 4049, 289; meaning of, in Writings differs from modern usage 290; "Lymphs" of infundibulum, possibly hormones 332; excrementitious, possibly gonadotrophins, i.e., hormones connected with sexual development 332

LYMPHATIC(S), an important part of body's economy and defence 198; are for cleaning 203; spirits 210, 213; include 213; similarity of responses in illness and health 215; an image of whole man 259

LYMPHATIC SYSTEM 440; brief study 198; function 201; absent from brain 290

LYMPHOCYTES 206-217, 262, 268; are cells from spleen and nodes 206; committed and uncommitted 211; committed c to persistent and impudent spirits 212; c to wandering spirits of province of lymphatics 213; incomplete 254; origin of, from stem cells 255, 257; short-lived, in thymus 255; concerned in auto-immune and auto-allergic diseases 255; many kinds of 259; like remains, are a defense 259; production of antibodies by, is a qualifying of goods according to truths 260; how like angels 263; how affected by antigens (Ref) 264; behavior of, analogous to memory (Ref) 264

LYMPHOID SYSTEM, thymus 252

LYMPHOID TISSUES 67, 258

LYMPHOPOIETIN 254

LYMPHS, number of 290; spirits of 333; excrementitious 333

MAC, in ref. to Most Ancient Church 326, 359, 425, 427; descendants of 187; more like animals 423; declined 429

MACROPHAGES are cellular scavengers 204

MACULA, most sensitive area of retina, c to Writings A519; natural light striking macula becomes spiritual light, and man views letter of Word not from self but from the Lord A519

MAMMILLARY processes differ from mammillary bodies; they are the olfactory tracts, important translation point 296

MAN, is viler than animals 56 (see also HUMAN); is a microcosm 86; the Grand 197; last things in receive influx last 246; internal communicates 258; apart from internal, is no other than an animal 444; each one is a population 466; imperfect 486

MARRIAGE, of love and wisdom 114, 350; of will and understanding 114, 130; of heart and lungs, illustrated by air cells of lungs 145

MARROW of bone, origin of stem cells 255, 257; not spinal marrow or medulla of AC 5717 & AC 8593; a very important distinction Fn 14 (257)

MARS, spirits of, respiration of, like circulation in embryo 193

MASCULINE NATURE AND FEMININE NATURE A533-A537

MEANS, EXECUTIVE 491, 496; are necessary for a cause to operate 492; are from realm of effect and they correspond 492; may be harsher than the cause 492; are interfaces 493; are further from the Divine than causes 497

MEDIATE and immediate influx 246

MEDITATION, thought of the spirit 142; looks down on bodily thought 142

MEDULLA OBLONGATA 124, 301, 337

MEMORY, long-term 385, c of 444, internal 465

MENDEL 490

MENINGES 416, 417

MENINGITIS 298, 417

MESENTERY 200

MICRO-ORGANISMS 217, 269; aid digestion in herbivores 443; digestion by, c to uses of evils and falsities 473; digestion by, c to combats in lower earth 478

MICROCOSM, man as a 86

MIND, attitude of viii; is spirit 6; mind ruled by affection, love, will 79; rational level of mind Fn 86; life of, depends on the will 103; workings of, simultaneous 147; dual structure of 163; divided, of modern man 183

MINERALS need no digestion 442, 458

MOHAMMEDANS 413

MOLECULES, small, pass out of the blood into tissues 76; various movements of in brain 291, due to diffusion 290; large, can move between brain cells 291; various may constitute various lymphs of AC 4050, 292; effect of splitting 431; of food 431; of starch 435; of proteins 437; from different foods can be the same 461; one, cannot represent one person 461

MOON, spirits from ix

MOST ANCIENT CHURCH different from spiritual church 156; structure of mind 159; had will and understanding united 160, 162; was celestial 1661; unity of mind in man of, c to unity of circulation in embryo 178; understanding in man of, c to respiration in embryo 179; as embryo of human race 190; doctrinal things 193; posterity of, wise but not instructed 425; posterity of, and role of limbic system 427; fall of, and changes in control of limbic system by cerebral cortex 428, 429

MOUNTAINS, c of 48

MUCOUS membrane 298

MUCOUS represents dull spirits 358; spirits relating to 414; once thought to be from brain, but it is not 415, 416, 417, 418; pituitary 418; uses of; c of 419; phlegm, pus, old usage suggests equivalence then 419; protection of stomach by 438

MUSCLES 276; c of 239; activated by nerve impulses 383

MYTHOLOGY and names of planets ix

NASAL mucosa, tissue spaces of, continuous with pia-arachnoid 297

NATURAL, relation to spiritual shown by muscular activity 489, by gastric ulcers 490

NATURAL GOOD, reformation of 155

NATURAL WORLD, produced by inward force from spiritual world 450

NATURE re-presents the world of spirit 1; illustrations from, were chosen by the Lord 2; produced in regular manner from world of spirit 3, 5, 6, 10; laws of have no exceptions 5; and spirit, relationship of, vaguely known and widely used 8, is subtle and complex 12; and spirit, a knowledge of both was needed for revelation 13; last things in, receive influx last 246; facts of, incomprehensible without knowledge 293; "red in tooth and claw" 499

NECK signifies communication, which must be controlled and bounded 302

NERVE(S), activity of, detectable by scientific instruments 7; are discretely different from the muscles they control 7; c between nerves and muscles 276; as terminals of arteries 305; not directly connected to cerebellum 382; vestibular 382, connected to cerebellum 382, 383; cochlear, auditory 383

NERVE PATHWAYS for vision 40% of total to brain A506; retina-optic nerves-chiasma-optic tracts-lateral geniculate bodies-visual areas in occipital and temporal lobes A520-A527

NERVE CELLS 271

NERVE FIBERS for vision 40% of total to brain A506

NEUROGLIA, also called glial cells 271

NEURONS 271, 278, 290, 308, 346; shapes and functions 271; connections 272; in the brain, connected into heavenly form 274; connections of, c to angels in truth, through whom those in good communicate 353

NEW WILL, formation of and importance of 164
NEWTON 14
NOAH 160, 182; the spiritual change of 163
NODE(S), sinuatrial 174; lymphatic, how they clean the lymph 204; c
    to spirits that do not wander 213
NON-FACT 35
NOSE nerves from 408; anatomy of 417; tissue spaces in, connection
    with brain 417, 420; not a source of mucus 417
NOSTRIL(S) 337, 358, 359, 414; interiors of, c of 359; province of 393; c
    to general or obscure perception 405; interiors of, are really brain
    and relate to a heavenly province and c to a better perception 406;
    represent 410; vision concerning (from AC 4627) 411, shows evil
    hindering perception 412, 415; and eyes, provinces of, connection
    in spiritual world 424

OBEDIENCE, unthinking, is of limited use 43; genuine internal of,
    from understanding 361; efficiency of the body is a form of 376
    connection with organs of balance 377; of body to organs of balance
    without thought 377; of body to organs of balance, involvement of
    cerebellum 377; represented by hearing 381, 389; to words, needs
    understanding, not involuntary 384, 385; of the most external spir-
    its, without reflection 385; not of ear itself 390; not of that part of
    brain that interprets sounds 390; meaning of 390; is more than
    performance of duty 390; from fear 390; follows conjunction of will
    and understanding 390, 391; function of 391; as a form of efficiency
    is not truly human 391; from willingness to serve from love 391
OBEDIENCES are spirits in province of ear 375
OBEDIENT spirits in the Grand Man must have free will; they enjoy
    life from the Lord 391
OBJECTS, spiritual, form images by spiritual light, which is truth 21,
    33
ODOUR(S), c to delights 393, 400; from spheres depend on observer
    401; exist only with those who smell them 401, 402; observed only
    when they change 402; contamination 404; enhanced by foul sub-
    stances 404 and emotions related to limbic system 430; 499
OLD WILL, continuation of 165
OLFACTORY, ref. to excretions in A.C. and S.D., 416; fluid spaces
    connected with brain 417, 420; epithelium 420; lobe in brain, control
    of by higher centres 422; mucosa not "interiors of nostrils" 405; lobe
    408; tract, like structures seen in spiritual world 408

OLFACTORY NERVE 283, 294; nerves in embryo 420; development
  of, and Lord's power of raising man 420, 421
OMATOTROPIN 309
OPTIC CHIASMA 369; A521
OPTIC NERVE(S) 282; nerve, separate strands of, allows transfer of
  retinal image in a certain form, to brain 19; is brain 364, 365;
  chiasma 369; pathway 369; decussation of 340; A520
OPTIC PATHWAY 367, 369
OPTIC RADIATION A524
OPTIC TRACTS A521
ORGANIC FORMS 444
ORGANS, heart rules in 73; in animals 444; rest of 73; as provinces 196
OXYGEN, supply of, from lungs through blood shows perfect union
  between heart and lungs 110, 111; function 241; c of 244

PACCHIONI (ref) saw connections between arachnoid granulations
  and pia mater 281, 289
PACEMAKER of heart 174
PANCREAS 435, 440; enzymes from 439
PARABLE(S) of the sower 4; deeper meanings revealed by knowledge
  of representations 2, 3, 4
PARADISE, can be seen in DLW Part V (see DLW 376) 114
PART(S), of spiritual things, form images of the whole 135; an image
  of the whole, illustrated by affection for truth 143; an image of
  whole illustrated by cells and DNA 259
PARTURITION, regeneration c to 180
PENDLETON, J & J. Ref. to useful letter concerning embryo 195
PEPSIN 439
PERCEPTION(S), is impossible without Divine Truth 30, 36; c to air
  ducts in the lungs 117; of truth: xi,117-147; interior 251; hearing,
  understanding, relationships 358, 361; meaning 394; wide range of
  394, 425; lowest form of is interior thought; in spiritual church;
  needs influx 395; by the evil through communication with heaven
  396; with the spiritual is conscience and is from truth 397; in the
  celestial, is knowledge by an inward way 398; by celestial angels -
  the things perceived 398; real, is celestial, the spiritual have enlightenment, what the differences are 398; in the spiritual world 399; of
  quality of others from their spheres 399; angelic and common -
  differences and similarities 400; awareness of odour 400; kinds of,

that c to nasal passages and bronchia 403, 404 (see also 139-141); kinds of that c to the nose 404; and wisdom, are together as sight and scent 423, 424; and understanding, marriage of, seen in c 424; understanding them by c 425; and "as-of-self" A539-A559; feed-back mechanisms and perception (diagram) A539-A548

PERIOSTEUM 417

PERSONALITY, change of, see breakdown, complexes, proprium; change by dissociation and re-building of complexes 466, 469, 471

PHAGOCYTES are cellular scavengers 204; important in lungs 205; properties, functions, circulation of, 205; c to wandering spirits of province of lymphatics 212, 213, 215; digestion by described in SD, 249, 250; digestion in c to mingling and separation of profane and holy 250; means 259

PHILOSOPHY, foolishness of when from mere terms 376; dancing by means of impossible 376

PHLEGM, a vague term in 18th Century 299; in brains, disorderly origin of 418; phlegm, pus, mucus, old usage suggests equivalence then 419; denoted lowest state of man 420

PHLEGMY or viscous excretions 416

PHLOGISTON, imaginary substance of negative weight 311

PHYSICS of solar radiation represents Divine accommodation 28, 29

PIA-ARACHNOID c to communicating spirits 285, communications 286

PIA MATER and arachnoid as one unit; structure 284; spirits of 285; contains channels of communication with brain 286; spirits related to 286; connection of, with longitudinal sinus; similarity of spirits 287

PINEAL gland 312

PITS, as part of lower earth 474, 475; beneath which they are 475; signify falsities 475; c to intestines 476; falsities removed there; a process c to digestion 476

PITUITARY gland 305, 308; see hypophysis cerebri 323; used to mean excretory, and in AC does not mean pituitary gland 418

PLACENTA etc. 122I, 191; c to posterities of Most Ancient Church that perished 192

PLEURA 120

POETIC images in the Word are c 49

POISONS 206; produced by intestinal bacteria c to the turning of good into evil in hell 480

POLYGAMY, as indicated by a bath 413

POSTERIOR things cannot flow into prior, nor lower into higher, nor exterior into interior, nor worldly and natural into heavenly and spiritual A502, A503

PRIESTS, evil, could represent the Lord 52

PRIOR things can inflow into posterior, higher into lower, lowest, and last, interior into exterior, heavenly and spiritual into worldly things; but not the reverse A502, A503

PROFANE and holy things, mingling and separation of 229, 248; c to phagocytes 250

PROLEPSIS 101

PROPRIUM 167, 404, 452, 481; is often the same as the old will 165; many things of, may be broken down 469

PROTEINS, examples, sources, uses, composition 211, 317, 433, 437; digestion of, 3 stages of 436, 438, 439; effect of stomach acid, is disorganization of molecule 438; digestion of, amino acids from make new proteins 439, 469

PROVIDENCE 454, 467, 481, 489; seen in c beforehand 183; Divine, seen in correspondences 194

PSALM 23, c in, easily understood 48

PSYCHOLOGICAL terms 257

PSYCHOLOGY, all of it included in c's of heart and lungs 96

PULMONARY arteries 127, 170, 172; refresh blood 120; form third arterial system 142; affections c to 143; completion 150

PULMONARY circulation 120

PUPIL A517, A519

PURER blood 320

PURIFICATION of new arrivals in the next life c to digestion 447, 487

PUS, phlegm, mucus, old usage suggests equivalence then, 419

PYRAMIDS, decussation of 335, 336

QUESTIONS, our own critical ones foreseen 109

RACE, see HUMAN

RACHEL 496

RATIONAL, affirmative 3; man becomes, through external ways 42; a higher spiritual mental function Fn 1 (86); is intermediate, like peripheral lymphoid tissues 258; spirits 387, 388

REALITY, inner or spiritual 1, 2, A509; natural A501

RE-SYNTHESIS 454

REBIRTH 181, 194

RECTUM 473, c of 476

RED, c of, is with red seen in the spiritual world 222

REFLECTION on natural knowledges to help appreciation of spiritual truths x

REGENERATION a new will 155; c to a new heart 155; like establishment of ancient churches 157; of spiritual man 164; c to conception, gestation, and parturition 180, formation of new will 485

REGURGITATION 438

RELATIONSHIPS, many incomprehensible ones are known 10

RELAY stations in brain, functions of 368; in optic pathway only one, is geniculate body 369; auditory pathway, several 370

REMAINS 263, 268; compared to lymphocytes 259; different kinds of 259, 261; c to antibodies; are truth adjoined to goods 260

REPRESENTATION(S), in the Word, are precise 1-5, 15, 49, 52; not necessarily true c 52; 324; beauty of, in province of eye 374; unpleasant, not to be ignored, are of proprium 481; richness and variety 498; seem to conflict 499; reasons for variety of 501, 502

REPRESENTATIVES x, 52; anatomical, are correspondences showing causes 410

RESPIRATION, see BREATHING; and molecular aspects 100, 110, 111; is motion from lungs in whole body 110; of the spirit 125; of embryo is through placenta 179, c to understanding in Most Ancient Church 179; internal before birth, external after 188; internal c to instruction through internal man, as in Most Ancient Church 189, 190, 191; internal, and cessation of (from AC 607-9) 189; of a child 195; external c to instruction by way of senses; c to the life of truth 245

RETICULAR FORMATION 347

RETINA(E) 17, 282; controlled by cerebral cortex 19; spiritual, receives images of spiritual things by light of truth 33; is brain 364, 365; image on, is in brain 367; communication of, with visual cortex, one half of each retina with one side of cortex 369; inmost tunic of eye, represents inmost sense of Word, or celestial heaven; its sensitive macula, representing the Writings, converts natural light into spiritual light; and its inmost fovea represents the Doctrine of the Lord A519

REVELATION, Divine ix-xi, chapter I, esp. 4, 8, 11, 13-15; is adjusted to capacity of recipients 11; confirmed 5, 15; must be in ideology of the time 14, 293, hence errors 295; applied to modern knowledge 198; makes best use of knowledge available currently 334; and psychology 465

RIBS, use in breathing Fn 6 (123)

RIGHT, denotes good 341; signifies the truth of good 342; various meanings listed 343; signifies good 344; and left, c of appear various 342, this is necessary 351; and left of brain c to four angelic categories 352; and left distinct but one as good and truth 354, 355

RIGHT (hand side) refers to good from which is truth 341; right hand signifies truth of good 342

RIGHT EYE c to affections of truth of understanding and to perception of good A508-A509, A567-568; and signifies the feminine nature of man A533; whereas the left eye c to perception of truths of understanding A508-A509, A567-568; and signifies the masculine nature A508, A509, A514, A532-A537, esp. A533

RODS 365

RULING LOVE 241, 448

RUMEN, and c of 443, 444

SALT, common, how different from the elements that combine to produce it 431

SARAH 42

SCENT and sight are together as wisdom and perception 423, 424

SCHWANN cells 365

SCIENCE, modern, a better confirmation of revelation than the lesser knowledge of earlier times 2, 14, 51

SCIENTIFICS as vessels of good 232-3; are Knowledges of External Memory (KEM) 323

SCIENTISTS, special use of in the New Church 2, 15

SCLERA 282; opaque white part of outer coat of eye, represents letter of Word, and natural heaven, and may also represent clouds of heaven, made transparent (cornea) from "as-of-self" effort A515, A519

SCRIPTURES, the, see Word of God

SEATS pertain to the life of love, or will 414

SECOND CONJUNCTION 117; affection for understanding 137; physiological correspondences 138; system which controls breathing 139; product 140

SEEING means understanding 9, 16; process of 17; depends on understanding 17; needs inflow of interior sight and hence of the Lord 18

SELF, destruction of by perversion of intellect no longer possible 163, nor by immersion in lusts 171

SELF-INDULGENCE 47

SEMICIRCULAR CANALS 376, 377, 383

SENSES, obedient response to 378

SENSUAL [degree] of man receives influx last 246

SERUM 317; blood 249

SEWAGE has uses; c to hell 480

SHERRINGTON, Sir Charles (ref.) 276

SIGHT, seems to re-create the environment inside the brain 19; of the body is the sight of the spirit led forth abroad 20; c to understanding 9, chapter II, 356; to societies in paradise 357; c of are especially glorious 363; sensory of, internal, is at back of head 364; internal, speech and, obedience and 386; and scent are together as wisdom and perception 423, 424; natural and spiritual A501, A505; of the eye is natural sight A501; spiritual, is faith A501, A504; spiritual, is sight of the understanding A501

SIGNIFICATION AND CORRESPONDENCE, similarities and differences 61, 62

SIGNIFICATIVES are often merely words 52; 324

SIMULTANEITY of mind's workings clarified by c 147, 153; like regularly repeated cycles 153

SINGLE WILL, bodily correspondence to 177

SINUATRIAL NODE 174

SINUS, longitudinal, connections with pia-arachnoid 287

SKULL, plates of bone 279; base of 407

SMELL, see ODOUR; sense of related to perception 358; c to those people in general perception 393, 405; sense of exhausted 402; sense of, organ of, is not interiors of nostrils 405; closer to animal nature of man 421, 423

SMILE 6, 10, 12, 13, 490; produced by love through the brain 6, 7, 10, 13; spiritual in nature 7

SOMATOTROPIN 309

SOULS, mixture of good and evil 465; novitiate, as food for the Grand Man; not to be understood materialistically 483

SOUND, immediate effect on will 380

SOWER, parable of 4

SPEECH uses natural things for spiritual meanings 8; stimulates the internal sight 386; translates into images 387

SPHERES, of spirits, how produced; perceived in various ways 399; of spirits and angels c to odours and are turned into odours when the Lord pleases 400; odours of, due to effect on observer (from the Lord) 401; of spirits due to contamination of Divine transflux 404

SPINAL CHORD 284, 337, 347

SPIRIT(S), of man is his mind 6; that sees 18; wandering 213; evil, in heaven, just before Last Judgement Fn 12 (229); many meanings of the word, e.g., an elusive substance 316; animal, perhaps the spiritual life of the body 320; obedient 391; newly arrived 446; individual, cannot c to individual molecules 461, do c to particular kinds of food 462; taken to pieces, cannot be destroyed 469

SPIRITUAL CAUSES of natural effects 5-10

SPIRITUAL FORCES both general and particular 54

SPIRITUAL MAN, sense of the Word seen only from the Lord 40; love 45; regeneration 155; after regeneration, cannot avoid consulting the understanding 182; will and understanding not united 184; state of childhood c of, 266; the, have enlightenment not perception 398

SPIRITUAL SIGHT, and natural A501, A502

SPIRITUAL WORLD is more real than the natural 1; is re-presented in nature 1; related to natural in an orderly consistent way 3, 5, 6, and subtle and complex ways 10; is the cause of the natural 10; vast and complex 11; seen by many but not understood 14; general awareness of 16; universe 86

SPIRITUOUS essences 316, 320

SPLEEN, lymphocyte production 206; related to lymphatics 225; white and red pulp c with wisdom and love 226; is like a giant lymph node 227; can store blood cells, mechanism of 227; destruction of erythrocytes by, and role of phagocytes 228; embryo 228; digestion of red cells; spiritual province of, abominations in 229; spirits of, commingle and separate things 248, 250; lymphocytes of 249; phagocytes of, act like corresponding spirits 249; function, purification of the blood by 249; relieves the liver, how 249; compared to thymus 252

STARCH and its digestion 435

STEM CELLS 255, 257
STOMACH 249, 250, 449
STRIATE AREAS A522-A525
STUDY of spiritual things 41
SUBSTANCE 431
SUCCESSIVE [things] are continual from the Lord to last things for
     the communication of Divine Truth 246
SUFFOCATION is temporary and disorderly 103, 104
SUGARS 434
SUN, the natural c to the spiritual sun in which is the Lord 28;
     illustrates accommodation of the Divine to man 28, 29; the spiritu-
     al, pours out Divine Love and Wisdom 27; of the spiritual world,
     and radiant belts of 246
SUNSET 45
SUPERIOR COLLICULUS A524
SUPERIOR SAGITAL SINUS 287
SWEDENBORG 15, 288, 293, 297, 299, 311, 312, 323, 324, 329, 336, 337,
     339, 351, 376, 415, 417, 418, 463, 470, 481; achievements, experiences
     under Divine auspices, was able to understand his spiritual experi-
     ences 13; expert in science, had no knowledge of future science,
     revelation through him limited to current knowledge 14; discredit-
     ed 14; contemporaries 293, 334; time 294; limited to science of his
     time 295; biased 298; misconceptions 311
SWEDENBORG'S works 15
SWOONING, is temporary and disorderly 103, 104
SYMPATHETIC nervous system controls arteries in pia 286
SYNTHESIS 452
SYSTEMS, various, that control breathing 124, 125, 149, are a form of
     conjunction of heart with lungs 139

TABERNACLE 301
TASTE c to perception and affection of spiritual food 362
TEMPTATION(S), 470, 471; when overcome c to acquirement of im-
     munity 216; equivalent to agitations 218; c to digestion 483
TERMS, various, from the Writings, arranges in a series 241; 18th
     Century 317
TETANUS 210
THINKING from c's ix, chapter III
THIRD CIRCULATION, search for 120

THIRD CONJUNCTION 118; product 144; may c to the pulmonary arteries 141, 145

THORACIC DUCT 199

THOUGHT(S), spiritual, impossible without the Word 15; impossible without influx from the Lord 30; assist 39; from c is universal 44, is the only sound way to spiritual ideas 50; c to bronchia and to air saccules of the lungs 117, 118, 139; produced by affection for seeing truth 142; of the spirit meditation 142; of the body is below that of the spirit 142; c to minutest air saccules, e.g., air cells, of lungs 144; a partitioning of conscience 144; every one a marriage of will and understanding 145; idle, c to quiet respiration 145; relation of, to KEM 239; c to alveoli of lungs 240; many different kinds of 242; expandable like alveoli to draw in the spirit 242; as forms of transport for the spirit like erythrocytes 230-242

THREE CONJUNCTIONS, products of 146, psychology of 147, repeating simultaneous cycles 153

THYMUS (gland), celestial associations of; important in infants; how it remains undisturbed during turmoils 251; is the essential principal organ of lymphoid system 252, 253; anatomy and physiology of 252; protection of from substances in blood 252; is essential for development of immunity 253; loss of 253; hormones of; lymphocytes and competence 254; tranquility of, due to blood-thymus barrier 256; represents 258; unable to operate defence by itself, like the celestial 258; development 265

THYROID 308

TISSUE, growth and repair 156; fluid, origin of 201

TORMENT due to dissociations in next life 470; avoidance 472

TOUCH 368

TOXINS 216, 220

TREE, c of 48

TRUTH(S), genuine, not possible in the understanding of man 21; is spiritual light 22; is the form of good 23, 38; purpose, is for the sake of good 24; many varieties of shown by c 25; lowest form of is facts about physical objects 26; highest form 27; Divine, is both spiritual light and sight 30; image of 34; innumerable 38; by which forms of good are seen 38; acceptance of 42; activated by loves, good or evil 100; not activated is in man at beginning of regeneration 100; not activated c to respiration in embryo 100; and wisdom, distinction between 100, 101; internal appreciation 112; affection for, produces thought 142; affection for, perception of, 147; its closeness to good in its vessels 234; spiritual truth 241; rational truth 241; natural truth 241; scientific truth 241; immediately from the Lord cannot be received 246; that flows into the highest heaven flows also into the last things of order without successive formations 246; in youth qualify goods; when adjoined c to competent lymphocytes 268; of good, signified by right hand 342; without good 353; the Lord's must be broken down by man for acceptance 485; can be joined in faulty ways by man 486; Divine flows in with, and without successive degrees 495

ULCERS 489
UNDERSTANDING (see also WILL), frequently meant by seeing and by the eye 9, 16, 17; c to sight 21; takes truths as eye takes images 21; function 22; impossible without Divine Truth 30, 36; will and, confusion regarding distinction 87; a receptacle, especially of Divine Wisdom 88, 89, 94; the seat of intellect 88; the, has a range of meanings 89; is activated by love from the will 94; respiration of the lungs 100; importance of 102; as well as will is needed for normal life 104, 105; growth of, in childhood, before conjunction with the will 130; growth of, is by affections which c to bronchial arteries 131; is biased by love from the will 132; refreshment of in adult c to bronchial arteries 133; in descendants of Most Ancient Church became perverted when will became corrupt 162; in Most Ancient Church c respiration in embryo 179; the, ought not to suffer violence 363; perception 424; dispensed with by limbic system 427
USE, c to exercise 141, induces a desire for truth, as does exercise for air 141

VAN DUSEN, W. (ref.), "The Presence of Spirits in Madness" 79, 495
VASOPRESSIN, hormone produced in protected form 309, 317
VASTATION 474
VEIL in tabernacle, barrier and communication 301
VEINS, regarded as part of heart 75; bronchial, anatomical details 122; pulmonary, connections with bronchial arteries 171
VENA CAVA 172
VENOUS SINUS 287
VENTRICLES, right and left, of the heart 120; of brain 288, 289; spirits of 290; of brain, anatomy of 312

VERITIES, spiritual, appreciated by reflection from natural knowledges x, 11, 86

VESSELS and contents, c of, similarities and differences 61, 90-95; blood, growth of, 130

VESTIBULAR nerve 382-383

VESTIBULE and canals are organs of balance or orientation 382, 383

VESTIBULOCOCHLEAR nerve Fig. 22 (383)

VICKERS, Rev. P. V. (ref.), *God-Talk and Man-Talk* 79

VIEUSSENS 297

VIRUSES 209

VISION, angelic explanation of, is natural within which is the spiritual 324; the, about nostrils shows evil hindering perception 415; process including the retina, brain, muscles, whole organism A506-A507

VISUAL AREAS A520-A529; and perception A540-A552; visuo-sensory area (area 17) A521

VISUAL MEMORIES from words 373

VISUAL PATHWAYS, retina-to-cerebral cortex, represent ways Lord reforms and regenerates man A520

VISUAL PROCESS, vision A514-A529, A530-A561;

3 degrees of eye globe of Word of heavens

A.Skeletal: holds image letternatural

B.Visceral: defines image interior sensespiritual

C.Cortical: interprets image inmost sense celestial

process including retina, brain, muscles, whole organism A506-A507; related to conjugial love A527, A531-A561

VITAMINS need no digestion 442, examples of 458

WASTE DISPOSAL 204

WATER is an essential mineral in photosynthesis 4, and c to truth that is also essential 458

WATER OF LIFE 4

WHITE c of, is equivalent to colourless in some cases 224; white matter of brain 346

WHOOPING COUGH 210

WILL, new, is in understanding as heart in lungs 14; ruling influence 79; c to the heart and its kingdom throughout the body 87, 92; emotions 88; a receptacle of Divine Love 88, 89, 90; the, the word itself has a range of meanings 89; is the whole of man 91, and his very life 102; is filled with many loves 92; primary importance of 107; never acts without the understanding 107; flows into the understanding as blood into lungs 119; new, is needed for regeneration, c to a new heart 155, 168; new, given by regeneration, c of (in 14 propositions) 156; new, implanted in intellectual part 162, 166; and intellect, separation of 164; old and new, both remain after regeneration 165, 167; the old evil will is necessary 166, set aside, not destroyed 166; restrained 167; unable to destroy man by immersing the understanding in lusts 171; the new of regenerated spiritual man cannot avoid consulting the understanding 182; old and new 184; things of, on right side of brain 338; and intellect, not to be divorced 339; the, effect of sound on 380, 381; connection with cerebellum 381; life of, indicated by sitting 414

WILL AND UNDERSTANDING, confusion regarding distinction 87; are together in whole of mind as heart and lungs work for whole body 110, 113; conjunction of, is like a marriage 115; conjunction of takes place by means of three affections which c to blood vessels related to the lungs 116; 1st conjunction of 116; 2nd conjunction of 117; 3rd conjunction of 118; products of conjunction 146; both invigorated after conjunctions are completed 151; were united in Most Ancient Church 160, 162; never united in spiritual man 185; c to heart and lungs 185; union of c to union of heart and lungs (as in DLW) 185; union of is a marriage, hence includes conjunction and disjunction 186; with distinction c to circulation of blood in the adult 187

WIND(S) c to spirit 190; in reference to the Lord denotes the proceeding Divine, but in reference to man it signifies the life of truth 245; in the spiritual world, effect separation of good and evil etc. 245; connection of, with proceeding Divine and Sun of the spiritual world 245

WINE, spirits of 316

WISDOM, things of, are spiritual objects 33; is from the Word 42; and perception are together as sight and scent 423, 424

WOMB 195

WOOFENDEN, Rev. Dr. W. R. His idea that early part of Word may c to prenatal life 195

WORCESTER, John. Ref. to his book on anatomy called *Physiological Correspondences*, Fn 12 (229); statements about auditory nerve and cerebellum 379, 382, 387

WORD (OF GOD) is a Divine Allegory whose meaning is revealed through Swedenborg, written by the same c that operate in creation 15; the, the spiritual sense of is seen only from the Lord 40; inner sense 49; the, denoted by a well and by a cloud 327, 328, functions like the infundibulum 330; Hebrew 445; its 3 degrees related to 3 coats of eye globe, and to the 3 degrees of the visual process A513-A528
WORDS, visual memories from 373
WORK increases the need for air, as use does for truth 141
WRITINGS, the, for list please see last page; errors in 295

YOUTH, goods of, stored in interiors 267; not qualified, c to uncommitted lymphocytes 268